Quest

English as a Second Language

Gillian Baxter
Cynthia Beyea
Claire Maria Ford

Secondary Cycle Two
Year Three

Student's Book

GRAFICOR
CHENELIÈRE ÉDUCATION

Quest
English as a Second Language
Secondary Cycle Two, Year Three

Student's Book

Gillian Baxter, Cynthia Beyea, Claire Maria Ford

Editor: Susan Roy
Project managers: Jeanine Floyd, Lee Ann Balazuc, Michèle Devlin, Roberto Blizzard
Proofreaders: Jocelyne Lauzière, My-Trang Nguyen
Copyright researcher: Marc-André Brouillard
Photo researchers: Rachel Irwin, Micheline Roy
Cover and book designer: Micheline Roy
Illustrator: Stéphane Jorisch
Printer: Imprimeries Trancontinental

Acknowledgements

The publisher would like to thank the following people for their valuable contributions to the publication of *Quest*, Year Three.

Teresa Capparelli, co-author of Quest, Year 1, pedagogical consultant, Commission scolaire de Montréal

Carolyn Greene, ESL consultant

Marie-Christine Guay, teacher, École secondaire Donnacona, Commission scolaire de Portneuf

Martine Jean-Gilles, teacher, École secondaire Louis-Riel, Commission scolaire de Montréal

Tollof Nelson, teacher, Académie Ste-Thérèse

Ronald Patterson, consultant

Patricia Pratt, teacher, École secondaire du Mont-Bruno, Commission scolaire des Patriotes

Martin Roy, teacher and ESL resource person, École secondaire Augustin-Norbert-Morin, Commission scolaire des Laurentides

Aphrodite Vlachakis, teacher, École secondaire des Patriotes, Commission scolaire de la Seigneurie-des-Mille-Îles

GRAFICOR
CHENELIÈRE ÉDUCATION

7001 Saint-Laurent Blvd.
Montréal (Québec) Canada H2S 3E3
Telephone: 514 273-1066
Fax: 450 461-3834 / 1 888 460-3834
info@cheneliere.ca

ISBN 978-2-7652-1325-3

Dépôt légal : 2e trimestre 2009
Bibliothèque et Archives nationales du Québec
Bibliothèque et Archives Canada

Printed in Canada

1 2 3 4 5 ITIB 13 12 11 10 09

We acknowledge the financial support of the Government of Canada through the Book Publishing Industry Development Program (BPIDP) for our publishing activities.

Government of Quebec – Tax credit for book publishing – Administered by SODEC.

Member of the CERC

Member of the *Association nationale des éditeurs de livres*

ASSOCIATION NATIONALE DES ÉDITEURS DE LIVRES

TABLE OF CONTENTS

Unit 8 When Human Rights Go Wrong

How can you stand up for human rights?

Explore what it means to have rights, and what happens when these rights are abused.

Options:
- ● Write a declaration of rights.
- ■ Write or record a persuasive editorial about a human rights issue.
- ◆ Create a video to promote human rights.

Grammar Adverbs and Their Position

Unit 9 Fast Forward 20

What will your life be like 20 years from now?

Take a walk into your future and see how different the world is. Measure your success.

Options:
- ● Describe a Fast Forward 20 product or service.
- ■ Write your autobiography @ 37.
- ◆ Create a comic strip about life @ 30-something.

Grammar Conditional Sentences

Section 2 Reading Folio

Texts Related to the Units and Workshops **202**

Three texts at different levels related to the theme of each unit. A selection of novels and non-fiction books is suggested for extra reading.

Texts of General Interest **274**

Texts from different genres for extra reading: novel excerpts, short stories, poems, biographies, magazine and newspaper articles.

Section 3 Reference Section

Grammar **302**
Vocabulary **332**
Strategies **340**
Processes **348**
Text Types **356**

OVERVIEW OF QUEST, YEAR THREE

Section 1 The Units and Workshops

The Opening Spread

You will find nine units and three workshops in *Quest* which are sure to appeal to different learning styles.

Each unit and workshop starts with a two-page spread. It tells you what you will be doing and learning.

The unit number and title help you identify the unit.
One large and three smaller photos give you ideas about the theme.
The title gives you an idea of what the unit is about.
Three questions start the conversation and activate your prior knowledge.
The introduction starts you thinking about the theme.
The guiding question presents you with a quest that you will discover as you go through the activities.
The unit overview describes the tasks that you will do and explains the final challenge.
This section refers you to the extra readings in the Reading Folio. Read more about the theme and practise your reading skills. The readings may also help you reach the conclusion of your quest.
UNIT 6
SONGS OF CHANGE
How can songs bring about social change?
How do you think musicians affect people's views?
What issues are musicians of your generation addressing?
How can music change the world?
Unit Overview
Reading Folio

The Phases of Learning

Each unit and workshop has three phases.

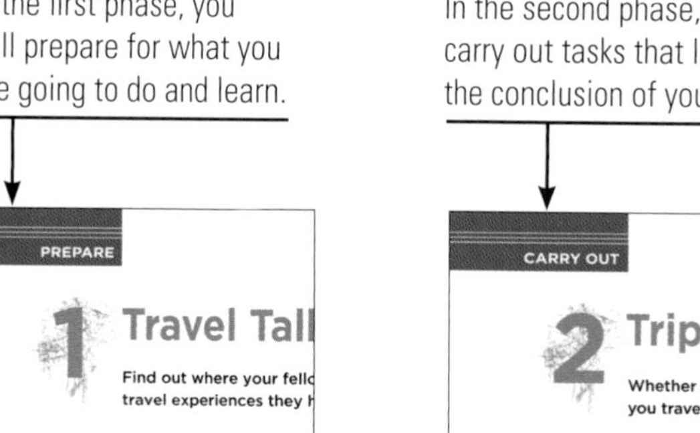

In the first phase, you will prepare for what you are going to do and learn.
In the second phase, you will carry out tasks that lead to the conclusion of your quest.
PREPARE
1 Travel Tal
CARRY OUT
2 Trip of a

In the final phase, you will integrate everything that you have learned.
INTEGRATE
YOUR Quest

The Tasks

Each phase includes one or more tasks.

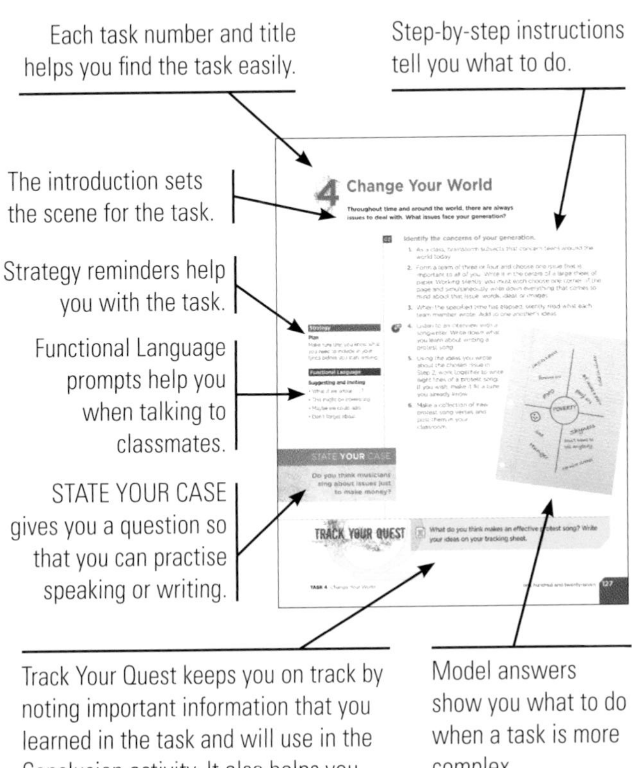

Each task number and title helps you find the task easily.
Step-by-step instructions tell you what to do.
The introduction sets the scene for the task.
Strategy reminders help you with the task.
Functional Language prompts help you when talking to classmates.
STATE YOUR CASE gives you a question so that you can practise speaking or writing.
4 Change Your World
TRACK YOUR QUEST
Track Your Quest keeps you on track by noting important information that you learned in the task and will use in the Conclusion activity. It also helps you reflect on your work.
Model answers show you what to do when a task is more complex.

Culture Capsule

Each unit includes a bonus reading for extra information.

The Culture Capsule tells you about aspects of English culture related to the unit.
CULTURE CAPSULE
Give Peace a Chance: John and Yoko in Montréal
The vocabulary helps you understand the text.

Integrated Grammar

Each unit includes two grammar pages.

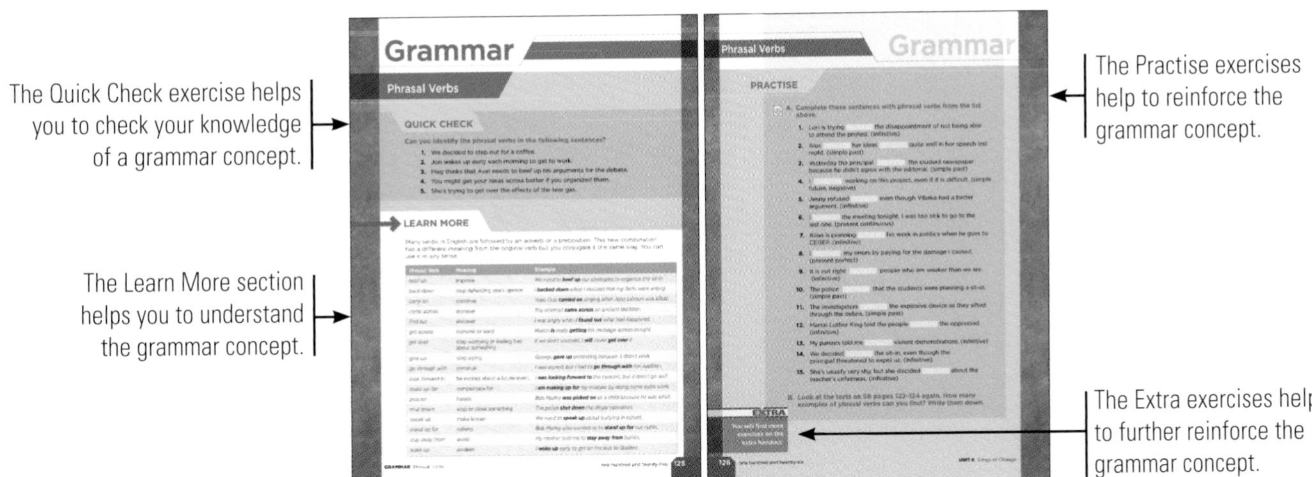

The Quick Check exercise helps you to check your knowledge of a grammar concept.
The Learn More section helps you to understand the grammar concept.
Grammar
Phrasal Verbs
QUICK CHECK
LEARN MORE
PRACTISE
EXTRA
The Practise exercises help to reinforce the grammar concept.
The Extra exercises help to further reinforce the grammar concept.

Your Quest......The Conclusion

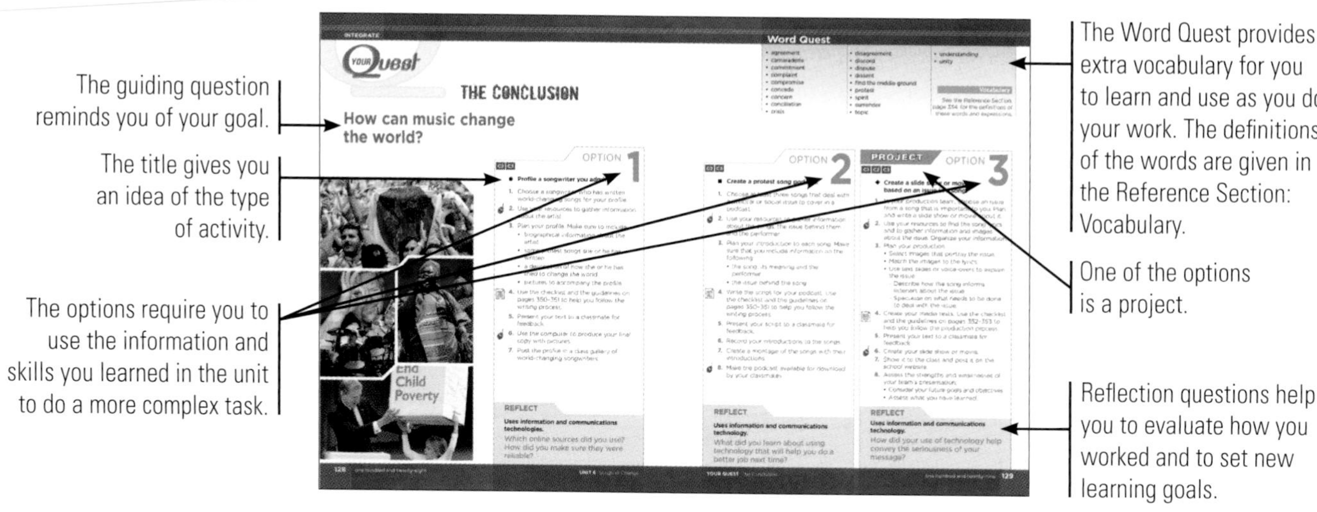

The guiding question reminds you of your goal.
The title gives you an idea of the type of activity.
The options require you to use the information and skills you learned in the unit to do a more complex task.
The Word Quest provides extra vocabulary for you to learn and use as you do your work. The definitions of the words are given in the Reference Section: Vocabulary.
One of the options is a project.
Reflection questions help you to evaluate how you worked and to set new learning goals.
THE CONCLUSION
How can music change the world?
Word Quest
OPTION 1
OPTION 2
PROJECT
OPTION 3
REFLECT

The Icons

Icons provide information quickly and easily.

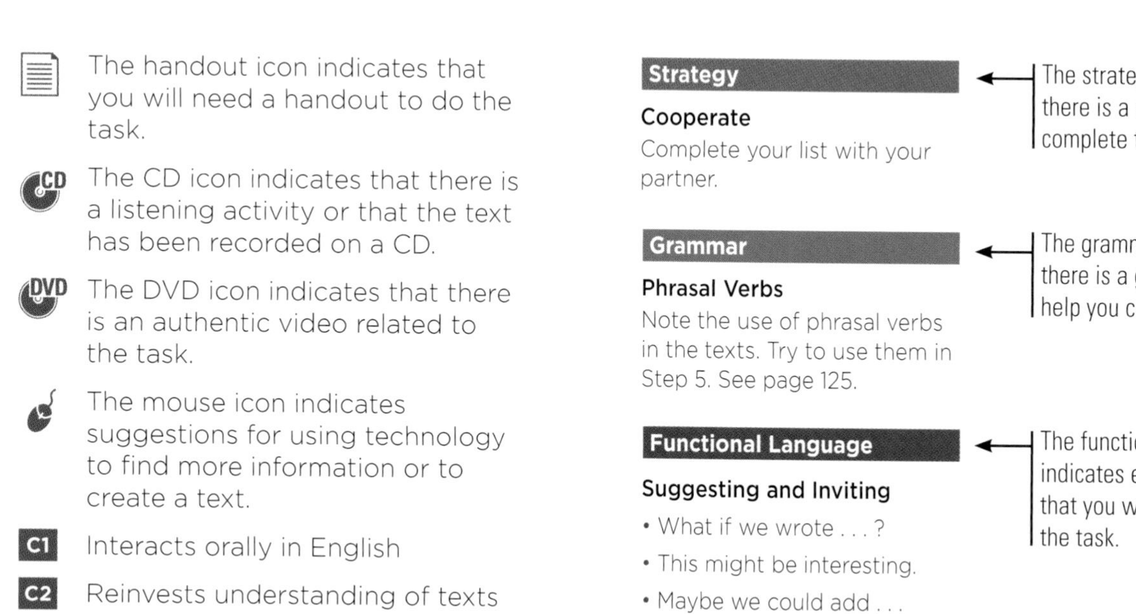

The handout icon indicates that you will need a handout to do the task.

The CD icon indicates that there is a listening activity or that the text has been recorded on a CD.

The DVD icon indicates that there is an authentic video related to the task.

The mouse icon indicates suggestions for using technology to find more information or to create a text.

C1 Interacts orally in English

C2 Reinvests understanding of texts

C3 Writes and produces texts

Strategy

Cooperate
Complete your list with your partner.

The strategy icon tells you that there is a strategy to help you complete the task.

Grammar

Phrasal Verbs
Note the use of phrasal verbs in the texts. Try to use them in Step 5. See page 125.

The grammar icon tells you that there is a grammar section to help you complete the task.

Functional Language

Suggesting and Inviting
- What if we wrote . . . ?
- This might be interesting.
- Maybe we could add . . .

The functional language icon indicates examples of language that you will need to complete the task.

Vocabulary

hurl: throw
drag: pull along the ground

The vocabulary icon indicates definitions of keywords from reading texts.

Section 2 Reading Folio

This section contains supplementary texts related to the units and workshops, as well as other texts of general interest. They will give you more information about the units and workshops and help you improve your reading skills.

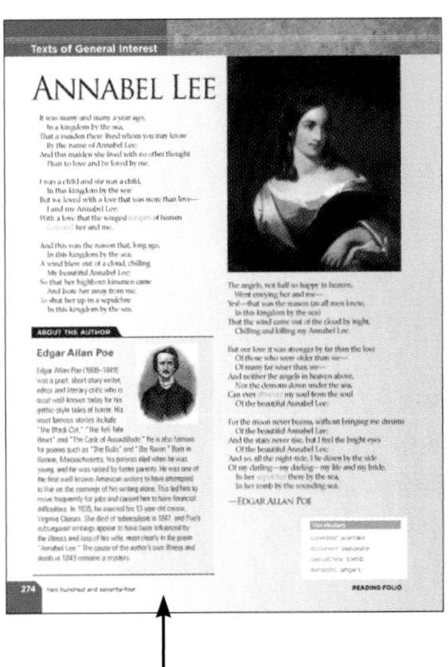

The Read-On feature suggests a novel or non-fiction book for you to enjoy.

The About the Author feature gives you extra information about the author's life and works.

Section 3 The Reference Section

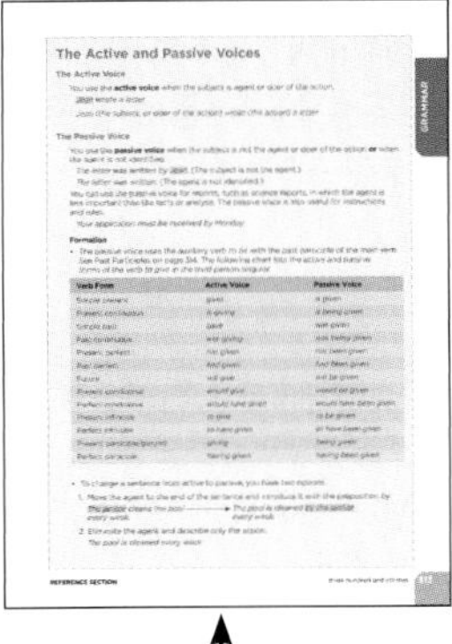

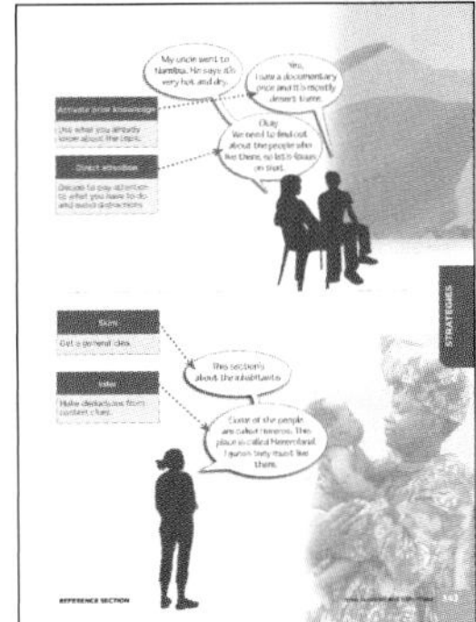

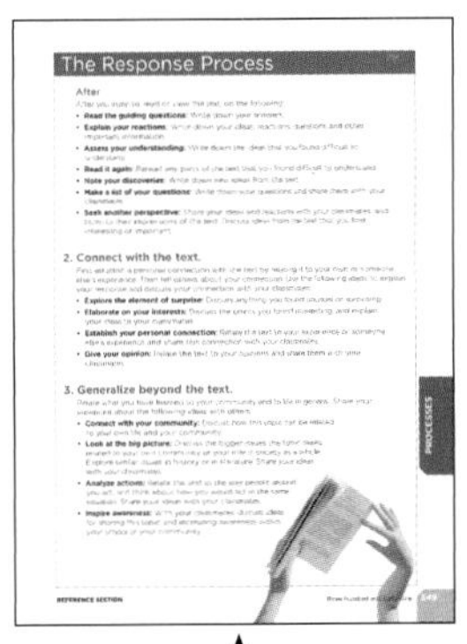

The grammar notes help you use English correctly.

The vocabulary helps you understand the text.

Learning and communication strategies help you learn English and communicate with others.

The processes help you respond to texts and write and produce them.

The text type examples explain and illustrate the different text types that you will encounter in the units and workshops.

UNIT 1

TICKET TO THE WORLD

- How does travel fit into your life plans?
- Which part of the world would you like to see?
- How would you like to experience this place?

Welcome! You are embarking on your last year of high school. Through the door of graduation, the whole world awaits you. Where will you go? How will you bring your memories home?

Do you dream of going on a safari in Kenya to enrich your career in zoology, or studying for a year in Spain to discover your family roots, or maybe spending time in the rainforests of Honduras as you take a year to decide what you really want to do in life? The world is closer than ever.

Choose your ticket and get ready for the travel experience of a lifetime.

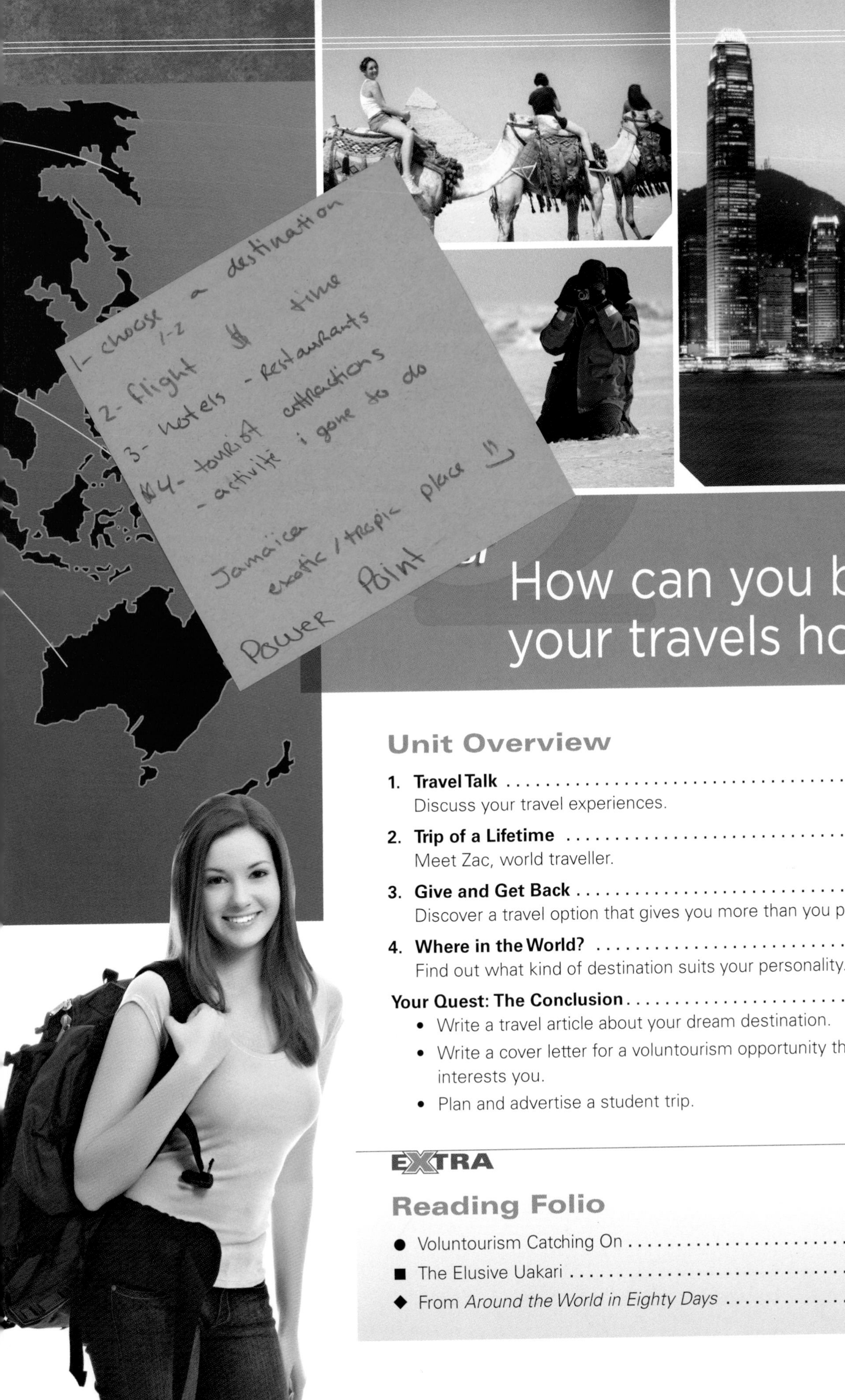

How can you bring your travels home?

Unit Overview

EXTRA

Reading Folio

Travel Talk

Find out where your fellow classmates have been and what travel experiences they have had.

Strategy

Practise

Think of different types of questions to ask to get different information.

Grammar

Indirect Speech

Change your classmates' responses to indirect speech when you report them to the other team. See pages 5-6.

Functional Language

Indirect Speech

- Melina said that . . .
- He told me that . . .
- She asked if . . .
- He explained that . . .

C1

Talk about where you have been.

1. Write down six questions to ask a classmate about his or her travel experiences and then interview your classmate.
2. Take turns reporting on your classmate's experiences to another team of two.

3. As you listen to your classmates' travel experiences, identify their destinations on a map. If you are not sure where they are, ask them questions about the location.

4. Find out approximately how many kilometres your team has travelled.
5. Compare your team's total travel distance with other teams to discover which team has travelled the furthest.
6. Discuss the reasons that you and your classmates travel.

Wizard Island, Oregon

Tadoussac, Québec

TRACK YOUR QUEST

On your tracking sheet, write the three most common reasons for travelling. Add examples of your classmates' destinations.

Grammar

Indirect Speech

QUICK CHECK

Can you change the following sentences to indirect (reported) speech?

1. She asked, "Do you like travelling?"
2. "The fifth person to call in will win a trip to Hawaii," announced the radio host.
3. "Where do we send our application forms for the Belize trip?" asked the students.
4. "I may never get another chance like this," Angel exclaimed.

LEARN MORE

Use

You use indirect (reported) speech to repeat what someone says without using the exact words. To do this, you need to make certain changes.

Direct speech: *"I always have a fabulous time in Cuba," Jonathan said.*

Indirect speech: *Jonathan told me that he always had a fabulous time in Cuba.*

Formation

1. Remove the quotation marks.
2. Change the tense of the verb in the direct speech if necessary.
3. Change pronouns and possessives from the first or second person to the third person, unless a speaker is reporting his or her own words.

   Direct speech: *"I met my cousin in Peru," said Mary.*

   Indirect speech: *Mary said that she had met her cousin in Peru.*

Direct Speech	Indirect Speech
Simple present *"I never go by train," he said.*	Simple past *He said that he never went by train.*
Present continuous *"I'm making reservations online," she explained.*	Past continuous *She explained that she was making reservations online.*
Present perfect *"I have already bought my ticket," Nash said.*	Past perfect *Nash said that he had already bought his ticket.*
Present perfect continuous *"I have been saving for the trip for months," said Marie.*	Past perfect continuous *Marie said that she had been saving for the trip for months.*
Simple past *"I cycled to Ottawa last summer," said Jacob.*	Past perfect *Jacob said that he had cycled to Ottawa last summer.*
Future (modal) *"I will leave when I finish my exams," said Kim.*	Past (modal) *Kim said that she would leave when she finished her exams.*
Future continuous (modal) *"I'll be arriving in Liberia on Independence Day," said Hussein.*	Past continuous (modal) *Hussein said that he would be arriving in Liberia on Independence Day.*

Note: In spoken English, we can often leave the verb in the original tense unless this causes confusion.

Grammar

4. Change time indicators to the past.
   Direct speech: *"I'm leaving tomorrow," said Guy.*
   Indirect speech: *Guy said that he was leaving the next day.*
   Direct speech: *"I'll be arriving this week," promised Anna.*
   Indirect speech: *Anna promised that she would be arriving that week.*
5. If there is no introductory verb, add an appropriate verb to introduce the speech, such as *to announce, to declare, to exclaim, to reply, to say, to warn.*
6. Add the word *that.*

To report a question

1. Make changes 1–4 above.
2. Remove the question mark.
3. If there is no introductory verb, add a verb of inquiry, such as *ask, inquire, wonder.*
4. If there is no question word, add the word *if.*
   Direct speech: *"What is in your bag?" asked the customs officer. "Did you pack it yourself?"*
   Indirect speech: *The customs officer asked me what was in my bag and if I had packed it myself.*

PRACTISE

 **Change the following sentences from direct to indirect speech.**

1. Marc asked, "Are there any travel sites that welcome new bloggers?"
2. The travel writers reported, "We have arrived in Morocco for a two-week stay."
3. The youth travel organizer answered, "Teens from 16 to 19 are welcome to apply."
4. Jeff wrote, "We were evacuated from the Playa Del Carmen Hotel yesterday because of the hurricane."
5. "Flight AC407 from Shanghai has been delayed because of the snowstorm," announced the sound system.
6. The poster at the currency exchange desk stated, "Canadian dollars are now accepted in Cuba."
7. The documentation explained, "To enter the U.S.A., you must have a valid Canadian passport now."
8. Claudia and Audrey complained, "We aren't comfortable at our hostel because the renovators are making too much noise and mess."

You will find more exercises on the extra handout.

Trip of a Lifetime

Whether you travel alone or with a group, by boat or by bike, the way you travel greatly affects your impressions.

C2 **Learn about Zac Sunderland's voyage.**

1. What does the word *circumnavigate* mean? Look at the prefix, then the root word.

2. Watch the story of a young adventurer who has travelled around the world. Write notes about:
   - Zac's goal
   - how he prepared for the voyage
   - his mother's feelings about the adventure
   - what makes him unique
   - his motivation
   - his challenges.

Strategy

Direct attention
As you watch the video, listen carefully to find information you need, and avoid all distractions.

Zac Sunderland, 2008

3. Discuss your ideas with your classmates. Use these questions to guide you.
   - What do you think Zac learned from his voyage?
   - How does his example encourage you to travel?
   - Would his example influence your choice of destination?

Strategy

Stall for time
Take time to think about your answer.

C2 **Learn how travel experiences differ.**

4. Look at the article on page 8. Use the photo, title and quotation to predict what it is about.
5. Read the article. Use the questions beneath the text to guide your reading.
6. Compare this journey with Zac's and think about:
   - the reason for each trip
   - which experience is more exciting
   - which experience would have the greatest impact on your life
   - which trip you would prefer and why
   - which country or area you would like to discover this way.
7. Share your view with your classmates. Support your ideas with examples from the two journeys.

Strategy

Compare
Look for similarities and differences between the two journeys.

Sea to Sea Riders Tell of Hard Pedalling and Stunning Beauty

Over two hundred cyclists set off on the Sea to Sea Bike Tour this morning. The journey covers 6246 km, for an average of 116 km per day. It requires some hard pedalling and climbing a 1236-m peak. The goal of the tour is to raise funds to help reduce poverty and to increase awareness of poverty worldwide.

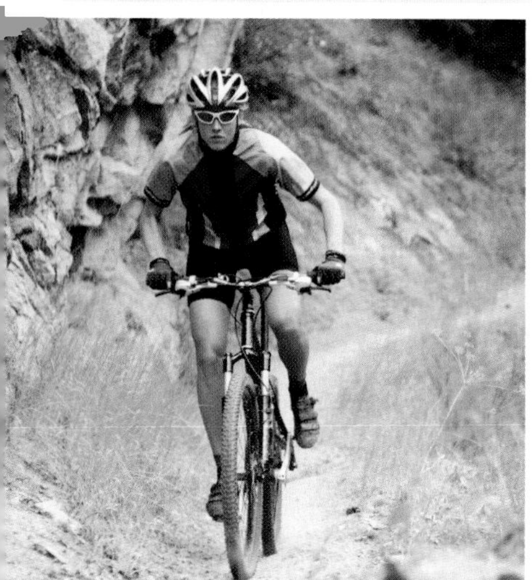

"We went up and then up and then up some more, over Stevens Pass and then down for a long time. It was a really hard day and I am whooped."

After a gruelling first day during which Sea to Sea riders had to conquer their first mountain pass, they hit the road for the 93-km trek to Ellensburg, Washington. Blogs posted on the Sea to Sea website give a glimpse of what riders are experiencing on the tour that will cross the United States and part of Canada.

"It was gorgeous as we climbed up Stevens Pass in Washington State," writes Nathan Beach of Ann Arbor, Michigan, in his blog. "The climb is a fairly steep incline for 11 km and we gained about 1000 m in altitude. The Cascade Mountains are filled with waterfalls, flowers, wildlife and beautiful whitewater rapids. It's spectacular."

Tyler Buitenwerf from Grand Rapids, Michigan, says in his blog how beautiful the ride has been so far. But it's also been tough. "We went up and then up and then up some more, over Stevens Pass and then down for a long time. It was a very hard day and I am whooped. Tomorrow is more climbing but 36 fewer km, so it should not be too bad."

One of the highlights, along with the scenery and fellowship, was being able to stop for ice cream, writes Randy DeWolde, a rider from Chilliwack, British Columbia. From there, he says, it was on to camp and some much-needed rest. "The last people came in to a rousing cheer just as supper was starting."

For Gayle Harrison, the ride included a snowball fight near Stevens Pass and a chance to breathe air that smelled of Christmas trees. She is from London, Ontario.

Jo Tipple, a rider from Ghent, New York, says there are varying levels of cycling abilities on the tour, but people are hanging together. For her, the descent from Stevens Pass "echoed to the roar and majesty of the whitewater of the Wenachee River as storm clouds rolled in above."

Vocabulary

awareness: knowledge
fellowship: friendship
glimpse: idea
gorgeous: beautiful
gruelling: exhausting
hanging together: encouraging each other
rousing: encouraging
trek: long or difficult journey
whooped: exhausted

1. What was the purpose of the bike ride?
2. How was the trip challenging?
3. What made the riders want to continue the gruelling ride day after day?
4. How do you think the experience changed the riders?
5. Whose experience can you most relate to and why?

C1 Plan a trip around the world.

8. Choose various means of transportation to travel around the world.
9. Plan your trip, making stops in 10 different countries. Mark your route on your map. Be ready to justify your choices.
10. Decide how long you would spend in each place and what you would do there.
11. Present your journey to your classmates and give reasons for your choices. Answer your classmates' questions.
12. There is a proverb that says, "They that travel far know much." Do you agree with this proverb? Discuss your answers with your classmates.

Functional Language

Asking for Clarification and Clarifying

- What do you mean exactly?
- Can you repeat that, please?
- I don't understand what you just said.
- Can you give an example?

TRACK YOUR QUEST

What can you learn by travelling? Write your ideas on your tracking sheet.

Give and Get Back

Travel is not only about postcards and sightseeing. Learn about a different kind of travel opportunity.

Strategy

Activate prior knowledge
Think of what you already know about voluntourism before you listen to the recording.

C1 C2 Learn how visiting a place can challenge your personal views and values.

1. Have you ever heard of *voluntourism*? What root words do you recognize? What does it mean?
2. In groups of four, write down all the voluntourism opportunities that you know about.

3. Listen to Tricia Sharpe and find out how a work placement in Sri Lanka changed her life.
4. With a classmate, discuss what you should find out before your trip so that you avoid negative surprises.

Strategy

Infer
Use the title, subtitles and photos to predict what you will learn from the poster.

C2 Find out about voluntouring opportunities.

5. Read the poster on page 11 to find out more about opportunities to help others while you travel. Choose an opportunity that appeals to you.
6. Use your resources to research the opportunity you have chosen. Think about why it appeals to you and discover what you can do to help.
7. Write about your choice and the reasons you made it. Use these questions to guide you:
   - What attracts you to this project?
   - What could you do to make a difference?
   - How could the experience challenge you?
   - What would you hope to learn from it?

STATE **YOUR** CASE

Who benefits more from voluntourism: visitors or local inhabitants?

EarthWorks

For teens who want to change their world!

How can I make today count? How can I make a difference?

EarthWorks has the answer . . . and an invitation. We are a non-profit organization looking for 16- to 19-year-olds who have from one week to one year to give in order to help create a better future for people in need.

Every day you read about pollution, endangered species and fragile ecosystems. News reports show graphic images of war and poverty. Markets are unstable and sometimes the future doesn't appear too bright.

Many people are looking for ways to make a better tomorrow. You're probably no exception. You don't want to just sit around and talk about things. You want to roll up your sleeves and get in there!

EarthWorks appeals to voluntourists rather than to people who just want to visit popular tourist destinations and get a tan. A voluntourist is someone who wants to see the world, but also give back.

Do you have the heart of a teen voluntourist?

Then check us out. Depending on the type of training and experience you have, we can plug you into one of our exciting volunteer opportunities around the globe.

Take a look at some of these examples:

- **Protecting the rainforest in Puerto Rico**
- **Teaching English or French in Senegal**
- **Rebuilding schools and caring for schoolchildren in Morocco**
- **Working in an orphanage in Romania**

Each project involves three parts: community work, recreation opportunities and team meetings. EarthWorks alumni have the following to say about their experience:

When I arrived in Churchill, I wasn't really sure I was cut out for working in such a cold place, but when I saw the appreciation on the faces of the people who were working with us, I knew I had to continue.
Mandy, 16

It was the best trip I have ever taken. It wasn't just fun—it made me realize what I want to do with my life.
Simon, 17

Ideal EarthWorks candidates are:

- between 16 and 19
- high school, college or university students
- in excellent health
- enthusiastic, open and service-oriented
- young people with a wide world view
- able to raise financial support to pay their way
- looking for a challenge that will change their world and their lives!

If this sounds like you, just ask for an application form.

TRACK YOUR QUEST

What voluntourism opportunities appeal to you? Write your ideas and feelings on your tracking sheet.

4 Where in the World?

Who you are colours the places you visit and what you do there. What kind of destination suits you?

Strategy

Skim

First read the texts quickly to identify keywords and important ideas.

Discover your classmates' dream destinations.

1. Look at the photos on pages 13–14 and rank the places by order of preference. Compare your preferences with a classmate.

2. Read the articles. Choose one of the destinations or find another and fill in your travel ticket.
3. Post your ticket on the board and read your classmates' to find:
   - the most popular destination
   - the most common form of travel.
4. Use the information from the articles and your own ideas to answer the question, How does your choice of destination suit your personality?

Dream Destinations

You live only once, so where are you going to go? What are you going to do?

Dream Destinations

1 Photography Lover

Skeleton Coast, Namibia

Photographers in search of the dramatic need look no further. This African region derives its name from the eerie whale bones found along the beach. The rapidly changing weather, often foggy coast, ghostly shipwrecks and startling sand dunes create unforgettable shots. The shore along this part of the Atlantic Ocean is dotted with tiny villages inhabited mainly by people who fish for a living.

A huge national park spreading over 1.6 million hectares attracts visitors to the dunes, plains, canyons of volcanic rock, and mountain ranges. The park is divided into two parts. The southern part consists of a wilderness area which has excellent sea fishing and wildlife. The northern part is home to the Himba people, nomadic herders who still live as their ancestors did.

OTHER SUGGESTIONS
- Isle of Skye, Scotland
- Victoria Falls, Zimbabwe and Zambia
- Utah, U.S.A.

2 Extreme Adventurer

Mount Everest, Nepal and Tibet

Climbing majestic Mount Everest is a cherished dream of many mountain climbers for the oustanding challenge, the spectacular views and the incomparable feeling of accomplishment. Located in the Himalayas bordering Nepal and Tibet, this formidable mountain rises close to 8850 metres and was formed 60 million years ago. The Nepalese call it "goddess of the sky."

The first climbers to reach the top of Everest were Sir Edmund Hillary and Tenzing Norgay. The youngest is Ming Kipa Sherpa, who was only 15. Although the unforgiving mountain, with its life-threatening avalanches and fatal snowstorms, has been the burial site of many climbers, Everest continues to fascinate climbers of every age.

OTHER SUGGESTIONS
- Doing the Chomolhari Trek, Bhutan
- Surfing off the Canary Islands
- Snowboarding at Whistler, Canada

Vocabulary

burial site: place where a dead body is laid
eerie: strange
ghostly: phantom-like

3 | History Buff
Petra, Jordan

OTHER SUGGESTIONS
- Chitchen Itza, Mexico
- Pompeii, Italy
- Easter Island, South Pacific

Just east of ancient Israel, in Jordan, Petra is a UNESCO World Heritage Site that any serious history lover dreams of discovering personally. The city was founded by the Nabataeans, an Arab people, over 2000 years ago. It is strategically located between the Red Sea and the Dead Sea and was a key route for traders of silk, spices and other wares. Petra prospered until the Romans defeated it in the second century AD. It was rediscovered in the 1800s by a Swiss explorer. The rose-red stone city never fails to astonish visitors with its impressive monuments, magnificent architecture and majestic backdrop of rugged mountains. The city is one of the New Seven Wonders of the World and was featured in an Indiana Jones movie in 1989.

4 | Culture Freak
Montréal, Canada

As one of North America's oldest cities, Montréal is a culture lover's dream. Whether you want music, theatre, art, dance or film, this city has it. Many famous writers (Mordecai Richler, Gabrielle Roy), musicians (Oscar Peterson, Leonard Cohen), playwrights (Michel Tremblay) and classical music groups (I Musici, Opéra de Montréal) made or make Montréal their home. The city's many venues, such as the Bell Centre, Place des Arts and Salle Pierre-Péladeau, offer its cosmopolitan population popular shows and festivals throughout the year. Visitors are always delighted with its excellent museums, such as the Museum of Fine Arts, the Canadian Centre of Architecture and the Musée d'art contemporain.

OTHER SUGGESTIONS
- Paris, France
- London, England
- Salzburg, Austria

5 | Fun Lover
Bunyol, Spain

Feel like participating in a mega food fight? Spanish natives and intrigued visitors do just that once a year during La Tomatina. This exciting festival takes place in the last week of August in Bunyol in the southern province of Valencia. Bunyol is usually a quiet industrial town, but once a year organized chaos reigns as the streets turn into a major salsa dish! There are a number of theories as to how the riot began. One is that the festival started in the 1940s when a local political protest turned into a tomato-throwing incident. Another theory is that two friends were arguing and ended up throwing food at each other. However, the most likely explanation is that it was a kind of gang war between two groups of teens proving their loyalty. Now it is an annual event that attracts curious tourists from around the world. This is one festival party lovers just won't want to miss. Don't forget to bring a change of clothes!

OTHER SUGGESTIONS
- Mardi Gras, New Orleans, U.S.A.
- Carnivale, Rio De Janeiro, Brazil
- Fringe Festival, Edinburgh, Scotland

Vocabulary

astonish: surprise

playwrights: people who write plays

rugged: rough

venues: concert and meeting halls

Teaching English to Karen Hill Tribe Children, Thailand

Last summer some students in my English class travelled to Thailand to help teach English to children at the local school.

The project was based at the school in the small village of Guid, 105 km north of Chiang Mai. During our time volunteering at the school, we helped to teach a class of 20 to 25 students aged from 6 to 15 years. We taught in the mornings and in the afternoons we had time to prepare for the next day's lessons, explore the surrounding area—there is a beautiful waterfall in the village—or visit nearby towns.

In the village we stayed with a local family in their traditional Thai home. Accommodation was basic but comfortable; we had a mattress, a mosquito net and a fan. There was no running hot water in the village, so showering involved pouring rain water over ourselves from a barrel. The toilet was Asian style with no toilet paper. There was electricity, so we were able to charge cellphones and camera batteries. There was usually good cellphone coverage in the village.

Guid is a small village with a population of around 300. There are basic amenities such as a convenience store and small market. The nearest large town is Matong, 30 km away, where there are larger shops and Internet cafés. Buses run approximately every two hours between Guid and Matong and cost approximately 60 baht (three dollars) each way.

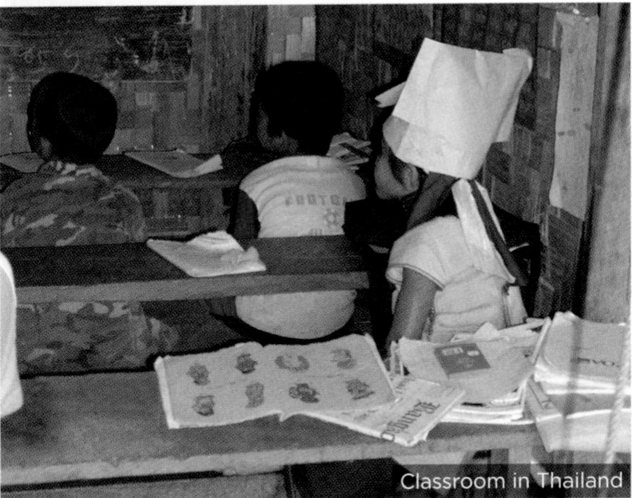
Classroom in Thailand

Helping to teach at the school was an immensely rewarding experience. The school has 10 classrooms and teaches around 250 local children. As volunteers we taught a class alone and prepared our own lessons. However, the school does have a full-time voluntary English teacher, Mr. Tony, who has been at the school for just over a year. He was our guide throughout the trip and advised us on lesson plans and teaching aids. We could easily contact him for help during class time. The children are extremely keen to learn English and to practise with an English-speaking person. Our time volunteering there was a great help to Mr. Tony, because the village cannot afford to pay for other teachers.

Vocabulary

keen: interested
rewarding: satisfying

How would a visit to your dream destination fit into your life goals? Write your answer on your tracking sheet.

THE CONCLUSION

How can you bring your travels home?

OPTION 1

C3

- **Write a travel article about your dream destination.**

1. Write a travel article for your school or local newspaper.
2. Determine your topic, purpose and audience.
3. If your destination is a place you have never visited, use the Internet or the library to gather information about it. If it is a place you have been to, gather photos and information from your trip.
4.  Plan your text. Use the checklist and the guidelines on pages 350–351 to help you organize your ideas. Make sure you include the following:
   - Introduction: topic, purpose
   - Development: unusual characteristics, fun places, interesting events
   - Conclusion: how you feel about this place and why the reader should visit it
   - Photos, if you wish.
5. Use persuasive language such as colourful adjectives to describe places and events. Use correct grammar and punctuation to communicate your ideas.
6. Publish your article.

REFLECT

Communicates appropriately.

Which codes, conventions and grammar rules did you integrate into your travel article?

Word Quest

- accommodation
- airline
- backpacking
- ballooning
- currency
- exchange
- fare
- handbook
- hitchhike
- journey
- landmark
- off the beaten track
- road trip
- sightseeing
- suitcase
- tour guide
- traveller
- trend
- wilderness

Vocabulary

See the Reference Section, page 332, for the definitions of these words and expressions.

OPTION 2

C3

■ **Write a cover letter for a voluntourism opportunity that interests you.**

1. Research voluntourism opportunities and choose one that interests you.
2. Write a cover letter to accompany your application form.
3. Refer to Task 3 to recall opportunities and ideas you would like to include in your letter.
4. Organize your ideas. Include the following:
   - Introduction: your name and age, the opportunity you are interested in
   - Development: three reasons you would like to participate (i.e. personal goals, things you would like to do, why you are an ideal candidate)
   - Conclusion: summarize how you think the experience would benefit you.
5. Remember to use an appropriate letter format. See the model in the Reference Section, page 362.

6. Use the checklist and the guidelines on pages 350–351 to help you follow the writing process.
7. Send your letter by mail or email.

REFLECT

Communicates appropriately.

How did you use the language from this unit to write an effective letter?

PROJECT OPTION 3

C3 C1

◆ **Plan and advertise a student trip.**

1. Work with a classmate to choose a class trip you would like to suggest for the end of the year.

2. Do a search to find out how to get to the place, what to do there, how much the trip would cost, and other details.

3. Decide on your ad media type: radio ad, school web page, electronic presentation or pamphlet. Use the checklist and the guidelines on pages 352–353 to help you follow the production process.
4. Plan and write the ad. Include an introduction and a conclusion.

5. Choose original images from the Internet, newspapers or travel magazines. Identify your images in the presentation.
6. Create your final media text.
7. Present your media text to a classmate.
8. Present your project, considering your choice of media type and audience.
9. Assess the strengths and weaknesses of your media text:
   - Consider your audience's reaction.
   - Decide what you would do differently next time.
   - Review your goals and objectives.

REFLECT

Communicates appropriately.

How did you decide which media type to use for your ad?

UNIT 2

BOUNCE BACK

1. What makes a survivor?
2. How can I be ready for life's unexpected events?
3. How can difficult situations make me a stronger person?

It has been said, "Tough times never last, but tough people do." News reports and reality shows demonstrate people's power to beat all odds. There is always something to learn from bad experiences, whether they are natural disasters, problems with a friend or personal upsets.

You're in transition between high school and the real world, between being a teenager and becoming an adult. How can you cope with the challenges? What do you need to know?

Everyday situations—measuring up to high standards, dealing with stressful exams, coping with unsuccessful dates, performing in challenging tournaments, maintaining good relationships, fighting the odds against illness and making difficult decisions—require personal strength. In the game of life, are you equipped to win?

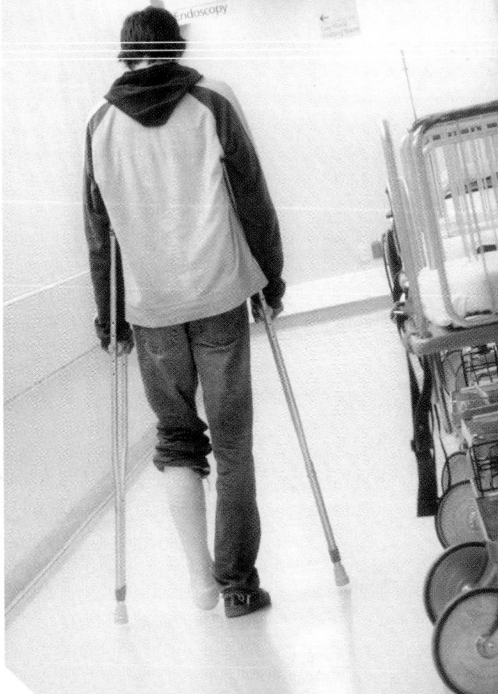

YOUR Quest

How can you bounce back in life?

Unit Overview

EXTRA

Reading Folio

Yes, We Can!

How you face life every day reveals who you are.

Strategy

Substitute
Use different words to express the idea of *human spirit*.

Functional Language

Agreeing, Disagreeing and Giving an Opinion
- I think that he/she . . .
- Yes, but they didn't . . .
- My point is that . . .
- I don't think so.
- That's true but . . .
- I'm not saying that . . . it's just that . . .

C1 Define a strong human spirit.

1. It has been said that the human spirit is stronger than anything that happens to it. What do the words *human spirit* make you think of?

2. In teams of four:
   - Take turns identifying people such as athletes, politicians and celebrities who have overcome obstacles and who exemplify a strong human spirit.
   - Identify their accomplishments and explain your choice.
   - Describe the obstacles and how the people overcame them.
   - Classify the obstacles and compare the ways of dealing with them.

C3 C1 Write about your own experience.

3. Think about how you would describe your own spirit. Use a graphic organizer to list the words you would use to describe yourself when facing adversity.

4. Write a short text describing a difficult situation you had to face and the qualities you demonstrated in dealing with it. Use the checklist and the guidelines on pages 350–351 to help you follow the writing process.
5. In a team of four, share what you wrote with your classmates and discuss the following questions:
   - How would you describe your classmates' spirit?
   - Are you all go-getters?
   - Who can you rely on to help you in difficult times this year?

Saku Koivu, 2002

TRACK YOUR QUEST

What are the characteristics of a strong human spirit? Write your answer on your tracking sheet.

2 The Winning Edge

Learn how some people find a way to turn discouraging situations to their advantage.

Strategy

Pay selective attention

Listen to the text and try to identify the clues that tell you how Raphael is coping.

Functional Language

Agreeing, Disagreeing and Giving an Opinion

- Why do you say that . . . ?
- I don't know. I think that . . .
- I don't think so because . . .
- That's what I think, too.
- That's my point exactly.
- It seems to me that . . .
- I still think that . . .
- That sounds . . . to me . . .
- All I'm saying is . . .

C2

Discover how hardship builds character.

1. What is *resilience*? Look it up in a dictionary if you need to. As a class, discuss: Why is it important to be resilient?
2. Think back to the situation you wrote about in Task 1, Step 4. Read the following questions and write your answers under your text:
   - Did you show resilience? Explain your answer.
   - What did you learn about yourself in the situation?
   - Did it help when you faced the next difficult situation?
   - Will you react the same way when you encounter another obstacle?

3. Listen to the story of a teen who faced a difficult challenge and find out how he coped with it.
4. Compare your reactions to a difficult situation with Raphael's. Would you have reacted in the same way? What do you think gave Raphael the winning edge? Discuss your answers with a classmate.
5. Write down your thoughts on the following, then discuss the issues with your classmates:
   - a similar experience you have heard of
   - how being in a difficult situation is different from supporting a person who has difficulties
   - how life's experiences can develop someone's character.

C2

Discuss secrets to survival.

6. Read about a teen who is coping with the aftermath of an accident. Use the questions beneath the text to guide your reading.
7. Compare Véronique's story with Raphael's in a Venn diagram. Include details about their challenges and treatment, the ways they helped others, their attitudes and their ingredients for the winning edge.
8. Compare your diagram with a classmate's. Discuss how these teens *might* have reacted to this type of situation compared with how they *did* react.
9. List ways that Raphael's and Véronique's examples inspire you to react to future challenges.

A Well-Kept Secret

Véronique is a 14-year-old with a secret: the skin on her back, legs, chest and abdomen is scarred for life. But this young teen won't stop smiling.

Véronique Potvin is someone who will probably never stop dancing through life. Two years ago she sustained deep, second-degree burns to her chest, abdomen, arms, back and thighs. But through it all she never lost her smile.

At the age of 12, Véronique was cooking pasta when she fainted and hit her head on the handle of a pot of boiling water. "The water splashed on me and I screamed my head off," she says. Her older sister called 911 and Véronique was rushed to the pediatric and adolescent trauma centre at the Montréal Children's Hospital.

Véronique was taken to the ICU where she was diagnosed with second-degree burns, which means that the top and deeper layers of skin were injured. Silver dressings—bandages that have antibacterial properties—were applied to Véronique's injuries. "She sustained burns to 30 per cent of her body," says Diane Richard, the Coordinator of the Burn Trauma Program, one of five trauma programs at the Montréal Children's Hospital. "But we also found out that Véronique had diabetes and she had fainted because her blood sugar level was very high."

Véronique stayed in the ICU for two days and was then moved to a ward where she remained for two and a half months while her burns healed. During this time she learned how to manage her diabetes, but she also learned that she had a bacterial infection in her back. "Because bacteria like sugar and Véronique's sugar levels were so high, it was hard to ensure she would not get an infection, even though she was on antibiotics and she had silver dressings on her burns," says Diane.

Unfortunately, owing to the infection, Véronique had to go into the operating room and have her wound scrubbed to remove the bacteria. "Because of the scrubbing, I had to have skin from my buttocks, legs and lower back grafted onto my back," says Véronique, who missed her first semester of school that year.

"Véronique was amazing," says Diane, "because through it all—the removal and placing of dressings every few days, which is never pain-free—she would be right back to smiling once we finished. She is a very beautiful person. She always puts her bright side forward."

Diane says it's difficult for the Trauma Program members, who include physiotherapists, occupational therapists, social workers, psychologists, child life specialists, plastic surgeons and nurses, to see young patients with burns. "We are used to seeing traumatic injuries, but burns are difficult emotionally because of the extreme pain the young patients have to endure," says Diane. "We treat over 200 burn victims a year. About 75 per cent are due to scald burns, the rest are due to fire."

This past summer, Véronique attended a burn jamboree for young burn victims. "There, I saw a lot of people with facial scars. Before this, I always felt very self-conscious about my scars, but this changed me forever. I saw these people just accepting and being happy in their skin regardless of the scarring. I decided then and there that this is my life and I will not live it for others—I will live it for me. I would tell all young burn victims to do the same."

Today, Véronique is back on track and excelling in school and dance. [. . .] And she wants to do well in school because one day she would like to become a nurse. "I want to help people get better," she says. "I want to see them smile. My friends tell me I have a poetic take on life. Maybe I do."

Today, Véronique is back on track and excelling in school and dance. "I really like ballet, jazz and hip hop," says Véronique, who is in a dance school where she practises these dances to popular music. And she wants to do well in school because one day she would like to become a nurse. "I want to help people get better," she says. "I want to see them smile. My friends tell me I have a poetic take on life. Maybe I do."

Source: The Montréal Children's Hospital Foundation

Vocabulary

fainted: fell unconscious
ICU: intensive care unit
jamboree: celebration, rally
scald burns: burns caused by hot water
scarred: badly marked
scrubbed: scraped
sustained: suffered

1. How did Véronique have her accident?
2. Why were her burns slow to heal?
3. Why did she need to have an operation and skin grafts?
4. How did Véronique react to her treatment?
5. In what ways does Véronique want to help others?

TRACK YOUR QUEST

How can your attitude make you a winner? Write your opinion on your tracking sheet.

3 Coping Skills

Have you ever thought that talking or writing about a difficult situation could help you cope with it?

Strategy

Infer

When you read the titles, use the keywords to determine the content of the articles.

Functional Language

Asking for Clarification and Clarifying

- So you're saying that you . . .
- What do you mean?
- Can you say that differently?
- That means . . .
- In other words . . .
- What they're saying is . . .

C2

Discover coping skills for difficult situations.

1. Look at the title of the article on page 25 to infer what it is about. Then read the article and take notes on how the writer deals with her feelings. Use the questions below the text to guide your understanding.
2. With a classmate, brainstorm how young people try to bounce back from difficult situations. List the ten most common ways.

3. Present your list to your classmates. Take notes as you listen to other teams and then, as a class, make a list of the five best skills.

4. Sometimes people react to major disappointments and challenges by becoming depressed. With your classmate, write down the signs of depression. Use your resources to find out more.
5. How could you help a friend cope with depression? Reread the list of skills from Step 3. Decide which skill would be most effective and why. Write down your answer.
6. As a class, discuss: Why is it important to develop coping skills?

The Struggle to Be Strong: How Writing Helps Me

Terry-Ann Da Costa

I think I developed a love of writing from my father. When I was a little girl he used to sit me on his lap, hold my hand, and help me write poems and stories.

I was raised by my father on the Caribbean island of Jamaica. I started writing when I was about four years old. When I was seven, my father gave me a diary to write in so that I wouldn't write on the walls or on his papers. I wrote at least three hours a day, and my father helped me whenever I wanted him to.

When I was twelve, I came to America to live with my mother. By then I was very good at writing. I wrote short stories about my family, my life, and my friends. I wrote poems about the things I was going through. If I had a bad day or a good day, I would write about what made the day so bad or so good.

I remember that whenever I wrote a poem, I would show it to my mother. She would crumple it up, throw it in the garbage, and tell me I couldn't have written it—and if I did, how did I know how to do it? When I told her that my father showed me and helped me with the poems, she would get mad and put me down.

She told me I wasn't going to be anything when I grew up, that I would only be a burger flipper. That really hurt my feelings. I couldn't understand why she was saying these things to me.

But that never stopped me from writing. I wrote about all the bad and good things she said and did to me. If she told me she loved me, I would write about how good that made me feel. If she bragged about me to her friends, I would write about how special I felt to have a mother who was not ashamed to have me for a daughter. Soon I had five diaries filled with poems and stories.

My favourite writer is Stephen King because I like to read and write about horror. My favourite book is *Carrie*, and my favourite poet is Edgar Allan Poe. I like Poe's poems because he writes with irony, like I do. You won't understand most of his poems if you read

When I was twelve, I came to America to live with my mother. By then I was very good at writing. I wrote short stories about my family, my life, and my friends. I wrote poems about the things I was going through. If I had a bad day or a good day, I would write about what made the day so bad or so good.

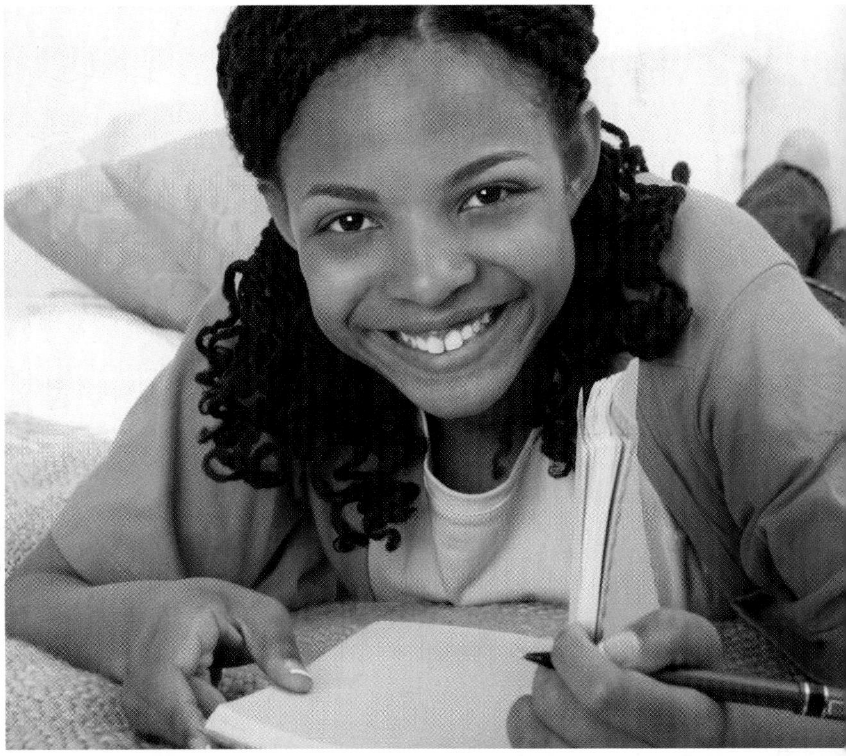

them only once. But if you read them over and over, you'll eventually understand what he's saying.

Sometimes when I'm in a bad mood and I can't think of anything to write, I choose a passage from one of my diaries and read it—or maybe I'll read all five diaries. That makes me feel better because it's like talking to a friend.

Writing has helped me through a lot. I remember one day I was really depressed. I wrote about what made me feel that way, and then I read over what I'd written. That helped me feel a lot better, because when I read it I couldn't believe I was capable of having those harmful, dangerous thoughts and feelings about myself.

Writing helped me when I was going through difficult times with my family—when they didn't or couldn't understand me, or when they didn't understand why I would cry for no reason. Writing helped me when I needed someone to talk to. Writing is like both my friend and my family because it's always there for me whenever I need it.

My mother still doesn't believe I can write on my own. She thinks I copy my poems and stories from someone else. My sisters think I'm crazy because they don't see how writing words on a piece of paper could help me with my problems.

But my cousin understands me. When she was going through a difficult stage, I made her read one of my poems about the beauty of life. She said it really helped her and made her look at herself in a new way. She was also very impressed with my poems.

I would like to be a writer someday. When I publish a story or a poem, I'll give it to my mother so she can see she was wrong about me being nothing when I grow up. She'll see I can write on my own, that I didn't copy anyone's poems or stories. She won't be able to say I'm lying because my name will be right there on the cover.

There's another reason I would like to be a writer. I know that if someone has a problem and they read my story or poem, it might make them feel a little (or even a lot) better about themselves.

Source: FreeSpirit Publishing: *The Struggle to Be Strong*

Vocabulary

ashamed: embarrassed

bragged: boasted

burger flipper: person who works in a fast-food restaurant

irony: double meaning

lying: not telling the truth

1. How did Terry-Ann start writing?
2. How did her mother react to her poems?
3. What kinds of things does she express in writing?
4. How does Terry-Ann use writing to help herself?
5. Why do you think her mother doesn't believe that Terry-Ann can write poems and stories?

TRACK YOUR QUEST

You have just discussed how important it is to have effective coping skills. What did you learn about your own skills? Write your answers on your tracking sheet.

Being Tough

Life is a game of win or lose. What character traits do you have to help you be a winner?

Strategy

Encourage yourself and others

Listen carefully and give positive feedback to your classmates.

Functional Language

Encouraging Others

- Wow, you're really brave!
- You're great!
- I couldn't have done it as well as you did.
- That's really impressive!

Grammar

Modals

Use modals to help you write your ideas. See page 30.

C2

Identify your character traits.

1. Read the poem on page 28. Check your understanding by discussing the questions below the text with a classmate.
2. List the character traits mentioned in the poem. Add other traits that help a person build resilience. Rank them all in order of importance.

3. With your classmate, talk about situations in which you or someone you know demonstrated any of these traits. Write down the situations and traits.
4. Keep a journal for a week. Write down difficult situations and disappointments that you experience and how you reacted to them.
5. Think about the character traits that helped you or could have helped you during the week. Write down what you could have done differently.

STATE **YOUR** CASE

When someone is faced with a problem, what is more important: attitude or actions?

Inspirations

Tom Krause

Courage is the discovery that you may not win.
And trying when you know you can lose.

Honour is standing for what you believe—
Not for what you know.

Life isn't about living without problems.
Life is about solving problems.

If you plough the field every day—
The only thing that grows is resentment.

Compassion is passion with a heart.

The only thing in the whole universe people need to
control is their attitude.

How a person wins and loses is much more important
than *how much* a person wins and loses.

If you only do what you know you can do—
You never do very much.

There are no failures—
just experiences and your reactions to them.

Getting what you want is not nearly as important
As giving what you have.

Going on a journey with a map requires following direction—
going on a journey without one requires following your heart.

Talent without humility is wasted.

If you don't want it bad enough to risk losing it—
You don't want it bad enough.

When life knocks you down you have two choices—
Stay down or get up.

Compassion is passion with a heart.

Source: Jack Canfield, *Chicken Soup for the Teenage Soul III*

Vocabulary

journey: travel

knocks down: pushes to the ground

plough: prepare for planting

standing for: defending

1. What is the author implying when he says, "If you only do what you know you can do, you never do very much"?
2. What is one practical way that you can live by the principle of giving what you have instead of getting what you want?
3. What two ways does the author say you can travel?
4. What other title could you give to this poem? Why?

Which traits do you think are the most useful in meeting everyday challenges? Write a short explanation of your choices on your tracking sheet.

Bounce Back Comedian **Jim Carrey**

What happens when life hands you lemons? Make lemonade and serve it with a smile! Jim Carrey, born near Newmarket, Ontario, in 1962, is somewhat of an expert in making lemonade, and using humour to do it.

Jim Carrey, who is known for his amazingly elastic features, lunacy and unbelievable antics has acted in numerous comedies over the past decade. But Carrey has not always had it easy. He is the youngest of four children and even when he was young, his outgoing personality made waves. When he was just ten years old, he sent his resumé to a TV comedy show and in junior high was given permission to do stand-up routines for ten minutes at the end of the day to entertain his classmates, on condition that he didn't disturb classes the next day.

His parents decided to move to Scarborough, a suburb to the east of Toronto. The entire family got jobs at a tire factory. Even Carrey worked a full shift after school and his school marks and morale both dropped. Then his parents quit their jobs and the family was forced to live in a trailer for a while. Carrey didn't let that get him down. He started using his twisted sense of humour to do gigs at the local comedy clubs, which improved his performing skills and helped him make contacts. This is where he met the comedian Rodney Dangerfield, who gave him the opportunity to open the show for a period of time.

After two unsuccessful marriages and dissatisfied with the comedy club scene, Carrey needed to do something positive with his life. That is when he tried to get into movies. He played roles in several movies but got poor reviews. Undeterred, he played roles in other minor films before finally becoming a star in 1994.

Failure is no joke, but in the case of Jim Carrey, it was his crazy sense of humour that gave him the opportunity to bounce back once and for all!

Vocabulary

features: facial characteristics

gigs: shows, performances

undeterred: not discouraged

Grammar

Modals

QUICK CHECK

Can you complete the sentences with appropriate modals?

1. You ______ (ability) either defeat your problems or let them defeat you.
2. Sara ______ (possibility) accept her disease by learning more about it.
3. Jonathan ______ (obligation) give Dr. Chan a call.
4. Aurélie ______ (possibility) be suffering from depression.
5. Laughing about problems ______ (ability) help relieve stress.

LEARN MORE

Use

You can use a modal before a main verb to modify its meaning.

A modal can express:

Ability	*can, could*	*You **can** always call me if you want to talk about it.*
Advice/suggestion	*should*	*Antoine **should** stop drinking so many energy drinks.*
Obligation	*must, have to*	*In emergencies, you **must** stay calm.*
Permission	*may*	***May** I go to the yoga class with you?*
Possibility	*might, may*	*Sadie **might** get out of the hospital next week.*

Formation

Affirmative

Use the modal auxiliary with the base form of the verb.

*You **should** focus on the positive.*

Negative

Add *not* between the modal and the main verb.

*You may **not** enjoy negative events, but you can learn from them.*

Interrogative

a) To form an information question, follow this pattern:
question word + modal + subject + main verb + rest of sentence
Why can't Hugo remember what happened that night?

b) To form a yes/no question, follow this pattern:
modal + subject + main verb + rest of sentence
Should I call an ambulance?

PRACTISE

A. Write three sentences for each situation, using appropriate modals. Consider what might happen in the situation. How would the person feel? What suggestions would you make?

1. Your friend has a teacher who gives difficult assignments.
   - You should speak to your teacher.
   - You could ask a classmate for help.
   - Can you plan your work better?
2. A friend has just lost his or her part-time job.
3. A classmate loses a parent.
4. A friend seems to have stopped eating.
5. Your best friend has just broken up with his or her boyfriend or girlfriend.
6. Your car breaks down in the middle of the countryside at night.
7. You and your parents don't agree on your curfew.
8. You can't decide which program to take at CEGEP.
9. Your brother is thinking about quitting school.
10. A cousin is isolating himself or herself more and more.

B. Complete the text with appropriate modals. Choose from *can, could, should, would, must, have to, might* and *may.*

When Kevin had his accident, he faced a dilemma: **1.** Would he let it get him down, or **2.** ______ he decide to be positive? He wondered how he **3.** ______ ever be optimistic when he **4.** ______ use his legs anymore. He **5.** ______ never be able to use a bike again.

The bicycle accident wasn't his fault. He had been riding along when a car suddenly sideswiped him. The doctors told him that he was lucky to be alive. He **6.** ______ have been killed. The nurse encouraged him every day. She reminded him that he **7.** ______ stay in his bed and be depressed or he **8.** ______ work hard and learn to walk again. "You **9.** ______ do whatever you set your mind to," she told him.

You will find more exercises on the extra handout.

The physiotherapist said that he **10.** ______ be able to get a special bike and learn to ride again. She inspired him when she said, "If you train hard, you **11.** ______ even participate in the Special Olympics one day." That thought gave him the hope he needed. He never looked back.

THE CONCLUSION

How can you bounce back in life?

OPTION 1

C3

- **Create a self-help guide for younger students.**

1. Write a guide to help new high school students cope with the expected and unexpected events of school.
2. Determine your topic, audience and purpose. Think about your own experience and what you have learned in this unit and throughout your high school years.
3. Choose a media type: pamphlet, blog or awareness ad in your school newspaper.
4. Prepare an outline and write your guide. Use the checklist and the guidelines on pages 350–351 to help you follow the writing process.
5. Discuss ways to improve your self-help guide with your classmates and teacher.
6. Write a final copy and present your guide to a Secondary Cycle One student or class.

REFLECT

Solves problems.

What kinds of suggestions did you give in your self-help guide to help students analyze and choose solutions?

Word Quest

- addiction
- conquer
- cope
- disease
- faith
- friendship
- hardship
- help line
- obstacle
- ordeal
- overcome
- peer pressure
- psychologist
- resort to
- self-esteem
- skill
- social worker
- substance abuse
- support network

Vocabulary

See the Reference Section, page 332, for the definitions of these words and expressions.

OPTION 2

C3

■ **Write a narrative.**

1. Write a story about a teen who coped successfully with a difficult situation.
2. Determine your topic, audience and purpose.
3. Prepare an outline, using a plot diagram. Be sure to describe the difficult situation clearly and to propose appropriate coping strategies. Make sure your story has a proper conclusion.
4.  Use the checklist and the guidelines on pages 350–351 to help you follow the writing process.
5. Choose illustrations and/or photos to add to your text.
6. Discuss ways to improve your text with your classmates and teacher.
7.  Write a final copy and publish it in a class collection of stories.
8. Present your book to another group of students or to visitors during your school's Open House event.

REFLECT

Solves problems.

What made you choose that particular problem to write about?

PROJECT OPTION 3

C3 C1

◆ **Produce a life strategies card game.**

1. Work with a classmate to decide on the type of game you would like to produce.
2.  Decide on the content of your game (i.e. situations, consequences, decisions and events). Refer to your tracking sheet for ideas.
3. Determine your audience and purpose and choose the media type: paper or electronic.
4. Plan and prepare your game and the answer key. Use the checklist and the guidelines on pages 352–353 to help you follow the production process.
5.  Don't forget to write clear instructions on how to play and win the game. Create your final version.
6. Exchange games with another team of classmates and play the game.
7. Assess the strengths and weaknesses of your game:
   - Consider your audience's reaction.
   - Decide how you would improve it next time.
   - Assess how well you met your objectives.

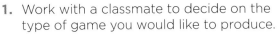

REFLECT

Solves problems.

Which ideas from the unit helped you prepare your life strategies card game?

WORKSHOP 1

WRITE A NARRATIVE

Everyone has a story to tell. It may be about yourself, a family member, or someone you have heard about. Writing a narrative is a great way to share that story.

The aim of this workshop is to help you learn how to use the writing process to write a narrative. First, you will learn how to write an introduction that will catch your readers' attention, and explore the concept of point of view. You will then review how to develop and structure your story and how to use descriptive language to create a dynamic and colourful account. At the end of the workshop, you will have all you need to write a narrative about a memorable experience.

YOU WILL LEARN TO:

- Write an introduction.
- Identify point of view.
- Recognize the features of a narrative.
- Structure events.
- Use a thesaurus to make your writing more effective.
- Write a narrative.

THEME

Walk in Someone Else's Shoes

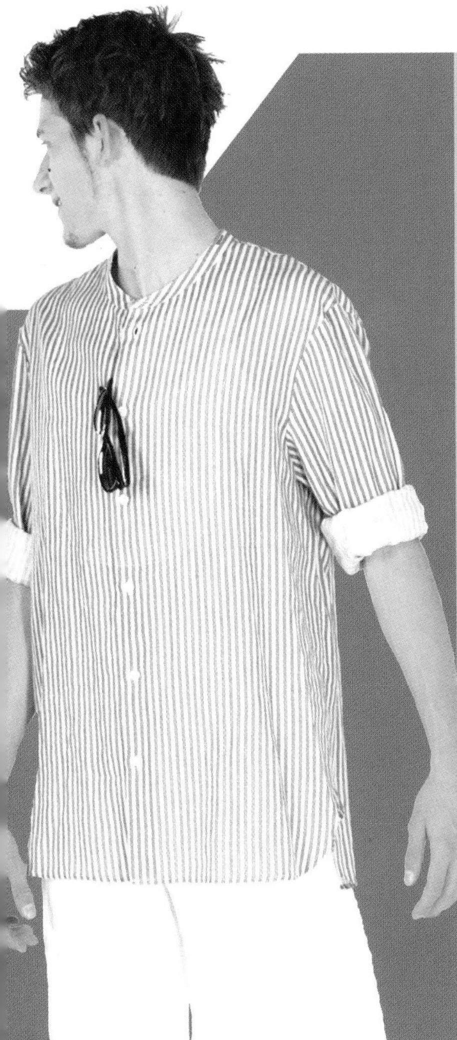

Have you ever read a story that made you feel angry or sad about what the character went through? Maybe it made you want to get involved, or it affected your attitude toward a group of people or a social class. How did the writer do this? Writers present events from a particular point of view so that readers can feel what the characters feel. They choose language and words carefully to help readers experience the story's highs and lows. An effective narrative does more than present events and actions: It explores inner feelings and thoughts.

Whose story would you tell if you could step into someone else's shoes?

EXTRA

Reading Folio

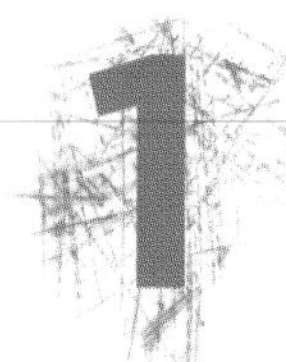

From Idea to Introduction

Think of a story that caught your attention from the start and learn how to write an effective introduction.

Strategy

Activate prior knowledge
Think about how stories have caught your attention.

Strategy

Set goals and objectives
Decide what you need to work on to become a good writer.

C2

HOW TO

Learn about introductions.

1. Think about stories you have read and enjoyed. How did they capture your attention? Write down your answer.
2. Read the three introductions on pages 36–37. Write down how the three authors introduce their stories. Compare these introductions with the introductions to your favourite stories.
3. Discuss these questions as a class:
   - Considering the introductions, which story would you like to read? Why?
   - Why is a good introduction important?
4. Think about how you would hook the readers' attention if you wrote a story. How would you introduce it? Why? Write down your answer and save it to help you later.

Text 1

"Last night I dreamed," said LVX-1, calmly. Susan Calvin said nothing, but her lined face, old with wisdom and experience, seemed to undergo a microscopic twitch.

"Did you hear that?" said Linda Rash, nervously. "It's as I told you." She was small, dark-haired, and young. Her right hand opened and closed, over and over.

Calvin nodded. She said quietly. "Elvex, you will not move nor speak nor hear us until I say your name again."

There was no answer. The robot sat as though it were cast out of one piece of metal, and it would stay so until it heard its name again.

Source: Isaac Asimov, *Robot Dreams*

Text 2

My name is Francis Joseph Cassavant and I have just returned to Frenchtown in Monument and the war is over and I have no face.

Source: Robert Cormier, *Heroes*

Text 3

And then, after six years, she saw him again. He was seated at one of those little bamboo tables decorated with a Japanese vase of paper daffodils. There was a tall plate of fruit in front of him, and very carefully, in a way she recognized immediately as his "special" way, he was peeling an orange.

Source: Katherine Mansfield, *A Dill Pickle*

HOW TO

How to Write an Introduction

What?

The goal of the introduction is to motivate the reader to read the complete narrative. The introduction provides information about the plot, setting, characters and action, and establishes the point of view.

How?

Capture your readers' attention by involving them in the story immediately. Here are some effective openings:

- a **description:** *She knew it was going to be a bad day when the cat scratched her face to wake her up.*
- an **action:** *William turned and glared at me. Then he took the jug of milk and poured it over my head.*
- **speech** or **dialogue:** *"What do you mean, Mindi?" whined Leo pitifully. "Just what I said!" Mindi snapped.*
- an **interjection** or a **sound:** *Ouch!* or *Ding dong. I hurried to the door.*
- a **question:** *Have you ever wondered how it would feel to be living out in the cold?*
- an **interesting fact:** *A teen driver with two or more teen passengers is four times more likely to crash than a teen driver alone in a car.*

2 Whose Point of View?

You never really know someone until you walk in their shoes. Learn about point of view. Whose shoes is the author wearing?

C1

Read an excerpt from a story and explore the idea of point of view.

Strategy

Delay speaking
Take the time to listen to your classmates' answers and then share your own.

Strategy

Compare
Comparing different characters' points of view will help you choose the point of view to use in your story.

Strategy

Substitute
Give the general idea of what you mean if you do not know the exact words or expressions.

HOW TO

1. Think about the introductions you have just read. Discuss these questions with your classmates:
   - From whose perspective is each story told?
   - How would each story be different if the author told it from another character's point of view?

2. Read the excerpt from *My Darling, My Hamburger* on pages 39–40. The author is describing a high school graduation ceremony. As you read, identify the point of view and find evidence to justify your answer.
3. Reread the excerpt. Write down Mr. Zamborsky's and Miss Blair's thoughts as the students pass them.
4. As a class, discuss how the story would be different if the writer had described the scene from the point of view of Maggie's mother or father or Mr. Zamborsky. Give examples by using information from the text.
5. Choose Maggie's mother or father or Mr. Zamborsky. Write down the information the author would need to describe the scene from his or her point of view. Find two classmates who chose the other characters and compare your answers.
6. Write five lines about the ceremony from the point of view of the character you chose. The model below will help you. Then, share your text with your classmates and discuss this question: Does writing from a different point of view change the story? Compare your answers with your conclusions from Step 4.

Model

Maggie's mother

At last some students opened the auditorium doors. Maggie would be arriving soon . . .

How to Identify and Use Point of View

What?

Point of view refers to the perspective from which a story is told. It colours the way readers will experience the story. An author can write the same story from different points of view.

How?

1. By using *I*: You can tell a story by writing from the point of view of one of the characters. The events are filtered through the thoughts and feelings of the chosen character. This is called a *first-person narrative*. Text 2 in the first task is an example of first-person narration.
2. By using *he* or *she*: You can tell a story by describing the events and the characters' actions, feelings and thoughts from the outside. This is called a *third-person narrative*. The extract below is an example of third-person narration.

Understanding the internal and external features of a narrative

Components of the text

Title → From the title, predict what the story will be about.

Author

Introduction The author uses speech to start the story.

Action The author develops the events, and cause and effect.

From My Darling, My Hamburger

Paul Zindel

"Keep your voices down," Mr. Zamborsky shouted. "They'll hear you in the auditorium!" He blew his whistle several times and darted between the lines of boys and girls.

"Students! Make sure you're in the same place assigned at rehearsal. Boys on the left side of the hall. Girls on the right. Hurry." Wwwwrrrrrrrrrr!

Suddenly a silence spread down the corridor. The band had started to play. At rehearsals, everyone had howled at the screeching clarinets. They had hooted the homely little girl who played the cymbals and laughed at the spectacled boy who pounded the big bass drum. They had jeered and dismissed every part of the ceremony. But now, trancelike, almost terrified, they took their places in line. Mr. Zamborsky gave a signal. The marshals opened the rear doors of the auditorium, and the music leaped out with deafening volume.

The slow sounding of the drum pervaded everywhere like the heartbeat of a giant, and the lines began to move, slowly, solemnly. Miss Blair stood at the entrance, making certain each student was in step. Hundreds of parents and relatives stood facing the rear of the auditorium as the first boy and girl stepped into view.

Purpose: to entertain

Audience: teens, high school students

Culture: high school

Action •⟶

The author develops the events, and cause and effect.

Vocabulary

aisle: passageway
darted: moved quickly
deafening: very loud
dismissed: gave up as useless
hollow: without significance
hooted: laughed loudly
intruded on: disturbed
jeered: scorned
marshals: officials
pervaded: filled
rehearsal: practice
screeching: sharp strident noise
shallow: not deep
trancelike: dazed

Resolution •⟶

The author brings the story to an end.

"Good luck, ladies and gentlemen," Miss Blair whispered as the graduates passed by. Several of the girls began to cry. The boys pulled back their shoulders and set their jaws. They hadn't rehearsed that. It was automatic, a reflex. For some, this was the first time they had felt the power of ritual.

At first, Maggie couldn't find the beat. Finally, near the entrance, she fell in step. "An arm's length between me and the girl in front of me," she kept repeating to herself. As she moved farther into the auditorium she saw her mother and father smiling from their seats near the middle aisle. There was such pride in their smiles. It was all she could do to keep from bursting into tears. She gave a smile in return and pretended not to notice the tears running down her mother's face. Flashbulbs were going off, and Maggie had to close her eyes from moment to moment to erase their blinding stains. The entrance seemed to be lasting forever. Then finally she turned into an empty row and was thankful when she reached her seat. She had to stand in front of it until the rest of the graduates had entered. During the singing of the national anthem she couldn't help but look back again at her mother. After a short prayer the audience was given the signal to sit down.

Maggie sat perfectly still. She kept her hands on her lap and tried to concentrate on all the speeches. It seemed to be making polite sense, but so much of it sounded hollow, shallow. She tried to understand exactly why, and the only word she could think of was disappointment. Perhaps that was it.

This should be such a big day, she thought. Everyone talks about it, writes about it. I don't feel so joyous. She could see Dennis now across the auditorium in the same row as she was. She was on the right side, and he was on the far left—across the centre aisle. There were dozens of other profiles between them, each one protruding a fraction of an inch farther than the one before it. It reminded her of looking into a set of double mirrors at a carnival. When she leaned forward, she was able to see Sean on the far side, three rows behind. He was so tall, and Mr. Zamborsky had made everyone line up according to size.

For a moment the principal's voice intruded on her thoughts. " . . . and last but not least, tonight represents a triumph for your parents who have loved you, encouraged you and prayed for you to reach this exciting and marvellous time in your lives . . ."

Source: Paul Zindel, *My Darling, My Hamburger*

Action!

The plot of a story is a series of events or actions connected by cause and effect. Learn how to structure the plot of your narrative.

Strategy

Direct attention
When scanning the story, pay attention to cause and effect.

Learn about the role of the plot.

1. Scan the excerpt again and list the events and actions. Use the features of the story to help you.
2. Compare your work with a classmate. Discuss the following questions and justify your answers:
   - Do events and actions alone tell a story? Why or why not?
   - Are the events or actions in chronological order?
   - Could this text be the introduction to the book?
   - Could this text be the conclusion of the book?
   - How would changing the position of the excerpt in the book result in a different story?

3. Place the events and actions you listed in Step 1 on a plot diagram. Identify the elements. Share your diagram with your classmate and add to it if necessary.
4. As a class, discuss this question:
   - Why would a writer start a story with the event that occurs last?

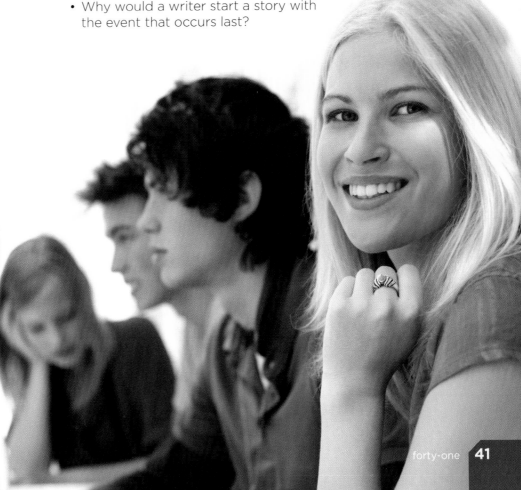

HOW TO

How to Sequence the Events in a Narrative

What?

A story follows a particular structure, or plot. The plot is divided into five parts: introduction, rising action, climax, falling action and resolution. If you follow this pattern when you write a story, readers can follow and understand the story and the message you are trying to convey.

How?

1. **A simple narrative pattern**
   - **Introduction:** The writer presents the information needed to understand the story (characters, setting, issue to be resolved).
   - **Rising action:** The events are presented in the order in which they occur. Interest builds as conflict develops.
   - **Climax** or **turning point:** The conflict reaches its highest point and the main character is transformed in some way.
   - **Falling action:** The issue is clarified.
   - **Resolution:** The issue is resolved.

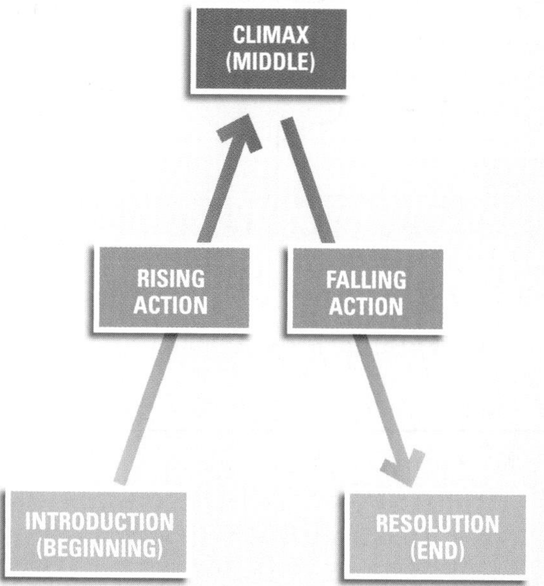

2. **A complex narrative pattern**
   - The events are not always described in chronological order. They can be described from last to first, or there can be flashbacks.
   - Events can also be described in order of importance: with the most important or the least important at the beginning.

The Power of Words

An effective narrative essay does not only describe events. It explores a series of emotions and experiences that convey a message to the reader. Every word has to add interest and credibility.

C2 Learn how writers add colour to a story.

Strategy

Infer

Focus on keywords to understand how the characters are feeling.

1. Work with a classmate. Scan the third paragraph of the excerpt from *My Darling, My Hamburger* and write down descriptive words that help you understand what the characters are thinking and how they are feeling. Identify the words as adjectives, adverbs or verbs.

2. Choose five adjectives and two adverbs from your list. With the help of a thesaurus, replace these words with synonyms or antonyms. Choose words that will stimulate your reader's imagination. Rewrite the paragraph with your new words.

Strategy

Take risks

Try to find unusual or interesting words when you write your paragraph.

3. Exchange your paragraph with a classmate. Read each other's texts. How is your classmate's different from yours? How are they different from the author's?

How to Use a Thesaurus

What?

Writers use descriptive words to add impact to a text and help readers imagine what they read more vividly. You can use a thesaurus to find high-impact words at the writing or the editing stage.

How?

1. Decide which words you wish to replace with others that are more precise, colourful or evocative.
2. Use the index in the thesaurus to find your original word.
3. Scan the list of synonyms provided. Choose the one that best conveys what you mean and find the correct form (noun, verb, adjective or adverb).
4. For each word, ask yourself:
   - Is this what I want to say?
   - Is it appropriate in the context?
   - Is it better than the word originally used?
5. Replace the old word and read the new sentence. Ask yourself if it produces the effect you want.

Write a narrative about an episode in someone else's life.

C3 **Write a narrative from someone else's point of view.**

1. Choose an experience you want to write about.
2. Choose your point of view. Whose shoes will you be wearing as a writer?
3. HOW TO Brainstorm details of the following:
   - the introduction: setting, characters and issues to be resolved; ways to start the story and capture the reader's interest
   - the plot: simple or complex
   - the climax
   - the resolution.
4.  Plan your narrative, using a plot diagram.
5.  Write a first draft. Add descriptive words to create impact and help readers experience the characters' feelings.
6.  Revise and edit your draft. Use the checklist and the guidelines on pages 350–351 to help you follow the writing process.
7. Exchange your text with a classmate and comment on his or her text. Use the peer-editing guide on page 355 for help.
8. Read the comments on your text and ask for clarification if necessary.
9.  Make adjustments and prepare the final copy.

C2 **Present and publish your narrative.**

1. Exchange your story with another student.
2. Use what you learned during this workshop to decide how effective your classmate's story is. Think about the structure, introduction, point of view and use of descriptive words.
3. Publish your story in a class anthology of stories, or share it in a reading circle.

REFLECT

Communicates appropriately.

1. Which language resources did you find most helpful when you corrected and improved your story?
2. How did you take your target audience into account as you wrote your story?
3. Which strategies suggested in this workshop did you use as you wrote your story?
4. What steps did you take to make sure your story was clear and logical?

HOW TO

How to Write a Narrative

What?

A narrative tells a story about someone's experience. For the story to be credible and dynamic, you need to include details that capture the readers' imagination. Choosing clear, accurate and descriptive words will help readers experience a segment of the person's life.

How?

1. Begin with an effective introduction. Refer to Task 1 for help.
2. Choose the point of view. From whose perspective will you tell the story? Refer to Task 2 for help.
3. Structure the events in a logical fashion, from the introduction, through the rising action, climax and falling action to the resolution. Refer to Task 3 for help.
4. Make sure that you end with an effective concluding statement.
5. Use your thesaurus or dictionary of synonyms to find vivid language that helps readers imagine the characters' actions, thoughts and feelings. Refer to Task 4 for help.
6. Don't forget to add a catchy title.

UNIT 3

GENDER STEREOTYPES

1. What are your views about men and women and their roles?
2. What do the media tell us about our gender roles?
3. How do stereotypes affect how we see each other?

Do you ever get the impression that there are rules about how people should look and behave: rules that say that women need to be feminine and pretty and men need to be masculine and tough? You just have to look at the advertising that surrounds us, turn on the television or watch a movie to get this message. Are the media entirely to blame, however, or are we just acting the way we were born to act?

In this unit, you will explore gender stereotypes and some of the influences that shape who we are. You will reflect on the movies and stories you were exposed to as a child and examine messages in advertising. Finally, you will consider whether there is anything we can do about the situation.

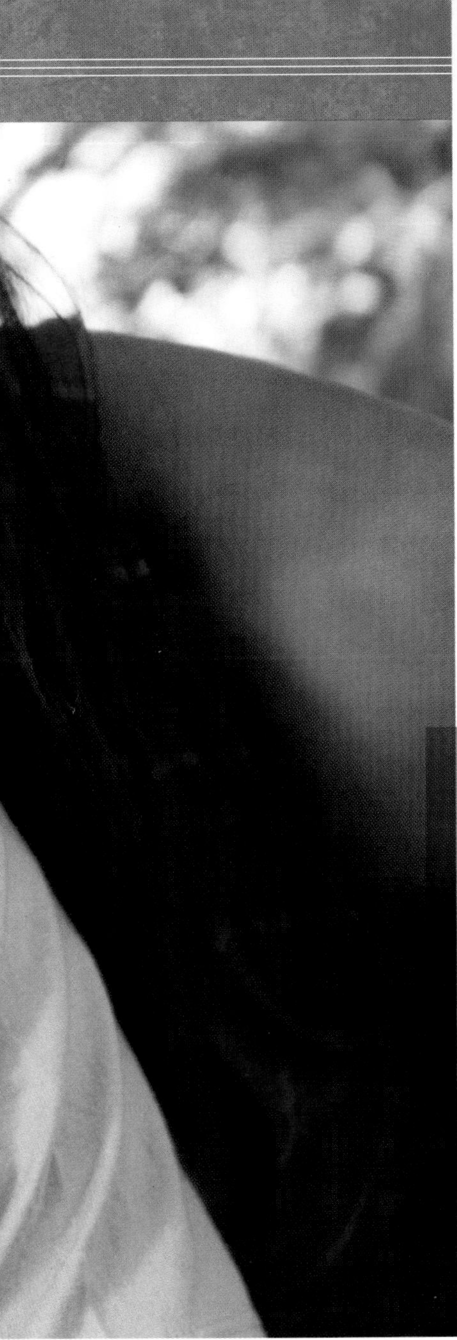

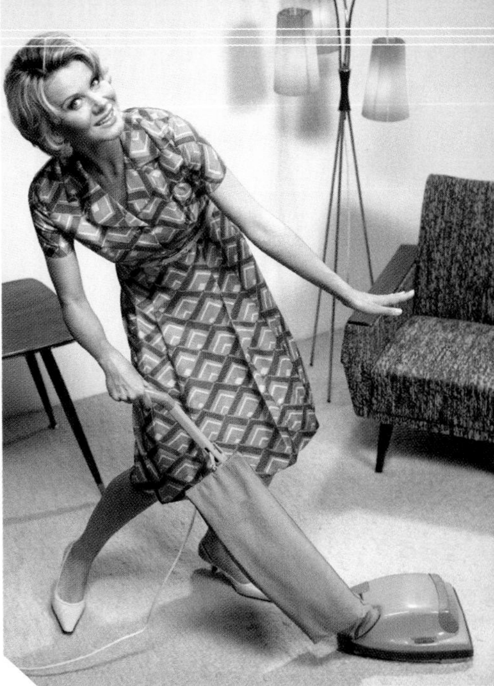

YOUR Quest

How can you change the gender stereotypes in your life?

Unit Overview

Reading Folio

1 Your View of the Sexes

What are your perceptions of men and women? Share your views on some common stereotypes.

C1

Confront some assumptions.

1. Read the definition of *stereotypes* below. Then read the statements on page 49. Write down whether you agree or disagree with each statement and give a reason or an example to support your opinion.
2. Form a team with three classmates, including both genders if possible. Takes turns discussing each statement. Refer to your notes for help.
3. Discuss the following question:
   - How are these assumptions fair or unfair to men and women?
4. Individually, list as many advantages and disadvantages of being a man that you can think of. Then list the advantages and disadvantages of being a woman.
5. Reread your list. Is life easier for males or females? Write down your answer to help organize your ideas. Then, defend your opinion in a class discussion.

Strategy

Delay speaking
Think about what you want to say before speaking. Use your notes for help.

Functional Language

Making Suggestions

- If you think about . . .
- Did you consider . . . ?

Grammar

Comparatives
Comparatives can help you as you talk about the differences between the genders.
See pages 318 and 325.

Stereotypes

Stereotypes are oversimplified generalizations about an individual or a group based on gender, race, religion, social class or sexual orientation. Stereotypes can be harmful if they put down the members of a group, or show or encourage prejudice. They do not respect an individual's uniqueness.

Gender Fact or Fiction?

a) Women have fewer responsibilities than men.

b) Women are more intuitive than men.

c) Men are less nurturing than women.

d) Men are better leaders than women.

e) Women are better bosses than men.

f) Men are better at math and science than women.

g) Women don't work as hard as men.

h) Women are better teachers and nurses than men.

i) Men are not as good at housework as women.

j) Women are better parents than men.

k) Women have less authority than men.

l) Men are better at sports than women.

m) Men are less fashionable than women.

n) Men experience more stress than women.

o) Women are crueller than men.

Vocabulary

gender: male or female
intuitive: instinctive
nurturing: caring
prejudice: judging people before getting to know them
put down: humiliate

TRACK YOUR QUEST

Do you think life is easier for men or for women? Explain the reasons for your answer on your tracking sheet.

2 Growing Up With Stereotypes

We receive messages about how we should behave from the day we are born. What do they tell us?

C1 C2 Examine your childhood role models.

1. With a classmate, take notes as you discuss story, television, movie and toy characters that you liked as children.
   - Which masculine or feminine qualities appealed to you, such as Superman's strength or a doll's prettiness? Write down your answers.
   - When you were young, how did you try to behave like your heroes?
2. Think of the different gender role models that you saw as a child. Which do you think had the strongest influence on you?
3. Read "The Hero and the Clown" on page 51. With your classmate, think of characters who fit these stereotypes from the article:
   - typical male heroes
   - incompetent or comic males
   - female characters who support or admire males.
4. Make a list of movies or stories that portray these stereotypes. Can you name any that contradict the stereotypes?

Strategy

Activate prior knowledge

Relate new ideas in the text to things you have experienced in the past.

Functional Language

Reflecting

- We should focus on . . .
- I understood this because . . .
- This stereotype should be changed because . . .

The Hero and the Clown: Male Characters in Children's Movies

What movies did you watch over and over as a child? Which were your favourites? Chances are, they involved a hero—a dominant male character—and he fit a certain mould.

The most popular children's movies glorify one male body type: chiselled abs, a barrel chest and big biceps. Men have deep voices, they are powerful and they prove their dominance by imposing themselves on others. Men who don't fit the stereotype are portrayed as bumbling or comic figures. They are rarely heroes but often the hero's sidekick.

These images we see as children do have an influence on our perceptions. It doesn't happen overnight, but when these messages are repeated time after time, they eventually shape our view of the world and ourselves.

There has been much talk about the effect that stereotypes have on girls, but less about how they influence young males, and boys' perceptions of females. Constant exposure to these stereotypes teaches boys that there are two roles for women: as objects of pleasure or as servants to men.

There are usually two variations to the storyline in children's cartoons: either the man needs to resolve a conflict or solve a problem, or he needs to fight for or protect a woman. The role of the woman is to support the man and admire his strength and masculinity. A woman who tries to dominate or play the role of a man quickly realizes what defines maleness: strength, speed and aggression. She usually ends up needing the help of a man to achieve her goal.

Using violence to prove dominance is an important theme in most children's movies. The climax of the movie often involves a battle between males, either to maintain status or to win a woman's approval. If one of the male characters is unwilling to fight or to prove his dominance, he is seen as weak and pitiful and he is mocked.

A dilemma arises when young boys do not fit the stereotype of violence and dominance, which ironically are not acceptable traits in our real-life interactions at school and work. Our society values caring and compassion, but these traits contradict the media messages. What is a young man to do?

Vocabulary

bumbling: not competent
chiselled: sculpted
climax: high point
mocked: laughed at
mould: pattern or type
pitiful: pathetic
portrayed: shown

C2 Examine childhood fairy tales.

5. Read the fairy tale "The Princess and the Pea" on page 52. Work with your classmate to identify the stereotypes which describe the prince and the princess.
6. Suggest ways that the fairy tale could be changed to eliminate the stereotypes. The model answer below will help you.

Model

Stereotype	Change
The prince has to search for a princess.	They meet through friends.

7. Which other fairy tales or stories are based on stereotypes? Share your answers with the class.

8. Write down your answers to the following questions:
   - How do the stories and images we encounter as children reinforce gender stereotypes?
   - How did fictional characters influence you as a child?

The Princess and the Pea

Hans Christian Andersen

There was once a prince who wanted to marry a princess, but she had to be a real princess. He travelled right around the world to find one, but there was always something wrong. There were plenty of princesses, but he had great difficulty discovering whether they were real princesses. There was always something which was not quite right about them. So at last he had to return home, and he was very sad because he wanted a real princess so badly.

One evening there was a terrible storm. The thunder roared and the lightning flashed and the rain poured down in torrents; indeed it was a fearful night. In the middle of the storm somebody knocked at the castle door, and the king himself went to open it.

There stood a princess, but she was in a dreadful state from the the wind and the rain. The water streamed from her hair and her clothes. It filled her shoes and ran out through her worn-down heels. However, she insisted that she was a real princess.

"Well, we shall soon see if that is true," thought the queen, but she said nothing. She went into the bedroom, took all the bedclothes off and laid a pea on the bedstead. Then she took twenty mattresses and piled them on top of the pea, and then piled twenty featherbeds on top of the mattresses. This was where the princess was to sleep that night. In the morning they asked her how she had slept.

"Oh, terribly badly!" said the princess. "I hardly closed my eyes the whole night. Heaven knows what was in the bed. I seemed to be lying upon some hard thing, and my whole body is black and blue this morning. It was awful."

They saw at once that she must be a real princess because she had felt the pea through twenty mattresses and twenty feather beds. Nobody but a real princess could have such delicate skin. So the prince took her to be his wife, for now he was sure that he had found a real princess. The little pea was put into the museum, where it may still be seen if no one has stolen it.

Now this is a true story.

Vocabulary

heels: parts of shoes

streamed: ran down

TRACK YOUR QUEST

Which stereotypical gender traits appealed to you and your friends when you were children? Write your answer on your tracking sheet.

Buying an Image

As a young adult, you are surrounded by advertising of all types. Have you ever thought about what it tells you about your own gender role?

Functional Language

Giving and Asking for Opinions

- I have (not) often seen . . .
- Have you ever noticed . . . ?
- I had/hadn't realized that . . .
- I have felt that . . .
- I had/hadn't thought that . . .

Strategy

Transfer

Use what you learn to help you understand the messages in advertising.

Grammar

The Present Perfect and Past Perfect

Use the present perfect and past perfect to express your impressions of advertising. See pages 55–56.

C2

Deconstruct a print advertisement.

1. Look at the advertisement on page 54. Read the four steps. Then, with a classmate, answer the questions to help you analyze the messages it conveys.
2.  Choose an ad from a magazine, the Internet or a newspaper. Follow the four steps and analyze the ad.
3. Present your analysis to another team and explain how your ad reinforces gender stereotypes.
4. Think about the following questions and write down your response. Give reasons to support your opinions.
   - Can you identify hidden messages in advertisements easily?
   - What surprised you about the hidden messages in advertising?

INTERNAL FEATURES

Step One

EXAMINE THE AD.

Components

- Examine the images: people (age, gender, race), objects, setting.
- Who is in control? Who is not?

Language

- What does the text say or suggest? Is there a logo or brand name mentioned?

INTERNAL FEATURES

Step Two

IDENTIFY THE TOPIC.

- What product is being sold?
- Do you find the product appealing? Why or why not?
- Who is the target audience: males, females, teens or adults?
- What feelings is the ad trying to associate with the product? Does this work? Why or why not?

EXTERNAL FEATURES

Step Three

IDENTIFY THE ASSUMPTIONS THE AD MAKES AND THE MESSAGES IT CONVEYS.

- What assumptions does the ad make about gender?
- Do these assumptions reinforce or challenge stereotypes?

EXTERNAL FEATURES

Step Four

CONSIDER THE CONSEQUENCES OF THE MESSAGES THE AD CONVEYS.

- What are some possible consequences?
- Do the messages create unrealistic expectations for people? Why or why not?
- How do the messages in the ad reinforce or challenge gender stereotypes?

TRACK YOUR QUEST

How has this task changed the way you view ads? Write your thoughts on your tracking sheet.

Grammar

The Present Perfect and Past Perfect

QUICK CHECK

Can you identify the verb errors in these sentences and correct them?

1. I have attend fashion shows five times.
2. Gerry is at the garage since eight o'clock.
3. Did you ever thought about why we are so different?
4. By the time he called, I have already left with somebody else.
5. I been different ever since I was little.

LEARN MORE

The Present Perfect

Use

You use the present perfect to describe a past action in relation to the present.

Pascale ***has joined*** *an all-girl band.*

Formation

- Use the simple present of the auxiliary verb *to have* (*have* or *has*) with the past participle of the main verb. See Participles on page 314 and Common Irregular Verbs on page 317.
- To form a negative statement, add *not* after the auxiliary verb.
- To ask questions, start the sentence with the auxiliary verb.

Affirmative	Negative	Question
I, You, We, They ***have*** *played.*	*I, You, We, They* ***have not*** *played.*	***Have*** *I, you, we, they played?*
He/She/It ***has*** *played.*	*He/She/It* ***has not*** *played.*	***Has*** *he/she/it played?*

Note:

In informal English, you can contract the auxiliary verb *to have* in the affirmative and negative as follows: *I've, You've, We've, You've, They've* / *He's/She's/It's* — *I, You, We, You, They haven't* / *He's/She's/It hasn't*

You can use time markers such as *ever, never, already, before, since, for, always, yet, lately, recently.*

The Past Perfect

Use

You use the past perfect to describe a past action in relation to the past.

We ***had seen*** *the movie before, but we still enjoyed it.*

The Present Perfect and Past Perfect

Formation

- Use the simple past of the auxiliary verb *to have (had)* with the past participle of the main verb. See Participles on page 314 and Common Irregular Verbs on page 317.

Affirmative	Negative	Question
I, You, He/She/It, We, They ***had*** *played.*	*I, You, He/She/It, We, They* ***had not*** *played.*	***Had*** *I, you, he/she/it, we, they played?*

Note:

In informal English, you can contract the auxiliary verb *to have* in the affimative and negative as follows: *I'd, You'd, He'd /She'd, We'd, You'd, They'd* *I, You, She/He/It, We, You, They hadn't*

You can use time markers such as *ever, never, already, before, for, always, when, as soon as, the moment, until.*

PRACTISE

Complete the story with the past perfect form of the verbs in parentheses.

I **1.** walk in and sat down before I noticed that nothing looked as if it **2.** be there for long. I **3.** feel strange about the whole thing, from the moment I **4.** receive that phone call to the time I **5.** arrive at the office and been sent to the costume department. Now I was here, dressed in these crazy clothes, wondering what was going to happen. "Next!" called a voice from inside the office.

"Hello," I said, somewhat nervously. "Are you here for the audition?" a grandmotherly woman asked. "Yes," I replied. "How do you feel?" she asked. "Well, . . ." I began nervously. I **6.** follow the instructions to put on the clothing and **7.** come in here, but I **8.** question (negative) what the audition was for.

I **9.** consider never that I would be participating in an ad like this! I felt a little silly. I **10.** imagine myself shooting a cool ad, looking tough. Now I just felt awkward. It turned out that they wanted to reverse our typical roles. The girl who **11.** walk in behind me was dressed as a construction worker. I wasn't so sure about being a secretary, but then I said, "Hey, why not? This is the 21st century!"

You will find more exercises on the extra handout.

Scarecrow **Melissa Etheridge**

Melissa Etheridge wrote this song after learning of the kidnapping, torture and murder of a 21-year-old university student named Matthew Shepard. Matthew was attacked because he did not fit the typical male stereotype. His body was dumped in a field after the attack and the passerby who found him thought at first that he was a scarecrow lying on the ground. Matthew later died in hospital.

The evidence presented against his attackers in court showed that he had been targeted because of his sexual orientation by young men who were known to be homophobes. The song carries a powerful message. As the songwriter said, "Love yourself, that's where tolerance begins. It's [feeling] strong enough in yourself . . . that you have room enough for everyone else's wants and needs and no desire to hurt or ridicule anyone else."

Showers of your crimson blood
Seep into a nation calling up a flood
Of narrow minds who legislate
Thinly veiled intolerance
Bigotry and hate

But they tortured and burned you
They beat you and they tied you
They left you cold and breathing
For love they crucified you

I can't forget hard as I try
This silhouette against the sky

Scarecrow crying
Waiting to die wondering why
Scarecrow trying
Angels will hold, carry your soul away

This was our brother
This was our son
This shepherd young and mild
This unassuming one
We all gasp, "This can't happen here"
We're all much too civilized
Where can these monsters hide?

But they are knocking on our front door
They're rocking in our cradles
They're preaching in our churches
And eating at our tables

I search my soul
My heart and in my mind
To try and find forgiveness
This is someone's child
With pain unreconciled
Filled up with father's hate
Mother's neglect
I can forgive but I will not forget

Scarecrow crying
Waiting to die, wondering why
Scarecrow trying
Rising above, all in the name of love

Vocabulary

bigotry: prejudice
crimson: dark red
gasp: sudden breath in shock or surprise
scarecrow: a life-sized figure put in a field to scare birds away
seep: flow gradually
shepherd: person who looks after sheep
unassuming: humble, not pretentious
unreconciled: not accepted
veiled: hidden

4 The Dating Game

How large a role do you think stereotypes play in dating?

Strategy

Self-evaluate

Pay attention to how well you are able to express your opinions. What do you need to improve?

Functional Language

Asking for Opinions

- Have you ever heard . . . ?
- Do you think . . . ?
- Had you ever thought about . . . ?

Vocabulary

cringe: move away in fear or disgust

nerd: uninteresting person ridiculed as studious and weak

players: people who like to date many people

STATE **YOUR** CASE

Are men and women equal in our society? Does *equal* mean *the same*?

C2 **Confront dating stereotypes.**

1. With a classmate, read the dating stereotypes below. Agree or disagree with each point and compare it with your generation's dating habits.

2. Watch the video about dating, "Hooking Up and Hanging Out." On a T-chart, make notes about what the males and females say about themselves and dating. Discuss the following questions with your classmates:
   - How do these teens' experiences compare with your own?
   - Which stereotypes do these teens respect?
   - How do you think stereotypes affect dating?
   - What would you like to change about dating today?

10 Common Stereotypes About Teen Dating

1. Females can't hear "I love you" enough, and males **cringe** from it.
2. All females want is a relationship, and all males want is fun.
3. Females are content with one man, and males are **players**.
4. **Nerds** can date only other nerds, popular people can date only other popular people, etc.
5. Looks are critically important.
6. Teens should date people who like the things that they like.
7. Males must ask females out.
8. Males should pay for everything.
9. Females adore poetry.
10. It is impossible to find true love at this age.

TRACK YOUR QUEST

Which stereotypes do you think are the most harmful to healthy relationships? Write your ideas on your tracking sheet.

5 Nature or Nurture?

Now that you have explored gender stereotypes, do you think that we are entirely defined by our environment? There are differing opinions about how we become the way we are.

Functional Language

Expressing Opinions

- I have seen . . .
- Most men/women seem to . . .
- Men/women are definitely . . .
- I really believe that . . .

C1 C2 Learn about nature vs. nurture.

1. With your classmates, think about jobs which are perceived as typically male or typically female. Discuss these questions:
   - Why do you think some jobs are thought to be suitable for one gender rather than the other?
   - How are these stereotypes changing? Is it more acceptable or common today for people to do work once considered unsuitable for their gender?
2. Read the following description of the nature-nurture issue.

Nature vs. Nurture

This issue refers to two popular theories of human development.

According to the **nature** theory, people are born with certain traits and their environment does little to change them as they mature.

According to the **nurture** theory, people are born without tendencies and preferences. How they develop is determined by their environment and the people around them.

Strategy

Take notes

Write brief notes to remind yourself of key information.

3. Listen to an interview with two psychologists.
   - As you listen, identify which side of the nature-nurture debate each expert supports and write down at least five reasons and examples given for each side.
4. Use your notes to help you discuss these questions with your classmates:
   - What did you learn that might help you understand the other sex better?

     Do you think individuals have a choice about how masculine or feminine they are?

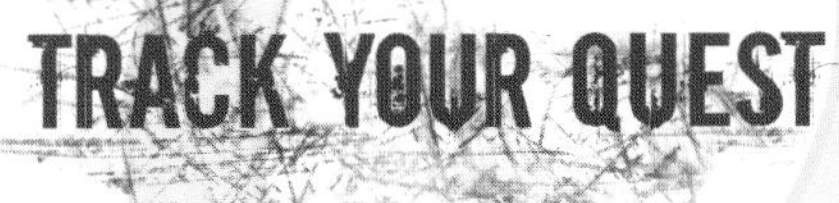

Which of your own gender traits do you think result from nature rather than nurture? Write your ideas on your tracking sheet.

THE CONCLUSION

How can you change the gender stereotypes in your life?

OPTION 1

C3

- **Create ten dating tips for the new millennium.**

1. Think of beliefs about dating that you would like to change.
2. Brainstorm ideas for your new dating tips.
3. Decide which software to use to present your information.
4. Plan your text. Make sure to do the following:
   - Write down each tip.
   - Explain in a few sentences why it is important.
5.  Use the checklist and the guidelines on pages 350–351 to help you follow the writing process.
6. Present your text to a classmate or your teacher for feedback and adjust your final copy.
7. Contribute your tips to the school news-paper or submit them to your favourite teen magazine.

REFLECT

Achieves his or her potential.

Which of your own values were most important in developing your list?

Word Quest

- communication
- compassion
- consideration
- femininity
- ignorant
- interaction
- machismo
- masculinity
- oblivious
- perceptive
- thoughtful
- understanding

Vocabulary

See the Reference Section, page 333, for the definitions of these words.

PROJECT OPTION 2

C1 C3

■ **Create an anti-ad which eliminates gender stereotypes.**

1. Work with a classmate to create an anti-ad which eliminates gender stereotypes. Refer to your handouts and tracking sheet to remind you of the different issues.
2. Choose a gender stereotype you think is harmful to young people and decide what message you would like to send about it.
3. Decide on your audience.
4. Decide how best to present your work: as a print ad or an audio or video advertisement.

5. Use the checklist and the guidelines on pages 352–353 to help you follow the production process.
6. Present your work to a classmate or your teacher for feedback and adjust your final product.
7. Post your print ad in the school or present it to the class. Be prepared to explain why you chose the stereotype and how your ad refutes it.
8. Assess the strengths and weaknesses of your team's project:
   - Consider your future goals and objectives.
   - Assess what you have learned.

REFLECT

Achieves his or her potential.

Which stereotypes do you think are the most harmful to young people?

OPTION 3

C3

◆ **Rewrite a story to eliminate gender stereotypes.**

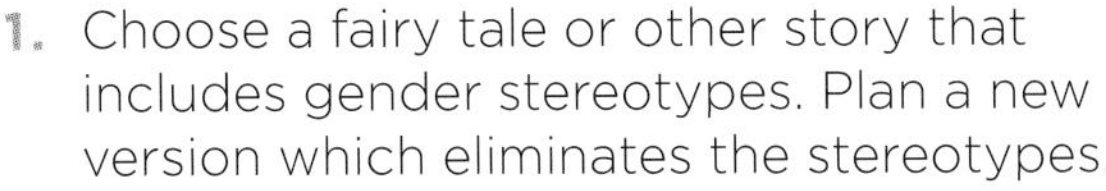

1. Choose a fairy tale or other story that includes gender stereotypes. Plan a new version which eliminates the stereotypes.

2. Decide how to present your work: as a paper or electronic storybook.

3. Use the checklist and the guidelines on pages 350–351 to help you follow the writing process.
4. Combine your text with visual elements to create a storybook.
5. Present your story to a classmate or your teacher for feedback.
6. Contribute your story to a class collection of gender-neutral stories and send it to an elementary school ESL class.

REFLECT

Achieves his or her potential.

How does your new story reflect your own ideas about gender?

UNIT 4

MOVING ON

1. How do you define *adulthood*?
2. How can you organize your new adult life?
3. What do you need to know before moving on?

You're almost there: Just a few more months and your high school years will be history. This is an exciting time as you consider the new opportunities and experiences that are just around the corner. You might have a clear idea of what you're going to do next, or maybe you're still working out the details. Either way, one thing is for sure: You're on the road to adulthood! Which doors will you choose to open? What do you want to know before you move on? In this unit, you will reflect on what it means to be an adult, examine some potential obstacles and figure out how to avoid them. Get ready to move on!

What's your next step?

Unit Overview

EXTRA

Reading Folio

1 Who's a Grown-Up?

You're at the end of your adolescence and will soon be considered a young adult. What does it take to be considered a grown-up?

C1 C2 Define *adulthood.*

1. When does a person become an adult? What does it mean to be an adult? Write down as many criteria as possible.
2. Participate in a class discussion to choose the five criteria that best define adulthood.

3. Read the "Five Transitions to Adulthood" from Statistics Canada your teacher gives you. Compare them with the class criteria and state whether you agree or disagree with them.
4. Read the statements on page 65 that describe adulthood around the world. Then discuss them with a classmate.
   - Share your thoughts about each statement.
   - Think of an example to support or contradict each statement.
   - Be prepared to say which statement surprised you the most and why.
5. As a class, make adjustments to your list and write down your final definition of adulthood.

Strategy

Self-monitor

Pay attention to how well you are able to use the functional language prompts.

Functional Language

Giving an Opinion

- I think being an adult means . . .
- Maybe it could be . . .
- Perhaps it means to . . .
- This is accurate because . . .
- This is ridiculous because . . .

STATE **YOUR** CASE

Is there an age when young adults should be forced to move out of their parents' homes?

Adulthood at Home and Abroad

1. Today in Canada, people are becoming adults from three to five years later than 30 years ago.
2. Women generally become adults earlier than men by taking a partner and having children at a younger age.
3. Men generally leave school and start full-time work earlier than women.
4. Today's young adults are more likely to stay in school longer than the previous generation.
5. Only about half of young adults get married by age 25.
6. In Québec, about 30% of couples live in common-law relationships compared with about 12% in the rest of Canada.
7. In certain parts of South Africa, you aren't considered a man until you have a child.
8. In certain parts of South Africa, a woman is not considered to be an independent adult until her husband and brothers die.
9. Over 60% of American students said they would continue to live with their parents after graduating.
10. In Canada, about 60% of young men and women aged 20–24 still live at home.

12. In Italy, some people believe that leaving home to study or work is not acceptable. Marriage is the only good reason.
13. In many cities, a job that pays $10 an hour isn't enough to cover the basic cost of living.

Vocabulary

common-law: cohabitation without a legal marriage

C2 **Read about recent graduates.**

6. Read the five profiles of recent high school graduates on pages 66–68. Use the class criteria to determine which individuals have reached adulthood.

7. Will you consider yourself to be an adult next year? Use the class criteria to analyze your own situation and write down your answer.

Strategy

Scan

Look quickly through the text to find the information you need.

Grammar

The Simple Future and Future Continuous

Use the simple future and future continuous to express your answer. See page 69.

Profile 1

Suneeti Kumar

AGE: 18

OCCUPATION: Full-time CEGEP student

This year, I'm studying full-time at CEGEP in Sainte-Thérèse. I'm in the Multimedia program and really enjoying it.

The biggest thing for me is my freedom. With my own car, I can come and go as I please.

LIVING SITUATION: My father lives in Saint-Sauveur, which isn't too far away from the college. With money I saved from working last summer and some help from my parents, I bought a car and I drive to school. I also kept my job working as a dishwasher at a local restaurant on the weekends.

HOW I'VE MOVED ON: The biggest thing for me is my freedom. With my own car, I can come and go as I please. I'm also responsible for my own expenses—except for school expenses. Luckily, my parents pay for those. The other thing is responsibility. It's up to me to get to class and do my assignments. My teachers don't babysit me as much as they did in high school, and neither do my parents.

Profile 2

Laurence Parenteau

AGE: 19

OCCUPATION: Katimavik participant

When I finished high school, I knew I wasn't ready to continue studying right away. I did some research and found out about Katimavik. This program lasts most of a year. We have the chance to spend a few months in three different communities (two anglophone, one francophone) throughout Canada. We get to practise our second language, and we do volunteer work in the community.

LIVING SITUATION: There are 11 of us—girls and guys—sharing a house, along with a coordinator. We take turns preparing meals and even baking our own bread.

HOW I'VE MOVED ON: This is my first experience living away from my family, so it's been an adventure. I'm living in new communities and practising my second language. It's also the first time that I've had to feed people. (We take turns.) I've had to plan the menu, buy groceries, everything. I'm definitely feeling more grown-up!

I did some research and found out about Katimavik. This program lasts most of a year. We have the chance to spend a few months in three different communities throughout Canada.

Profile 3

Serge Alarie-Cohen

AGE: 18

OCCUPATION: Student/employee

LIVING SITUATION: Apartment in my parents' basement

I have my own apartment—sort of. I still go up and raid my parents' fridge sometimes. They say they're going to put a lock on it!

HOW I'VE MOVED ON: I've not quite finished high school. I still have to complete a math course I failed last year. The deal I've made with my parents is that I work full-time, I pay rent on my apartment, cover my own car payments and expenses, and take the math class at night. They give me a discount on the rent and sometimes let me raid the fridge! I have to manage my own money and keep my place clean—I haven't been too successful yet, but I'm learning. My job is okay, but I wouldn't want to do it for the rest of my life. I'm on the road to independence.

I have my own apartment—sort of. I still go up and raid my parents' fridge sometimes. They say they're going to put a lock on it!

Profile 4

Charlotte Conitsioti

AGE: 18

OCCUPATION: Student and page for the Parliament of Canada

Because I had really good marks in my last year of high school, I was accepted right away at the University of Ottawa, in the Environmental Studies program. I also applied and was accepted in the Page program in the House of Commons. It's a really great part-time job where I help members of parliament by running errands, giving out documents—things like that. I see first-hand how our government works.

LIVING SITUATION: University residence

I have a tiny little room but at least it's all mine. I have to share the bathroom and I eat my meals in one of the university cafeterias or cafés. I'm definitely independent, but it's nice to have the community feeling of the residence. There's always someone around to talk to.

HOW I'VE MOVED ON: Just living away from my family is a huge experience. My page job also requires me to be very professional.

It's a really great part-time job where I help members of parliament by running errands, giving out documents—things like that.

Profile 5

Vincent Girard

I finished high school last year. My father is a contractor and he offered me a full-time job with his company so I could learn the ropes.

AGE: 19

OCCUPATION: Construction worker

I finished high school last year. My father is a contractor and he offered me a full-time job with his company so I could learn the ropes. I am learning to build houses. It's hard work and sometimes it gets cold working outside, but I like the fact that I'm making my own money and building a career. I really enjoy working with my hands.

LIVING SITUATION: At Christmastime I had enough money to move into an apartment with a friend, who is studying at CEGEP. I saved enough money during my last year of high school to get an old truck and I love having my independence.

HOW I'VE MOVED ON: I have my own place, a job and a truck. I don't need anything else. In a couple of years I'd like to go back to school to study construction management so I can take over my father's business someday.

Vocabulary

discount: price reduction

House of Commons: the lower house of the Parliament of Canada

learn the ropes: get experience

raid: steal from or attack

sort of: in a way

You now have some different ideas about the ways young adults move on and what it means to be an adult. Write your ideas on your tracking sheet.

Grammar

The SImple Future and Future Continuous

QUICK CHECK

Can you correct the verb errors in these sentences?

1. When I turn 25, I was applying to work at the United Nations.
2. Next weekend I have been skiing.
3. By this time next week, I sat on a beach in Cuba.
4. In fifteen minutes, I go home on the bus.
5. When I finish university, I am 22 years old.

LEARN MORE

The Simple Future

Use

You use the simple future to express an action or situation that will happen in the future. You can use it with or without a time reference.

Formation

Use the future form of the verb *to be* (*will*) with the base form of the main verb.

Affirmative	I ***will get*** a job when I'm older.
Negative	I ***will not get*** a job this summer.
Question	***Will*** you ***get*** a job this summer?

The Future Continuous

Use

You use the future continuous to express an action that will be in progress over a period of time in the future. A time or another event is usually mentioned.

Formation

Use the simple future of the verb *to be* (*will be*) and add *ing* to the main verb.

Affirmative	I ***will be attending*** CEGEP next year.
Negative	I ***will not be attending*** CEGEP next year.
Question	***Will*** you ***be attending*** CEGEP next year?

Note:

In informal English, you can contract the auxiliary verb *to be* in the affirmative and negative as follows:

I'll, You'll, He'll/She'll/It'll, We'll, You'll, They'll *I, You, She/He/It, We, You, They won't*

You can use time markers such as *tomorrow; on Saturday; next week/month/year/summer; in two days' time/2015.*

The Simple Future and Future Continuous

PRACTISE

A. Complete each sentence with the appropriate future tense in the negative or the affirmative.

1. By this time next year, . . .
2. When I am older, . . .
3. When I have saved $1000, . . .
4. On July 1, 2020, . . .
5. In three hours from now, . . .
6. When I am fully bilingual, . . .
7. After I finish high school, . . .
8. When I retire, . . .
9. When people are able to live in outer space, . . .
10. On the first day of summer vacation, . . .
11. When I make my first million dollars, . . .
12. On January 1, 2050, . . .
13. When I take a trip around the world, . . .
14. Next September, . . .
15. After I become a parent, . . .

B. Choose five of the prompts and write questions to ask your classmates about their future.

C. Complete the text with the appropriate future tense of the verbs in parentheses. Use the contracted form.

When I leave my parents' house, I **1.** be ready to support myself. I **2.** end up (negative) like the boomerang generation I've heard about lately: people who move out and then decide to move back in with their parents a couple of years later. I **3.** make sure that I have everything organized. You **4.** see + never me coming back home. Once I'm out, I **5.** stay out. I'm sure you **6.** hesitate (negative) to remind me if I seem to be changing my mind!

You will find more exercises on the extra handout.

Get Moving

Part of becoming an adult means becoming financially independent, and to do that you will need a job. You will be more confident if you know how to handle a job interview.

C1

Find out about job interviews.

1. As a class, discuss the following questions:
   - Which of you has had a job interview?
   - What happens at a job interview?
   - Do you think that all job interviews follow the same pattern?
   - What do most job interviews have in common?

2. Work with a classmate. Read the topics on the list your teacher gives you and brainstorm ideas. Write down two or three of your best ideas about each topic.
3. Meet with another team to compare what you wrote. Add any new ideas to your list.
4. Review your notes and circle the most useful job-interview tips. Be prepared to discuss them in class.

Functional Language

Offering Advice

- Don't ever . . .
- Don't forget to . . .
- I think you should . . .
- It's important to never . . .

C1

Role-play a job interview.

5. Think of a job that interests you or choose one from the list your teacher gives you. Tell a classmate which job you chose. Then:
   - Think about possible topics that could arise in the interview for the job chosen by your classmate.
   - Think of pertinent interview questions to ask your classmate about this job. Use your list from Step 3.
6. Take turns role-playing the job interview by answering each other's questions.
7. Decide if you would hire your classmate and give each other feedback.
8. Participate in a class discussion about the following questions:
   - Which questions were the most difficult to answer well?
   - What can you do when you're not sure how to respond?
   - How important is it to practise for a job interview?

Strategy

Practise

Practise answering the interview questions until you are happy with the results.

Strategy

Gesture

Use head or hand gestures to help communicate your message.

TRACK YOUR QUEST

You have discussed and reflected on some of the keys to a successful job interview. Write the most important tips on your tracking sheet.

3 Budget Busters

Managing money is challenging for people of any age. Following a budget is a great skill to learn, but what happens when life surprises you?

C1 Balance your books.

1. According to your plans for next year, calculate your monthly income from a full-time or part-time job.
   - Decide on a realistic salary.
   - Calculate the number of hours you will work each week and multiply by four for a month's income.

2. Write down your monthly income and subtract thirty per cent for basic income taxes. Note that this percentage rate varies from year to year and by province and is determined by your salary level.
3. With your class, make a list of all possible monthly expenses and estimate their costs.
4. Choose the expenses you expect to have, estimate how much they will cost and add them to create your own budget for next year. The model below will help you.

Model

Expense	Amount
Bus pass	$50
Groceries	$300

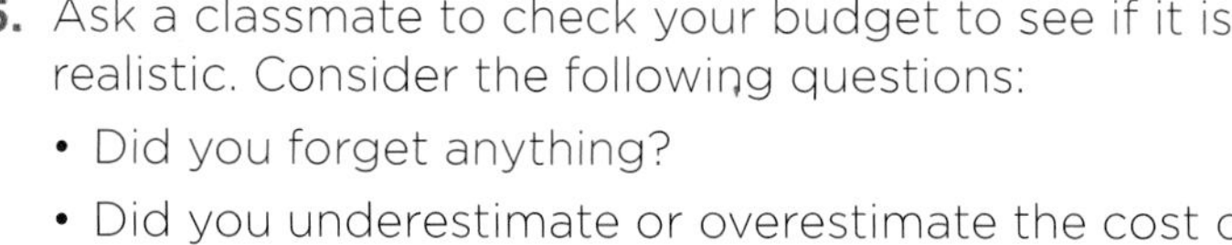

5. Ask a classmate to check your budget to see if it is realistic. Consider the following questions:
   - Did you forget anything?
   - Did you underestimate or overestimate the cost of any items?

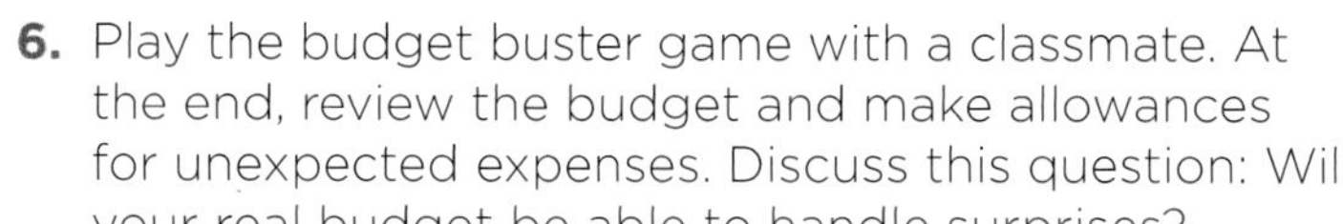

6. Play the budget buster game with a classmate. At the end, review the budget and make allowances for unexpected expenses. Discuss this question: Will your real budget be able to handle surprises?

Functional Language

Using If-Sentences

- If I calculate . . . , my budget will . . .
- If I included . . . , my budget would . . .
- I won't have enough if . . .
- I will be able to . . . if . . .

Strategy

Direct attention

Focus on what you are doing so that you do not forget any numbers or miscalculate your totals.

C2 Find out about credit cards.

Grammar

Conditional Sentences
Use conditional sentences in your replies. See the Reference Section, page 309.

DVD **7.** Watch the video clip and learn about one student's experience with credit cards. After viewing, discuss the following questions with your classmates:

- What are the consequences of Robin's use of credit cards?
- Robin says, "If you live like a professional in college, you'll live like a student when you get out." What does she mean by this?

8. Work with one or two classmates. Take turns reading the statements about credit cards below and decide whether each statement is true or false. Give reasons or examples to support your answer. As a class, discuss and correct your answers.

Credit Cards: Fact or Fiction?

a) You can have many credit cards at the same time.

b) You must pay the entire amount you owe on a credit card each month.

c) Credit card companies provide students with low-interest cards.

d) If a store charges you twice by mistake, you do not have to pay the extra charge when you pay your bill.

e) If you mail your payment on the day it is due, you will not have to pay interest charges.

f) You can use your card in another country for no extra charge.

g) More than 20% of students have over $7000 in credit card debt when they graduate.

h) You can get a cash advance on your credit card without paying any extra fees or interest if you pay it all back when your bill is due.

i) If you owe $2000 on a credit card and you pay only the minimum monthly payment, it will take about eight years to pay it off.

j) If someone steals your card or card number and uses it, you are responsible for the charges.

k) A credit card is a good way to pay for college expenses.

l) If you always pay your entire bill on time, you will not have to pay any interest.

Money management is an important issue for everyone. Will you be able to follow a budget? Write what you want to remember on your tracking sheet.

A Great Balancing Act

Adult life can be busy and stressful. How can you find a balance and stay cool?

C2 **Decide what you need to balance.**

1. Think about the following questions and write down your ideas.
   - How will you balance all the different activities in your life, such as work, sports and entertainment?
   - What elements will be added next year?
2. Read the advice about time management below and choose the five tips that you think are the most useful. Write them down.
3. Read the students' profiles on pages 74–75. List all their activities and the time needed for each of them. Then, think about the tips you learned about time management.
4.  Create a one-week schedule for each student.
5. Form a group with three classmates and compare the schedules you made. Discuss the following questions and share your answers with the class.
   - Which schedule is the most balanced?
   - How did you decide that this schedule was the most balanced?
   - Which priorities did your group consider the most important?
   - Which time management tips were the most useful?

Strategy

Scan

Look quickly through the article to find the information you need. Spend more time on the ideas that interest you.

Time Management Made Easy

Sometimes it feels as though there are too many things to do and not enough time to do them. What would you say if someone told you that you could be a full-time student, have a part-time job, carry out household chores, start a new hobby, and have time for socializing, all in the span of one week? It's not impossible. The trick lies in being able to manage your time. Just think, there are 24 hours in a day, 144 hours in six days, and one day left for pleasure.

Monday to Saturday = 144 hours

Class time: 21 hours per week
Sleep & meals: 66 hours in six days
Part-time job: 20 hours per week
Hobby: 7 hours per week
Clubbing & socializing: 10 hours per week
Total: 124 hours

- Pay attention in class and be an active listener by taking careful notes. You can cut your studying time in half by doing this!
- On your way home from school, review all the notes you took during the day. You'll remember more this way and understand the material better.
- Make a schedule for yourself that includes everything you have to do, including homework, studying, working part-time and even sleeping.
- What's the point of making a schedule if you don't follow it? Stick to your schedule! Don't make excuses or look for reasons for not following it.
- Always keep your agenda with you and constantly remind yourself of the assignments you have to do.
- When you're trying to figure out a certain assignment, think about it whenever you can: while you're taking a shower, eating dinner or walking the dog.
- Make studying part of your regular routine. It should be an integral part of your day.
- Figure out the best time to study. Most people don't study well late at night, so early afternoon is probably better.
- Get enough sleep. If you're studying and start nodding off, you probably need sleep and should go to bed. If you try to keep studying, you probably won't remember much.
- Don't have marathon study sessions; take frequent short breaks when studying for a test. Go get a glass of water or do some push-ups to wake up your brain.
- When you have to read a novel, read it carefully and make sure you don't just skim through it. This way, you won't have to reread it when it's time for the test.
- Your social life is important too, but it's also limited. You have to be selective in your choices because you can't do everything.

Source: Vanier College Learning Centre

The trick lies in being able to manage your time. Just think, there are 24 hours in a day, 144 hours in six days, and one day left for pleasure.

Profile 1

Luc

Luc is in his first year of CEGEP and he loves the social side of things so much that now his marks are slipping. He really needs a schedule to get him back on track. He has three assignments due next week, so he will need some extra time to complete them—about nine hours. Plus, he asked to work a few extra hours this week at his job because he's planning a big trip during spring break to go skiing and he needs the cash. This puts him up to 27 hours. He also needs time to spend with his new girlfriend. Luc needs at least three visits to the gym to keep up his training; it's open every day from 6 a.m. to 10 p.m. His soccer team practises Monday, Wednesdays and Fridays from 4 p.m. to 6 p.m and there's no way he can miss that. Finally, of course, he needs to sleep for at least eight hours a night.

Luc needs at least three visits to the gym to keep up his training.

Kiana

Kiana has a lot on her plate and needs help getting organized. She has a full-time course load, plus a 20-hour-a-week job at a restaurant. It is important to her to volunteer at a local children's hospital twice a week for a total of eight hours. She also visits her grandfather once a week because he is often alone. She needs about three hours for that.

Kiana plays the electric bass in a rock band that rehearses Tuesday and Thursday nights from 7 p.m. to 10 p.m. It takes her a half-hour on the bus to travel to the rehearsals. Finally, if she wants to stay in shape, she needs to get to her one-hour exercise class at least three times a week. She could go at either 7 a.m. or 3 p.m., Mondays, Wednesdays and Fridays. Kiana tries to get at least eight hours' sleep.

She has a full-time course load, plus a 20-hour-a-week job at a restaurant.

Vocabulary

a lot on her plate: many responsibilities or things to do

back on track: in the right direction

slipping: going down

Time management is no easy task! Add a useful tip that you would like to remember to your tracking sheet.

Meet Richard Lee, Gap Year Student

Richard Lee, from England, is participating in a gap year program at Mont Tremblant. He agreed to talk to *Quest* about his experience.

QUEST: Hello there, Richard. We'd like to ask you a few questions about gap years, why British students take them, and your own experience.

RICHARD: Great, go ahead.

QUEST: What is a gap year? Why do British students take them?

RICHARD: It's the year between finishing high school and starting university. Many students use this year to work or travel. It helps them gain maturity and broadens their experience of the world.

QUEST: What percentage of students take a gap year?

RICHARD: Well, it's hard to tell, but I'd say it's a good portion of the kids who are planning to go to university.

QUEST: Why did you choose to come to Québec?

RICHARD: Lots of British kids choose to travel around Europe because it's close to us, but I wanted to come to Canada because it's further away. I also wanted to learn French and experience the culture of Québec. Coming here is more exotic for me than staying close to home.

QUEST: What do you hope to get out of your gap experience?

RICHARD: I chose to take a three-month ski program at Mont Tremblant. By the end of the program, I'll be a qualified coach. It's a qualification that is recognized by ski resorts around the world. There are different specialties as well, such as becoming a racing coach or a coach for skiers with disabilities. There's a lot of depth to my program. We also get the chance to travel around the province and experience life in Québec.

QUEST: What will you do when you leave Tremblant?

RICHARD: At the beginning of April, when the program ends, I hope to head to New Zealand to teach skiing. After that, I'll be going home to study physiology.

QUEST: When you finally return to England, will you be living with your parents or going away to school?

RICHARD: Most British kids go away to university rather than continue to live at home while studying, which many students seem to do here. I will be living in a hall—a residence—for the first year or two. Usually, by the middle of their university programs, students have moved into a house they share with friends.

QUEST: What are the positive and negative sides of gap years?

RICHARD: For me, one positive thing is the qualification I will have that I can use later. I'm enjoying doing something I'm passionate about—skiing. Some kids do volunteer work during their gap years, and helping in this way is obviously a good thing. As for negative points, I've never heard of anyone who didn't enjoy their gap experience.

THE CONCLUSION

What's your next step?

OPTION 1

C2 C3

- **Create a "moving on" care package for a friend.**

1. Choose a friend who will soon be moving on and would appreciate a care package.
2. Determine 10 needs they may have, based on what you learned in the unit.
3. Choose one object to represent each need and assemble all the items in a box.
4. Write a letter to your friend explaining the choice of items.

5. Use the checklist and the guidelines on pages 350–351 to help you follow the writing process.

6. Produce your final copy using a computer.
7. Present your text to a classmate or your teacher for feedback and revise your final text.
8. Present your care package to classmates who have prepared similar packages and ask them for feedback.
9. Give your care package to your friend.

REFLECT

Adopts effective work methods.

What steps did you follow in preparing your care package?

Word Quest

- advice
- career
- conscientious
- dependability
- dilemma
- endeavour
- exploit
- guidance
- independence
- occupation
- predicament
- quest
- trade
- volunteering

Vocabulary

See the Reference Section, page 333, for the definitions of these words.

OPTION 2

C2 C3

■ **Write a "day in the life" narrative essay about your future.**

1. Decide what you will be doing next year, what activities you plan to be involved in and what challenges you may have, and write about them.
2. Plan a typical day. Make sure to include the different aspects of your life: academic, social, work, health and financial.
3.  Write a narrative essay describing your day. Use the checklist and the guidelines on pages 350–351 to help you follow the writing process.
4. Present your text to a classmate or your teacher for feedback.
5.  Produce your final copy using a computer.
6. Put your text away in a safe place and plan to read it again a year from now.

REFLECT

Adopts effective work methods.

Which steps of the writing process could you pay more attention to in order to improve your writing?

PROJECT OPTION 3

C3 C1

◆ **Produce a video or a radio commercial about the risks of credit cards for young adult consumers.**

1. In your team, decide what message about using credit cards you wish to send.
2. Determine the audience for your video or radio commercial.
3. Choose your medium: radio or video.
4. Use your resources to research the issue and then organize the information.
5.  Use the checklist and the guidelines on pages 352–353 to help you follow the production process.
6.  Use a storyboard to plan the commercial.
7. Prepare your final script and ask another team for feedback. Make adjustments if necessary.
8. Practise the commercial before recording it.
9. Record your commercial and post it on your school website.
10. Assess the strengths and weaknesses of your teamwork:
    - Decide how you could improve it.
    - Assess what you have learned from working in a team.

REFLECT

Adopts effective work methods.

What did you do to make sure your commercial met the requirements of the task? What could you improve next time?

WORKSHOP 2

WRITE A PERSUASIVE EDITORIAL

Every day the radio, TV and newspapers present stories involving controversial issues. You often hear about issues such as bullying, steroid use and media influence on teens. These issues raise ethical questions that make you think about moral standards and use your judgment about what is right and what is wrong. Writing a persuasive editorial is an effective way to share your opinion on these topics.

The aim of this workshop is to help you learn how to use the writing process to write a persuasive text. You will become a better writer by using strategies and learning how to reach your goal. You start by expressing your point of view on a topic, making sure that your facts are straight. Then, you gather information as you carry out the tasks in the workshop. At the end of the workshop, you use the information to support your opinion and justify your point of view in a persuasive editorial.

YOU WILL LEARN TO:

- Use quick writes to brainstorm ideas about a topic.
- Distinguish fact from opinion.
- Identify the features of a persuasive editorial.
- Write a thesis statement.
- Use the research process to find information.
- Prepare arguments to defend an opinion.
- Participate in a discussion and defend your ideas.
- Write a persuasive editorial.

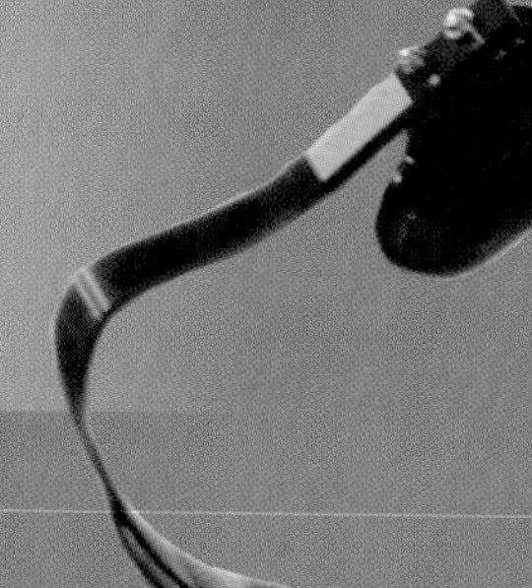

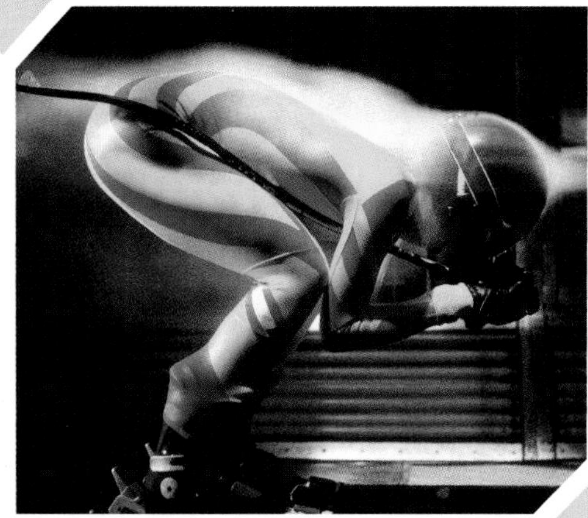

THEME

Technology in Sports

Technology has changed the face of sports in many ways. Developments such as high-tech equipment and around-the-clock media coverage certainly benefit athletes and spectators alike. Progress in technology has also given physically challenged athletes the opportunity to participate in international competitions. Technology is revolutionizing the world of sports. But are there limits to how far we should go?

EXTRA

Reading Folio

What Makes a Champion: Talent or Technology?

Think about what you already know about your topic. This is the first step in the writing process.

C3 C1 Discuss technology in the world of sports today.

1. Do a quick write to gather your ideas about successful athletes. If you need help, use the following questions to guide you:
   - Who are some world-champion athletes today?
   - What makes these athletes successful?
   - What qualities or attributes do they have?
   - How are they similar to or different from successful athletes of the past?
2. Choose a classmate. Take turns sharing your ideas about the world's most successful athletes. Refer to your quick write for help. Add some new ideas to your quick write to use later on.
3. Now think about technology and its impact on sports today. Do another quick write. If you need help, use the following questions to guide you:
   - What kind of technology is used in sports today?
   - How has technology changed sports for athletes and spectators?
   - How do athletes use technology to enhance their performance?
   - Have any of the world-champion athletes mentioned in your first quick write used technology or other performance enhancers to win?

Strategy

Activate prior knowledge
Think about the ways that athletes use technology to improve their performance.

Joannie Rochette, 2008

Florence Griffith-Joyner, 1988

Strategy

Use semantic mapping
Organize the information from your quick writes by grouping similar ideas together.

4. Share your ideas from both quick writes with your classmates. As you listen to your classmates' ideas, write them down on a graphic organizer. This will help you organize your ideas. The model below will help you.

5. Think about the ideas you gathered during the class discussion. Use them to support your answer to the question:
   - What makes a champion: talent or technology?

HOW TO

How to Do a Quick Write

What?

A quick write is a brainstorming strategy. During a quick write, you have a specific amount of time to write down as many ideas as you can about a particular topic or idea or in response to a question. Thinking about your topic is the first step in the writing process.

How?

1. Choose a topic or find out from your teacher what you have to write about.
2. When your teacher gives you the signal to start, write down everything you know about the topic at hand. Do not worry about punctuation or mechanics. It is more important to note down as many ideas as you can.
3. Do not stop writing until your teacher says so.

2 Technology in Sports

Think about the text you will write. Learn about the features of a persuasive editorial and how to find information to support your ideas.

C2

HOW TO

Read about technology in sports today and discuss the issues with your classmates.

1. Read the statements below and decide if each statement is a fact or an opinion.
   a) Athletes will do anything they can to win a competition.
   b) Steroid use should be legalized for professional athletes.
   c) There is an increase in steroid use among teenage athletes.
   d) Progress in technology has given physically challenged athletes the opportunity to compete in international events.
   e) Taking dietary supplements is a safe and acceptable way to enhance performance.
2. Decide if you agree or disagree with each of the statements and discuss them with your classmates.
3. Read one of the two texts on pages 86–89 and take note of the features of a persuasive editorial.
4. Find five facts and five opinions about technology and sports today. Write down your ideas in a T-chart. The model below will help you.

Strategy

Scan

Look for facts and opinions about technology and sports today.

T-Chart

Fact	Opinion
1. In 2008, Michael Phelps became the first swimmer to win eight gold medals in the same Olympics.	1. Steroids and other performance-enhancing drugs are an unfortunate part of every major sports competition.
2.	2.

Functional Language

Agreeing, Disagreeing and Giving an Opinion

- In my opinion, . . .
- I think that . . .
- I don't think that . . .
- I agree that . . .
- I disagree with you.
- According to the text, . . .

5. Form a team with at least two other classmates who have read the other text. Discuss:
   - the impact of technology on athletic performance
   - the five statements from Step 1 again.
6. Find information in the text to support your opinions if possible.

How to Distinguish Fact From Opinion

What?

A **fact** is true information about something that really happened or existed or still happens and exists. Facts can be used to support an opinion. Using facts to justify your point of view will help you provide solid arguments.

An **opinion** is a statement of belief or an expression of a judgment formed in someone's mind. When you express your opinion in a persuasive editorial, you must use facts to support your ideas.

How?

1. Look for certain words that can help you determine if a statement is a fact or an opinion. Opinions may be introduced by words such as *think, believe* and *suggest.* Other words that are often used in opinions are words that show judgment such as *always, never, best* and *worst* or descriptive words such as *funny, sad* and *beautiful.*
2. When you read a statement, ask yourself the question, "Can I find proof that this statement is true?"
3. Think about different resources you can use and then find evidence that the statement is true.

Understanding the internal and external features of a persuasive editorial

Components of the text

Title
From the title, predict what this text will be about.

Introduction
The main idea is usually in the first paragraph.

Thesis statement
The thesis statement presents the topic and viewpoints.

Paragraphs
Paragraphs present arguments from the writer's point of view and include facts that support the writer's opinion.

Language
Transition words help the reader make connections between thoughts.

Option 1

Swifter, Higher, Stronger

The Olympic motto "Swifter, Higher, Stronger" certainly held true at the 2008 Beijing Olympics and perfectly describes the world of sports today. Marked by record-breaking performances, outstanding feats and high-tech equipment, these Games were a far cry from the first ones held in Greece so long ago. **Although today's athletes are achieving unprecedented performance levels, there may be something more than sheer talent and hard work at play.**

These days athletes want more, coaches want more and fans want more. Consequently, many athletes will use anything they can to improve their performance and maximize their chances of success. Technology certainly has a part to play, helping coaches create personalized plans designed to optimize athletes' nutrition, training and techniques. Developments in sports nutrition also mean there is no shortage of "harmless" dietary supplements, protein shakes and energy gels to choose from. There are also steroids and performance-enhancing drugs—an unfortunate part of every major sports competition. The life of a professional athlete is arduous and gruelling. It's no wonder that some athletes go to great lengths to keep themselves, their coaches and their fans happy.

Michael Phelps, Olympic gold medal winner, 2008

Topic: the impact of technology on sports

Language: technical terms related to sports and technology; transition words

Purpose: to persuade

Culture: world of sports and technology; ethical questions regarding the use of technology in sports

Fans were certainly not disappointed by the spectacular performance of one American in the Beijing Games. Millions of spectators from around the world waited eagerly to see if Michael Phelps would live up to their expectations. Phelps did indeed, becoming the first swimmer to win eight gold medals in the same games. How did a mere mortal perform such an outstanding feat? Phelps's success was no doubt due to hours of training, a carefully calculated diet and adequate rest. However, watching Phelps in his slick high-tech bodysuit also made us wonder how much his attire had to do with his performance.

High-tech bodysuit

For years, swimmers shaved off their body hair, hoping to shave off precious seconds from their times. They also wore skimpy bathing suits, believing that less was more. Nowadays, swimmers wear more clothes! Many swim records have been broken by athletes wearing bodysuits that imitate shark skin and provide even less resistance in the water than their own smooth skin. There seems to be no doubt that athletes are benefitting from new high-tech products that promise maximum comfort and better performance. However, it makes you question whether today's world of sports is marked by better athletes or better products.

In the end, today's athletes may very well be getting by with a little more than sheer talent and hard work, but no one can blame them for doing what they can to be the best they can be. Nonetheless, the use of technology in sports certainly raises questions. And given the speed at which technology is advancing, the world has definitely not heard the last of this debate.

Vocabulary

- **arduous:** difficult
- **attire:** clothes
- **feats:** extraordinary acts
- **go to great lengths:** try very hard
- **gruelling:** exhausting
- **mere:** simple
- **sheer:** pure
- **slick:** smooth, slippery

Conclusion

The conclusion restates the thesis and summarizes the important points.

Components of the text

Title
From the title, predict what this text will be about.

Introduction
The main idea is usually in the first paragraph.

Thesis statement
The thesis statement presents the topic and viewpoints.

Language
Transition words help the reader to make connections between thoughts.

Option 2

Athletes of the Future:

Track-and-field coach Bill Bowerman once said, "If you have a body, you are an athlete." His comment holds true today more than ever before. Not so long ago, the idea that anyone with a physical disability could compete in an international sports event was only a dream. Today, increasingly complex technology has turned that dream into reality—physically challenged athletes are now able to participate in some of the world's greatest sports events. **Technology has opened up a world of possibilities, but has also created controversy as to where we should draw the line.**

One of Québec's most admired athletes has had the opportunity to fulfill her dreams because of progress in the world of technology. Chantal Petitclerc continually amazes fans with her achievements in wheelchair racing. Indeed, technological advances and high-tech equipment now allow athletes like Petitclerc to continually strive to be "swifter, higher and stronger." The world watches in awe as these athletes defy their physical limits. No one would surely begrudge them the opportunity to compete alongside the world's best. Needless to say, these high-tech developments have also created controversy, making us wonder how far athletes will go to win that gold medal.

Chantal Petitclerc, Paralympic gold medal winner, 2008

Vocabulary

able-bodied: having no severe physical disabilities
ailments: physical disorders
bar: exclude
begrudge: resent
deemed: judged
outperform: do better

How Far Can We Go?

Topic: the impact of technology on sports

Language: technical terms related to sports and technology; transition words

Purpose: to persuade

Culture: world of sports and technology; ethical questions regarding the use of technology in sports

Oscar Pistorius,
Paralympic gold medal winner, 2008

Science and technology also provide athletes with medical options that did not exist in the past. Nowadays, surgery is available to cure a number of physical ailments that would have previously prevented athletes from achieving their best. Few would criticize athletes who take the necessary means to improve their chances of success.

It may come as a surprise then that a high-tech device was at the centre of controversy before the 2008 Beijing Games. South African amputee runner Oscar Pistorius made history when his request to qualify for the Games was refused. The athlete was deemed ineligible to compete because of his artificial legs. Although the athlete's prosthetic blades, made of aluminum and carbon-fibre, were not designed to boost athletic performance, officials claimed that they actually gave Pistorius an unfair advantage over his able-bodied counterparts. The decision to bar Pistorius from the competition was later overruled, but the case certainly raised questions about the future of physically challenged athletes and their participation in international competitions. It also raised questions about the concept of fairness in sports today and tomorrow.

Paragraphs
Paragraphs present arguments from the writer's point of view and include facts that support the writer's opinion.

The irony is that breakthroughs in science and technology may very well allow physically challenged athletes to outperform their able-bodied competitors. Using technology to increase a human's ability to perform, known as "techno-doping," is becoming more and more common. In fact, one concern is that some athletes may one day voluntarily resort to techno-doping just to maintain their competitive edge. All athletes strive to enhance their body's ability to perform in competition. The question is, just how far are they willing to go?

Conclusion
The conclusion restates the thesis and summarizes the important points.

For or Against?

Use your resources to gather all the information you need to discuss your topic.

Strategy

Cooperate
Work with your classmates to write a thesis statement about the use of technology in sports.

C3 C1 Use the research process to gather information for a discussion about sports technology.

1. With your classmates, decide which aspect of sports technology you would like to talk about in a class discussion.
2. Think about some controversial issues or "hot topics" related to sports technology that provoke thought and promote discussion.
3. Write a thesis statement about the topic. Make sure the statement is carefully written to provide both sides with the opportunity to defend their position. The model below will help you.

HOW TO

Model

All swimmers in international competitions should wear high-tech bodysuits.

How to Write a Thesis Statement

What?

A **thesis statement** is a sentence that presents the topic you want to discuss. It states your main idea and the point you want to make.

How?

1. Think about a topic related to sports technology that interests you.
2. Identify a controversial aspect of this topic and people's opinions on the issue.
3. Take a position on the issue and make a statement that will provoke reaction and lead to discussion.

4. Share your statement with the class. Together, select four statements to discuss in the next task. Sign up for the topic you would like to discuss. Each topic will be discussed by two teams.

5. Form a team of four with classmates who have chosen the same topic as you.

6. Use the research process to research your topic. Find at least three arguments for and three arguments against the issue. Provide details such as facts, statistics and examples to support your arguments.

HOW TO

How to Apply the Research Process to Find Supporting Details

What?

When you present your arguments during a discussion, it is important to have details such as facts, statistics and examples to support your opinion. Conducting research to find supporting details will help you build a solid case. During the discussion, you can use the information to support your arguments and refute your opponent's arguments.

How?

1. Think about the topic that you will research.
2. Plan your research: Identify accessible and reliable sources such as books, newspapers, magazines, dictionaries, encyclopedias, websites and TV reports and documentaries.
3. Choose or design tools for collecting your information such as graphic organizers, index cards and tables.
4. Gather the information and classify it. Use your critical judgment to help you separate facts from opinions.
5. Make sure you find at least three arguments for and three arguments against the issue. Find details (facts, statistics and examples) to back up your arguments. Indicate the sources.
6. Get ready to communicate the results of your research.

Talk About It

Talk about the issue you will write about to understand it better and get more ideas from others.

C1 C2 Share your ideas in a team discussion and defend your position on an issue related to sports technology.

1. Return to your team of four. Share the results of your research and present the details you found to support your arguments both for and against. Add your classmates' ideas to your notes.
2. Rate your supporting details for each argument from strong to strongest.
3. With one member of your group, form a new team of four with two other classmates who chose the same discussion topic as you.

4. Decide who will argue for and who will argue against the issue during the discussion. Work with the classmate who will defend the same side as you and organize your presentation.
5. Decide how you will divide the presentation. Start by writing an opening statement to present your position on the issue.

6. Prepare your arguments. Use the information gathered in Step 1 to help you.
7. Write your closing statement.
8. Think about the possible arguments that your opponents might use and how you will respond to them.
9. Practise your presentation. Pay attention to pronunciation and intonation.
10. Return to your team of four. Discuss the issue and take turns presenting your arguments to each other. As you listen to the opposing side, take notes and think about how you will respond to their arguments.
11. Respond to your opponents and defend your point of view.

Strategy

Pay selective attention
Focus on your opponents' arguments and prepare your response.

Functional Language

Transition Words

- First of all, . . .
  Furthermore, . . .
  In addition, . . .
  In the end, . . .
- However, . . .

HOW TO

How to Present Arguments When Discussing Issues

What?

Participating in a discussion about a controversial topic gives you the opportunity to present arguments and share your opinions. Talking about a topic can also help you organize ideas to use in your writing later on. Listening to your classmates' ideas will also provide you with information to use in your editorial.

How?

1. Write a statement to introduce your point of view. Make sure that you state your position clearly.

2. Present your arguments from strong to strongest. Use transition words to emphasize your points and to connect your ideas.
- To introduce an argument, use words such as *first of all, to begin with.*
- To connect your ideas use words such as *next, in addition, also.*
- To conclude, use words such as *in conclusion, finally.*

3. Listen to your opponents' arguments.

4. Respond to your opponents' arguments and provide information to support your point of view.

Write a persuasive editorial about technology in sports.

HOW TO

C2 C3 **Use your information to write a persuasive editorial about one aspect of sports technology.**

1. Think about the topic you discussed in the previous task and the information you gathered in your research and during the discussion.
2. Decide which position you will defend in your editorial; you may write in favour of or against the issue at hand. Use your notes from previous tasks to help you write your editorial.
3. Think about the arguments you will use to support your opinion.
4. Choose three arguments to support your opinion.
5. Make sure you have three supporting details (such as facts, statistics, examples or quotations related to the subject) for each of your main arguments.

6. Write the outline of your editorial.

7. Write your first draft. Use the checklist to help you follow the writing process and refer to the features of a persuasive editorial described on pages 86–89.
8. Use transition words to express your ideas logically and make your text coherent.
9. Revise and edit your text. Confer with others and use their feedback to help you improve your text.

10. Make adjustments and prepare the final copy of your editorial.

C3 **Present and publish your editorial.**

1. Share your editorial with a classmate and read his or her text.
2. Use what you learned during the workshop to decide if your classmate's editorial is convincing or not.
3. Publish your editorial on the school web page or in your school newspaper.

REFLECT

Adopts effective work methods.

1. Did the information in the "how to" boxes help you complete the tasks? If so, how did it help? If not, why didn't it help?
2. Did participating in a discussion help you write your editorial? If so, how did it help? If not, why didn't it help?
3. How well did your notes help you defend and support your opinion in your persuasive editorial?

HOW TO

How to Write a Persuasive Editorial

What?

An editorial is a news article in which the author reacts to a current event or controversial issue. As in all news articles, an editorial presents the basic facts of a story: the *who, what, when, where* and *why*. News articles involve an objective report of the event in question. However, in a persuasive editorial, the writer tries to convince the readers by sharing his or her point of view about the subject.

How?

1. Write an **introduction** to your editorial.
   a) First of all, develop a thesis statement.
      - A thesis statement is the heart of your editorial.
      - It presents the main idea and the point that you are trying to prove.
   b) Present the facts of the issue objectively.
      - Think of the five wh-questions.
   c) State your opinion as well as the main arguments you will use to support your position. Try to provide at least three reasons to prove that your thesis statement is true.
   d) Write a sentence that ensures a smooth transition to the next paragraph.
2. Write **three paragraphs** in which you present your arguments and support them with valid information.
   a) Present your arguments in order from strong to strongest.
   b) In each paragraph, clearly state your viewpoint and support it adequately.
   c) Stick to your opinion and defend it solidly throughout your editorial. When appropriate, acknowledge that some opposing points are also valid but don't start to defend them yourself.
   d) Include a sentence to conclude each paragraph and to serve as a transition to the next one.
3. Write a **conclusion** to your editorial.
   a) Summarize the most important points and state your thesis once again.
   b) Conclude your editorial with a strong statement that will leave your audience convinced of your point of view.

UNIT 5

HUMANS, ANIMALS AND ETHICS

1. How are animals important to people?
2. In what ways do humans use animals?
3. What is right and wrong about the human relationship with animals?

The human relationship with animals is a complex one. Animals have fascinated people for thousands of years. Most of us have loved a pet or admired animals in nature, but animals play more functional roles as well. They are raised and slaughtered for food and clothing. They are used for testing products from cosmetics to drugs that enhance or even save human lives. They are hunted for sport and trained for our entertainment. We control how animals live and when they die. Many ethical questions surround the way we use and treat them. How far do you think we should go in our use of animals? Do you think that we have already crossed the line?

YOUR Quest

What is your position on our relationship with animals?

Unit Overview

EXTRA

Reading Folio

The Animal-Human Connection

Most people have been close to an animal at some point in their lives, but animals are more than just companions. What do you know about the different ways human beings interact with animals?

Strategy

Create practice opportunities
Sharing information with a partner is a great opportunity to practise your language skills.

Strategy

Take notes
When exploring a text, ask yourself the five wh-questions to identify key ideas.

Functional Language

Giving an Opinion
- If there were no animals, . . .
- The world would be different because . . .
- If we didn't have them, we would . . .

C1 Explore animals' roles.

1. Look at the pictures on pages 96–97. Think about the following questions and exchange your ideas with a classmate:
   - What roles do animals play in our lives?
   - Which animals play these roles?
2. As a class, discuss what life would be like if we did not have animals. What would we replace them with?

C2 Discover how animals help humans.

3. What stories have you heard about animals' unique ability to sense danger and death?
4. Choose one of the articles on pages 99–101.
   - Read it and identify how the animal was able to help humans.
   - Be prepared to explain your article to classmates who read different texts and to describe one way in which animals are important.
5. Form a team with classmates who chose other texts and share what you learned. Combine the ideas you learned from the texts with your own ideas and write a list of all the reasons animals are important.
6. Choose the main reason that animals are important to you. Circle it and share it with your classmates. Justify your choice.

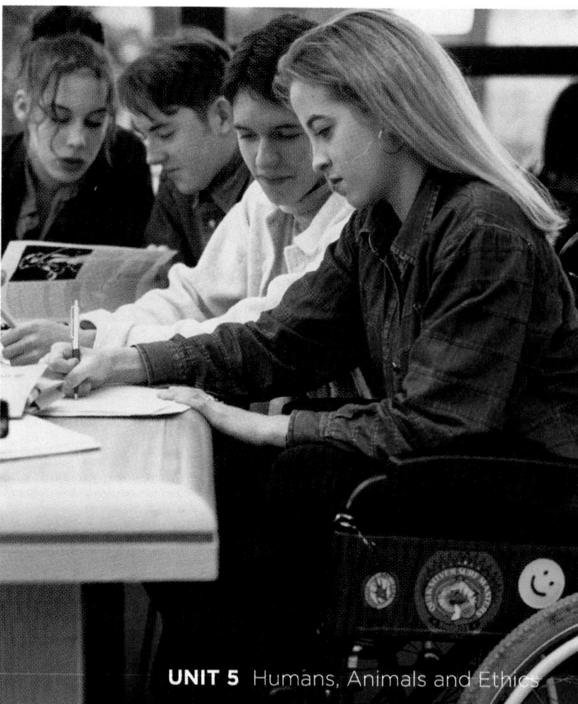

Oscar the nursing home cat can sense death

CTV NEWS

His name is Oscar. He's not the friendliest cat. But he has an uncanny knack for predicting within hours when nursing home patients with whom he lives are about to die.

When he senses that someone is near death, he will jump onto the bed and curl up beside the patient.

Oscar lives at the Steere House Nursing and Rehabilitation Center in Providence, Rhode Island, and is the subject of a fascinating essay in this week's issue of the prestigious medical journal, *The New England Journal of Medicine.*

What makes Oscar special is his ability to sense when one of the hospice residents is about to die. Every day, Oscar makes his rounds among the patients, entering each room and giving each patient a sniff. When he senses that someone is near death, he will jump onto the bed and curl up beside the patient. Within hours, without fail, he or she will die.

Oscar has demonstrated his prognostication skills at least 25 times. He's considered so accurate that nursing home staff will immediately call family members once Oscar has chosen someone, since it usually means they have less than four hours to live.

Dr. David Dosa, a geriatrician from Brown University in Providence, tells Oscar's story, noting that the feline has never been wrong yet.

"His mere presence at the bedside is viewed by physicians and nursing home staff as an almost absolute indicator of impending death," Dosa writes.

Raised at the nursing home since he was a kitten, Oscar is described as aloof—even, at times, grouchy. But when he is on a death watch, he is as warm as can be. He will nuzzle a dying patient and purr, perhaps trying to offer whatever comfort he can.

"For his work, he is highly regarded by the physicians and staff at Steere House and by the families of the residents whom he serves," Dosa writes.

The staff appreciates Oscar so much that a local hospice agency has even erected a plaque to him that reads, "For his compassionate hospice care, this plaque is awarded to Oscar the Cat."

Source: CTV News

Vocabulary

aloof: cold, unfriendly

geriatrician: doctor for older people

grouchy: in a bad mood

hospice: nursing home for people who are close to death

impending: about to happen

nursing home: residence for very old or sick people

nuzzle: rub against

prognostication: prediction

uncanny knack: mysterious or strange ability

1. How long before a death does Oscar go to the patient?
2. How does Oscar treat the dying patient?
3. How does he generally treat people who aren't dying?
4. How has the staff recognized Oscar?
5. What do you think causes Oscar to play this role?

Dogs smell cancer in patients' breath, study shows

STEFAN LOFGREN

Dogs can detect if someone has cancer just by sniffing the person's breath, a new study shows.

Ordinary household dogs with only a few weeks of basic "puppy training" learned to accurately distinguish between breath samples of lung-cancer and breast-cancer patients and healthy subjects.

The results of the study showed that the dogs could detect breast cancer and lung cancer between 88 and 97 percent of the time.

"Our study provides important evidence that cancers hidden beneath the skin can be detected simply by [getting dogs to smell] the odour of a person's breath," said Michael McCulloch, who led the research at the Pine Street Foundation.

Early detection of cancer greatly improves a patient's chances of survival, and researchers hope that our best friend, the dog, can become an important tool in early screening.

"Cancer cells emit different waste products than normal cells," said Nicholas Broffman, executive director of the Foundation. "The differences between these metabolic products are so great that they can be detected by a dog's keen sense of smell, even in the early stages of disease."

The researchers used food as a reward to train five ordinary household dogs. When they smelled breath samples captured in tubes, the dogs gave a positive identification of a cancer patient by sitting or lying down in front of a test station.

The results of the study showed that the dogs could detect breast cancer and lung cancer between 88 and 97 percent of the time.

"It did not seem to matter which dog it was or which stage of cancer it was, in terms of our results," Broffman said.

Researchers predict that dogs could be used in doctors' offices for preliminary cancer detection. According to James Walker, director of the Sensory Research Institute at Florida State University, canines' sense of smell is generally 10 000 to 100 000 times superior to that of humans.

"There are lots of experimental treatments," Walker said. "This could be an experimental diagnostic tool for a while, and one that is impossible to hurt anyone with or to mess up their diagnosis with."

Broffman hopes to build on the current study to explore the development of an "electronic nose."

"Such technology would attempt to achieve the precision of the dog's nose," he said. "Such technology would also be more likely to appear in your doctor's office."

Source: National Geographic News

Vocabulary

accurately: precisely
achieve: replicate
screening: checking for disease
waste products: unwanted by-products

1. How long does it take to train a dog to smell cancer?
2. What odour is identified by the dog?
3. What does a dog do to show it has found cancer?
4. How accurate are the dogs in detecting cancer?
5. What does Broffman hope will develop as a result of the study?

Option 3

Pet rabbit saves couple from death in fire

CITYNEWS

He doesn't have a very original name. (He's a pet rabbit known as "Rabbit.") In fact, he doesn't appear to be very extraordinary at all. But this honey of a bunny is famous in Australia after saving his owners' lives in a fire.

This honey of a bunny is famous after saving his owners' lives.

It happened early Thursday morning in the city of Melbourne, when Gerry McLeod came home exhausted at the end of a night shift and went straight to bed.

About half an hour later, around 6 a.m., he was awakened by the odd sound of a soft but anxious thumping and reluctantly got up to investigate the cause. It was his pet rabbit, Rabbit, making the noise, but that wasn't what got McLeod's attention. Instead he was startled to find that part of his hallway was filled with smoke and that a fire was blazing away in a back room—and spreading quickly.

Without much time, McLeod woke his wife, Michelle Finn, and they ran out of the house to safety. And he admits if it hadn't been for his furry best friend he might not be here to tell the tale.

They pleaded with the firefighters to go in and rescue the hero. One of the firefighters finally found the black bunny right in the line of fire but miraculously unharmed. The house wasn't quite so lucky—it suffered extensive damage.

The couple had been renovating the place and the key smoke alarm that might have told them what was going on had been temporarily disconnected while the ceiling was being worked on.

Rabbit was penned up but made sure to make enough noise to wake the sleeping duo. "He is in his cage at night, which is in our lounge room," Finn explains, "He was just thumping around in his cage and he can be pretty boisterous when he wants to be."

The couple had been working on the renovation project for two years and were just six days away from finally completing everything.

Michelle now plans to give her hero a special treat. "Some fruit I think," she says, holding the adorable fur ball. "Some sweet stuff, just for now."

Investigators believe that a heater may have started the fire and agree that the rabbit not only saved his owners' lives but allowed them to escape without injury.

Source: CityNews

Vocabulary

blazing: burning brightly
boisterous: active and noisy
penned up: in a cage
reluctantly: unwillingly
startled: surprised
thumping: dull hitting sound
unharmed: not injured

1. How did Rabbit wake his owners?
2. The owners saved Rabbit. True or false?
3. Why didn't the smoke alarm go off?
4. How does Michelle plan to reward Rabbit?
5. What caused the fire?

What do you think are the most important roles that animals play? Write your ideas on your tracking sheet.

2 To Be or Not to Be Vegetarian

Many humans rely on animals as an important source of food. What are the alternatives?

Strategy

Plan

Make sure you know what you are looking for before you start to read.

Grammar

Transition Words

These words are used to link ideas and to help a text flow. See page 104.

C2

Give your opinion.

1. Do you think people should use animals for food? Write down reasons to support your opinion.
2. Read the newspaper opinion articles on page 103 and compare each opinion with your own.

3. For each text, identify and write down:
   - the question behind the issue
   - the arguments used
   - the reasons and examples the author uses to support his or her opinion.
4. Read the explanation of "pros and cons" below. Then, list the arguments the writers make for and against vegetarianism.
5. Put a checkmark beside the ideas you agree with and an X beside the ideas you disagree with. Compare your ideas with a classmate.

Pros and cons

Pros and cons are arguments for and against an issue. Listing pros and cons before making an important decision can help you make a better-informed choice.

Including the pros and cons of an issue in your persuasive writing shows that you have considered all sides of the issue and are confident about your opinion.

In a debate, knowing the pros and cons helps you predict what your opponent will say and refute it.

Eating meat: A necessary evil?

PATRICK LAMARCHE

Meat is a large part of the human diet, and leather and fur are commonly worn. Do animals exist to be a source of food and clothing for humans? Some people think so. Others feel that eating meat and wearing leather or fur are wrong, so they prefer to live as vegetarians and avoid all animal products. Why do most human beings continue to consume animal products?

First of all, human beings need protein to grow and live, and animal protein is a natural source. By eating meat, young people become strong and healthy. In fact, the Canada Food Guide suggests eating 2–3 servings of meat products every day to maintain a healthy lifestyle. Therefore, since teens are still growing and need to develop their muscle mass, it is important for them to eat meat.

Secondly, meat is a traditional food in North American culture. Our ancestors evolved by eating meat, so eating meat is in our genes. Moreover, we enjoy the smell of meat cooking and its taste: It's genetic! In fact, the majority of cultures throughout the world enjoy meat as a part of their diet. What traditional family dinner doesn't involve a big piece of meat?

Finally, eating meat supports farmers. Provided that you make an effort to buy local, organically produced meat and that the animals are well-treated, meat is good for you. Not all meat has to come from giant farms where animals are not treated well. We need to support farmers who take good care of their animals and feed them healthy food.

In conclusion, eating meat is part of being human. We evolved from meat eaters, so it is natural for us to eat meat today. It keeps us healthy and it makes us happy, especially if we buy organic meat from local farmers.

Meat: Necessity or luxury?

ELLEN DEJONG

Traditionally, meat is eaten and enjoyed by most families in North America. Meat plays a large role in our culture. Many people love to eat hamburgers and hot dogs, but others feel repulsed by the thought of eating meat. Is eating meat really essential? Let's explore this question.

Firstly, the body is healthier on a plant-based diet and it is perfectly capable of using plant-based food as a source of protein. As a matter of fact, complete protein can be created by combining certain plant foods, for example, corn and beans. Some civilizations, such as the Hindus in India, have survived for thousands of years without eating meat. Some studies have also found lower rates of cancer among vegetarians, whereas meat eaters have more health problems.

In addition, eating meat is cruel. Most meat is produced by giant factory farms, where the conditions under which animals are raised are totally inhumane. Chickens are crammed into small cages and sometimes their beaks are cut off. Cows or pigs are packed together and never get to be outside and enjoy life, which is really unnatural. Animals feel pain and can be afraid, so killing them is completely heartless.

Finally, eating meat is bad for our planet and its people. Cows produce huge amounts of methane gas when they digest their food. Since this gas pollutes the atmosphere, it contributes to global warming. Furthermore, it takes at least 10 kilograms of grain and 43 500 litres of water to produce a kilogram of beef. If that wasted grain and water went to feed people, a lot of lives would be saved.

To conclude, if we all became vegetarians, the world would be a better place. There would be less pollution and poverty, and people would be healthier. So stop eating meat today!

Vocabulary

crammed: packed tightly
repulsed: disgusted

TRACK YOUR QUEST

Now that you have explored another important role animals play in our lives, use your tracking sheet to write down your ideas about the merits of eating meat or being vegetarian.

Grammar

Transition Words

QUICK CHECK

Can you identify the illogical sentences and use better transition words to make them logical?

1. Jimmy really enjoys eating meat, even though it's good for his muscle development.
2. We shouldn't eat meat because it means killing animals.
3. We should eat more tofu. In addition, we prefer meat.
4. Eating meat is natural for humans, despite the fact that it is a good source of protein.
5. Although we love hamburgers, we don't eat them every day.

LEARN MORE

Transition words link sentences and show the relationship between the ideas in them. They add clarity and flow to writing and speech. They also indicate whether the idea that follows is more important, less important, of equal importance or in contrast to what has already been written.

Transition Words	Function	Position Within Sentences
1. *also, in addition, additionally, furthermore, besides, moreover*	Adds another idea.	Beginning of sentence
We enjoy eating meat. ***Furthermore,*** *meat is an important part of our diet.*		
2. *however, on the other hand, in contrast, yet, on the contrary, nevertheless, instead*	Indicates a contrast between two different ideas.	Beginning of sentence; *instead* can go at the end
On the other hand, *some people think eating meat is bad.*		
3. *although, even though, despite the fact that*	Indicates an unexpected contrast (or concession).	Beginning of sentence or second clause
Despite the fact *that our bodies can use plant protein, people continue to eat meat.*		
4. *because, since, as*	Indicates a reason.	Beginning of sentence or second clause
Meat remains an important part of our diet ***because*** *human beings have developed as omnivores.*		
5. *therefore, consequently, as a result, hence, thus, for this reason, because of this, so*	Indicates a consequence.	*Beginning of sentence*
For this reason, *we need to have a better relationship with our animal friends.*		

Transition Words	Function	Position Within Sentences
6. *if, as long as, provided that, assuming that*	Expresses a condition.	Beginning of sentence
***As long as** we pressure politicians, things will improve.*		
7. *as a matter of fact, in fact, indeed, of course*	Reinforces an idea.	Beginning, middle or end of sentence
*Animals, **in fact,** are necessary to humans.*		
8. *first, firstly, first of all, second, secondly, third, next, finally, in conclusion, to conclude*	Puts ideas in a logical order.	Beginning of sentence
***In conclusion,** people need to stop eating meat.*		

PRACTISE

A. Use an appropriate transition word to link the two ideas.

1. We love animals. We should take care of them.
2. I would love to have a pet. I have very bad allergies.
3. I love animals. I love to eat meat.
4. I am fond of animals. I don't eat meat.
5. I could never be a vegetarian. I love hamburgers too much.
6. I've stopped eating so many hamburgers. I've lost a little weight.
7. I haven't eaten meat for two years. I still miss it.
8. She doesn't eat any animal products. They are locally raised.
9. You can be healthy as a vegetarian. Eat enough protein.
10. Our bodies get enough protein from plant sources. We shouldn't need animal protein.
11. I'm a vegetarian. I love the smell of cooked mushrooms.
12. Leather clothing looks great. I would never wear it.
13. I buy leather shoes. I feel guilty about it.
14. Wearing fur is controversial. Jen wears it anyway.
15. We work together. We can make life better for animals.

B. Go back to the newspaper articles on page 103. How many transition words can you find? List them and identify their roles.

EXTRA

You will find more practice exercises on the extra handout.

Cat Aids Crew of HMS *Amethyst*

Cats have always been valued on ships for their rat-catching abilities and their furry friendliness. During wartime, when a seaman was far from hugs at home, a cat could bring a lot of comfort. Some cats even became war heroes. Maybe you've never thought of a cat as a hero? Think again! Simon became the most celebrated and honoured cat of our time.

He was born in 1947 in a busy Hong Kong dockyard and adopted by a seaman who brought him back to his British ship, HMS *Amethyst*, to kill some of the rats on board. Simon did his job well and also became a cuddly friend of the men.

The *Amethyst* was sent to protect the British people on the Yangtze River in China, but one day in April, the ship was attacked. During the battle, some of the seamen were killed and the ship ran aground. The men tried to escape from the ship, but many were killed as soon as they left the *Amethyst*. About 50 men remained on board, some of whom were hurt. The ship was heavily guarded by the enemy for three months.

Simon stayed on board with the men. He was injured, too, but he continued to do his job. He caught at least one rat a day, often more, which helped improve the crew's spirits because he was helping to save their food supply.

Simon also found another job. Several of the seamen lay unwell in the sick bay, in shock and wounded from their experiences under fire. The doctor on board thought Simon could help and he encouraged the cat to sit on their bunks, where he would knead the bed and purr, and take care of his own wounds. His own injuries helped the sailors relate to him and they started to welcome his visits, which helped them get over their own injuries.

After 101 days, the seamen were finally able to escape and sailed the *Amethyst* back to Hong Kong. News about Simon and the crew was picked up by newspaper and radio reporters and shared with the world.

Simon became famous. Letters and gifts from around the world were sent to him and there were even poems written about him! He was soon awarded the Dickin Medal, an award for animal bravery—the only cat ever to receive this honour. A special cat collar in the colours of the medal ribbon was made for him.

Simon was due to be presented with the Dickin Medal in December 1949 but the cat-hero died the month before. The *Amethyst* crew was very sad and upset. They buried Simon with full naval honours in a pet cemetery near London, England. When Simon's death was announced, his photograph and the story about his deeds appeared in *Time*, a magazine read by millions of people around the world.

Simon the *Amethyst*'s Cat

There are many heroes in the world
To whom you raise your hat
But I'd like to say "well done" to one
For he was a gallant cat.

They called the hero Simon
He was on the Honours list,
So give three cheers for the little Puss
Who belonged to the *Amethyst*.

Yes! Simon he was wounded
But he still caught mice and rats,
He never shirked his duty
Did that splendid little cat.

But alas! poor little Simon died
Like many a brave man
And his Pussy soul has passed away
To some far-off Pussy land.

Mena McAllen, Northern Ireland

Source: Veteran Affairs Canada

Vocabulary

- **alas:** unfortunately
- **bunks:** beds
- **dockyard:** place where ships are built
- **fire:** attack
- **hugs:** embraces with arms
- **knead:** push and press
- **on board:** on the ship
- **passed away:** died
- **Puss/Pussy:** cat
- **ran aground:** sailed into the land
- **seaman:** sailor
- **shirked:** didn't do
- **wounds:** injuries

Animals in Science

Animals play an important role in science as both objects of study and objects of experiments. How necessary are animals to our learning?

Give your opinion of animal testing.

1. What kinds of tests are performed on animals, and why? Discuss what you know with a classmate. You will confirm your answers by listening to a podcast debate about the subject.
2. The first time you listen to the discussion about animal testing, write down the arguments used by each side of the debate.
3. Listen a second time and write down the rebuttal of each argument.
4. With your classmate, decide if each rebuttal is strong or weak. If it is weak, give a contradictory reason or example to illustrate why you disagree.
5. Which side of the debate do you support? Write down your ideas to back your opinion in a class discussion.

Strategy

Direct attention

Listen carefully to how the arguments are refuted.

Functional Language

Giving an Opinion

- This is (un)acceptable because . . .
- That argument is (in)valid because . . .

STATE **YOUR** CASE

Should students be obliged to dissect animals in science class?

In this task, you discussed the importance of animal testing. Write any thoughts or ideas you have about the issue on your tracking sheet.

4 Keepers of the Earth

Some people feel that it is our responsability to act as caretakers of the planet. Others feel that we interfere with things that we should stay out of. Are human beings responsible for managing animal populations?

C2 C1 Find out about the protection of animals.

1. How far should we go to protect animals? Think about your answer and share your opinion with your classmates. Support it with a reason or an example.
2. DVD Watch the three short videos about endangered giant tortoises. Take notes about what the scientists did to help or hurt them.
3. Work with a classmate to refute these statements:
   - The scientists helped the turtle population.
   - The scientists hurt the turtle population.
4. Compare your ideas with your classmates.

C2 Win your case.

5. Read the newspaper clippings on page 109.
6. With a classmate, choose one of the issues concerning the management of animal populations. Decide who will be for and who will be against the issue.
7. Write down one argument to support your side of the issue.
8. Exchange papers with your partner. Write down a rebuttal of your partner's argument as he or she writes a statement that refutes yours. Continue exchanging the papers and adding arguments and rebuttals until you can't think of any more.
9. Together, read what was written and decide who had the better arguments for each issue.
10. Change classmates and repeat the activity, using a different proposal.
11. As a class, discuss what makes a good rebuttal.

Strategy

Plan

Try to imagine which arguments your partner will use so that you can refute them.

Functional Language

Agreeing and Disagreeing

- That is not true because . . .
- If we look at the other side of the question, . . .
- On the contrary, . . .
- But on the other hand, . . .
- Nevertheless, . . .

Alaskan wolves to be hunted from airplanes

Hunters in Alaska have won the right to shoot wolves from airplanes. They claim that wolves are ruining their hunting by killing young moose.

Cost of sterilizing animals to increase

Higher costs to veterinarians are responsible for a big jump in the fee for having a pet sterilized. Animal rights groups fear that this will cause pet owners to avoid the procedure, leading to an increase in abandoned animals.

Dozens of dogs rescued from puppy mills to be euthanized

The local animal shelter will be obliged to kill many dogs saved from illegal puppy mills earlier this year. There are simply not enough families willing to adopt dogs.

Australia contemplates culling 3000 kangaroos to protect endangered species

High numbers of these jumping giants in a protected wildlife area are causing problems for two species of reptiles as well as the golden sun moth. The hungry kangaroos are destroying the habitat of these endangered animals.

Kelowna to cull city's wild rabbit population

Citizens have been complaining about their gardens and lawns being damaged by the overpopulation of wild rabbits. The city has decided to reduce the population by dramatic means.

Hundreds of Canada geese to be exterminated near New York's LaGuardia Airport

Canada geese are causing major headaches for pilots near New York's busy airport. The geese fly into engines and can cause planes to crash. Animal rights groups say that other means should be taken to discourage the birds.

Vocabulary

cull: select animals to kill

puppy mills: high-volume dog-breeding operations with poor conditions

TRACK YOUR QUEST

Human beings control the lives of animals in many ways. Write your thoughts and ideas about this issue on your tracking sheet.

THE CONCLUSION

What is your position on our relationship with animals?

OPTION 1

C2 C3

- **Write a newspaper profile of an animal that plays a role in the lives of humans.**

1. Choose an animal that plays a role in the lives of humans for your profile.
2. Use your resources to gather information about the animal and use the texts on pages 99–101 as models.
3. Plan your text. Make sure to include the following information:
   - Present the animal and its role.
   - Explain the facts behind the story.
   - Explain any issues surrounding the role of this animal.
4. Use the checklist and the guidelines on pages 350–351 to help you follow the writing process.
5. Produce your final copy using a computer.
6. Present your text to a classmate or your teacher for feedback.
7. Contribute your article to your class or school newspaper.

REFLECT

Uses critical judgment.

How did you know which facts were credible?

Word Quest

- accountable
- animal kingdom
- attachment
- bond
- contact
- cruel
- essential
- harvest
- inevitable
- issue
- link
- required

Vocabulary

See the Reference Section, page 333, for the definitions of these words and expressions.

OPTION 2

C2 C3

■ **Write a persuasive editorial about a moral debate that arises from our use of animals.**

1. Choose an animal-human relationship issue about which to write a persuasive editorial.
2.  Prepare your article by:
   - researching the issue
   - organizing your information
   - making a list of pros and cons to clarify your opinion
   - planning your arguments from strong to strongest.
3. Clearly state your point of view and support it throughout the editorial. Refer to Workshop 2 for help.
4. Use the checklist and the guidelines on pages 350–351 to help you follow the writing process.
5. Present your text to a classmate or the teacher for feedback.
6.  On a computer, combine your text with visual elements to create your final copy.
7. Contribute your article to your class or school newspaper.

REFLECT

Uses critical judgment.

What question did you attempt to answer in your article?

PROJECT OPTION 3

C1 C2 C3

◆ **Produce a radio or TV interview about an animal-human issue.**

1. Choose an animal-human issue on which to base a radio or TV interview.
2.  Form a production team with two classmates who have different opinions about the issue. Use the checklist and the guidelines on pages 352–353 to help you follow the production process.
3. Determine the interview audience.
4. Choose your media type: radio or video.
5.  Use your resources to research and gather information about the issue. Then organize it.
6. Prepare the interview questions and give them to your classmates so that they can prepare their answers.
7. Prepare your final script and ask another team for feedback. Make adjustments if necessary.
8. Practise the interview before recording it.
9.  Record your interview as a radio or TV show and post it on your school's website.
10. Reflect on the strong and weak points of your teamwork:
    - Consider your goals.
    - Assess what you have learned.

REFLECT

Uses critical judgment.

How did you phrase questions to elicit arguments for both sides of the issue?

UNIT 6

SONGS OF CHANGE

- How can songs bring about social change?
- How do you think musicians affect people's views?
- What issues are musicians of your generation addressing?

A song plays on the radio. You have never really paid attention to the lyrics before, but this time you realize that there is more going on here than just a cool beat. The musician is singing about an important issue, an issue that touches people around the world, an issue that touches you. You already know something about it, perhaps because you have read about it in a newspaper, seen something on TV or learned about it at school. You have never really thought you could do anything to help; it just seemed like "one of those things," a sad story destined for history books. But this singer is making you see things differently. What if you started paying more attention to what was going on? What if there was something you could do? That is the power of song.

YOUR Quest

How can music change the world?

Unit Overview

EXTRA

Reading Folio

1 Sing a Song of Change

Some songs try to bring about change through their words or their style. What songs do you know that have a message of change?

C1

Think of the protest songs that you know.

1. Look at the pictures on pages 112–113. As a class, discuss these questions:
   - What songs do you know that convey messages of change (protest songs)?
   - What issues do song writers deal with?
   - Do you know of any musicians who support social causes?

2. On your protest song log, write down all the social problems you have heard musicians talk or sing about. Add the names of the artists and their songs.
3. Share your ideas with a classmate and then with another team. See how many protest songs you can think of. Categorize the songs on your protest song log according to the issues and indicate if they are newer or older songs.

Strategy

Cooperate

Complete your list with your classmate.

Functional Language

Asking for Information, and Agreeing and Disagreeing

- Have you heard of . . . ?
- Yes, I have./No, I haven't.
- Do you think . . . ?
- I have noticed . . .
- I think it might be . . .
- I agree/disagree with you.

C2 C1

Discover a songwriter's perspective.

4. Before you watch the video, think about these questions and discuss them with a classmate:
   - Why do you think musicians sing about issues?
   - How do you think music can bring about change?
5. After you have watched the video, compare the issues that Dave mentions with the list you made in Step 2 and add any new ones.
6. Dave says, "Activism is our rent for living on the planet." What do you think he means by this? Discuss your ideas with your classmates.
7. Think about the following statements and write down your response to each idea. Share your responses with your classmates to find out if you have the same opinions.
   - Musicians have a responsibility to use their music to make the world a better place.
   - Music is just for entertainment.

TRACK YOUR QUEST

Which issues addressed in songs seem the most important to you? Keep track of the songs to help you make a choice for Your Quest and keep looking for messages in the songs you listen to.

Blast From the Past

Musicians have always been involved in social change. Investigate these songs of change to discover the messages they convey.

Strategy

Infer

Look for metaphors (symbols and images that represent other ideas) and try to work out what they mean.

Functional Language

Giving an Opinion

- I think that they are (not) successful because . . .
- I feel that . . .
- They will be . . .
- They might be . . .
- Our group concludes that . . .

Investigate the lyrics of a classic protest song.

1. Read the introduction to Jared's podcast below. Then, choose one of the songs on the following pages and read the background information and lyrics. Write down:
   - the issue the song talks about
   - keywords and expressions that identify the issue.

2. Add the song you chose to the appropriate category on your protest song log. Find classmates who chose different songs, share your information and add their songs to your log.

C2 C1

Discuss what progress has been made.

3. Select one of the songs. Decide if you think the problem in the song has been solved or if there is still work to be done.
4. Discuss the following questions in teams of three or four. Take turns writing notes. Be prepared to share your answers with the class.
   - Do you think that songwriters succeed in making the world a better place? How do they do this?
   - What issues do you think songwriters will be talking about 15 years from now? Will they be the same issues as today?
   - Why have these songs become so popular?

Pete Seeger

Bob Marley

Sarah McLachlan

Bruce Springsteen

Hello, everybody. My name is Jared. Today I'm going to present some of my favourite protest songs. I'll give you short biographies of the songwriters and explain some of the issues behind the songs.

1962

Where Have All the Flowers Gone?

Pete Seeger

Where Have All the Flowers Gone? 

Where have all the flowers gone?
Long time passing
Where have all the flowers gone?
Long time ago
Where have all the flowers gone?
Girls have picked them every one
When will they ever learn?
When will they ever learn?

Where have all the young girls gone?
Long time passing
Where have all the young girls gone?
Long time ago
Where have all the young girls gone?
Taken husbands every one
When will they ever learn?
When will they ever learn?

Where have all the young men gone?
Long time passing
Where have all the young men gone?
Long time ago
Where have all the young men gone?
Gone for soldiers every one
When will they ever learn?
When will they ever learn?

Where have all the soldiers gone?
Long time passing
Where have all the soldiers gone?
Long time ago
Where have all the soldiers gone?
Gone to graveyards every one
When will they ever learn?
When will they ever learn?

Where have all the graveyards gone?
Long time passing
Where have all the graveyards gone?
Long time ago
Where have all the graveyards gone?
Covered with flowers every one
When will we ever learn?
When will we ever learn?

My first song is by a guy who is probably the most important protest song writer of all time. Pete Seeger has been a source of inspiration for protesters for over 60 years. He has written songs about the labour movement, the civil rights movement, anti-war movements and the environment. He is a voice of social conscience. In the 1950s the United States government became suspicious of his social activism and prevented his music from being played on the radio and television. This made him even more determined to fight for freedom. His major influence was Woody Guthrie, the popular protest singer of the 1930s and 1940s.

The song "Where Have All the Flowers Gone?" was written in 1961 and quickly became a symbol of the United States' involvement in the Vietnam War. North Vietnam, a communist country, was at war with South Vietnam. The U.S. government did not want North Vietnam to win, so they became involved in trying to stop the communists.

It turned into a terrible conflict: More than 58 000 American soldiers died and more than 300 000 were wounded. Between three and four million Vietnamese died, most of them civilians. Many young Americans protested against the war at home and it became a national issue. Many songs were written to inspire and mobilize protesters. The United States eventually withdrew from the conflict in 1975 and the communist government took power over South Vietnam.

Vocabulary

activism: campaigning for social or political change

civil rights: equality for all people

labour: working people

1977

Guiltiness

Bob Marley

The second song is "Guiltiness" by Bob Marley. Marley had a black Jamaican mother and a Caucasian British father. He was the victim of discrimination and bullying because of his mixed racial heritage and short stature. However, he became an icon for oppressed people in many countries and his popularity spread internationally. His songs carried messages of peace and tolerance. At one point, he even succeeded in bringing together politicians at one of his concerts to try to stop violence in his home country of Jamaica.

In the song "Guiltiness," Bob Marley sings about poverty and oppression in Jamaica. Jamaica is a beautiful island nation, but a large portion of its population remains poor while a small minority controls most of the wealth. This poverty and unfairness have caused riots and violence. Bob Marley was an advocate for a peaceful solution to his country's problems and for better services and living conditions for the poor.

Bob Marley was diagnosed with cancer in 1977. He refused certain treatments because of his religious beliefs and died in 1980 at the age of 32. His last words to his son Ziggy were "Money don't buy life."

Vocabulary

'bout: about
bullying: intimidation
Caucasian: a person with white or pale skin
downpressors: oppressors
icon: idol
sorrow: sadness
woe: unhappiness

Guiltiness

Guiltiness (talkin' 'bout guiltiness)
Pressed on their conscience. Oh yeah.
And they live their lives (they live their lives)
On false pretence every day:
Each and every day. Yeah.

These are the big fish
Who always try to eat down the small fish,
Just the small fish.
I tell you what: they would do anything
To materialize their every wish.
Oh yeah-eah-eah-eah.

Say: woe to the downpressors:
They'll eat the bread of sorrow!
Woe to the downpressors:
They'll eat the bread of sad tomorrow!
Woe to the downpressors:
They'll eat the bread of sorrow!
Oh, yeah-eah! Oh, yeah-eah-eah-eah!

Guiltiness
Pressed on their conscience.
Oh yeah. Oh yeah.
These are the big fish
Who always try to eat down the small fish,
Just the small fish.
I tell you what: they would do anything
To materialize their every wish.
Oh, yeah-eah-eah-eah-eah-eah.

But woe to the downpressors:
They'll eat the bread of sorrow!
Woe to the downpressors:
They'll eat the bread of sad tomorrow!
Woe to the downpressors:
They'll eat the bread of sad tomorrow!
Oh, yeah-eah! Oh yeah-e-e-e-e-e!
Guiltiness. Oh yeah. Ah!
They'll eat the bread of sorrow every day.

World on Fire

2004

Sarah McLachlan

Sarah McLachlan is a Canadian singer and songwriter who lives in Vancouver, British Columbia. She wrote the third song I have chosen today, "World on Fire," which I chose because of the eye-opening video the artist made to accompany it. The video opens with McLachlan, dressed in jeans and a T-shirt, sitting alone in an undecorated room playing her guitar and singing. We learn that it costs $150 000 to make a typical music video. We then see clips that illustrate the breakdown of costs involved in making a music video, such as $3000 for one day of catering in Los Angeles—an amount of money that would buy 10 950 meals for street children in Calcutta. Or $5000 for make-up and hairstyling for one day, which would pay for 145 Afghan girls to attend school for a year.

We then discover that the "World on Fire" video cost only $15. McLachlan donated the $150 000 that she saved to 11 different charities around the world. Her song and actions convey a powerful message: She wants us to think about how we spend money here in the West and how it could be put to better use.

McLachlan has been involved in a variety of humanitarian projects during her career. In 1997, she founded the Lilith Fair concert tour, which promoted female artists. Over three years the tour raised over $7 000 000, which were donated to women's shelters and other non-profit organizations across North America. In 2009, Sarah McLachlan was recognized at the JUNO Awards (Canada's annual music awards) for her outstanding humanitarian contributions.

World on Fire

Hearts are worn in these dark ages
You're not alone in this story's pages
Night has fallen amongst the living and the dying
And I try to hold it in, yeah I try to hold it in

[Chorus]

The world's on fire and
It's more than I can handle
I'll tap into the water
(I try to pull my ship)
I try to bring more
More than I can handle
(Bring it to the table)
Bring what I am able

I watch the heavens and I find a calling
Something I can do to change this moment
Stay close to me while the sky is falling
Don't wanna be left alone, don't wanna be alone

[Chorus]

Hearts break, hearts mend
Love still hurts
Visions clash, planes crash
Still there's talk of
Saving souls, still the cold
Is closing in on us

We part the veil on our killer sun
Stray from the straight line on this short run
The more we take, the less we become
A fortune of one that means less for some

Vocabulary

catering: food brought in
shelters: temporary homes for abused women
wanna: want to

2007

Last to Die

Bruce Springsteen

Last to Die

We took the highway till the road went black
We marked Truth or Consequences on our map
A voice drifted up from the radio
We saw the voice from long ago

Who'll be the last to die for a mistake
The last to die for a mistake
Whose blood will spill, whose heart will break
Who'll be the last to die for a mistake

The kids asleep in the backseat
We're just countin' the miles you and me
We don't measure the blood we've drawn anymore
We just stack the bodies outside the door

Who'll be the last to die for a mistake
The last to die for a mistake
Whose blood will spill, whose heart will break
Who'll be the last to die for a mistake

The wise men were all fools
What to do

The sun sets in flames as the city burns
Another day gone down as the night turns
And I hold you here in my heart
As things fall apart

A downtown window flushed with light
Faces of the dead at five (faces of the dead at five)
A martyr's silent eyes
Petition the drivers as we pass by

Who'll be the last to die for a mistake
The last to die for a mistake
Whose blood will spill, whose heart will break
Who'll be the last to die

Who'll be the last to die for a mistake
The last to die for a mistake

Darlin' your tyrants and kings form the same fate
Strung up at your city gates
And you're the last to die for a mistake

My final choice is "Last to Die" by the great American rocker, Bruce Springsteen, whose music has been popular for about four decades. He usually sings straight-ahead rock and ballads, but he has recorded some more folk-style songs. Springsteen celebrates the struggles of everyday life and his music has become more and more political. He recorded a tribute album to Pete Seeger in 2006, and in 2009 he opened the Obama Inaugural Celebration concert in Washington DC.

"Last to Die" is based on a speech made by Senator John Kerry, who ran for president of the United States in 2004. Kerry made the speech against the Vietnam War in 1971. What is interesting about the speech, and probably the reason that Springsteen based a song on it, is the parallel with the Iraq War, which was still being waged in 2007. The line, "How do you ask a man to be the last man to die for a mistake?" from Kerry's speech shows that he was against the Vietnam War and thought it was wrong. Springsteen is saying the same thing about the war in Iraq.

Vocabulary

spill: fall out like a liquid
stack: make a pile
straight-ahead: basic, clear
struggles: difficulties
tribute: homage
Truth or Consequences: a town in New Mexico
waged: fought

TRACK YOUR QUEST

What similarities have you noticed between protest songs? Write all the songs on your tracking sheet. They will help you choose songs for Your Quest.

Give Peace a Chance: John and Yoko in Montréal!

In 1969, during the Vietnam War, John Lennon, one of the Beatles, and his wife, Yoko Ono, held two widely publicized bed-ins. One took place at the Queen Elizabeth Hotel in downtown Montréal. At that time, sit-ins were a popular form of protest. Protesters would peacefully occupy public places, just sitting on the floor for long periods of time, and refuse to move. John and Yoko's version meant staying in bed. They had just married and they were very much against the war. They knew that their fame would attract a lot of attention for the peace movement, so they spent a week in bed in their pyjamas. They invited the media to visit between 9 a.m. and 9 p.m., when they answered journalists' questions and gave interviews.

As they predicted, the event attracted a huge amount of attention for their cause, although some of the media didn't take them too seriously. Some reporters even made fun of them and said that they were crazy hippies. People realized only later what a historic event had taken place when they heard one of John Lennon's most famous songs, "Give Peace a Chance," which he wrote that week.

The end of the bed-in was capped off with a spontaneous recording of the song, in which the background singers were mostly just people who happened to be there at the time. The song has since become a classic peace anthem which has inspired generations of peaceful protesters. The hotel has renamed the rooms that John and Yoko used "The John Lennon Suite" and they can be rented for several hundred dollars a night. The bedroom is basically the same as it was in 1969, and features pictures of the event on its walls.

A Montréal teenager, Gail Renard, and her friend were able to sneak past security into the hotel by climbing through a window from the fire escape and then using the stairs to get to the right floor. Ono invited Gail into the room and she ended up running errands and taking care of Ono's little girl for eight days. As a gift, Lennon gave her the envelope on which he had written the lyrics to "Give Peace a Chance." He said that she should keep them because they might be worth a lot of money someday. He was right: In 2008 she sold the envelope with the original lyrics for $841,000.

Vocabulary

anthem: song of devotion or loyalty

capped off: finished with a decisive action

fame: being well-known, a celebrity

running errands: getting things

sit-ins: peaceful protests at which people occupied a public building and refused to move

We Were There

Here are personal accounts from three people who were touched by the social issues mentioned by songwriters.

Strategy

Compare

Notice what is similar and different about the experiences.

Functional Language

Giving an Opinion

- I would (not) have participated because . . .
- I think this is important because . . .
- There are (no) other ways to express . . .

Grammar

Phrasal Verbs

Note the use of phrasal verbs in the texts. Try to use them in Step 5. See page 125.

C2 C1 Compare three people's experiences.

1. Before reading, think about the following questions:
   - What protests have you heard about in songs, in the news or in history?
   - What were the issues behind the protests?
   - Can you think of any songs or musicians who were associated with the protests?
2. Read one of the texts on pages 122–124. Use the questions beneath the text to guide your reading.

3. Find classmates who read the other two texts and compare the three people's experiences. Write down your ideas. Are there songs on your protest song log that deal with similar themes? Add them to the chart. Discuss:
   - How do you think music made the protests more meaningful to the participants?
4. Discuss the following statements with a classmate. Agree or disagree with each one and support your opinions with reasons and examples.
   - I would have participated in those protests.
   - There is no issue I would protest against.
   - Protesting is the only way to tell politicians what we think.
5. Work with a classmate to think of slogans that could be used to protest against each of the issues presented in the texts. Make the slogans into bumper stickers and post them around the class.

Joan Baez, 1968

Option 1

Darcy Bortman Geders, Kent, Ohio

In the spring of 1970, I was finishing my first year at Kent State University. There had been many protests that year against the Vietnam War. Many of us felt that the government was fighting a war that could not be won and it was costing too many young American lives. Many singers were singing songs of protest. They motivated us all to think that we could do something about the terrible events we were **witnessing**. On April 30, the United States invaded Cambodia and students held protests across the country.

On May 4, following a fire and some **rioting** on campus the previous weekend, the National Guard arrived. We were told that we should not attend the demonstration, which just had the effect of making everybody go there! We were amazed to see soldiers and tanks. I had never been very politically active, but out of curiosity my boyfriend and I joined the thousands of students in the common area. The **rally** began with chanting and singing. Then we heard the university president telling us to break up the rally and leave. If we did not, the National Guard would arrest us. We did not take the threats seriously and nobody moved. After all, we thought that this was a peaceful rally.

To make us move, the soldiers threw **tear gas** canisters into the crowd. We were stunned and terrified. I ran inside, struggling to breathe as the yellow smoke burned my throat and nostrils. When we heard gun shots, I thought that they were firecrackers. When things were quiet, I went outside and was told that the school was closed indefinitely and we must all go home. People were saying that some students had been wounded, possibly killed. I was in shock and I called my parents to come and pick me up. Later I learned that four students had been killed and nine injured. To this day, every time I hear Neil Young's song "Ohio," I remember May 4, 1970, and I weep.

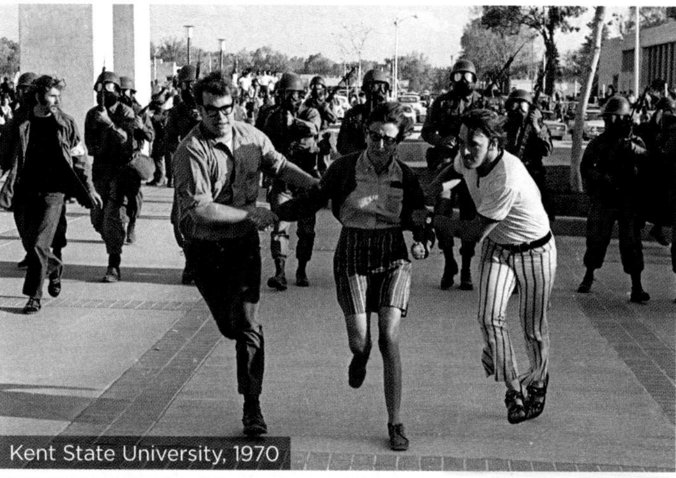
Kent State University, 1970

To make us move, the soldiers threw tear gas canisters into the crowd. We were stunned and terrified.

1. What were students protesting against?
2. Why did the National Guard come to the campus?
3. Why did Darcy and her boyfriend attend the protest?
4. Why did the students not react to the president's threats?
5. What two forms of violence did the National Guard use against the students?

Vocabulary

rally: public meeting

rioting: noisy, violent public disorder

tear gas: gas that burns the eyes, used against rioters

witnessing: seeing something happen

Madeline Hendrickson, Chino Valley, Arizona

The year was 1952. It was a dream come true for a very enthusiastic, naive 16-year-old: a real job.

I was **hired** at the F.W. Woolworth store in Bloomington, Illinois. The job title was *extra girl*; the job description was to work wherever I was needed, and that included the lunch counter.

I arrived at work on a Saturday morning and was informed that I would be working at the lunch counter.

I was advised by my supervisor that serving "negroes" was not allowed. [. . .] I was angry and confused.

Lunch counter, 1952

My training was brief, and I was very nervous. It was my first experience as a waitress. Around noon, I noticed a black couple sitting at the next station. They had been there for quite a while and had not yet been served. I decided to **wait on** them, even though I had been told not to leave my station without permission.

Almost immediately, I was **summoned** to the office, where I was advised by my supervisor that serving "negroes" was not allowed. She then told me that if I had waited a little longer they would have left. I was angry and confused. I asked why they were treated differently. My supervisor just looked at me angrily and said that I should understand. I fully expected to **be fired**. I was not, but I have never forgotten the day, the order, or the incident. It made me a strong supporter of the civil rights movement.

The action of an innocent, compassionate teenager did not change anything. The practice of discouraging blacks from dining there continued. I never knew for how long. There were many protests. The people would **picket** businesses like this one, marching and singing songs.

Some years later, thanks to the work of the civil rights movement, I was able to sit down at the same lunch counter, at that same station, with my daughter. A black mother and her daughter sat next to us. The little girls shared their ice cream.

1. Why did the black couple wait so long before being served?
2. What was the supervisor's reaction to the waitress serving the couple?
3. What did the supervisor mean when she said the waitress "should understand"?
4. What was the waitress's reaction to the incident?
5. How do you think the waitress felt years later, when she returned to the counter and sat beside an African-American woman?

Vocabulary

be fired: lose a job
be hired: get a job
picket: protest against
summoned: called for
wait on: serve

François St-Charles, Sainte-Adèle, Québec

When I was in my first year of CEGEP, I had the chance to attend the protests over the 2001 World Trade Organization (WTO) meetings in Québec. At that time, the leaders of the Western world were trying to negotiate a new free-trade agreement to unite most of the countries of the West. The problem that I and many others had with that agreement was simple. We felt that it would give far too much power to the big multi-national corporations at the expense of regular workers. Poverty would increase and Canadian jobs would be sent to countries where workers were paid less and could be exploited. The songs of the band Rage Against the Machine were being played, and that pumped us up.

WTO protest, 2001

That day, there were thousands of students and activists protesting in the city. Some say there were as many as 150 000. There were supposed to be zones where it was safe to protest but that was not always the case. The authorities were ready for us. They were armed with tear gas and pepper spray, batons and rubber bullets. On our side, we had a **catapult** which we used to **hurl** teddy bears at the police and soldiers.

Most of us were doing our best to remain peaceful, but there were a few people who were shaking things up. Many of them repeatedly broke down the fences. They were arrested and taken away or sprayed with tear gas. At one point, our group demanded to see the text of the document the politicians were working on. We chanted together, "Please let us in," but of course no one opened the door. The police started to **drag** away our leaders and then they used tear gas and rubber bullets to disperse the crowd. I was later told that they used so much tear gas that even the people inside the building felt its effects.

The authorities were ready for us. They were armed with tear gas and pepper spray, batons and rubber bullets.

Vocabulary

catapult: large weapon that works like a slingshot

drag: pull along the ground

hurl: throw

1. Who were participating in the WTO meetings?
2. What issue were the protesters demonstrating against?
3. What consequences of globalization were the protesters against?
4. What weapon did the protesters use against the police?
5. What weapons did the police use against the protesters?

Protest songs are inspired by difficulties faced by real people all over the world. Do you agree that protests are the only way to get a message across? Write your thoughts on your tracking sheet.

Grammar

Phrasal Verbs

QUICK CHECK

Can you identify the phrasal verbs in the following sentences?

1. We decided to step out for a coffee.
2. Jon wakes up early each morning to get to work.
3. Meg thinks that Axel needs to beef up his arguments for the debate.
4. You might get your ideas across better if you organized them.
5. She's trying to get over the effects of the tear gas.

LEARN MORE

Many verbs in English are followed by an adverb or a preposition. This new combination has a different meaning from the original verb but you conjugate it the same way. You can use it in any tense.

Phrasal Verb	Meaning	Example
beef up	improve	*We need to* ***beef up*** *our strategies to organize the sit-in.*
back down	stop defending one's opinion	*I* ***backed down*** *when I realized that my facts were wrong.*
carry on	continue	*Yoko Ono* ***carried on*** *singing after John Lennon was killed.*
come across	discover	*The scientist* ***came across*** *an ancient skeleton.*
find out	discover	*I was angry when I* ***found out*** *what had happened.*
get across	transmit or send	*Martin* ***is*** *really* ***getting*** *his message across tonight.*
get over	stop worrying or feeling bad about something	*If we don't succeed, I* ***will*** *never* ***get over*** *it.*
give up	stop trying	*George* ***gave up*** *protesting because it didn't work.*
go through with	continue	*I was scared, but I had to* ***go through with*** *the audition.*
look forward to	be excited about a future event	*I* ***was looking forward to*** *the concert, but it didn't go well.*
make up for	compensate for	*I* ***am making up for*** *my mistake by doing some extra work.*
pick on	harass	*Bob Marley* ***was picked on*** *as a child because he was small.*
shut down	stop or close something	*The police* ***shut down*** *the illegal operation.*
speak up	make known	*We need to* ***speak up*** *about bullying in school.*
stand up for	defend	*Bob Marley also wanted us to* ***stand up for*** *our rights.*
stay away from	avoid	*My mother told me to* ***stay away from*** *bullies.*
wake up	awaken	*I* ***woke up*** *early to get on the bus to Québec.*

PRACTISE

A. Complete these sentences with phrasal verbs from the list on page 125.

1. Lori is trying ______ the disappointment of not being able to attend the protest. (infinitive)
2. Alex ______ her ideas ______ quite well in her speech last night. (simple past)
3. Yesterday the principal ______ the student newspaper because he didn't agree with the editorial. (simple past)
4. I ______ working on this project, even if it is difficult. (simple future, negative)
5. Jenny refused ______ even though Vibeka had a better argument. (infinitive)
6. I ______ the meeting tonight. I was too sick to go to the last one. (present continuous)
7. Allan is planning ______ his work in politics when he goes to CEGEP. (infinitive)
8. I ______ my errors by paying for the damage I caused. (present perfect)
9. It is not right ______ people who are weaker than we are. (infinitive)
10. The police ______ that the students were planning a sit-in. (simple past)
11. The investigators ______ the explosive device as they sifted through the debris. (simple past)
12. Martin Luther King told the people ______ the oppressed. (infinitive)
13. My parents told me ______ violent demonstrations. (infinitive)
14. We decided ______ the sit-in, even though the principal threatened to expel us. (infinitive)
15. She's usually very shy, but she decided ______ about the teacher's unfairness. (infinitive)

B. Look at the texts on SB pages 122–124 again. How many examples of phrasal verbs can you find? Write them down.

EXTRA

You will find more exercises on the extra handout.

Change Your World

Throughout time and around the world, there are always issues to deal with. What issues face your generation?

C2

Identify the concerns of your generation.

1. As a class, brainstorm subjects that concern teens around the world today.
2. Form a team of three or four and choose one issue that is important to all of you. Write it in the centre of a large sheet of paper. Working silently, you must each choose one corner of the page and simultaneously write down everything that comes to mind about that issue: words, ideas or images.
3. When the specified time has elapsed, silently read what each team member wrote. Add to one another's ideas.

4. Listen to an interview with a songwriter. Write down what you learn about writing a protest song.
5. Using the ideas you wrote about the chosen issue in Step 2, work together to write eight lines of a protest song. If you wish, make it fit a tune you already know.
6. Make a collection of new protest song verses and post them in your classroom.

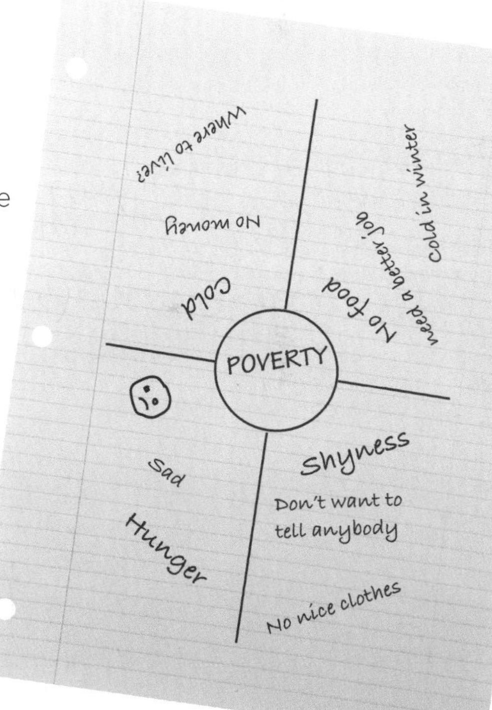

Strategy

Plan

Make sure that you know what you need to include in your lyrics before you start writing.

Functional Language

Suggesting and Inviting

- What if we wrote . . . ?
- This might be interesting.
- Maybe we could add . . .
- Don't forget about . . .

STATE YOUR CASE

Do you think musicians sing about issues just to make money?

What do you think makes an effective protest song? Write your ideas on your tracking sheet.

THE CONCLUSION

How can music change the world?

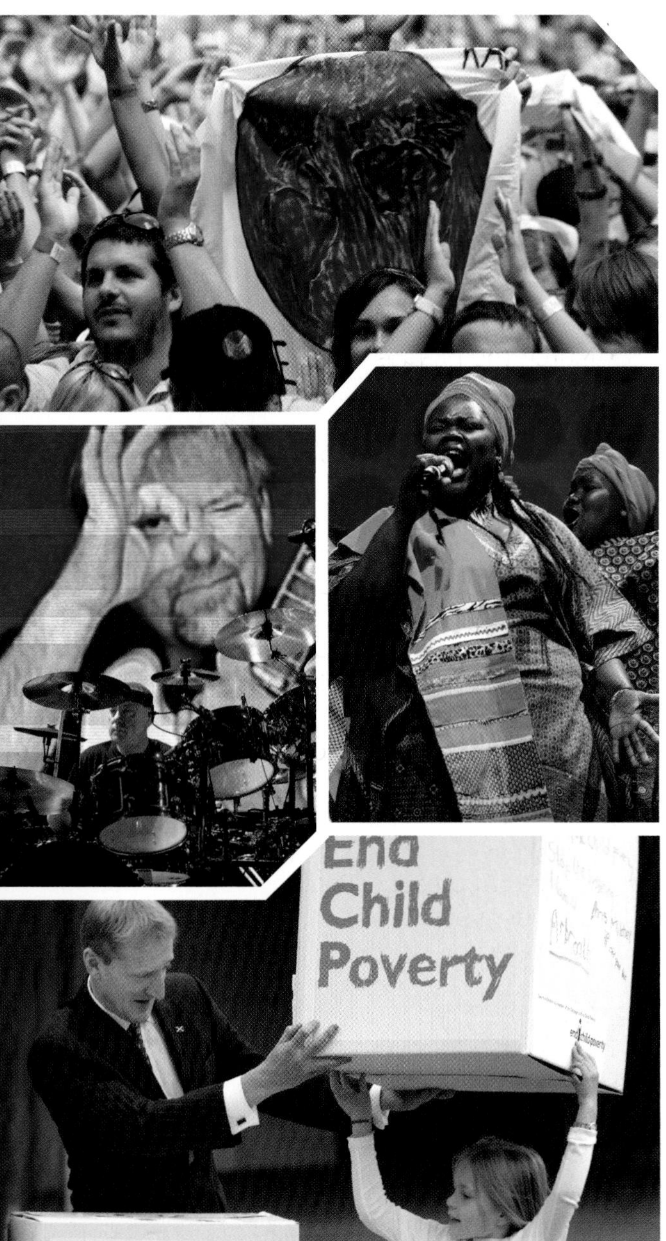

OPTION 1

C2 C3

- **Profile a songwriter you admire.**

1. Choose a songwriter who has written world-changing songs for your profile.
2. Use your resources to gather information about the artist.
3. Plan your profile. Make sure to include:
   - biographical information about the artist
   - some protest songs she or he has written
   - a description of how she or he has tried to change the world
   - pictures to accompany the profile.
4. Use the checklist and the guidelines on pages 350–351 to help you follow the writing process.
5. Present your text to a classmate for feedback.
6. Use the computer to produce your final copy with pictures.
7. Post the profile in a class gallery of world-changing songwriters.

REFLECT

Uses information and communications technologies.

Which online sources did you use? How did you make sure they were reliable?

Word Quest

- agreement
- camaraderie
- commitment
- complaint
- compromise
- concede
- concern
- conciliation
- crisis
- disagreement
- discord
- dispute
- dissent
- find the middle ground
- protest
- spirit
- surrender
- topic
- understanding
- unity

Vocabulary

See the Reference Section, page 334, for the definitions of these words and expressions.

OPTION 2

C2 C3

■ **Create a protest song podcast.**

1. Choose at least three songs that deal with a political or social issue to cover in a podcast.
2. Use your resources to gather information about the songs, the issue behind them and the performer.
3. Plan your introduction to each song. Make sure that you include information on the following:
   - the song, its meaning and the performer
   - the issue behind the song.
4. Write the script for your podcast. Use the checklist and the guidelines on pages 350–351 to help you follow the writing process.
5. Present your script to a classmate for feedback.
6. Record your introductions to the songs.
7. Create a montage of the songs with their introductions.
8. Make the podcast available for download by your classmates.

REFLECT

Uses information and communications technology.

What did you learn about using technology that will help you do a better job next time?

PROJECT OPTION 3

C1 C2 C3

◆ **Create a slide show or movie based on an issue in a song.**

1. In your production team, choose an issue from a song that is important to you. Plan and write a slide show or movie about it.
2. Use your resources to find the song lyrics and to gather information and images about the issue. Organize your information.
3. Plan your production.
   - Select images that portray the issue.
   - Match the images to the lyrics.
   - Use text slides or voice-overs to explain the issue:
     - Describe how the song informs listeners about the issue.
     - Speculate on what needs to be done to deal with the issue.
4. Create your media texts. Use the checklist and the guidelines on pages 352–353 to help you follow the production process.
5. Present your text to a classmate for feedback.
6. Create your slide show or movie.
7. Show it to the class and post it on the school website.
8. Assess the strengths and weaknesses of your team's presentation:
   - Consider your future goals and objectives.
   - Assess what you have learned.

REFLECT

Uses information and communications technology.

How did your use of technology help convey the seriousness of your message?

WORKSHOP 3

WRITE A CHARACTER ANALYSIS

When you explore works of literature, you meet characters who bring stories, poems and plays to life. Learning to understand a character will help you appreciate the texts that you read, listen to and view. It will also help you the next time you write a story and create characters of your own.

The aim of this workshop is to help you develop your ability to analyze characters and to use the writing process to improve your essay-writing skills. It will also show you how to make a plan and use strategies to reach your goal.

You will start by thinking about some famous literary characters and about your own favourites. Then, you will read a play and gather information about the characters. At the end of the workshop, you will use the information to write a character analysis.

YOU WILL LEARN TO:

- Describe a character.
- Identify the components of a play.
- Identify different types of characters.
- Explore the characters in a play.
- Analyze a character.
- Write a character analysis.

THEME

Playing the Part:
Character Analysis in Literature

When you think about your favourite stories, you probably remember colourful characters and how they made you smile, laugh, cry or shake with fear. From Dr. Jekyll and Mr. Hyde to fairy-tale princesses and fantastic superheroes, the world of literature is full of memorable characters who teach you about life in their time and place. Their actions, speech and thoughts not only expose you to a wide range of emotions but can also help you better understand the society in which they lived.

EXTRA

Reading Folio

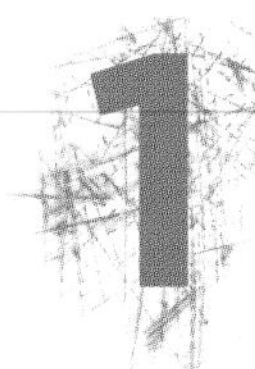

A World of Characters

Identify some famous literary characters and describe your favourite characters in books and movies.

Strategy

Scan

Look for words or phrases that describe the character.

Functional Language

Agreeing, Disagreeing and Giving an Opinion

- I think that . . .
- I don't think that . . .
- I agree that . . .
- I disagree with you.
- What do you think?

C1 C2 Talk about some famous literary characters.

1. With your classmates, make a list of well-known literary characters.
2. Read the descriptions of three famous characters and decide who they are. Use the images on pages 131–133 for help.
3. Find the words and phrases that helped you make your decision and write them down. Discuss your ideas with a partner.

1. "He is not easy to describe. There is something wrong with his appearance; something displeasing, something downright detestable. I never saw a man I so disliked, and yet I do not know why. He must be deformed somewhere; he gives a strong feeling of deformity, although I couldn't specify the point. He's an extraordinary-looking man, and yet I really can name nothing out of the way. No, sir; I can make no hand of it; I cannot describe him. And it is not want of memory; for I declare I can see him this moment."

2.

The wife of a rich man fell sick. Before she died, she called her only daughter to her and said, "Dear child, always be good and I will be near you." Every day, the girl went out to her mother's grave and wept, and she remained good.

By springtime, her father had taken another wife, who brought two daughters with her. The daughters made life miserable for the poor girl. They took away her pretty clothes and made her wear an old grey nightgown and wooden shoes.

They took her into the kitchen where she worked hard from morning till night. She had to get up before daybreak, carry water, light the fire, cook and wash. In the evening, she had no bed to go to. She had to sleep by the hearth in the cinders and so she always looked dusty and dirty.

3.

There stood a tall old man, cleanshaven save for a long white moustache, and clad in black from head to foot, without a single speck of colour about him anywhere. The old man motioned me in, saying in excellent English, "Welcome to my house!" He moved impulsively forward, and holding out his hand, grasped mine with a strength which made me wince, an effect which was not lessened by the fact that it seemed cold as ice, more like the hand of a dead man than a living man.

His face was strong and sculpted, with an aquiline nose and strangely arched nostrils. His eyebrows were massive, almost meeting over the nose, and with bushy hair that seemed to curl in its own profusion. The mouth was fixed and rather cruel-looking, with peculiarly sharp white teeth. These protruded over the lips. His ears were pale, and at the tops extremely pointed. The chin was broad and strong, and the cheeks firm though thin.

I had noticed the backs of his hands and they had seemed rather white and fine. But seeing them now close to me, I could not but notice that they were rather coarse, broad, with squat fingers. Strange to say, there were hairs in the centre of the palm. The nails were long and fine, and cut to a sharp point.

Vocabulary

aquiline: curved and prominent

cinder: ashes

clad: dressed

coarse: not refined

displeasing: unpleasant

grasped: took

hearth: fireplace

profusion: abundance

squat: short and thick

want of memory: forgetfulness

wince: grimace with pain

C1 Discuss your favourite characters in books and movies.

4. Think about two of your favourite characters in stories, books or movies. Use the graphic organizer to help you answer the following questions:
   - What does the character look like?
   - How does the character act? What are some of his or her habits and preferences?
   - Describe the character's personality. What are some of his or her character traits? What are some of his or her strengths and weaknesses?
   - What does the character say that shows something about him or her? What are some of his or her favourite sayings or catch phrases? What does the character think about himself or herself and others around him or her?
   - How does the character represent the typical behaviour and attitudes of that society and time?
   - What do the other characters say about him or her? How do they react to him or her?

5. Discuss your favourite characters with a classmate. Choose two characters to compare and complete the graphic organizer with information about them.

HOW TO

How to Prepare a Character Sketch

What?

Interesting characters are the key to a successful story. A character sketch is a description of a character in a work of literature. An artist paints or draws a picture of a character, but a writer uses words to bring a character to life. Providing a description of a character helps the readers create a mental image of him or her.

How?

1. Think about the character you will describe.
2. Make a list of adjectives that describe the character's physical appearance and personality.
3. Think of verbs that describe what he or she does.
4. Think about how the other characters react to him or her.

A Wicked Woman

Learn about the components of a play.

Strategy

Predict
Based on the title, say what you think the play is about.

C2

Read the play *A Wicked Woman.*

1. Before you read the play, write down your answers to the following questions:
   - Judging from the title, what do you think the play will be about?
   - How do you imagine the character described in the title? What mental image comes to mind?
   - Look at the illustrations on pages 137–145. When do you think the play takes place? What do you know about the roles of men and women at that time?

2. Silently read the script of *A Wicked Woman*. Pay attention to the components that help you understand the play.

How to Identify the Components of a Play

What?

All texts have internal and external features that help you analyze them and understand them better. The internal features of a play include components such as scenes, stage directions, dialogue, characters and setting.

How?

1. Scan the script of the play *A Wicked Woman*.
2. Look for these text components:
   - title
   - cast of characters
   - setting
   - scene numbers
   - stage directions
   - dialogue.

C2 **Share your ideas about the events and characters in the play.**

3. Check the predictions you made in Step 1 and write down how your ideas changed.
4. Now, participate in a class reading theatre. If you are a reader, speak clearly and with expression. Use the information provided by the narrator and in the stage directions to help you bring the character to life for your audience.
5. Read the statements below. Place the events in the order in which they happen in the story. Write down your answers.
   a) Loretta believes that she must marry Billy to save her reputation.
   b) Ned tries to talk seriously to Loretta but is interrupted by Jack and Alice.
   c) Alice confesses to Ned that she invited him to stay in the hope of playing matchmaker.
   d) Loretta confesses to Ned that she let Billy kiss her at least five times.
   e) Loretta and Ned stay at the Hemingways' house in Santa Clara, California.
   f) Loretta is distressed because she does not love Billy, but he has convinced her that she is a wicked woman.
   g) Ned finally proposes to Loretta and then takes her in his arms and kisses her.
   h) Loretta refuses to let Ned kiss her for fear of creating another scandal.
   i) Billy arrives at the Hemingways' house to persuade Loretta to marry him.
   j) Ned learns that Billy had been Loretta's fiancé.
6. As a class, discuss how the characters in the play depict the gender stereotypes of the early 1900s. Do you think this story could take place in today's society? Explain your answer.

Functional Language

Giving an Opinion

- I was surprised that . . .
- I don't understand why . . .
- I found it interesting that . . .
- I enjoy/don't enjoy reading plays because . . .
- My favourite character is . . . because . . .
- The character . . . should/should not . . . because . . .
- I think/don't think this story could take place in today's society because . . .

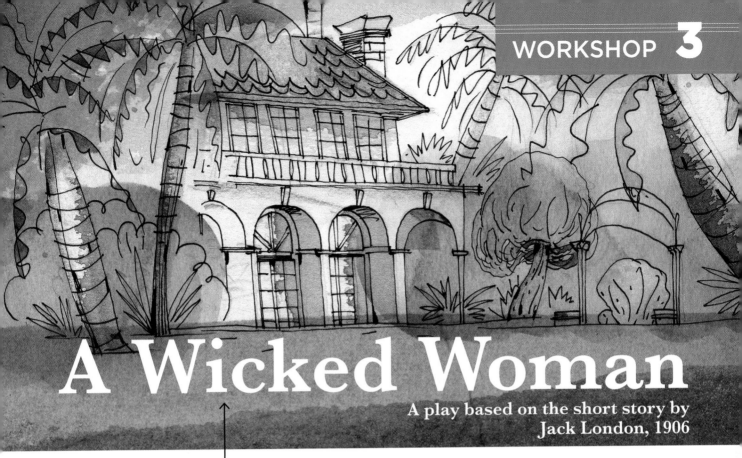

A Wicked Woman

A play based on the short story by Jack London, 1906

Understanding the components of a play

Title

From the title, you can predict what the play will be about.

Cast of Characters

The characters are presented at the beginning of the play. You will find the names of the characters and a short description of each one.

Setting

The setting provides information about where and when the play takes place.

CD

CHARACTERS

Loretta:
A sweet, innocent young woman about nineteen years old. Slender, delicate.

Ned Bashford:
A cynical, world-weary young man who has no faith in women.

Billy Marsh:
A boy from a country town who is just about as innocent as Loretta. A positive youth but also awkward and immature.

Alice Hemingway:
A good-hearted society woman, a matchmaker.

Jack Hemingway:
Alice Hemingway's husband.

Josie:
A domestic servant.

SETTING

Place:
Santa Clara, California

Time:
A summer afternoon in 1910.

Vocabulary

awkward: not graceful

matchmaker: someone who tries to bring two single people together

SCENE 1

Scene numbers

Plays are divided into scenes. Each scene is numbered.

Stage directions

Stage directions provide extra information about the characters and how the scenes should be carried out.

They are usually written in italics and presented in square brackets.

Look for clues in the stage directions to help you understand the play.

Dialogue

The dialogue is the exchange between the characters in the play. It brings the plot to life for the audience.

NARRATOR: The curtain rises on the living room of a country house in California on a summer afternoon. It is the Hemingways' house in Santa Clara. The year is 1910.

Loretta is seated at a grand piano, facing Ned Bashford, who is standing. Loretta has been sent to stay with the Hemingway family after her recent breakup with Billy Marsh. Ned is also staying at the Hemingways' house, invited by Alice Hemingway, who hopes to play matchmaker to her two guests.

LORETTA: No, I won't go fishing. It's too warm.

NED: Oh, come on. It's not warm at all. And anyway, we won't really fish. I want to tell you something.

LORETTA: You always want to tell me something.

NED: Yes, but this is different. This is serious. Our . . . my happiness depends upon it.

NARRATOR: Loretta looks serious but delighted. She is hoping for a marriage proposal.

LORETTA: Then don't wait. Tell me right here.

NED: Shall I?

LORETTA: Yes.

NARRATOR: Ned looks around apprehensively as though fearing an interruption. He clears his throat and takes Loretta's hand. Loretta is startled and timid. She cannot hide her love for him.

NED: Loretta. I . . . ever since I met you, I have—

NARRATOR: Jack Hemingway appears from the left. Ned suddenly drops Loretta's hand. He looks exasperated, and Loretta seems disappointed by the interruption.

NED: What do you want now?

JACK [*enthusiastically*]: Come fishing.

NED [*abruptly*]: No. It's too warm.

JACK [*going out*]: You don't need to take a fellow's head off!

LORETTA: I thought you wanted to go fishing.

NED: Not with Jack.

LORETTA: And you told me it wasn't warm at all.

NED: That isn't what I wanted to tell you, Loretta. [*He takes her hand.*] Dear Loretta—

NARRATOR: Alice Hemingway suddenly enters the room.

ALICE: Goodness! I thought you'd both gone fishing!

LORETTA [*sweetly*]: Is there anything you want, Alice?

NED [*trying to be courteous*]: Anything I can do?

ALICE: No, no. I only came to see if the mail had arrived.

LORETTA AND NED: No, it hasn't arrived.

LORETTA: I will go see.

SCENE 2

NARRATOR: Ned flings himself disgustedly into a chair.

ALICE: What have you been saying to her?

NED: Nothing.

ALICE [*threateningly*]: Now listen to me, Ned.

NED: On my word, Alice, I've been saying nothing to her.

ALICE: Then you ought to have been saying something to her.

NED: Look here, Alice, I know your game. You invited me down here to make a fool of me.

ALICE: Nothing of the sort, sir. I asked you down to meet the sweetest, most innocent girl in the world.

NED: That's what you said in your letter.

ALICE: And that's why you came. Jack had been trying for a year to get you to come. He did not know what to put in his letter.

NED: If you think I came because of a line in a letter about a girl I'd never seen—

ALICE [*mockingly*]: The poor, jaded, world-weary man, who is no longer interested in women and girls! The poor, tired pessimist who has lost all faith in the goodness of women—

NED: For which you are responsible.

ALICE [*incredulously*]: I?

NED: You are responsible. Why did you throw me over and marry Jack?

ALICE: Do you want to know?

NED: Yes.

ALICE: First, because I did not love you. Second, because you did not love me. And third, because there were just about twenty-seven other women at that time that you loved, or thought you loved. That is why I married Jack. And that is why you lost faith in the goodness of women. You have only yourself to blame.

NED: You talk so convincingly. I almost believe you as I listen to you. And yet I know all the time that you are like all other women—faithless, dishonest and immoral.

ALICE: And how about Loretta?

NED [*sincerely*]: Loretta is an exception, I confess. She is all that you said in your letter. She is a little fairy, an angel. It is remarkable to find such a woman in this day and age.

ALICE: She is so naive.

NED: Yes, isn't she?

ALICE: She cannot conceal anything. Do you know that she loves you?

NED [*excitedly*]: Do you think so?

Vocabulary

conceal: hide
incredulously: not believing
jaded: exhausted
ought to: should

ALICE [*laughing and rising*]: And to think I once went out with you for three weeks!

NARRATOR: Ned rises. Josie enters from left with letters, which she brings to Alice Hemingway.

ALICE [*looking over the letters*]: None for you, Ned. Two for me, and three for Loretta. [*Speaking to maid*] Put them on the table, Josie.

NARRATOR: Josie puts the letters on table and exits stage left.

NED [*with shade of jealousy*]: Loretta seems to have quite a correspondence.

ALICE: Yes, but I did not notice any from Billy.

NED: Billy?

ALICE: Of course she has told you about him?

NED: She has had boyfriends . . . already?

NARRATOR: Alice laughs and puts her hand on Ned's arm.

ALICE: Now don't be alarmed. She doesn't love Billy at all.

NARRATOR: Loretta enters the room and Alice hands her three letters. Loretta sits down, opens the letters and begins to read.

NED [*suspiciously to Alice*]: But Billy?

ALICE: I am afraid he loves her very much. That is why she is here. They had to send her away. Billy was making life miserable for her. They were little children together—playmates. And Billy has been, well, importunate. And Loretta, poor child, does not know anything about marriage. That is all.

NED [*reassured*]: Oh, I see.

NARRATOR: Alice and Ned walk toward the door together.

ALICE: Are you going fishing, Loretta?

NARRATOR: Loretta looks up from her letter and shakes her head.

ALICE [*to Ned*]: Now is your chance to say what you want to say.

NARRATOR: Alice leaves the room.

SCENE 3

NARRATOR: Ned watches Loretta as she reads her letters. Loretta finishes reading the last one and puts it back in the envelope. She looks up and sees Ned.

LORETTA: Oh! I thought you were gone.

NED: I thought I'd stay and finish our conversation.

LORETTA: Yes, you were going to—

NED [*taking her hand, tenderly*]: I little dreamed when I came down here visiting that I was to meet my destiny in—

NARRATOR: Josie enters the room. Ned abruptly releases Loretta's hand.

Vocabulary

importunate: persistent

Josie [*to Loretta*]: A gentleman to see you. He doesn't have a card. He said for me to tell you that it was Billy.

Narrator: Ned rises to his feet and prepares to go.

Loretta: Oh! . . . Ned!

Ned [*courteously*]: If you'll excuse me now, I'll wait until later to tell you what I wanted.

Loretta [*in dismay*]: What shall I do?

Ned: Don't you want to see him? [*Loretta shakes her head*] Then don't.

Loretta [*slowly*]: I can't do that. We are old friends. We . . . were children together. [*to Josie*] Send him in. [*to Ned, who has started to go out toward right*] Don't go, Ned.

[*Josie exits stage left.*]

Ned: I'll come back.

Narrator: Ned leaves the room to the right. Loretta looks agitated.

SCENE 4

Narrator: Billy enters the room from the left and stands in the doorway for a minute. His shoes are dusty and he looks hot and tired. His face brightens at the sight of Loretta.

Billy: Loretta!

Loretta [*not very enthusiastic*]: You never said you were coming.

Narrator: Billy shows that he expects to kiss her, but she merely shakes his hand.

Billy: I walked from the station.

Loretta: If you had let me know, the carriage would have been sent for you.

Billy: If I had let you know, you wouldn't have let me come.

Narrator: Billy looks around the stage cautiously and then tries to kiss her.

Loretta [*refusing to be kissed*]: Won't you sit down?

Billy: Go on, just one kiss. [*Loretta shakes head.*] Why not? We're engaged.

Loretta [*decisively*]: We're not. You know we're not. You know I broke it off the day before I came away. And . . . and . . . you'd better sit down.

Narrator: Billy sits down. Loretta sits by the table. Billy moves his chair to face Loretta, his knee touching hers. He leans toward her, but she moves her chair back slightly.

Billy [*with supreme confidence*]: That's what I came to see you for—to get engaged over again. Now look here, Loretta, I haven't any time to lose. I've got to leave for that train in ten minutes. And I want you to set the day.

Loretta: But we're not engaged, Billy. So there can't be any setting of the day.

Vocabulary

dismay: distress, shock

BILLY [*with confidence*]: But we're going to be. Oh, Loretta, if you only knew how I've suffered. That first night I didn't sleep a wink. I haven't slept much ever since. I walk the floor all night. Loretta, I don't eat enough to keep a canary bird alive. Loretta—

LORETTA: I know it, Billy. But . . . [*She glances toward letters on table.*] Captain Kitt, my sister's husband, doesn't want me to marry you. He says—

BILLY: Never mind what he says. He wants you to stay and be company for your sister. He doesn't want you to marry me because he knows she wants to keep you.

LORETTA: Daisy doesn't want to keep me. She wants nothing but my own happiness. She says—

BILLY: Never mind what Daisy says—

LORETTA: And Martha says—

BILLY: Never mind Captain Kitt and Daisy and Martha and what they want. The question is, what do you want? Do you want to marry me? [*He looks at his watch.*] Just answer that.

LORETTA: Aren't you afraid you'll miss that train?

BILLY: I didn't come all the way here for a train. I came for you. Now just answer me one thing. Do you want to marry me?

LORETTA [*firmly*]: No, I don't want to marry you.

BILLY [*with assurance*]: But you've got to, just the same.

LORETTA [*defiantly*]: Got to?

BILLY [*still confident*]: That's what I said—got to. And I'll see that you do.

LORETTA [*blazing with anger*]: I am no longer a child. You can't bully me, Billy Marsh!

BILLY [*coolly*]: I'm not trying to bully you. I'm trying to save your reputation.

LORETTA: Reputation?

BILLY: Yes, reputation. [*He pauses for a moment, then speaks very solemnly.*] Loretta, when a woman kisses a man, she's got to marry him.

LORETTA: Got to?

BILLY: It is the custom.

LORETTA: And when . . . a . . . a woman kisses a man and doesn't . . . marry him?

BILLY: Then there is a scandal. That's where all the scandals you see in the papers come from.

NARRATOR: Loretta sits in silent despair.

LORETTA [*shakily*]: You are a good man, Billy. [*Billy shows that he believes it.*] And I am a very wicked woman.

BILLY: No, you're not, Loretta. You just didn't know.

LORETTA [*with a gleam of hope*]: But you kissed me first.

BILLY: It doesn't matter. You let me kiss you.

LORETTA [*hope dying*]: But not at first.

BILLY: But you did afterward and that's what counts. You let me—

LORETTA [*with anguish*]: Don't! Don't!

BILLY: —kiss you when you were playing the piano. You let me kiss you that day of the picnic. And I can't remember all the times you let me kiss you good night.

LORETTA [*beginning to weep*]: Not more than five.

BILLY [*with conviction*]: Eight at least.

LORETTA [*reproachfully, still weeping*]: You told me it was all right.

BILLY: So it was all right, until you said you wouldn't marry me after all. Then it was a scandal, only no one knows it yet. If you marry me no one ever will know it. [*looks at watch*] I've got to go. [*stands up*] Where's my hat?

LORETTA [*sobbing*]: This is awful.

BILLY: You bet it's awful. And there's only one way out. [*looks anxiously about for hat*] What do you say?

LORETTA [*brokenly*]: I must think. I'll write to you. The train? Your hat's in the hall.

NARRATOR: Billy looks at his watch and then tries to kiss Loretta. He succeeds only in shaking her hand.

BILLY: All right. You write to me. Write tomorrow. Remember, Loretta, there must be no scandal.

[*Billy exits stage left.*]

Vocabulary

gleam: small sign
reproachfully: disapprovingly
weep: cry

SCENE 5

NARRATOR: Loretta sits in the chair, quietly weeping. She slowly dries her eyes, rises from the chair, and stands, undecided as to what she will do next.

Ned enters from the right. He discovers that Loretta is alone, and comes quietly across stage to her. When Ned comes up to her, she begins weeping again and tries to turn her head away. Ned puts an arm around her shoulder and draws her to him.

NED: There, there, Loretta, don't cry.

LORETTA: Oh, Ned, if you only knew how wicked I am.

NED: What is the matter, little one? Has your dearly beloved sister failed to write to you? [*Loretta shakes her head.*] Then it must have been that caller of yours? [*long pause, during which Loretta's weeping grows more violent*] Tell me what's the matter, and we'll see what I can do.

LORETTA [*sobbing*]: I can't. You will despise me. Oh, Ned, I am so ashamed.

NED: Let us forget all about it. I want to tell you something that may make me very happy. My fondest hope is that it will make you happy, too. Loretta, I love you.

LORETTA: Too late!

NED [*surprised*]: Too late?

LORETTA: Oh, why did I? I was so young. I did not know the world then.

NED: What is it all about anyway?

LORETTA: Oh, I . . . he . . . Billy . . . I am a wicked woman, Ned. I know you will never speak to me again.

NED: This . . . er . . . this Billy—what has he been doing?

LORETTA: I . . . he . . . I didn't know. I was so young. I could not help it. Oh, I shall go mad, I shall go mad!

NARRATOR: Loretta buries her face in her hands and starts crying again.

NED: I . . . I do not understand.

LORETTA: I am so unhappy!

NED: Why unhappy?

LORETTA: Because . . . he . . . he wants to marry me.

NED: That should not make any girl unhappy. Because you don't love him is no reason—of course, you don't love him? [*Loretta shakes her head vigorously.*] What?

LORETTA: No, I don't love Billy! I don't want to love Billy!

NED [*with confidence*]: Because you don't love him is no reason that you should be unhappy just because he has proposed to you.

LORETTA: That's the trouble. I wish I did love him.

NED: Now my dear child, you are worrying yourself over trifles. Because you have changed your mind, or did not know your mind, because you have—to use an unnecessarily harsh word—jilted a man—

LORETTA: Jilted? Oh Ned, if that were all!

NED: All!

NARRATOR: Ned's hands slowly retreat from hers. He opens his mouth as though to speak further, then changes his mind and remains silent.

Vocabulary

despise: detest
jilted: rejected

LORETTA [*protesting*]: But I don't want to marry him!

NED: Then I shouldn't.

LORETTA: But I ought to marry him.

NED: **Ought** to marry him? *[Loretta nods.]* That is a strong word.

LORETTA [*nodding*]: I know it is. *[Her lips are trembling, but she strives for control and manages to speak more calmly.]* I am a wicked woman. A terrible wicked woman. No one knows how wicked I am . . . except Billy.

NED: Tell me about it. You must tell me all of it.

LORETTA: And . . . will . . . you . . . ever . . . forgive . . . me?

NED [*drawing a long breath, desperately*]: Yes, I'll forgive you. Go ahead.

LORETTA: If I had only known.

NED: Yes, yes. Go on.

LORETTA: We were together almost every evening. We were with each other so much . . . If I had only known . . . There was no one to tell me . . . I was so young . . . *[breaks down crying]*

NED [*jumping to his feet, explosively*]: The scoundrel!

LORETTA [*lifting her head*]: Billy is not a scoundrel. He . . . he . . . is a good man. It was all my fault. I should never have let him. I was to blame.

NARRATOR: Ned paces up and down for a minute, stops in front of her, and speaks with resignation.

NED: All right. You have been very honest. It is . . . er . . . commendable. But Billy is right, and you are wrong. You must get married.

LORETTA: To Billy?

NED: Yes, to Billy. I'll see to it. Where does he live? I'll make him. If he won't, I'll . . .

LORETTA: But I am the only one who doesn't want to marry Billy.

NED [*severely*]: You must. And Billy must. Do you understand? It is the only thing.

LORETTA: That's what Billy said.

NED [*triumphantly*]: You see! I am right.

LORETTA: And if . . . if I don't marry him . . . there will be . . . scandal?

NED [*calmly*]: Yes, there will be scandal.

LORETTA: That's what Billy said. Oh, I am so unhappy!

NARRATOR: Loretta breaks down into violent weeping. Ned paces grimly up and down, now and again twisting his moustache.

LORETTA: I don't want to leave Daisy! I don't want to leave Daisy! What shall I do? What shall I do? How was I to know? He didn't tell me. Nobody else ever kissed me. [*Ned stops pacing to listen. As he listens his face brightens.*] I never dreamed a kiss could be so terrible . . . until . . . until he told me. He only told me this morning.

NED: Is that what you are crying about?

LORETTA: N-no.

NED: Then what are you crying about?

LORETTA: Because you said I had to marry Billy. I don't want to marry Billy. I don't want to leave Daisy. I don't know what I want.

NED: Now look here, Loretta, be sensible. What is this about kisses? You haven't told me everything after all.

LORETTA: I . . . I don't want to tell you everything.

NED: You must.

LORETTA: He . . . I . . . we . . . I let him, and he kissed me.

NED [*desperately, controlling himself*]: Go on.

LORETTA: He says eight, but I can't think of more than five times.

NED: Yes, go on.

LORETTA: That's all.

NED [*with great incredulity*]: All? I mean . . . er . . . nothing worse?

Vocabulary

scoundrel: very dishonest person

LORETTA: [*puzzled*] Worse? As though there could be. Billy said that my . . . our . . . our . . . our kisses were terrible if we didn't get married.

NED: What else did he say?

LORETTA: He said that when a woman permitted a man to kiss her she always married him. That it was awful if she didn't. It was the custom, he said; and I say it is a bad, wicked custom, and it has broken my heart. I shall never be happy again. I know I am terrible, but I can't help it. I must have been born wicked.

NARRATOR: Ned takes Loretta's hands and leans forward to kiss her.

LORETTA [*with horror, repulsing him*]: No! No!

NED [*surprised*]: What's the matter?

LORETTA: Would you make me a wickeder woman than I am? There will be another scandal. That would make two scandals.

NED: To kiss the woman I love . . . a scandal?

LORETTA: Billy loves me, and he said so.

NED: Billy is a joker . . . or else he is as innocent as you.

LORETTA: But you said so yourself.

NED: I?

LORETTA: Yes, you said it yourself, with your own lips, not ten minutes ago. I shall never believe you again.

NARRATOR: Ned puts his arm around her and draws her toward him.

NED: And I am a joker, too, and a very wicked man. Nevertheless, you must trust me. There will be nothing wrong.

LORETTA: And no . . . scandal?

NED: Loretta, I want you to be my wife.

NARRATOR: Ned waits anxiously. Suddenly, Jack, in fishing costume, appears from the doorway on the right and looks on.

LORETTA: I will . . . if—

NARRATOR: Alice appears from the doorway on the left and looks on.

NED [*in suspense*]: Yes, go on.

LORETTA: If I don't have to marry Billy.

NED [*almost shouting*]: You can't marry both of us!

LORETTA [*sadly*]: Then, Ned, I cannot marry you.

NED [*stunned*]: W-what? There is nothing to prevent you.

LORETTA [*with sad conviction*]: Oh, yes, there is. You said yourself that I had to marry Billy. And isn't it the custom . . . what . . . Billy said?

NED: No, it isn't the custom. Now, Loretta, will you marry me?

LORETTA: Don't be angry with me, Ned. [*He gathers her into his arms and kisses her.*] I wish it were the custom, because now I'd have to marry you, Ned, wouldn't I?

THE END

Vocabulary

puzzled: confused

3 Who's Who?

Learn about the different types of characters in a play.

C2 Complete the chart with information about the characters in the play *A Wicked Woman*.

1. Read about the different types of characters found in a play.

Type of Character	Description
Major	A major character is involved in many of the conflicts presented in the story. The character is well-described and changes as the plot progresses.
Minor	A minor character contributes to the story in different ways. A minor character always has a particular function. He or she may hold certain knowledge about the major characters or play an important role in moving the story along.
Protagonist	The protagonist is the central character in a story who struggles with various conflicts.
Antagonist	The antagonist creates conflict for the protagonist.
Static or flat	A static or flat character is one who can be described in a few words. This is usually a minor character who does not change during the story.
Round	A round character is usually a major character. He or she is a complex character who changes as the story develops.

Strategy

Take notes

Write down important information about each of the characters in the play.

Functional Language

Expressing Decision and Indecision

- Have you made a decision?
- I'm not sure what type of character he/she is.
- I can't decide.
- I'm quite sure he/she is . . .

2. With a classmate, scan the play and complete the chart. Look for words and sentences in the dialogue and information in the stage directions to help you.
3. As a class, discuss your answers and add any new information to your chart.

Characters Revealed

Learn about the different methods authors use to reveal characters in works of literature.

Analyze one of the characters in the play *A Wicked Woman*.

1. Choose one character from the play. This is the character you will write about in the final task.
2. Scan the play for information about this character. Note down any words or phrases that describe him or her. Pay attention to how the other characters react to him or her.

How to Analyze a Literary Character

What?

A character analysis is a detailed study of a literary character. There are different types of characters in literary works.

How?

Authors use different methods to provide their readers with infomation about the characters.

a) Direct characterization

The author **tells** the reader about the character. The character's thoughts, feelings and attitudes are described directly.

b) Indirect characterization

The author **shows** the reader what the character is like through his or her thoughts, speech and actions. The reader must then infer the character's traits from the information provided by the author. For example, in the play *A Wicked Woman,* Loretta believes that she must marry Billy because she let him kiss her. The reader can infer from this behaviour that Loretta is naive. A character can also be revealed through the other characters' reactions to him or her.

Strategy

Infer

Use the context and information provided to make deductions about the character.

3. Analyze the character in more detail. Look for three character traits and find evidence in the play to support each one. Use the questions below for help and write down your answers.
   - How is this character different from the others?
   - What does the character say about himself or herself?
   - With whom does the character interact?
   - What do the other characters say about him or her?
   - What are the character's attitudes about life?
   - What gender stereotypes does the character portray?
4. Read the analysis of John Conlan, the main character in Paul Zindel's *The Pigman,* on page 149. Use it as a model for your own character analysis.
5. Pair up with a classmate who chose the same character from the play. Compare your ideas and add any new information to your notes.

Understanding the components of a character analysis

The main characters in *The Pigman* by Paul Zindel are John Conlan, and Lorraine Jensen and an old man, Mr. Angelo Pignati. John, a lonely teen with a difficult home life, shows that despite his rebellious behaviour, he is capable of feeling compassion. Through his experiences with Mr. Pignati, John learns an important lesson about life.

John displays rebellious behaviour, such as playing pranks at school. From setting off stink bombs in the bathroom to writing on desks, to organizing the "supercolossal fruit roll" (p. 2), John demonstrates an exceptional talent for troublemaking. At home, John makes prank phone calls and glues the telephone. Lorraine describes him perfectly when she states that "he drinks and smokes more than any boy I ever heard of" (p. 8). She also remarks, "He pretends he doesn't care about anything in the world . . . but if you ask me, any real hostility he has is directed against himself" (p. 10).

John's behaviour is caused by his loneliness. No one understands John or cares about what he wants. His parents never encourage him nor give him any positive attention. They constantly compare him to his brother Kenneth who, according to his mother, never gave them any trouble. When John finds the nerve to tell his father about his dream of becoming an actor, his father responds, "An actor? . . . Thank God, Kenneth isn't a lunatic" (p. 66). Although John lives with his two parents, he has a very lonely existence.

John welcomes his relationship with Mr. Pignati because he discovers a loyal friend and father figure. As their friendship develops, John reveals the compassionate side of his nature that Lorraine always knew was there. As Mr. Pignati lays dying, John kneels beside him and notices that "a small trickle of saliva had started from the corner of his mouth" (p. 160). John takes his handkerchief, gently wipes away the saliva and turns Mr. Pignati's head. This sensitive gesture proves that John will take care of his friends.

Thanks to the Pigman, John realizes that he is responsible for his actions and his life. He understands that he can choose to combat his loneliness with rebellion or with compassion for those he loves.

Source: Paul Zindel, *The Pigman*

Title
Provide the title of the literary work and the author's name.

Introduction
Present the main idea: In the thesis statement, present the character and the three character traits that will be developed in the essay.

Paragraphs
In each of the development paragraphs, present the character trait and provide supporting evidence for each one. Give examples of the character's actions, thoughts and speech. Provide information about how the other characters react to him or her.

Conclusion
Restate the thesis and summarize the three character traits.

Write a character analysis.

C3 **Use your information to write a five-paragraph character analysis.**

1. Think about the character in *A Wicked Woman* that you chose in Task 4.
2. Use your notes from the previous tasks to decide which character traits you will focus on in your essay. Make sure you have at least two examples from the text to support each of the traits.
3. Write an outline of your character analysis. Use the checklist and the guidelines on pages 350–351 to help you follow the writing process and refer to the features of a character analysis described on page 149.
4. Write your first draft. HOW TO
5. Revise and edit your text. Exchange it with your classmates and use their feedback to help you improve it.
6. Make adjustments and prepare the final copy of your essay.

C1 C3 **Present and publish your character analysis.**

1. Form a group of four with classmates who analyzed the same character as you.
2. Present your essays to each other.
3. Listen to your partners. Compare the information in your essay with the information they give.
4. Write down the character traits and supporting evidence that your partners chose.
5. With your partners, discuss the traits that describe the character the most accurately and the evidence that best supports each one.

REFLECT

Uses information.

1. Did the information in the "how to" boxes help you complete the tasks? If so, how did it help?
2. How did you use information from the play *A Wicked Woman* to support the ideas you presented in your character analysis?

HOW TO

How to Write a Character Analysis

What?

A character analysis is a text in which you present a character's most important traits and give examples from the work of literature. Developing a character analysis allows you to describe a character from a different perspective or point of view. It gives you the opportunity to explore the text in more detail and find evidence to support your ideas. It also provides your reader with a more thorough understanding of a character.

How?

1. Write an introduction to your character analysis.
   - First of all, mention the author's name and the title of the work.
   - Then, present the character and the traits that you will explore in your essay.
   - Write a thesis statement.
   - Write a sentence to ensure a smooth transition to the next paragraph.
2. Write three paragraphs in which you present the character traits and support them with evidence from the text.
   - Present one character trait in each paragraph.
   - Use information from the play shown through direct and indirect characterization as proof that the character displays each of the traits. There are different ways in which you can use information from the play. You can quote, paraphrase or summarize. Always give credit to the author and include the page reference in parentheses (p. 00).
     - When you quote, use the author's exact words directly from the text, between quotation marks (" . . . ").
     - When you paraphrase, use your own words to express what the author meant.
     - When you summarize, give the main ideas briefly in your own words.
   - Try to include a sentence that concludes each paragraph and serves as a transition to the next one.
3. Write a conclusion to your character analysis.
   - State your thesis again.
   - Conclude your essay with a statement that summarizes the three character traits you have presented.

UNIT 7

SHAKESPEARE LIVES ON

1. Who was Shakespeare?
2. What do you know about his life?
3. What kinds of works did he write?

Imagine this: A man born in the 16th century, with no university education, is considered to be the greatest playwright of all time. What could he possibly have to say to a 21st century teen?

In this unit, you will learn who Shakespeare was and what kind of life he had. You will discover some of his work and compare it with today's box office hits. You will have the opportunity to look at a timeline of film adaptations of his plays and see how interpretations of Shakespeare's work have evolved. You will also discover some new ways to present Shakespeare's works and talk about whether he is relevant to teens today.

Get ready to make a few unexpected discoveries!

YOUR Quest

Why is Shakespeare still important today?

Unit Overview

EXTRA

Reading Folio

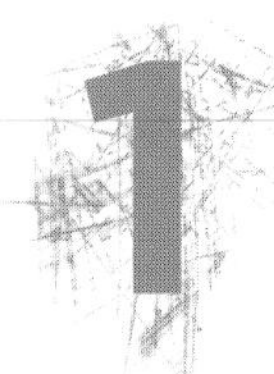

1 Meet Will

Get to know Shakespeare and learn about his life.

C1 C2 Learn about Shakespeare to create a trivia game.

1. Do a quick write to gather your ideas about Shakespeare. Think about his life and his work. Use the following questions to guide you:
   - Where did he come from?
   - When did he live?
   - What did he write?
   - What plays do you know?
2. Share what you know with a classmate. Refer to your quick write if you need help.
3. Read the biography of Shakespeare on pages 154–155 and take notes as you read.
4. With your classmate, review your notes to make sure you understood the text. Then, write 10 questions based on the text to create a trivia game.
5.  Using your resources (e.g. the library, the Internet, the Reading Folio), read more about Shakespeare and each write another five more challenging questions about his life and accomplishments. Write the answers on another sheet of paper.
6. Join another team of two. Take turns asking your questions and answering theirs. Make adjustments to your questions if they are too easy or not clear.
7. Combine the questions and exchange them with another team of four. Play the trivia game. Give feedback to the other team on their game.
8. Return to your quick write to add any new information you have learned about Shakespeare.

Strategy

Ask questions

Use a variety of yes/no and information questions to quiz your classmate.

Grammar

Information Questions

Try to use different information questions in Step 4. See page 328.

Functional Language

Making Suggestions

- Maybe the answer is . . .
- I think it is . . .
- We could answer that . . .
- Maybe it was . . .

Profile of a Playwright: Meet William Shakespeare

William Shakespeare was born in Stratford-upon-Avon in England. Although the precise date of his birth is unknown, we know that he was baptized on April 23, 1564.

Shakespeare's parents were Mary Arden and John Shakespeare. John Shakespeare was a tradesman who made and sold leather goods. He was also a moneylender who had a bad reputation for charging high interest rates. Shakespeare's father was involved in local politics and was elected to the town council while his son was still young. Because of his father's status, Shakespeare attended the Stratford grammar school until he was fifteen. Lessons were given in Latin and he was taught to read Italian and French, too, which was useful in his later writing career.

When he was only 18, Shakespeare married Anne Hathaway, who was 26. Some Shakespearean scholars believe that some of his 154 sonnets, which were published in 1609, convey his feelings for Anne. They had three children: two daughters, Susanna and Judith, and a son, Hamnet. Hamnet died at the age of 11 and his twin sister, Judith, married against Shakespeare's will. Susanna, Shakespeare's favourite daughter, inherited all of Shakespeare's property when he died.

Nothing is known about Shakespeare's life from 1585 to 1592, when he moved to London. This period is called the "lost years." Some people think, however, that he might have been a teacher in a rich person's household and that he became interested in drama when he had the opportunity to participate in a private theatre troupe.

Shakespeare started his first play, *Henry VI*, in 1592, his first year in London, and his last one, *Henry VIII*, around 1613. Like many of Shakespeare's historical plays, they are about English kings. In all, he wrote 37 plays, which are studied throughout the world. Some of the best-known are *Romeo and Juliet*, *Macbeth*, *A Midsummer's Night Dream* and *Anthony and Cleopatra*. One of his plays, *Cardenio*, was lost and has never been found.

Shakespeare loved to invent words when he could not find one that conveyed exactly what he meant. It is estimated that 1500 such words are part of our everyday vocabulary. He would definitely have a chuckle when hearing words that he invented, like *assassination* and *fair play*, used so casually today.

William Shakespeare died at the relatively young age of 52, on April 23, 1616. Although the cause of his death is a mystery, it was reported that he died of a fever, possibly the plague. Shakespeare wrote the epitaph for his own tombstone.

Good friend, for Jesus' sake forbear
To dig the dust enclosed here.
Blessed be the man that spares these stones,
And cursed be he that moves my bones.

Mystery and controversy surround Shakespeare and his life. Many modern scholars even question whether he wrote the poems and plays that carry his name. We cannot even be sure what he looked like—there is only one surviving portrait of him painted at the time.

Ben Jonson, another famous writer from that era, said of Shakespeare, "He was not of an age, but for all time."

Vocabulary

best-known: most famous
chuckle: laugh
convey: describe
cursed: be ill-wished
enclosed: contained
grammar school: school that taught Latin grammar, logic, rhetoric and literary style
inherited: obtained legal rights to
leather: animal skin
spares: leaves alone
tradesman: skilled craftsman

What did you find most interesting about Shakespeare? Write your answer on your tracking sheet.

CULTURE CAPSULE

The Theatre: Yesterday and Today

The First Theatre

The first theatre in England was built by James Burbage in 1576 and was named The Theatre. It had a fixed stage for the actors and a cobbled yard that provided seating and standing room for approximately 275 audience members. Vendors would sell refreshments such as water, gingerbread, apples and—the most popular—hazelnuts. Unlike today's classy theatres, there were no washrooms and no intermissions, so the theatre often smelt of urine, sweat and tobacco!

The Theatre During Shakespeare's Time

Shakespeare was a brilliant businessman. Not only did he write, produce and act in plays, but he was also part owner of the Globe Theatre. This theatre was built in 1599 by Shakespeare's company of actors, using wood from Burbage's theatre. It was a three-storeyed open-air amphitheatre that could hold 3000 spectators.

In 1613, the Globe burned to the ground during a presentation of *Henry VIII*, when a cannon exploded and set the thatched roof on fire. The original foundations of the Globe were discovered in 1989. In 1997, a reconstruction of the Globe was opened to the public as an example of a theatre at the time of Elizabeth I. Since then, it has become a monument to the greatest playwright of all time and icon of English literature. Thousands of tourists and drama lovers view plays there every year.

Modern Theatre Etiquette

Did you know that there is important etiquette to respect when you attend a play at the theatre? Here are some of the rules to follow the next time you go to see a play.

- Switch off your cellphone.
- Do not use any recording equipment (i.e. cameras or videocams).
- Do not eat or drink inside the theatre.
- Avoid unwrapping candy or gum during the show.
- Wear discreet perfume so that theatregoers with allergies aren't affected.
- Be quiet when the opening music signals the start of the play.
- Sit in the place your ticket indicates so that others won't be deprived of their own seat.
- Don't talk during the play because it can distract others.
- Address complaints to the theatre manager.
- Make sure you visit the washrooms before the play because leaving the auditorium disturbs others.
- Feel the emotion of the play and react accordingly to let actors know that their work is being appreciated.

Going to the theatre is supposed to be an entertaining experience. So, go with an open mind and a sense of curiosity. Enjoy yourself!

The Globe Theatre, 1599

Reconstruction of the Globe Theatre, 1997

Vocabulary

cobbled: paved with small stones

deprived: not able to have

hazelnuts: small round nuts

part owner: co-proprietor

thatched: made of straw

Shakespeare's Themes

From 1587 to 1616, Shakespeare wrote 37 plays and over 100 sonnets. Four hundred years later, his plays are still being performed. Find out what makes Shakespeare's work endure.

C2

Study the timeline of Shakespeare adaptations.

1. With a classmate, study the timeline of Shakespeare adaptations on pages 158–159. Identify the different kinds of productions, such as movies and musicals, and then answer the following questions:
   - Is there a production that you would you like to see? Explain your choice.
   - Why do you think Shakespeare's plays are so easy to adapt?

C2

Find the themes in Shakespeare's plays.

2. Skim through the play synopses on pages 160–162. Which of these plays have you seen or heard of? Share your answers with a classmate.
3. In his plays, Shakespeare deals with a number of universal themes, including those below. Read the list.

conflict, tragedy, fantasy, humour, friendship, love, jealousy, hatred, revenge, corruption, ambition, dreams, power, family relationships.

4. Read the play synopses. As you read, write down keywords.
5. Use the keywords to identify the main themes of each play. Compare your answers with a classmate. Which theme appears most often?

6. Are these themes explored in modern-day plays and movies? Write down your answers.

Strategy

Infer

Use the keywords in the synopses to identify the main themes of each play.

Grammar

The Active and Passive Voices

Practise using the passive voice when you write about Shakespeare's themes. See pages 163–164.

STATE YOUR CASE

Is Shakespeare relevant today?

1899: First film adaptation of Shakespeare, a four-minute segment of *King John,* produced by Sir Herbert Beerbohm

1929: *The Taming of the Shrew,* directed by Sam Taylor and starring Douglas Fairbanks and Mary Pickford

1936: *As You Like It,* directed by Paul Czinner and starring Laurence Olivier and Elizabeth Bergner

1948: *Hamlet* directed by and starring Laurence Olivier

1957: *West Side Story* Broadway musical

1961: Movie version of *West Side Story,* directed by Jerome Robbins and Robert Wise and starring Natalie Wood and Richard Beymer

1967: *The Taming of the Shrew,* directed by Zeffirelli and starring Elizabeth Taylor and Richard Burton

1968: *Romeo and Juliet,* directed by Franco Zeffirelli and starring Olivia Hussey and Leonard Whiting

1972: *Macbeth,* directed by Roman Polanski and starring Francesca Annis, Terence Bayler and Jon Finch

1900 1910 1920 1930 1940 1950 1960 1970

1993: *Much Ado About Nothing,* directed by Kenneth Branagh and starring Richard Briers, Denzel Washington, Kate Beckinsale and Imelda Staunton

1996: *William Shakespeare's Romeo & Juliet,* directed by Baz Luhrman and starring Leonardo Di Caprio and Claire Danes

1996: *Hamlet,* directed by Kenneth Branagh and starring Riz Abbasi, Richard Attenborough, Judi Dench, Billy Crystal and Kate Winslet

1998: *Shakespeare in Love,* directed by John Madden and starring Gwyneth Paltrow, Geoffrey Rush and Judi Dench

1999: *10 Things I Hate About You* (based on *The Taming of the Shrew*), directed by Gil Junger and starring Julia Stiles and Heath Ledger

1999: *A Midsummer's Night's Dream,* directed by Michael Hoffman and starring Calista Flockhart and Michelle Pfeiffer

1985: *Ran* (based on *King Lear*), directed by Akira Kurosawa and starring Tatsuya Nakadai, Akira Terao and Jinpachi Nezu

1980

1990

2000

There have been a number of other creative adaptations:

1989: *Shakedown Shakespeare,* produced by the Nakai Theatre, a First Nations group

2002: Rave theatre production: *Romeo and Juliet Remixed,* Toronto

2003: Hiphop production, *A Bombitty of Errors,* presented in London, England

2005: Joe Hillyer production *Bard Americana: The Songs of Shakespeare,* folk and bluegrass styles

2005: Rufus Wainright's classical guitar and vocal production "Go Ask Shakespeare" (based on *Sonnet 29*) on Burt Bacharach's album *At This Time*

2006: Jazz CD by Diane Nalini, University of Guelph professor from Montréal, *Shakespeare's Songs of Sweet Fire*

2007: Manga Shakespeare books

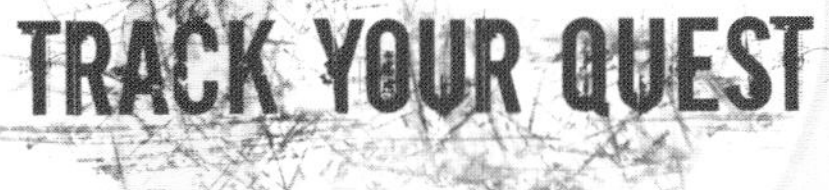

What do all these Shakespeare adaptations tell you about the writer? Write your answer on your tracking sheet.

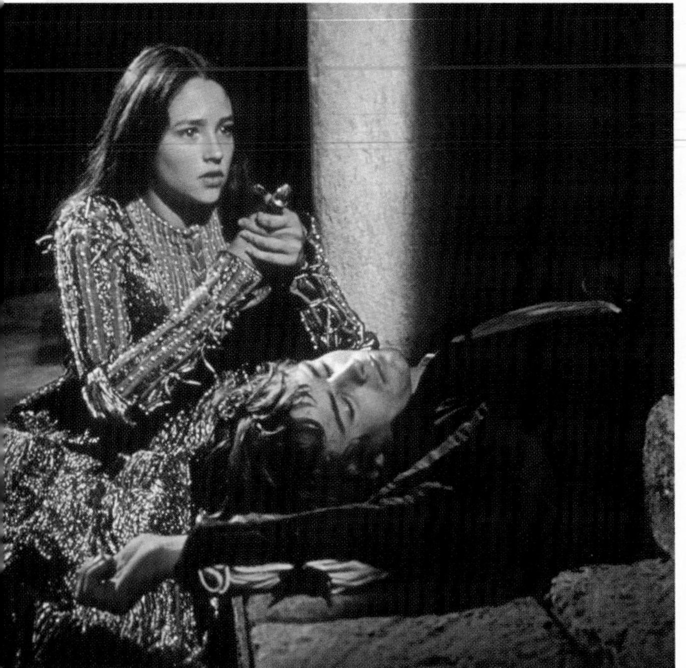

Synopsis 1

Romeo & Juliet

In Verona, Italy, two families are trying to help their teens. The Montague family learns that their son, Romeo, is depressed because the woman he loves is not interested in him. The Capulet family is trying to convince their daughter, Juliet, to marry a family friend. Romeo's family decides to hold a party so that he can meet other women. At the party, Romeo and Juliet meet and fall in love, but their families are enemies and their love is forbidden.

Romeo's confidant, Friar Lawrence, gives Juliet a potion to make her fall asleep and appear dead until she and Romeo can run away and marry. However, Romeo hears only that she is dead. When he arrives at the tomb, he is heartbroken and drinks poison. Juliet wakes up and sees that he is dead. She plunges Romeo's dagger into her heart and joins him in death. The families are devastated by the loss of their children and they end their feud.

Synopsis 2

A Midsummer's Night Dream

A young couple, Lysander and Hermia, run away into the forest so that Hermia won't have to marry Demetrius, the man her father has chosen. Demetrius and Helena, Hermia's best friend, follow them. There are many other people in the forest: a group of tradesmen rehearsing a play; Titania, the fairy queen, and her court; and Puck, an elf.

Oberon, the fairy king, creates a magic potion to turn one of the tradesmen into a donkey and make the fairy queen fall in love with it. Oberon tells Puck to give the potion to "a young man" so that he falls in love with the first woman he sees. Puck gives it to the wrong man and makes Lysander fall in love with Helena. There is much confusion until Oberon and Puck reverse the magic. In the end, the lovers wonder if what happened to them was real or just a dream.

Vocabulary

dagger: short pointed knife
feud: prolonged dispute
forbidden: not permitted
rehearsing: practising
run away: leave without saying where they are going

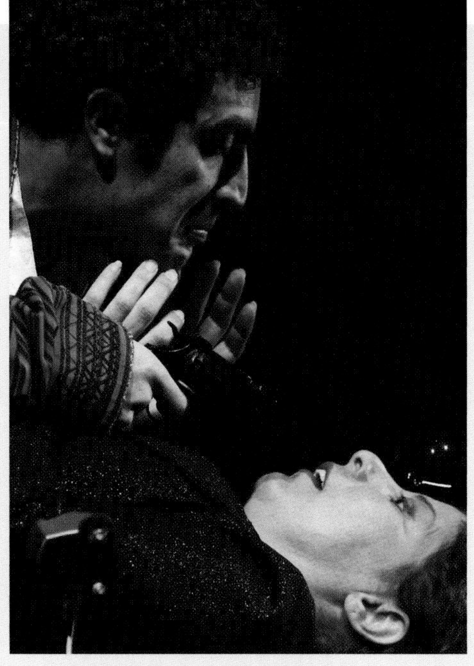

Synopsis 3

Hamlet

Hamlet is the son of the king of Denmark. He returns home from university to discover that his father is dead and that his mother has married Claudius, his uncle, who is the new king. A ghost tells Hamlet that Claudius murdered his father and Hamlet is determined to prove this. He fakes madness and has a group of actors present the murder, hoping that it will push Claudius to confess.

When Hamlet's mother tries to reason with him, he kills a man spying on them, thinking that it is the king. Claudius sends him into exile and orders two men to murder him, but Hamlet kills them. In a final duel with the king's men, Hamlet is fatally wounded with a poisoned sword, but he kills Claudius and names a new king of Denmark before he dies.

Synopsis 4

King Lear

In this tragic story, King Lear decides to divide his kingdom among his three daughters. He tests them by asking them how much they love him. The first two, Goneril and Regan, lie and flatter him profusely. The third, Cordelia, who is the king's favourite, is honest and remains silent. She says that she cannot describe how much she loves her father. Lear is outraged and banishes her from the kingdom. She then marries the king of France.

Cordelia's hypocritical sisters and their husbands plan to seize the kingdom from Lear and his allies, and war breaks out. Cordelia returns from France with her husband to fight on her father's side. Eventually, King Lear goes insane, and he and Cordelia are captured. Goneril and Regan commit suicide and Cordelia is killed in prison. King Lear dies of grief.

Vocabulary

grief: sadness

kingdom: territory under his power

outraged: very angry

profusely: a lot

Synopsis 5

Julius Caesar

This play is set in ancient Rome when Julius Caesar was dictator. The play opens with the townspeople celebrating Caesar's victory in war and he arrives with three of his supposed supporters, Brutus, Cassius and Mark Antony.

Cassius, who is very ambitious and wants to rule Rome himself, tries to turn Brutus against Caesar. He flatters him and tells him that he is as good as Caesar, but Brutus is a loyal friend and refuses to believe this. Then Cassius tricks Brutus by planting letters in his house. These letters are supposed to be from citizens complaining that Caesar has become too powerful. Brutus is influenced by them and agrees to join Cassius's plot to kill Caesar.

Caesar's wife warns him not to go to the Senate, but he ignores her and Brutus assassinates him there. The conspirators turn against each other and eventually Caesar's son defeats Cassius and Brutus, who both commit suicide rather than admit defeat.

Synopsis 6

Macbeth

As the play opens, two Scottish generals, Macbeth and Banquo, are returning from successful battles. They meet three witches who prophesy that Macbeth will become a nobleman and eventually king of Scotland, and that Banquo's descendents will become kings.

When the first prophecy comes true, Macbeth begins to believe the others and tells his wife about them. She is very ambitious and wants her husband to be king. Macbeth refuses to harm the reigning king, Duncan, but his wife accuses him of cowardice. She persuades him to invite Duncan to their castle, where Macbeth kills him.

Macbeth becomes king but he realizes that he has to kill Banquo to stop the third prophecy coming true. As Macbeth becomes increasingly violent, killing anyone who opposes him, the Scottish nobles flee to England and form an army under Duncan's son, Malcolm. In the meantime, guilt drives Lady Macbeth insane and she commits suicide. Finally, Macbeth is killed and Malcolm becomes king.

Vocabulary

cowardice: lack of courage
flee: run away
nobleman: aristocrat

Grammar

The Active and Passive Voices

QUICK CHECK

Can you rewrite the following sentences in the passive voice?

1. Shakespeare's company of actors built the Globe theatre.
2. The video company classifies the movies according to content.
3. People of all ages enjoyed the theatre production.
4. Within three hours of opening, the box office had sold all the concert tickets.
5. The director considered five leading actors for the important role.

LEARN MORE

Use

You use the active voice to emphasize the agent—the doer of the action. You use the passive voice when you want to indicate that the subject is unknown or not important.

Active: Shakespeare wrote *Anthony and Cleopatra* in 1609.

Passive: *Anthony and Cleopatra* was written in 1609.

Formation

The passive voice uses a form of the verb *to be* with the main verb. The following chart lists the active and passive forms of the verb *to write* in the third person singular.

Tense	Active Voice	Passive Voice
Simple present	*writes*	*is written*
Present continuous	*is writing*	*is being written*
Simple past	*wrote*	*was written*
Past continuous	*was writing*	*was being written*
Present perfect	*has written*	*has been written*
Past perfect	*had written*	*had been written*
Future	*will write*	*will be written*
Conditional	*would write*	*would be written*
Perfect conditional	*would have written*	*would have been written*
Present infinitive	*to write*	*to be written*
Perfect infinitive	*to have written*	*to have been written*

To change a sentence from active to passive, you have two options:

1. Put the subject at the end of the sentence and introduce it with the preposition *by*.
   The King's Men first performed Macbeth *in 1611.* → Macbeth *was first performed by the King's Men in 1611.*
2. Eliminate the subject and describe only the action.
   People often call Macbeth *"the Scottish play."* → Macbeth *is often called "the Scottish play."*

PRACTISE

A. Rewrite the following sentences in the passive.

1. Laurence Olivier played Hamlet in the 1948 production of *Hamlet*.
2. Jerome Robbins choreographed the original Broadway musical of *West Side Story*.
3. Elizabeth Taylor took the role of Kate in *The Taming of the Shrew* in 1967.
4. Kenneth Branagh directed *Much Ado About Nothing* in 1993.
5. The Nakai Theatre, a First Nations theatre troupe, put on *Shakedown Shakespeare*.

B. Rewrite the verbs in the following sentences in the active.

1. Theatregoers were amazed by the ultra-modern *Romeo and Juliet Remixed* in 2002.
2. A massive study of Shakespeare adaptations in Canada was undertaken by a group of scholars from the University of Guelph in Ontario in 2005.
3. Numerous articles and links to the Canadian adaptations are provided on a helpful website.
4. Scholars wonder what other wonderful Shakespeare adaptations will be produced in the future.
5. Vancouver's Ron Basford Park was turned into the Forest of Arden for a teen production of *As You Like It.*

C. Complete the text with the correct active or passive form of the verbs in parentheses.

School in Shakespeare's Day

Education **1.** (*consider*) a moral responsibility. Schools founded during this era **2.** (*call*) grammar schools. There were two types: public and private. Both rich and poor children **3.** (*attend*) the public schools which **4.** (*finance*) by rich people. Private grammar schools **5.** (*set*) aside for children whose parents **6.** (*pay*) the tuition. Students **7.** (*teach*) Latin and sometimes Greek. Usually, education **8.** (*limit*) to boys. Girls **9.** (*keep*) at home to help with household chores and arts. Only wealthy girls **10.** (*educate*).

You will find more exercises on the extra handout.

Shakespeare Reinvented

Modern productions have succeeded in keeping Shakespeare alive and accessible to everyone, including young people.

C1 **Participate in a teen forum.**

1. Think about these questions and then participate in a class discussion.
   - Have you ever heard or seen Shakespeare's work presented in a format other than a play? Which format was it? Did it appeal to you?
   - To get young people interested in Shakespeare's work, how could his work be presented differently?

2. Reread the synopses of Shakespeare's plays in Task 2. Then, listen to a recording of a musical adaptation of one of them. Listen for keywords that can help you identify the play and write them down.
3. As a class, discuss the keywords and themes and decide which play it is.
4. Share your answers to the following questions:
   - How does this adaptation demonstrate originality? Is it appealing?
   - What do you think of the voices? Did the music help you understand?
   - What did you like most about this adaptation?
   - What if anything, would you change?
   - Rate this adaptation on a scale of 1 to 10 and justify your answer.

Strategy

Develop cultural understanding

Be open to surprising new ways of presenting Shakespeare.

Functional Language

Asking for Help

- I don't understand this part. Do you?
- What did you put for . . . ?
- What does . . . mean?
- How do we explain . . . ?
- Can you help me answer this?

What did you like about the adaptation? Write your answer on your tracking sheet.

A Man of Our Era?

You have learned about Shakespeare's life and how his work is presented in various ways. How do you think he would fit into today's Hollywood?

Strategy

Practise

Practise English by talking about the familiar topic of the world of entertainment.

C1 C2 Imagine Shakespeare as a Hollywood producer.

1. As a class, discuss the following question and justify your answers:
   - If Shakespeare were alive today, do you think he would be in the movie business?
   - Would he be a well-known Hollywood producer? Or would he be doing something else? Explain your answer.

2. Read the editorial and discover a different opinion of this great playwright. As you read, identify the kind of controversy that surrounds Shakespeare. Write down your answers.
3. As a class, discuss your opinion of each of these charges: capitalism, plagiarism and entertainment industry victim. Use your note-taking chart to justify your arguments.

C1 C2 Ask Shakespeare himself.

4. Today's Shakespeare could very well be the topic of a report on a popular entertainment show on TV. As a class, discuss the following questions:
   - How do you think Shakespeare would fit into today's entertainment industry?
   - How does the controversy surrounding him compare with that of modern producers and entertainers?
5. Prepare for a role play by writing five interview questions to ask Shakespeare about these charges and his work. With a classmate, decide on eight questions and prepare the interview.
6. Role-play the interview for another team.

Functional Language

Agreeing, Disagreeing and Giving an Opinion

- I think that's ridiculous because . . .
- Shakespeare would probably . . .
- I'm not sure if Shakespeare would . . .

Controversial Hollywood Producer

If William Shakespeare were alive today, he might be in real estate.

Shakespeare made some money as a writer over the course of his career. But long-time Shakespearean actor Patrick Stewart notes that his real wealth seems to have come from owning shares in The Globe Theatre, as well as a substantial amount of property.

"He was a capitalist, no doubt about that," Stewart says.

Today, Shakespeare's works are in the public domain. But as a living playwright, he would be collecting thousands of dollars in royalties—just as Neil Simon does—from the hundreds of productions of his plays in the United States alone.

One theatre director in Denver, for example, said that his company's five-week run of *Measure for Measure* produced ticket sales of US$470 000. Shakespeare's royalty would have been about 10%, or US$47 000. That's just one theatre in a medium-sized market.

As for publishing, Shakespeare Incorporated would stand to sell several million books a year. Last year in the United States, Shakespeare titles sold more than 775 000 copies. Shakespeare is translated into more than 100 languages; publishing royalties would rake in at least $10 million a year.

Shakespeare would have been popular in Hollywood, too. Like Stephen King, the Bard has spawned a cottage industry of film and television productions. They don't always make money, but, a little like Woody Allen movies, they are seen as prestige opportunities for big stars.

However, Shakespeare might now find himself vulnerable to charges of plagiarism. Barbara Hodgdon, author of *The Shakespeare Trade*, notes that only three of Shakespeare's plays contained plots that weren't borrowed from somewhere else.

"So if he were writing in that way today," Hodgdon says, "he would certainly need a team of lawyers to handle lawsuits."

Another scholar, Gary Taylor, author of *Reinventing Shakespeare*, thinks the Bard would have made an ideal scribe for shows such as *The Sopranos* or *Deadwood*. Those shows, like many of Shakespeare's plays, revolve around men and power struggles.

Deadwood creator David Milch, however, says that he wouldn't even take Shakespeare's calls—unless he had a really powerful agent.

In the end, it's possible to imagine Shakespeare as both a rich, multimedia juggernaut and a victim of Hollywood power plays.

As Hollywood insider Bernie Brillstein put it, "Shakespeare? He's too talented to be successful in today's market."

Source: National Public Radio

Vocabulary

- **cottage industry:** basic commerce
- **juggernaut:** giant
- **lawsuits:** legal proceedings
- **real estate:** buildings and land
- **royalties:** percentage of profits from sales
- **spawned:** produced
- **the Bard:** Shakespeare

TRACK YOUR QUEST

Where do you see Shakespeare in the world of entertainment today? Describe his lifestyle briefly on your tracking sheet.

THE CONCLUSION

Why is Shakespeare still important today?

OPTION 1

C3

- **Write a newspaper editorial about Shakespeare's success.**

1. Write a newspaper editorial about Shakespeare's success in Hollywood today that demonstrates why he is still important.
2. Decide on the topic, audience and purpose. Use your tracking sheet and other resources to find more information, if necessary.
3. Reread the editorial on page 167 to review how to structure your text.
4.  Prepare an outline and then write your editorial. Use the checklist and the guidelines on page 350–351 to help you follow the writing process.
5. Discuss ways to improve your editorial with your classmates and teacher.
6.  Write a final copy and submit it to your school newspaper editor.

REFLECT

Uses creativity.

What objectives guided the content of your editorial?

Word Quest

- characterization
- comic relief
- houselights
- lead role
- musical
- part
- performance
- play
- playbill
- playwright
- plot
- script
- setting
- Shakespearean
- star
- storyline
- supporting actor
- theatregoers
- tragedy
- usher

Vocabulary

See the Reference Section, page 334, for the definitions of these words and expressions.

PROJECT OPTION 2

C1 C3

■ **Write and produce an entertainment show segment about Shakespeare.**

1. With your team, decide on the topic of your segment. Plan your outline to include a trivia question to pique the audience's interest, an excerpt of the Shakespeare song, play or movie you wish to feature and a brief interview segment with Shakespeare or an artist who performs in your segment.

2. Use your resources to find more information if necessary.
3. Write your outline and use it to produce your script.

4. Use the checklist and the guidelines on page 352–353 to help you follow the production process.
5. Discuss ways to improve your segment with your classmates and teacher.
6. Videotape your final copy and post it on the school website.
7. Assess the strengths and weaknesses of your media text.
   - Consider your audience's reaction.
   - Decide how you would improve it next time.
   - Assess how well you reached your objectives.

REFLECT

Uses creativity.

Which new strategies did you use to make your segment reflect Shakespeare's timelessness?

OPTION 3

C3

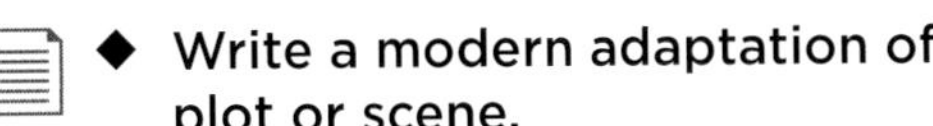

◆ **Write a modern adaptation of a plot or scene.**

1. Write a modern adaptation of a Shakespearean work as a rap song, a reader's play, a graphic novel or an illustrated children's story.
2. Decide on the play, audience and purpose and choose the media type. Use your resources to find information about other Shakespearean plays, if necessary.
3. Review the adaptations you read about or heard in the unit and the Reading Folio for examples of different forms.
4. Prepare an outline and then write your script or story. Use the checklist and the guidelines on pages 350–351 to help you follow the writing process.
5. Discuss ways to improve your adaptation with your classmates and teacher.
6. Write and publish your final text.

REFLECT

Uses creativity.

What risks did you take in choosing the form and content of your adaptation?

UNIT 8

WHEN HUMAN RIGHTS GO WRONG

1. What are human rights?
2. What do you know about human rights abuses?
3. Why should you care about human rights?

A high-pitched sound stops Montréal teenagers from meeting outside a corner store. Prisoners in Guantanamo Bay are held illegally and tortured until they confess to crimes they did not commit. A teenage girl in Pakistan is stoned to death because she is pregnant. What do these people have in common? They are all victims of human rights abuse.

The next time you watch the news, pay attention to how many stories involve human rights issues, and start observing what is happening at home. What rights do you think people should have, and how far should we go to stand up for them? In this unit, you will explore what it means to have rights, what happens when they are abused, and what you can do to protect them.

"THEY CAME FIRST for the Communists,
and I didn't speak up because I wasn't a Communist.

THEN THEY CAME for the Jews,
and I didn't speak up because I wasn't a Jew.

THEN THEY CAME for the trade unionists,
and I didn't speak up because I wasn't a trade unionist.

THEN THEY CAME for the Catholics,
and I didn't speak up because I was a Protestant.

THEN THEY CAME for me,
and by that time no one was left to speak up."

YOUR Quest

How can you stand up for human rights?

Unit Overview

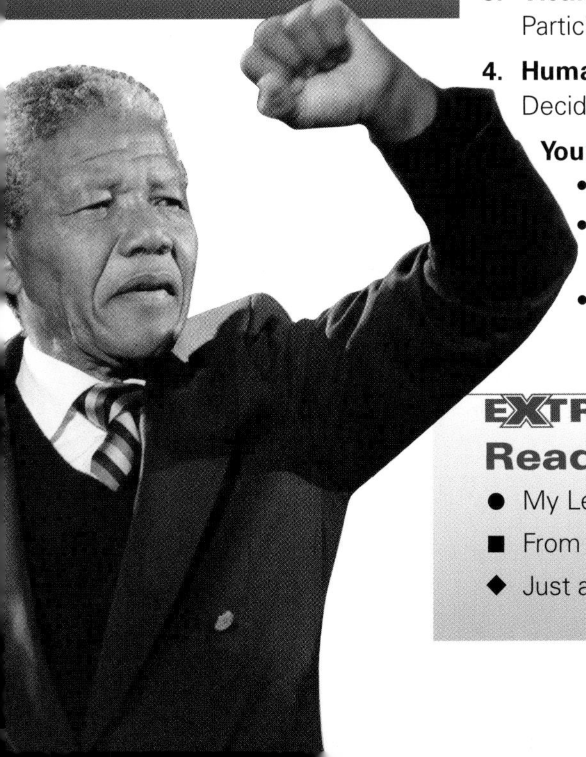

EXTRA Reading Folio

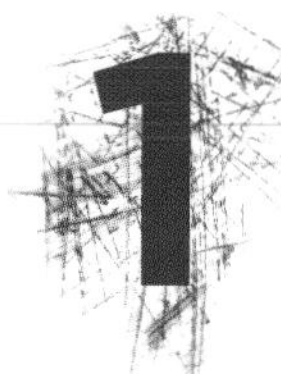

1 On the "Right" Track

Often people do not respect the rights of others. Who needs protecting, and from whom?

C2 C1 Consider human rights.

DVD **1.** Watch a music video and discuss the following questions with your classmates. Give reasons for your answers.
- What message about human rights does the video send?
- What message do you think the young boy would have written on the paper airplane?
- What message would you write? Who would you send it to?

2. List the rights you think all human beings should have. Next to each one, write the responsibility that goes with it. Be ready to justify your choices.

3. Form a team with three other classmates. Take turns sharing the information from your lists and explaining your ideas. As you listen, add more rights and responsibilities to your list.

4. As a team, circle the rights on your lists that you think are sometimes ignored. Discuss the following questions and justify your answers:
- Who ignores these rights?
- In what situations are these rights ignored?
- What are the consequences, if any?

5. Share your team's answers with the class.

C2 Determine how you see the world.

6. Read the statements in the survey on page 173. Write down the number that corresponds to your opinion. The number 3 means that you are neutral.

7. Add up your total score and read the results.

8. Compare your results with your classmates'. As a class, discuss:
- the reasons some people fight for human rights
- the reasons some people abuse human rights.

Functional Language

Working in a Team and Giving Feedback
- What do you think about . . . ?
- What you said makes me think . . .

Strategy

Cooperate

Listen to what your classmates have to say and build on each others' ideas.

Grammar

Adverbs

Use adverbs to add clarity and detail to your ideas. See pages 174–175.

Functional Language

Giving an Opinion
- This probably happens when . . .
- We could certainly see that . . .
- I'm not really sure about that because . . .

Survey

Strongly disagree 1 2 3 4 5 6 Strongly agree

a) I think people generally get what they deserve.

b) I think that if something unfair happens to people, they will eventually be compensated for it.

c) I generally find the world to be a fair place for most people.

d) I think most people try to be fair to everybody when they make important decisions.

e) I believe that justice always triumphs over injustice.

f) I think that injustices in life (at school, in families or in government) are the exception rather than the rule.

Results:

30–36 points: You think that the world is a fair place. As you complete the tasks in this unit, try to find current examples that confirm or modify your outlook.

21–29 points: You believe that the world is generally a fair place, but you don't think it is perfect. As you go through this unit, look for what could be done to improve the situation.

Fewer than 20 points: You feel that many people in the world are treated unfairly and you see it as an unjust place. Your goal will to be to discover what can or cannot be done to make things better.

What is your view of world justice? How fair do you think the world is? Write your thoughts on your tracking sheet.

Grammar

Adverbs and Their Position

QUICK CHECK

Can you identify and correct the adverb errors in these sentences?

1. He studied carefully the problem.
2. Jennifer will not tolerate definitely people who bully others.
3. I have wanted to travel to other countries always.
4. Many people violently were killed.

LEARN MORE

Use

You use adverbs to describe, intensify or clarify what you say and write. An adverb can modify a verb, an adjective or another adverb.

Formation

- You form many adverbs by adding *ly* to the end of an adjective. For example, *quickly, slowly, silently.*
- Some adverbs have the same form as the corresponding adjective. For example, *fast, good, late, early, hard.*
- Other adverbs have a completely separate form. For example, *always, perhaps, soon.*

Position

The position of an adverb depends on what it modifies. Many adverbs can be placed in different positions.

Position	Adverbs by Type	Examples
At the beginning or end of a sentence or clause	**Time:** *at once, yet, before, since, soon, eventually, lately, now, recently*	***Now** is the time for action!* *He will leave **eventually.***
	Manner: *somehow, anyway*	*We'll get it done **somehow.***
	Place/Direction: *anywhere, far, away, somewhere, nowhere*	*She is going **away.*** ***Anywhere** we go is fine with me.*
	Frequency: *once, sometimes, often occasionally, usually*	***Once** I met the Prime Minister.* ***Occasionally,** he writes me a letter.*
After the verb *to be* After an auxiliary verb Before a main verb	**Time:** *soon, eventually, lately, now, recently, still*	*Nash is **always** hungry.* *He is **still** working on his essay.*
	Frequency: *always, never, often, sometimes, once, repeatedly, usually*	*I **always** organize my ideas before I write.*
	Certainty: *actually, definitely, probably, perhaps, surely, frankly, totally*	*We **definitely** need a new office.*
	Degree: *almost, barely, enough, just, hardly, nearly*	*I **almost** forgot to call you about the meeting.*
	Manner: *reluctantly, quickly*	*He **quickly** took photos of the people.*

Adverbs and Their Position

Position	Adverbs by Type	Examples
After a verb	**Place/Direction:** *up, down, there, everywhere, west, away, across,* **Manner:** *sadly, angrily, bravely, hard, happily, tirelessly, well, softly, carefully*	*He walked* ***down*** *to the shore.* *She worked* ***tirelessly*** *all night.*
Before another adverb or an adjective	**Degree:** *almost, nearly, really, painfully, only, completely, absolutely, very, much, too, fairly*	*You are* ***absolutely*** *wrong about him.* *It is a* ***fairly*** *difficult issue to discuss in an hour.*
At the end of a sentence or clause	**Manner:** *well* **Time:** *early, immediately, late, yet*	*She knows that area* ***well****.* *We had to leave the meeting* ***early****.* *I haven't called him* ***yet****.*

Note: Do not place an adverb between a verb and its object.

You ~~speak well English~~.

PRACTISE

A. Rewrite each sentence with an adverb from the chart. Put the adverb in the correct position.

1. People's rights are violated. (frequency)
2. I am sure that this issue needs to be investigated. (degree)
3. I think that we could do more to promote justice in the world. (certainty)
4. This is a difficult subject for some people to talk about. (degree)
5. People will become more aware of the need for justice. (time)
6. We must work hard to make others understand our point of view. (manner)
7. Gillian travelled to learn more about injustice in the world. (place/direction)

B. Add adverbs from the chart to modify the underlined words.

When my aunt was younger, she was **1.** ______ aware of injustice in the world. Her family was **2.** ______ poor and she **3.** ______ went to school hungry. One day, the teacher discovered that my aunt had head lice and told her to move **4.** ______. She **5.** ______ slid her desk **6.** ______ from the others. The other children looked **7.** ______ at her, wondering if they would catch the lice. Despite the hardships, my aunt was **8.** ______ sure of one thing: She was going to succeed. After enduring many challenges and years of working **9.** ______, my aunt became a lawyer and later, a judge. She works **10.** ______ to help people improve their lives.

You will find more exercises on the extra handout.

Setting Standards

"All human beings are born free and equal in dignity and rights." At the end of the Second World War, the United Nations created the Universal Declaration of Human Rights. Find out about the Declaration and learn how people in many countries are still not treated equally and with dignity.

Functional Language

Asking for Help

- What does this article mean?
- How else could you describe . . .?
- What could you compare this with?

Strategy

Ask for help

Do not be afraid to ask for assistance if you have difficulty understanding.

C2

Explore the Universal Declaration of Human Right (UDHR).

1. Form teams of four. Together, read the excerpt from the UDHR on page 177.

2. Your teacher will give you a section of the UDHR to read silently. As you read, identify which articles correspond to the rights you listed in Task 1.
3. Read your section to your teammates. As you listen to your teammates, continue matching the rights with those on your list.
4. In your team, discuss:
   - How many of the rights from the UDHR did you include on your list from Task 1? Which ones?
   - Which rights did you not include? Why do you think you did not include them?
   - How would your life be different without these rights?

5. Watch the video clips. As you watch each one, identify the right it describes. After each clip, discuss the following questions and write down your answers.
   - How is the right being abused?
   - In which other situations have you seen or heard about the abuse of this right? Think about cases reported in the news or events that have happened in your community.

Children in Auschwitz, Poland, 1945

Refugees in Darfur, Sudan, 2009

Universal Declaration of Human Rights

Introduction

All people everywhere have the same human rights, which no one can take away. This is the basis of freedom, justice and peace in the world.

This Declaration affirms the dignity and worth of all people, and the equal rights of women and men. The rights described here are the common standard for all people everywhere.

Every person and nation is asked to support the understanding and respect for these rights, and to take steps to make sure that they are recognized and observed everywhere, for all people.

> his Declaration affirms the dignity and worth of all people, and the equal rights of women and men.

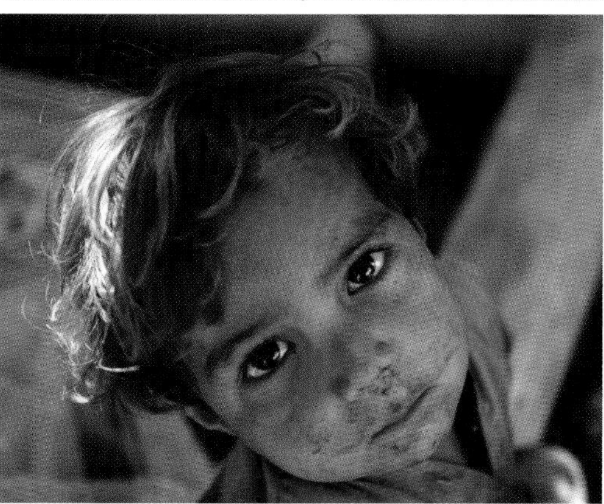

Article 1: You have the same human rights as everyone else in the world, because you are a human being. These rights cannot be taken away from you. Everybody, no matter who they are or where they live, should be treated with dignity.

Article 2: You should not be treated differently, nor have your rights taken away, because of your race, colour, sex, language, religion or political opinions. Your basic rights should be respected no matter what country you were born in or how rich or poor you are.

Section 1: Rights of the Individual

Section 2: Rights of the Individual in Civil and Political Society

Section 3: Spiritual, Public and Political Freedoms

Section 4: Social, Economic and Cultural Freedoms

Conclusion

Article 29: We all have a responsibility to the people around us, and we can only develop fully as individuals by taking care of each other. All the rights in the UDHR can be limited only by law and then only if necessary to protect other people's rights, meet society's sense of right and wrong, maintain order, and look after the welfare of society as a whole.

Article 30: There is nothing in the UDHR that justifies any person or state doing anything that takes away from the rights to which we are all entitled.

Source: Amnesty International Australia

Vocabulary

nor: and not
no matter: regardless
welfare: well-being

How important is the UDHR in your life? On your tracking sheet, write down the five rights which are most important to you.

3 Victims, Oppressors and Watchdogs

When human rights are abused, a complaint is often filed with the United Nations and may be investigated by someone called a Special Rapporteur. Learn about the role of this watchdog.

Functional Language

Using Adverbs

- I was recently a victim of . . .
- Something terrible happened to me once . . .
- She said she repeatedly . . .
- He often experienced . . .
- He never mentioned that he . . .

Strategy

Encourage yourself and others

Give positive feedback to your classmates and help them if necessary.

Grammar

Indirect Speech

Using indirect (reported) speech to relay the stories people have told you. See page 329.

C2 **Role play a human rights investigation.**

1. Read about the Special Rapporteurs on page 179 and write down the different aspects of their job.
2. Read the role card that your teacher gives you and write down the following information. Then, share this information with your classmates.
   - who you are and where you are from
   - the problem you have been having
   - your feelings about the situation.
3. Work with a classmate. Take turns playing the roles of human rights abuse victim and Special Rapporteur.
   - As a human rights abuse victim, tell your story to the Special Rapporteur. Answer the Rapporteur's questions to help him or her understand your particular situation and the abuse you believe you have suffered.
   - As a Special Rapporteur, ask questions to learn as much as possible about the victim's story and how his or her rights were violated. Write down what you learn.
4. Continue the role play with partners from other teams.
5. With your final partner, consider the cases you both recorded as Special Rapporteurs. Identify the rights that were abused, using the information about the Universal Declaration of Human Rights from Task 2.
6. As a class, compare your answers to see if you agree on the identification of the rights that were abused. Correct your answers if necessary, Discuss these questions:
   - Which rights are most commonly abused?
   - Which of the stories are similar to those you have heard about in the news or in your community?

Child labourer, Bolivia

The Role of Special Rapporteurs

Special Rapporteurs are dedicated individuals such as lawyers, academics or human rights workers who are chosen because they are highly respected in their fields and are passionate about human rights. Their job is sometimes dangerous and difficult because no country likes to be visited and investigated for human rights abuses. Special Rapporteurs need to be diplomats and investigators at the same time. When the United Nations Commission on Human Rights receives complaints that need to be investigated, Special Rapporteurs write to the governments involved, asking for clarification. If the Rapporteurs then decide that they need to investigate complaints personally, they have to request an invitation from the governments. When they arrive, the Special Rapporteurs may be hosted and assisted by NGOs (non-governmental organizations), which work to advance human rights.

Meetings are held with both government leaders and the complainants, who are often members of minority groups. The Special Rapporteurs investigate the problems and also recommend what actions need to be taken to resolve them. The interview process includes not only investigating the details of a complaint, but also asking victims what solutions they believe would solve their problems.

When their investigations are complete, Special Rapporteurs prepare reports which are submitted to the complainants' governments and also made public in the international community. This process has been quite effective in improving the living conditions of people in difficulty. The Special Rapporteurs' reports also guide the United Nations in deciding if further action needs to be taken against a country.

Special Rapporteurs have the authority of the United Nations but operate independently in order to remain objective. This is why they receive no payment or other financial reward for their work.

The Special Rapporteurs investigate the problems and also recommend what action needs to be taken to resolve them.

Source: Office of the United Nations High Commissioner for Human Rights

Vocabulary

complainants: people who file official complaints

Which role-play story touched you the most? Why? Write your answers on your tracking sheet.

CULTURE CAPSULE

Nelson Mandela and the End of Apartheid

For twenty-seven years, six months and six days, Nelson Mandela was a prisoner. During that time he became a symbol of resistance to apartheid in his home country of South Africa.

South Africa was colonized by English and Dutch settlers in the early 1600s and became one of the most prosperous countries in Africa. Although apartheid became law only in 1948, elected white governments started taking away the rights of some citizens as early as 1910, and later began classifying them according to race. People were classified as Black, White, Coloured (mixed race), Indians and Asians. Laws were passed denying "non-white" people basic rights and access to certain areas without special passes. Many jobs were listed as "whites only," only white people were allowed to vote, and interracial marriages were forbidden. Non-white children went to inferior schools. Black people were assigned to poor rural areas called *homelands*, and their South African citizenship was taken away. By 1990, white people made up only about one quarter of the country's population but controlled 87 percent of its land and three-quarters of the national wealth.

Nelson Mandela, born in 1918 and a lawyer by profession, campaigned against apartheid. He was elected leader of the African National Congress (ANC) in 1944. The ANC opposed the white government and its racist policies and fought for equal rights by organizing boycotts and strikes. Nelson Mandela was convicted of trying to overthrow the government and was sent to prison for life. While in prison he became a symbol of the anti-apartheid movement. On several occasions, he could have been released but he refused to compromise his political ideals to obtain freedom.

Nelson Mandela with Nobel Peace Prize medal, 1993

For years the international community, including Canada, pressured the South African government to free Mandela and to eliminate the racism which was part of its constitution. These sanctions, supported by the United Nations, greatly affected the nation's economy, sports and culture. In 1990, Mandela was finally released from prison by F.W. de Klerk, who was president at the time. Mandela went on to work closely with de Klerk to dismantle apartheid and bring about equality in South Africa. Both men were awarded the Nobel Peace Prize in 1993. Mandela went on to be elected president of the country himself in 1994, and served until 1999.

Mandela became widely recognized as the most significant leader on the continent of Africa and his messages of peace and tolerance continue to inspire people all around the world.

Vocabulary

apartheid: policy of segregation
dismantle: take apart
prosperous: affluent, rich
settlers: colonists

4 Human Rights at Home

Québec is the only province in Canada that has its own Charter of Human Rights and Freedoms. Despite this, do you know of cases in your community where human rights have been abused?

C1 C2 Examine a case.

1. As a class, discuss the following questions:
   - Have you heard of human rights being abused in your community?
   - Who were the victims?
   - How were their rights abused?

2. Read one of the texts on pages 182–183 about a device that discourages teenagers from gathering outside stores. As you read, write down the arguments for or against its use on a T-chart. Use the questions beneath the text to guide your reading.
3. Find a classmate who read the other text. Use your notes to discuss the device and its use, and add any missing information.
4. Individually, write down your response to the question below. Use examples from the texts, the UDHR and your knowledge of the Québec Charter of Human Rights and Freedoms to support your opinion.
   - Does the use of this device against teens constitute a violation of human rights?
5. As a class, decide if this is a case for the Human Rights Tribunal. Share your points of view.

Strategy

Rephrase

Describe the ideas in the text in your own words to be sure your partner understands.

Functional Language

Giving an Opinion

- I really think that the device is . . .
- It's definitely important to remember that . . .
- It surprises me/doesn't surprise me that . . .

STATE **YOUR** CASE

Should Canada refuse to do business with countries that violate human rights?

Option 1

Oussama Romdhani

I'm young, my ears are sharp and I don't miss much. The other evening I went to the corner store to meet a friend. I was standing there looking around, minding my own business, when suddenly I become aware of a high-pitched whine. "Hey, that hurts!" I said. "What's going on? Get me out of here." I had just been buzzed and it was not pleasant.

This new technology is being used against young people. A small box, mounted three metres above the ground, emits a high-frequency sound that can generally be heard only by the sensitive ears of young people. The noise is so annoying that it forces the people to leave the area. The device is being marketed to businesses and municipalities as a way to stop teens from doing what teens do best—hanging out with their friends.

I've had a chance to think about this and there are some serious problems. First of all, the device is being used as a weapon. Since when has it become acceptable for a country to attack its own citizens? All teens, no matter what their intentions, are being targeted by this device. It indiscriminately attacks all young people and makes it unpleasant for us to spend time in public places. Secondly, it is not only teens who suffer. Innocent children and babies are just as vulnerable to this horrible sound. Why should they be exposed to it? We also know that dogs have a very good sense of hearing. Are dogs now targets, too?

This type of attack can only be considered an abuse of human rights.

This type of attack can only be considered an abuse of human rights. In fact, in Great Britain, there is already a movement underway to stop the use of this type of device, which has been supported by the commissioner of children's rights there. Here in Québec, the Commission of Human Rights and Youth Protection has spoken out against its use, saying that it has been known to cause ear injuries and headaches and can be dangerous to pregnant women.

By attacking teens in this way, society is only widening the divide between the young and the old. We all know that some teens cause trouble, but this kind of persecution is only a temporary solution to an old problem. Teens might be chased away from a few places, but this will not solve anything.

Vocabulary

device: small machine

indiscriminately: randomly

1. In what places is the device being used?
2. What is the purpose of installing this device?
3. Why is the sound audible only to young people?
4. Who else would be affected by the device?
5. What health problems might the device cause?

Camille Lafontaine

Have you ever been hurt by vandalism? Perhaps a sports facility you use has been damaged, or a park you like has been closed because of the inconsiderate actions of other people. It recently happened to me. I went to play soccer with my friends one evening only to find that vandals had cut the nets on the goals. We are sure that this was done by a gang of guys who hang around there in the evenings.

It's a great, harmless way to make people disappear.

There is a new device designed to keep young people away from certain areas at certain times, and I think it is a great idea. We all know that vandalism is a real problem in our society and the sad truth is that it is usually caused by young people with nothing better to do. By installing this machine and using a timer to control when it is turned on, we can chase away people who have no business hanging out where they are not supposed to.

The emitter sends out a high-pitched sound at a frequency that can be heard only by young people. The noise is about 85 decibels (approximately the same level as traffic on a busy street, and a little less than a lawnmower) and it is really annoying. Doctors say that being exposed to 85 decibels of sound for long periods will damage your hearing, but the point of this device is that you will not stick around for very long. It's a great, harmless way to make people disappear.

My friend's father has been experimenting with one at his corner store. He is really happy to report that some annoying kids have stopped hanging around in the evenings. When I asked him about the effects of the machine on younger children, he told me that because he needs to turn on the machine only in the late evening, there are not many young children around. He did admit that one child complained about the sound and her mother did not understand why. When he explained it to her, she said that she preferred not having to walk through a big group of teens in order to enter the store, as long as her child's hearing would not be damaged.

Of course, the ultimate solution to this problem is not chasing away the teens, but keeping them busy with other activities. Even then, there will always be troublemakers around. This is a good way to start chasing them away.

Vocabulary

emitter: machine that makes a sound

stick around: stay in one place

1. What incident made Camille think that the device might be useful?
2. Why is hearing damage not likely to occur?
3. Why does Camille say that the device isn't generally a problem for young children?
4. What is the mother's attitude to the device?
5. What alternative solution does Camille suggest?

What factors contribute to human rights abuses? Write your thoughts on your tracking sheet.

THE CONCLUSION

How can you stand up for human rights?

OPTION 1

C2 C3

- **Write a declaration of rights.**

1. Choose a group for whom you would like to write a declaration of rights, and brainstorm human rights issues that you think they might face.
2. Review the information on your tracking sheet and use your resources to gather more information about these issues.
3. Plan your declaration of rights. Make sure that you do the following:
   - Identify the group and explain why you chose it.
   - Present each right and explain why it should be respected.
   - Explain what responsibilities, if any, come with the right.
4.  Use the checklist and the guidelines on page 350–351 to help you follow the writing process.
5. Present your draft to a classmate or your teacher for feedback and make any adjustments.
6.  Use appropriate computer software to produce your final copy.
7. Post your declaration of rights for other students to read or submit it to your school newspaper.

REFLECT

Cooperates with others.

Which suggestions from classmates or your teacher did you include in your declaration? How did you handle disagreement?

Word Quest

- acquittal
- conviction
- duty
- just
- pardon
- quandary
- reprieve
- resolution
- responsibility
- suffer
- warranted
- way out

Vocabulary

See the Reference Section, page 335, for the definitions of these words.

OPTION 2

C2 C3

■ **Write or record a persuasive editorial about a human rights issue.**

1. Identify a human rights issue that you would like to investigate and write or record a persuasive editorial about it.
2. Use your resources to gather more information about the issue.
3. Decide what you want to say about the situation.
4. Plan your text. Include the following information:
   - a description of the issue
   - your opinion about it
   - supporting facts and examples
   - reasons for people to take an interest.

5. Use the checklist and the guidelines on pages 350–351 to help you follow the writing process.
6. Present your text to a classmate or your teacher for feedback and make any adjustments.

7. Produce your final copy using a computer or record your editorial as a podcast.
8. Contribute your essay to your school newspaper or make the podcast available to your classmates.

REFLECT

Cooperates with others.

What new ideas did you learn about human rights by discussing them with others during the unit?

PROJECT OPTION 3

C1 C2 C3

◆ **Create a video to promote human rights.**

1. In your production team, choose a human rights issue that you would like to promote in a video. Refer to your tracking sheet for ideas.
2. Determine your audience.

3. Use the checklist and the guidelines on pages 352–353 to help you follow the production process.
4. Use a storyboard to plan your video.
5. Present your storyboard to a classmate or your teacher for feedback and make any adjustments to your plan.

6. Film and edit your video and add music.
7. Present your video to your classmates and post it on the school website.
8. Assess the strengths and weaknesses of your team's project:
   - Review your goals and objectives.
   - Assess what you have learned.
   - Assess the quality of your teamwork and decide how it could be improved in future projects.

REFLECT

Cooperates with others.

What differences of opinion were you able to reconcile in your group? How did you come to an understanding?

UNIT 9

FAST FORWARD 20

1. Where will you be 20 years from now?
2. What will your life be like?
3. What do you hope the future will bring?

It is 20 years from now. You are 37, high school days are far away and you have settled into your adult life.

You have made many major decisions since leaving school: whether to live in an apartment or a house, to buy a car or use public transportation, to remain single or to be in a relationship. You have decided if you want children and whether to work outside the home or to be a stay-at-home parent. You may live on the other side of the world, or just down the street from where you grew up. Is this what you planned?

What is life like as an adult? Are you happy with your accomplishments? Do you have any regrets? What is going on in the world? How has life around you changed?

There are so many decisions to make and options to look at. Take a peek!

YOUR Quest

What will your life be like 20 years from now?

Unit Overview

EXTRA Reading Folio

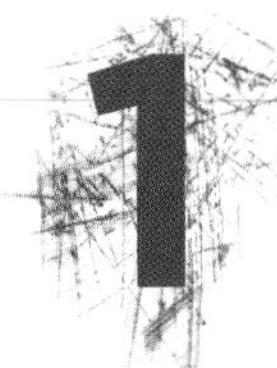

1 Me @ 37

Step into your life 20 years from now. You will be in your late 30s and well-established. What kind of life will you have?

C1 **Map your dreams and aspirations.**

1. Do a quick write about the dreams you hope will have come true and the discoveries you hope to have made by the time you are 37. To help you, think about:
   - your work
   - your travels
   - your personal life: your lifestyle, family and hobbies.
2. Create a life map to illustrate your life from high school graduation in June to where you will be at 37. Plot your path step by step. Use your quick write to help you.
3. Form a team. Share your life maps and discuss the following questions:
   - Whose life map surprised you and why?
   - Whose life map did not surprise you? Why not?
   - Are the dreams and wishes realistic and within reach? If not, what needs to happen to make them come true?
4. Post your life map in the classroom for your classmates to read.

Strategy

Use semantic mapping

Be creative in designing your life map.

Functional Language

Reflecting

- That surprises me because . . .
- I didn't expect . . .
- I'm not sure that is realistic because . . .
- You would need to . . .

What do you think are the three most important choices you will make in the next 20 years? Write your answers on your tracking sheet.

2 Discovering Change

Twenty years have passed. How has life changed?

Strategy

Recast
Repeat the information to make sure you understand it.

Functional Language

Reaching and Expressing a Consensus
- You say that . . . but I think . . .
- Do we all agree that . . . ?
- We all wrote that . . .
- So we've decided that . . .

C1 Explore the changes in your world.

1. Form a team with three classmates. Your teacher will give you a set of questions. Take turns drawing a question and answering it. Write down all your ideas on a large sheet of paper.
2. Reread your notes and complete them with more ideas if you can. For each question, agree on the most likely changes and circle them.
3. Report back to your classmates. How are your ideas about life at 37 similar? How are they different? Add new ideas to your notes to help you in the tasks that follow.

C2 Link your future to the choices you make now.

4. Read the poem "Lost Generation" on page 190. Take notes on the messages it communicates.
5. Now read the poem from the end, starting with the line "There is hope." What do you notice? Take notes on the messages again.
6. Compare the two versions and answer the following questions. Write down your answers.
   - What are the major differences between the messages?
   - Which version matches your idea of the future?

STATE **YOUR** CASE

Will the future be better than the present?

Lost Generation

Jonathan Reed

I am part of a lost generation.
And I refuse to believe that
I can change the world.
I realize this may be a shock, but
"Happiness comes from within"
Is a lie, and
"Money will make me happy"
So in thirty years, I will tell my children
They are not the most important thing in my life.
My employer will know that
I have my priorities straight because
Work
Is more important than
Family
I tell you this:
Once upon a time
Families stayed together
But this will not be true in my era.
This is a quick-fix society
Experts tell me
Thirty years from now, I will be celebrating the tenth anniversary of my divorce.
I do not concede that
I will live in a country of my own making.
In the future,
Environmental destruction will be the norm.
No longer can it be said that
My peers and I care about this Earth.
It will be evident that
My generation is apathetic and lethargic.
It is foolish to presume that
There is hope.

And all of this will come true unless
we choose to reverse it.

Source: AARP

Vocabulary

apathetic: indifferent
lethargic: lacking energy
quick-fix society: society that looks for immediate and easy solutions

TRACK YOUR QUEST

What will you enjoy most in your world 20 years from now? What will you miss most? Why? Write your answers on your tracking sheet.

Exploring Success

Everyone wants to succeed, but does success mean the same to everyone?

C2

Take stock of how you are doing.

1. At 37, have you lived up to your expectations? Use a graphic organizer to write down words that you associate with success. Define what being successful means to you.
2. Compare your ideas with your classmates. Do you share the same definition of success? As a class, agree on three essential ingredients of success and rewrite your own definition.
3. DVD Watch the video and listen to the interviews. As you listen, take notes with a classmate. One of you should take notes on what success is and the other should takes notes on what success is not. Share your answers with your classmate.
4. As a class, compare the interviewees' definitions with your class definition. What do you think accounts for the differences and similarities?

Strategy

Rephrase

Use your own words when you talk about the ideas expressed in the video.

Grammar

Conditional Sentences

To express conditions and results, we use if-clauses in conditional sentences. See page 194.

Functional Language

Politely Interrupting a Conversation

- Excuse me. I have something to say.
- Wait a minute, what about . . . ?
- Pardon me, but . . .

C2

Talk about regrets and how to avoid them.

5. Read the text on page 192 and find out how a man of 36 assesses his life. Note his conclusions. Use the questions beneath the text to guide your reading.
6. Share your answers with your classmates and then discuss the following:
   - How can we avoid having regrets?
   - How can we bounce back from bad decisions or missed opportunities?
   - How would you use the author's advice to make decisions in future?

Tomorrow You Will Regret Today (If Things Don't Change)

By Mike Michalowicz

I'm 36. I have regrets.

It seems like yesterday that I was in college [. . .]. I remember high school as though it were yesterday. It feels just moments ago that I was swinging from the jungle gym and enjoying naptime during my kindergarten class. But that stuff is far gone now . . . 10 years ago . . . 20 years ago . . . 30 years ago.

Looking back, I have clearly made mistakes. That doesn't bother me so much. I have learned from most of them. What do bother me are the missed opportunities. What bother me are the times I ran toward comfort instead of trying something new. What bother me are not the risks that I took, but the risks that I avoided.

My past is as dead as a stiff in a morgue. So is yours. There is nothing we can do to resuscitate our pasts. Don't waste your time trying and don't waste your time worrying. The only thing we can do is change our behaviour now. It is time to push away from the comforts of repeating your past, because until you do, you will regret what you missed.

Here is my little formula for living without regret (or at least with a whole lot less regret):

1. If your heart says yes and your head says no, go for it. This is the clearest sign you will get from your soul telling you what to do. Your head is just going into the protection mode of keeping you in the "tried and true" past. Lead with your heart!

2. If it won't go away, go for it. Sometimes life will present the same opportunity over and over. That can be a clear signal you should be giving it a shot.

3. Follow your heart, not your urges. I love jelly beans. When they are put in front of me, I go through a whole bag in seconds. Then I get sick as a dog. I followed my urge to devour the jelly beans, and not my heart, which was telling me to enjoy just a few. When temptation presents itself, make sure you are listening to your heart and not an urge.

What do bother me are the missed opportunities. What bother me are the times I ran toward comfort instead of trying something new. What bother me are not the risks that I took, but the risks that I avoided.

4. Fear the pressure of peer pressure. Just because everyone else is doing it, doesn't mean it is right for you. Your gut knows what's right; go with that.

5. If you regretted it once, don't regret it again. If you have regrets, it is a clear signal not to make that mistake again. If you are lucky enough for the opportunity to present itself again: Go for it! Go for it! Go for it!

Do you have any regrets? Do you regret something in your professional life? Or in your personal life? It's time to start living without regrets. It's time to push the limit today, so when you reflect back tomorrow, you smile.

Today I will wrap up with this famous quote from Mark Twain:

Twenty years from now you will be more disappointed by the things that you didn't do than by the ones you did do. So throw off the bowlines. Sail away from the safe harbour. Catch the trade winds in your sails. Explore. Dream. Discover.

Source: Obsidian Launch

Vocabulary

giving it a shot: trying it
gut: instinct
naptime: time for a short sleep
resuscitate: bring back to life
stiff in a morgue: a dead body
tried and true: proven
urges: impulses, desires
wrap up: conclude

1. What does the author say about his high school days?
2. How does the author feel about his past?
3. Why should you listen to your heart and not your head?
4. How does the author suggest that you react to peer pressure?

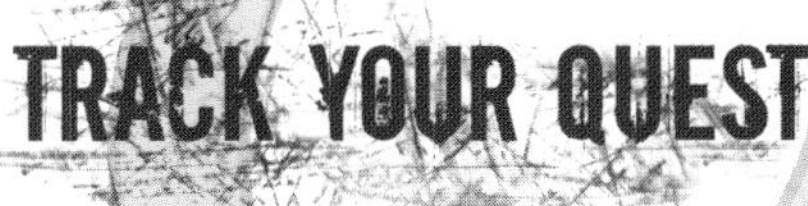

How has your definition of success changed as a result of this task? On your tracking sheet, write three statements that define success.

Grammar

Conditional Sentences

QUICK CHECK

Can you complete the sentences with the correct form of the verb?

1. If Li-Sum had accepted the position, she (*travel*) with you today.
2. If Corbin and Alex had decided to sell the company, they (*become*) millionaires.
3. Lauren's dress-making company would have succeeded if she (*persevere*).
4. The city (*develop*) faster if they had built the highway.
5. If you (*study*) to become a veterinarian, you could have opened your own clinic.

LEARN MORE

Use

You use conditional sentences with the perfect tense to talk about imaginary or unreal situations in the past.

If she had studied in Málaga for a year, she would have learned to speak Spanish well.

Formation

Conditional sentences have two parts: a condition and a result. You can start the sentence with either part.

- The if-clause describes the *condition.* It follows this pattern:
  if . . . + past perfect ⟶ *If she had studied . . .*
- The main clause describes the *result.* It follows this pattern:
  . . . + perfect conditional ⟶ *she would have learned . . .*

You can use *could* or *might* instead of *would* in the main clause.

The project ***might have worked*** *if we had planned it better.*

You can also use *could have* in the if-clause.

If I ***could have afforded*** *it, I would have travelled around the world.*

PRACTISE

A. Join the clauses to form conditional sentences. Change each verb in parentheses to the appropriate tense.

1. If Annie and Paul had decided to buy the house - they (*need*) a bank loan.
   If Annie and Paul had decided to buy the house, they would have needed a bank loan.
2. If Sarah had gone to university in Rimouski - she (*study*) natural sciences.
3. If you (*decide*) to get a dog - your whole family would have taken care of it.
4. Graduates (*find*) jobs more easily - if the economy had recovered from the recession.
5. Thousands would have lost their jobs - if the plant (*close*).
6. If he had decided to work in Brazil - he (*stay*) with his uncle for a while.
7. Cara might have been promoted - if she (*accept*) the job in Ottawa.
8. The couple (*add*) on to the house - if they had found out they were expecting a baby.

B. Complete the sentences with a condition or result.

1. If Julia had gone to the University of Ottawa, *she would have lived close to the Rideau Canal.*
2. Hugo would have lost all his investments if ____________
3. If Thomas hadn't met Solana in Rio di Janeiro, he ____________
4. If ____________, the Itos wouldn't have sold their house.
5. Jaci and Enrich would have visited Dubai if ____________
6. People ____________ If they had known the future.

You will find more exercises on the extra handout.

Poster Artist's Career Started by Accident

By Alan Hustak

Vittorio Fiorucci, one of the country's most acclaimed graphic artists—best known for the chuckling satyr that has become the mascot of the Just for Laughs comedy festival—died in Montréal on July 30, 2008. He was 75.

Fiorucci was a boulevardier, a raconteur and a gregarious self-confessed hedonist who owned seven vintage cars as well as an outstanding collection of antique mechanical toys. The little green man that became the symbol of the comedy fest was, he said, autobiographical—a self-caricature that evolved over 40 years.

"There are two types of people in the world, people who are themselves, and people who go through life pretending they are somebody else," he once said, "They can never say I was never myself."

During his career Fiorucci designed more than 300 art posters and turned out eight covers for *Time Magazine*. His work is a combination of the bawdy and the beautiful, the comic and the sad. It is represented in the permanent collections of the Museum of Modern Art in New York, the National Poster Collection in Ottawa, the Toronto Metropolitan Library and Montréal's Musée d'art contemporain.

Fiorucci was born in Zara, Yugoslavia, to Italian parents on November 2, 1932, and grew up in Venice, Austria. He came to Canada when he was 19.

"I thought I was going to be a short-story writer," he once said. "But when I came to Montréal, I couldn't speak English, I couldn't speak French, I couldn't rely on language, so I used cartoons without words to express myself. It just happened. I started doodling, and I started doing posters. It was an accident."

His first poster was a handbill he designed in the spring of 1962 to advertise Norman Mailer's visit to Montréal. Then he did the poster for Claude Jutra's film *À tout prendre*. He was hired by the fledgling Montréal World Film Festival as art director and, in 1964, won first prize in the Czech International Poster Contest for his stylized portrait of a member of the Italian Carbonari. He also designed posters for the Opéra de Montréal and the hot-air balloon festival in Saint-Jean-sur-Richelieu.

He often said he fulfilled his ambition to write short stories, but not as he had planned. "Posters are, after all, short novels of art."

Vocabulary

acclaimed: famous
bawdy: bold, uninhibited
chuckling: laughing
doodling: aimless drawing
fledgling: young
fulfilled: accomplished
gregarious: sociable
hedonist: person who loves pleasure
satyr: mythological creature

Source: Canwest News Service

The Future: Fact or Fiction?

What do you think of when you hear the word *future*? Explore how beliefs about the future affect people's decisions.

Strategy

Recombine
Find creative ways to express your understanding of the ideas.

C2 **Consider the future.**

1. Think of opinions, predictions and advice about the future that you have heard from your parents and teachers, or from economists. List these ideas.
2. Read the three comic strips below and identify what they say about the future. Write a sentence to summarize the message of each comic strip. Compare the messages with the ideas from Task 1. Are they similar or different?
3. Write a brief explanation of how these ideas affect the decisions you might make. Support your explanation with examples.

TRACK YOUR QUEST

On your tracking sheet, write three common beliefs about the future.

THE CONCLUSION

What will your life be like 20 years from now?

OPTION 1

C3

- **Describe a Fast Forward 20 product or service.**

1. Write a descriptive essay about a product or service you would find in 20 years.
2. Determine your topic, purpose and audience.
3. Use the information on your tracking sheet and other resources to write your description.
4. Plan your text. Answer the five wh-questions to help you organize your ideas. Make sure you include the following, and draw a sketch if you wish.
   - Introduction: statement of your topic and purpose
   - Development: description of the product or service, its purpose and usefulness
   - Conclusion: restatement of the topic.
5.  Use the checklist and the guidelines on pages 350–351 to help you follow the writing process.
6. Present your text to a classmate or your teacher for feedback and adjust it if necessary.
7.  Produce your final copy on a computer.
8. Post your text for other classes to read.

REFLECT

Achieves his or her potential.

How will the product or service you chose benefit the community?

Word Quest

- achievement award
- birth
- breakthrough
- childhood
- corporate world
- entrepreneurial
- fame
- fulfillment
- happiness
- high school sweetheart
- housing development
- income
- investments
- leisure
- parenthood
- relationships
- relocate
- scholarship
- single
- suburbs
- training

Vocabulary

See the Reference Section, page 335, for the definitions of these words and expressions.

OPTION 2

C3

■ **Write your autobiography @ 37.**

1. Write about your life at the age of 37. Brainstorm ideas of what you would like your life to be like 20 years from now and what you hope to have accomplished.
2. Organize your ideas by putting them in logical order and deciding which are realistic and which are not.
3. Plan your text. Make sure to include information about the following:
   - what you are known for
   - how you got to where you are
   - your lifestyle
   - how you feel about your life
   - your ideas about success.

4. Use the checklist and the guidelines on pages 350–351 to help you follow the writing process.
5. Present your text to a classmate or your teacher for feedback. Make adjustments if necessary.

6. Produce your final copy on a computer.
7. Circulate your autobiography in class. Read as many of your classmates' autobiographies as possible in the time available.

REFLECT

Achieves his or her potential.

What new things did you learn about yourself as you planned and wrote your autobiography?

PROJECT OPTION 3

C1 C3

◆ **Create a comic strip about life @ 30-something.**

1. In your production team, decide on a general idea about the future on which to base a comic strip.
2. Decide on your audience and the type of media document: photos, drawing, computer-generated comic strip.

3. Use a storyboard to plan the plot, setting and characters. Make sure that each scene creates suspense and leads to the final frame.

4. Create your comic strip. Use the checklist and the guidelines on pages 352–353 to help you follow the production process.
5. On the back of your comic strip, write the underlying idea and your message.
6. Present your text to a classmate or your teacher for feedback.
7. Place your comic strip in a class collection for other students to read.
8. Assess the strengths and weaknesses of your media text:
   - Consider your audience's reaction.
   - Decide what you would do differently next time.
   - Review your goals and objectives.

REFLECT

Achieves his or her potential.

How did you display autonomy and resourcefulness as you worked on your comic strip?

READING FOLIO

This section includes interesting and varied texts that will help you improve your reading skills. There are two different sections in the Reading Folio.

TEXTS RELATED TO THE UNITS AND WORKSHOPS include three extra texts linked to the theme of every unit and workshop.

TEXTS OF GENERAL INTEREST are other texts about different topics that you may enjoy reading for interest and pleasure.

Table of Contents

TEXTS RELATED TO THE UNITS AND WORKSHOPS

TEXTS OF GENERAL INTEREST

Voluntourism Catching On

By Emma Reilly

When Toronto resident Annette Bering went on safari in Tanzania in 2006, one of the most meaningful moments of her trip had nothing to do with witnessing the splendours of African wildlife.

Before returning home, Bering's tour group made an impromptu stop at a public school outside Arusha to drop off school supplies brought from Canada.

When the group learned the school was raising money to build a dormitory for its female students—who couldn't walk to school for fear of being assaulted en route—Bering and her 15 fellow tourists spontaneously passed a hat, leaving enough money to fund the dormitory in their wake.

"There was so much poverty. They had so little, yet they were happy," Bering said. "I came home feeling very humble from the trip, but very enthused to try and do more."

Whether it's a spontaneous gift or a planned gesture of help, a growing number of tourists are giving back to the countries they visit, said Lewie Gonsalves, president of a Toronto-based company that operates exotic tours.

Annette Bering stands with local people in a Masai village in Ngorongoro Conservation area, Tanzania.
Photo: Lewie Gonsalves/The Canadian Press

"People want to be more than just camera-carrying tourists who take pictures and go home," Gonsalves said.

"There's a spontaneous feeling of 'how can I make life better' or 'how can I help in a tangible sort of way,' which is different from being back in Canada and sending money to a large organization, where there isn't that immediate sense of having interacted and made a connection with somebody."

This trend—known as "voluntourism" —is gaining popularity among travellers seeking experiences that go beyond the regular holiday feeling.

One major hotel chain decided to implement a program offering half-day volunteering sessions at local charities. The "Give Back Getaways" cost the volunteer anywhere from US$70 to US$160, a portion of which is donated to a local charity.

The programs range from assisting at a music therapy session for disabled children in Istanbul to feeding endangered iguanas in the Cayman Islands.

"We had a number of instances where properties had developed local programs that guests had expressed an interest in," said Sue Stephenson, vice-president of the hotel chain's community footprint program.

"This was an opportunity to introduce the guests to the programs we're already involved in with our local communities."

Since the program began, about 300 people have participated, Stephenson said.

Critics of voluntourism say it's a short-term, feel-good experience for tourists who then return to the comfort of luxury hotels. They say there are more meaningful ways to help the needy in impoverished countries.

But Gonsalves argues that although many voluntourists do indeed enjoy luxurious vacations, their gifts are nonetheless meaningful.

He says the reaction of those people his clients choose to help says it all.

"You can tell by the reception you get, where the people are so excited—their eyes are sparkling," Gonsalves said. "That interaction is very genuine and very apparent."

Bering says her experience in Tanzania made a big impact on her—so much so that after returning to Canada she and her teenage daughter sent care packages to the school she visited.

"It's incredible the difference that one person can make in a country like that if they just took a moment to do it," Bering said.

Bering, who plans to travel to Africa or Southeast Asia with her daughter, says she plans to donate as much as she can while she's overseas.

"I have to. I feel in my heart I have to do that. Because I feel I have so much."

Vocabulary

endangered: at risk of disappearing

footprint program: program to reduce environmental effects of human behaviour

impoverished: extremely poor

wake: the trail left behind by something that has passed

Source: The Canadian Press

The [illegible]sive Uakari

Amazon Riverboat Exploration Diary

By Kris Dreessen

We walk along the machete-blazed path, our footsteps padding along the fallen leaves and dirt. Leaf cutter ants haul pieces of dime-sized greenery across the trail in straight [illegible] military style. We hike quietly and slowly so we don't spook the animals and don't [illegible]anything during four or five kilometres. We will rest for an hour, then hike back, [illegible]ing monkeys, wild pigs and other large mammals that may cross our path.

What we see will be combined with sightings by biologists and volunteers over several months to estimate how many species there are in Lago Preto, including the endangered red uakari monkeys. I wonder if we'll see a uakari. The highest concentration of red uakaris in the world is right outside our houseboat, but I'm one of the only volunteers who haven't seen one. A few days ago, they ate breakfast for an hour pretty much over Gerry's head.

It's my last day of field research, my last chance. Juan, our local guide, and Maribel lead Laura and me on the trail. Soon, Juan stops. He looks at us and points to a cluster of trees about 30 metres away. I see some movement, some fur. Uakari?

Squirrel monkeys. Lots of them.

[illegible]re crossing the trail in the treetops, tails pitched high in the air like prancing cats. [illegible] one, they emerge through the branches. A few stop for a second to look down and check out their visitors. Juan says it was a troop of 20, with four capuchins tagging along. He and the other guides are amazing. Juan sees things we don't and hears things we never will. He grew up on the river; the Amazon is his backyard. Sometimes he lives out here on a platform for months. He watches over the Lago Preto concession area, bringing only sugar and rice, and spears fish for the rest of his food. In the forest now, he mimics a bird call and the bird answers.

Laura and I sidestep ruts of mud, then give up and enjoy trudging on the trail in the ankle-deep gunk. It sounds like a vacuum as it nearly sucks my hiking boots clean off. Further down the trail, we are treated to another march of the same squirrel monkeys. The plants and trees are amazing and unlike anything I've seen. Trees look like braided ropes, vines like turtle tracks and bright green spaghetti noodles. An hour in, we hear the faint "chi chi" of uakaris. Jackpot!

Juan freezes and folds his hands across his mouth, imitating their call.

"Chi. Chi."

They come no closer. We wait, not moving a muscle.

"Chi. Chi."

Moments later the chatter fades into the forest. Out of luck. Juan asks me in Spanish, "Have you seen a uakari?" I shake my head. With a small wave he flips his machete to follow him. This is never going to work, I think. The monkeys are long gone. We bushwhack through branches anyway, ducking under spiderwebs and studded palm trees toward where we heard the last monkey conversation. After a few minutes, Juan stops. Ah well, we were close.

He stares at the forest floor as if in defeat, then points his hand to the trees above us as if ending a concerto. I follow his fingertips up to the treetops.

The uakaris! They are almost directly above us in *bacacho* trees, crossing to and fro, chowing down on fruit. Their fur is cinnamon, their faces cherry red. One is sitting down on a branch, staring at us. He seems only vaguely distracted from his fruit by us and soon turns and takes off, swinging from branch to branch, lunging with grace and a loud rustle of leaves in its wake. There are so few in the world and there must be 10 right here, eating lunch in the Amazon. They are too far to get a close-up look, so while I am with them, they are still a mystery.

My mind flashes to the close-up photos we saw on the boat during a slide presentation. Their similarity to our own faces was startling. Now, I can't make out their features so my imagination fills them in. Big brown eyes, distinct lines on the face, and a big forehead. The one above us is about the size of a Dalmatian. It soon reaches out with its arms and disappears into the trees too.

They make their way through the canopy and get further away. Some of them stop like the squirrel monkeys did to check us out. This is amazing. For a few moments, we've stepped into their world—or rather, below it. I mouth, "Wow!" to Juan, who flashes me a big grin.

When they move on, Juan and I mark the milestone with a photo: me with one arm up in triumph and the other arm around his shoulder, him with his machete in hand, chuckling.

Source: The Earthwatch Institute

Vocabulary

bushwhack: clear a path through vegetation

concession area: an area of land granted by a government for conservation

haul: carry

lunging: moving forward suddenly

milestone: a significant event or stage in a project

prancing: springing from the ground while walking

rustle: make a whispering noise

ruts: deep grooves

sightings: instances of observation

studded: thickly set

trudging: walking slowly, with difficulty

From

Around the World in Eighty Days

by Jules Verne

Chapter 37

IN WHICH IT IS SHOWN THAT PHILEAS FOGG GAINED NOTHING BY HIS TOUR AROUND THE WORLD, UNLESS IT WERE HAPPINESS

Yes; Phileas Fogg in person.

The reader will remember that at five minutes past eight in the evening—about five and twenty hours after the arrival of the travellers in London—Passepartout had been sent by his master to engage the services of the Reverend Samuel Wilson in a certain marriage ceremony, which was to take place the next day.

Passepartout went on his errand enchanted. He soon reached the clergyman's house, but found him not at home. Passepartout waited a good twenty minutes, and when he left the reverend gentleman, it was thirty-five minutes past eight. But in what a state he was! With his hair in disorder, and without his hat, he ran along the street as never man was seen to run before, overturning passers-by, rushing over the sidewalk like a waterspout.

In three minutes he was in Savile Row again, and staggered back into Mr. Fogg's room.

He could not speak.

"What is the matter?" asked Mr. Fogg.

"My master!" gasped Passepartout—"marriage—impossible—"

"Impossible?"

"Impossible—for tomorrow."

"Why so?"

"Because tomorrow—is Sunday!"

"Monday," replied Mr. Fogg.

"No—today is Saturday."

"Saturday? Impossible!"

"Yes, yes, yes, yes!" cried Passepartout. "You have made a mistake of one day! We arrived twenty-four hours ahead of time; but there are only ten minutes left!"

Passepartout had seized his master by the collar, and was dragging him along with irresistible force.

Phileas Fogg, thus kidnapped, without having time to think, left his house, jumped into a cab, promised a hundred pounds to the cabman, and, having run over two dogs and overturned five carriages, reached the Reform Club.

The clock indicated a quarter before nine when he appeared in the great saloon.

Phileas Fogg had accomplished the journey round the world in eighty days!

Phileas Fogg had won his wager of twenty thousand pounds!

How was it that a man so exact and fastidious could have made this error of a day? How came he to think that he had arrived in London on Saturday, the twenty-first day of December, when it was really Friday, the twentieth, the seventy-ninth day only from his departure?

The cause of the error is very simple.

Phileas Fogg had, without suspecting it, gained one day on his journey, and this merely because he had travelled constantly *eastward*; he would, on the contrary, have lost a day had he gone in the opposite direction, that is, *westward*.

In journeying eastward he had gone toward the sun, and the days therefore diminished for him as many times four minutes as he crossed degrees in this direction. There are three hundred and sixty degrees on the circumference of the earth; and these three hundred and sixty degrees, multiplied by four minutes, gives precisely twenty-four hours—that is, the day unconsciously gained. In other words, while Phileas Fogg, going eastward, saw the sun pass the meridian *eighty* times, his friends in London only saw it pass the meridian *seventy-nine* times. This is why they awaited him at the Reform Club on Saturday, and not Sunday, as Mr. Fogg thought.

And Passepartout's famous family watch, which had always kept London time, would have betrayed this fact, if it had marked the days as well as the hours and the minutes!

Phileas Fogg, then, had won the twenty thousand pounds; but, as he had spent nearly nineteen thousand on the way, the pecuniary gain was small. His object was, however, to be victorious, and not to win money. He divided the one thousand pounds that remained between Passepartout and the unfortunate Fix, against whom he cherished no grudge. He deducted, however, from Passepartout's share the cost of the gas which had burned in his room for nineteen hundred and twenty hours, for the sake of regularity.

That evening, Mr. Fogg, as tranquil and phlegmatic as ever, said to Aouda: "Is our marriage still agreeable to you?"

"Mr. Fogg," replied she, "it is for me to ask that question. You were ruined, but now you are rich again."

"Pardon me, madam; my fortune belongs to you. If you had not suggested our marriage, my servant would not have gone to the Reverend Samuel Wilson's, I should not have been apprised of my error, and—"

"Dear Mr. Fogg!" said the young woman.

"Dear Aouda!" replied Phileas Fogg.

It need not be said that the marriage took place forty-eight hours after, and that Passepartout, glowing and dazzling, gave the bride away. Had he not saved her, and was he not entitled to this honour?

The next day, as soon as it was light, Passepartout rapped vigorously at his master's door. Mr. Fogg opened it, and asked, "What's the matter, Passepartout?"

"What is it, sir? Why, I've just this instant found out—"

"What?"

"That we might have made the tour of the world in only seventy-eight days."

"No doubt," returned Mr. Fogg, "by not crossing India. But if I had not crossed India, I should not have saved Aouda; she would not have been my wife, and—"

Mr. Fogg quietly shut the door.

Phileas Fogg had won his wager, and had made his journey around the world in eighty days. To do this he had employed every means of conveyance—steamers, railways, carriages, yachts, trading-vessels, sledges, elephants. The eccentric gentleman had throughout displayed all his marvellous qualities of coolness and exactitude. But what then? What had he really gained by all this trouble? What had he brought back from this long and weary journey?

Nothing, say you? Perhaps so; nothing but a charming woman, who, strange as it may appear, made him the happiest of men!

Truly, would you not for less than that make the tour around the world?

Vocabulary

conveyance: transportation
dazzling: brilliant
fastidious: scrupulous in matters of proper procedure
grudge: feeling of resentment
pecuniary: financial
phlegmatic: calm, unemotional
staggered: walked unsteadily
wager: bet
waterspout: a gyrating column of water and spray formed by a whirlwind between sea and cloud

READ ON

Around the World in Eighty Days

by Jules Verne

On a bet, adventurer Phileas Fogg takes off with Passepartout, his servant, to travel all the way around the world, but there's one catch: he must do it in only eighty days! The journey proves to be full of excitement and unexpected events, challenging the unstoppable Fogg at every turn.

Don't Sweat the Breakups

by Richard Carlson, Ph.D.

I hesitated in titling this strategy because I didn't want anyone to think that I was minimizing how difficult it is to break up with a boyfriend or girlfriend. I can assure you, I am not. In fact, I know it's one of the hardest things that a teenager can go through.

I remember the day my first serious girlfriend and first true love broke up with me. I was devastated, and thought I was going to die. I thought I'd never get over it or meet anyone else.

But I did.

In fact, I'm glad. Had it not happened, I wouldn't have married Kris and wouldn't have my kids. The ex-girlfriend is glad too. She's happily married with three beautiful kids of her own. To this day, the two of us are close friends.

The only way that I'm aware of to make breakups more tolerable is to enhance one's perspective and to see that it's necessary. It's weird when you think about it, but if not for breakups, all of us would marry the very first person we were ever interested in! And obviously, in most cases, that's not in our best interests. The truth is, as hard as they can be, breakups are an essential part of life, for all of us.

When you put breakups into this perspective, it's a little easier to spend less energy mourning relationships that are over and, instead, to spend that same energy appreciating them. With appreciation, it's much easier to focus on the gifts of the relationship—the memories, growth and fun you shared—while at the same time letting go and moving on, realizing that, as painful as it might be, you will love again.

I've found that teens who are able to look at breakups like this are able to maintain a friendship—if not immediately, then at least later on. Rather than be angry that their boyfriend or girlfriend didn't turn out to be "the one," or getting angry, resentful or wanting revenge because someone changed or didn't live up to their expectations, instead they are able to keep alive a nice feeling for that person and to genuinely wish him or her well.

One of the ultimate tests of being human is to be able to wish someone else well—even when you may be hurt. If you can do this, you'll experience the magic of the healing power of love. You'll notice that you'll bounce back more quickly, feel happier and more self-confident, and even appear more attractive to others when your thoughts and wishes are positive. The love and forgiveness in your heart is more visible to others than any of us can possibly imagine.

So remember, even though it may seem like the end of the world, it probably isn't. It may take a while, but your breakups usually will end up seeming like a gift in disguise.

Source: *Don't Sweat the Small Stuff for Teens: Simple Ways to Keep Your Cool in Stressful Times* by Richard Carlson, Ph.D.

Vocabulary

devastated: overwhelmed, reduced to helplessness

genuinely: truly

mourning: grieving over

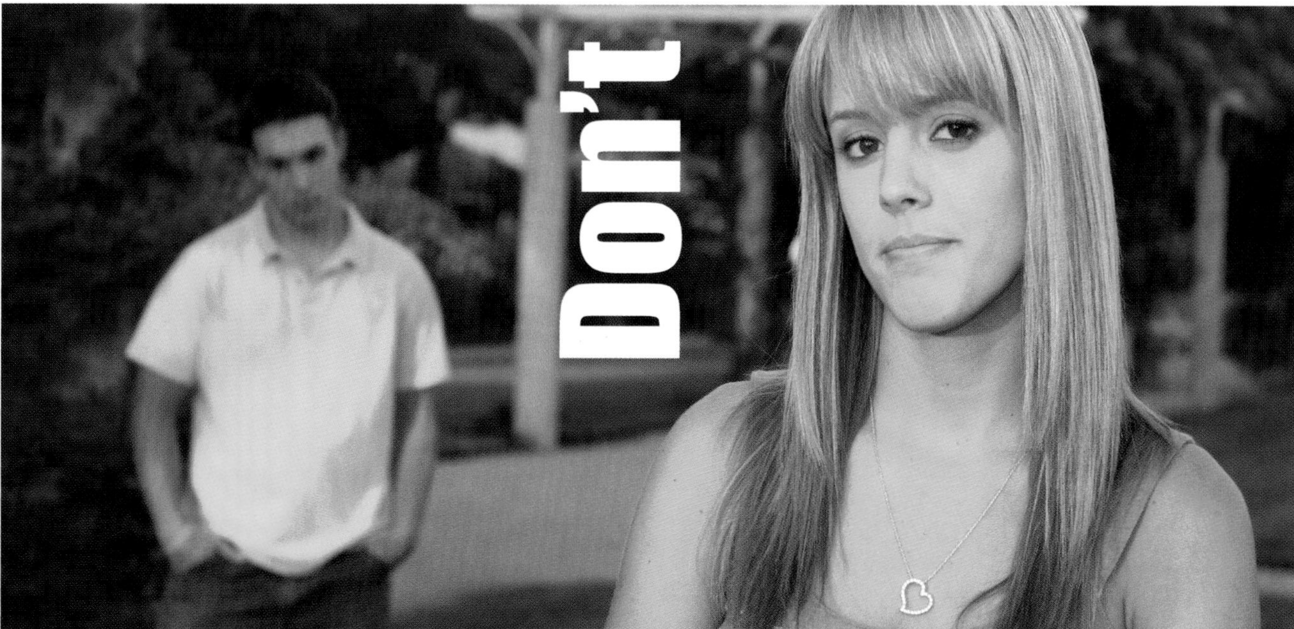

The Courage to Come Back

BY LORA GRINDLAY

Nanaimo's Emily White was seven when doctors told her that she had asthma. That diagnosis, the treatment and medical complications that followed, consumed her life throughout her elementary school years. She went from being an active kid to awaiting death, then back again to a full life. But the heavy doses of medications and their side effects were unnecessary. She was never as sick as doctors believed and only began to heal when told she would die. And in 2005, the then-18-year-old received a Courage to Come Back award in the youth category.

Source: *The Province*

Interviewer: Describe the years you were ill.

EW: The biggest thing that sticks out is that I was in a wheelchair and I was completely dependent. I couldn't feed myself, I couldn't walk, I couldn't bathe myself. I continued to get worse. The asthma medication was not working so they continued to up the doses until Grade 5, when I was on adult doses and I was on the ventilator about four times a day. I couldn't breathe and I was really weak. I was on heavy doses of prednisone. After lots of tests, I was diagnosed with Myasthenia Gravis, a neuromuscular disease and treated for that. Again, it was very high doses of really severe medications. Because I didn't need it, I continued to deteriorate. Finally they just said to me, "We don't know what's wrong. You have six months to live."

Interviewer: How did you react when told you would soon die?

EW: I didn't believe them. I said, "I have all these things I'm going to do in my life and you are wrong." We decided to take me off medications and let me die sooner. That was when, instead of dying, I got better. I moved to a walker from a wheelchair and started to develop my strength.

Interviewer: Was it ever determined what made you so sick?

EW: They figured I had a virus that would have taken six to eight months to go through my system. Because they started to treat me, I got sick. It just shows if you don't need [medical treatment] what it can do to you. I'm not having any problems now, but I get colds a lot because of all the medications that beat down my immune system.

Interviewer: What lessons did you learn?

EW: I'm so much more empathetic–some people think I'm too empathetic. I'll see the little tiny things and I'll get really upset about them. I can really put myself in that position because I've suffered. Even if the suffering isn't to do with illness or bullying or things that I've experienced, I can say, "I think I know how that feels."

Interviewer: What is the most challenging hurdle you've overcome?

EW: When I came back to school I was bullied and [was an] outcast, and people didn't want to be with me because I was the crippled kid. I really strived for excellence in academics and got involved in volunteering. I really had to learn two years ago, when I got depressed, that I need to balance myself and open myself up. I am starting to learn to think about myself before I can help other people.

Interviewer: How did you overcome the bullying and isolation when you returned to school?

EW: It was really tough. I tried for a while to keep fitting in and it just didn't work. It's just recently that I feel happier with the peer group I have. You have to not focus on those people and find other things.

Interviewer: What are your hopes for the years ahead?

EW: I want to help other people for the rest of my life. I'm going to go into special-education teaching. I want to travel the Third World and work on creating peace within countries and helping starving children and families. I don't know how far I'll get but I just want to reach as far as I can.

Vocabulary

bullying: abusive treatment
crippled: unable to use arms or legs
hurdle: obstacle
outcast: person who is not accepted by others
walker: a framework designed to support a disabled person

I'M A 17-YEAR-OLD THERAPIST

BY QUANTWILLA L. JOHNSON

When I was around eight years old, I hated going to therapy. I felt the therapist tried to pry my problems out of me instead of letting them come out. I swore to myself I would never become a therapist. But now that I'm 17 and out of therapy, my main thing is helping other people with their problems.

I never really saw the value in therapy until people began confiding in me. I knew exactly how to treat them—the same way I wanted to be treated when I was in therapy.

It all began when I first started going to church. Teenagers, adults and little kids would tell me their problems with boyfriends, family members, school, etc. The funny thing was that I didn't know why. I hardly knew them and they hardly knew me, so why were people I hardly knew confiding in me?

A friend of mine named Jamie came to me one day upset, telling me her boyfriend beat her. I told Jamie she had to leave him. I told her no one had the right to **lay a hand** on her, and she should not **allow** it under any circumstances.

Jamie didn't want to, but she finally did break up with him. She thanked me and said it was all for the best. But I still can't figure out why Jamie picked me to talk to. What really **puzzled** me was that she was older than me. At that time I was 14 and she was 19. Why would someone older ask me for advice? I hardly knew anything about boys at that age.

I also told Jamie she should talk to someone older, like Rev, the youth minister in our church. She said she would. About a week later Jamie came to me and thanked me for sending her to Rev. She said he helped her a lot. I was glad I helped her, but **befuddled** as to why she made such a big deal about it.

Pretty soon more people came to talk to me. I was shocked, wondering, why is everyone coming to me? But it didn't take long for me to get used to helping people, and besides, it became fun—I liked to do it. I think people passed the word about me being a good listener.

I'm a "therapist" now on a regular basis, because everyone seems to want to talk to me. I know how it can get when you don't know who to trust with your problems, so that's why I do what I do.

I think being in therapy helped me to help others. I had to help myself before I could help anyone else. Now when I think about it, I never really disliked therapy. It was the way the therapist went about getting information out of me that I didn't like. She didn't try to get to know me, just my business. She would force things out of me in a way that made me want to cry.

With my "patients," I establish trust—whatever you want to tell me will be of your own free will. I won't force anything out of you. I think I'm a good person to talk to because I do not pass judgment on anything you say, do, or let happen to you. I believe you must work at your own pace and let a friendship build before I start being **nosy**. When my " patients" and I talk, I don't think of myself as the "professional"—we both work together.

In the past, a lot of people have tried to help me with my problems, but then they disappeared and never came back. It really hurt not to be taken seriously. That's why I want to be there for people who need someone to listen.

I guess I get my ways from my godmother, Susan. Susan and I are there for each other. If she's not at home for me to talk to, I have her beeper number and cellphone number. If I have a problem, she's a very caring person who believes in making time. I do the same thing with my "patients"—try to always be there for them.

If one of my friends has a problem, first I try to get it off her mind by going somewhere with her to talk and giving her a shoulder to cry on.

The thing I hate most is when you tell your friends your problem, and to them it's nothing and they tell you to get over it. I think no matter what the problem is, if it's hurting your friend, don't say "get over it."

When my friend's dog died and she told her best friend, her best friend laughed at her. Then she came to me, **heartbroken**. I understood what she was going through. You don't know how something like that feels unless it's happened to you. I knew how she felt because I had a dog I loved very much that died.

Another friend of mine was going out with an older man, and now she thinks she might be pregnant. I know she must feel alone and hurt, because she already has a child and faces a lot of ridicule for it. All I can do is be by her side no matter what she faces.

The thing I want most now is to become a real therapist and help teenagers with their problems. I've been through a lot and I know I can relate. There are times when I think a professional should step in. There isn't always someone to talk to, and you may not find someone like me.

P.S.: I take all major credit cards!

Source: *The Struggle to Be Strong: True Stories by Teens About Overcoming Tough Times*, edited by Al Desetta, M.A. and Sybil Wolin, Ph.D.

READ ON

The Struggle to Be Strong: True Stories by Teens About Overcoming Tough Times

edited by Al Desetta, M.A., and Sybil Wolin, Ph.D.

The stories in this collection were all written by teens who have been through very difficult times, but came out on the other side and moved forward. The writers have one thing in common: the ability to be resilient, to bounce back from adversity. These inspiring tales of courage and strength will help you to build skills you need to overcome life's many battles.

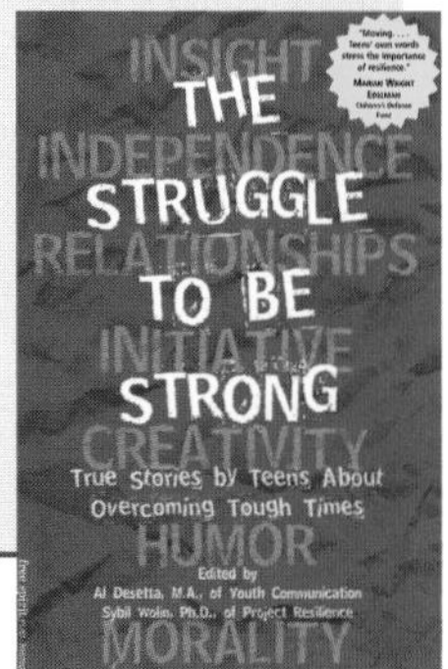

Vocabulary

allow: permit
befuddled: confused
heartbroken: very sad
lay a hand: hit
nosy: interested in the private lives of others
puzzled: confused

Empathize

by Richard Carlson, Ph.D.

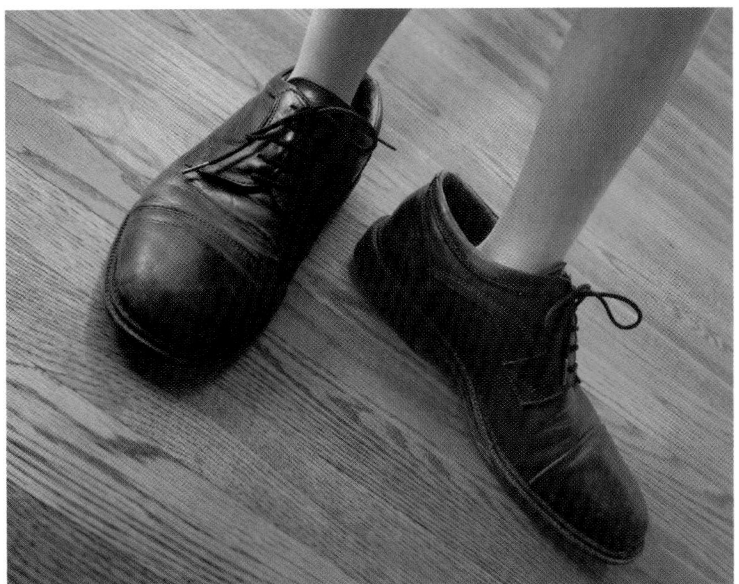

Learning to empathize is a great way to become not only a more gracious and thoughtful person, but a happier one as well. To empathize means that you attempt to put yourself in others' shoes, to experience something from their perspective. It doesn't mean you feel sorry for them, but that you seek to understand what it must feel like to be them—or what it must be like to be going through what they are going through.

Imagine, for a moment, that there is a new kid at school. He's awkward and lonely. He has no friends, no one to talk to. He's shy and frightened. To empathize with this person would mean you would imagine what it must be like to be him right now. You might think, "Gee, that would be tough," or something like that. Your empathetic feelings probably would translate into some type of thoughtful behaviour. You might go out of your way to say hello, for example, or you might suggest that others do the same. At the very least, you'd be absolutely sure to be sensitive to the fact that what he's going through is difficult, so you wouldn't even think of being insensitive or mean-spirited.

The opposite of empathy would be indifference, the feeling of, "So what, it's not me so why should I care?" This more selfish way of thinking about things tends to translate into equally selfish ways of acting. An indifferent person would never go out of his or her way to be welcoming or inclusive. In fact, it's possible such a person might even go out of his or her way to be cruel.

Empathy, then, is characterized by a sense of caring and interest in others, while indifference is made up of self-centredness and apathy.

It's fairly obvious why developing one's empathy increases one's character and warmth as a human being. It means you take some of your attention off yourself and put it on others. Doing so makes you a nicer person, easier to be around and more compassionate.

What's not so obvious, however, is that developing your empathy also serves to heighten your own level of happiness and to greatly reduce your stress.

Empathetic people care about others and their feelings, so they feel connected with others rather than isolated. This connection keeps them from feeling threatened when other people are successful, good-looking, or talented. Instead, they are able to share in the joy that other people experience. People are drawn toward empathetic people; they want to spend time with them, help them, listen to them.

Empathetic people are acutely aware of the fact that we're all human. Therefore, it's easy for them to be forgiving when people make mistakes or mess up. And they extend this perspective to themselves as well. Rather than beat themselves up or act overly self-critical, they instead learn from their mistakes and move on.

There's a real upside to becoming more empathetic, but no downside whatsoever. What's more, empathy is easy to develop. All it takes is the willingness to put yourself in the shoes of others. Take the step today. The benefits will last a lifetime.

Source: *Don't Sweat the Small Stuff for Teens: Simple Ways to Keep Your Cool in Stressful Times* by Richard Carlson, Ph.D.

Vocabulary

awkward: not fitting into a group

gracious: polite

mean-spirited: unkind

threatened: under attack

HOW TO WRITE FROM THE OPPOSITE GENDER

BY **BLAIR HURLEY**

Writing from the opposite gender can be one of the toughest challenges in fiction, for beginners and experts alike. No matter how many years you've been in the writing game, it is still possible to portray a person of the opposite gender in the completely wrong light. Just remember the tepid reception that Tom Wolfe got for his recent novel *I Am Charlotte Simmons*, about a college-aged girl. Many reviews pointed out that the gender was written all wrong and didn't seem genuine.

So does this mean men can't write about women and women can't write about men? Absolutely not: after all, men and women have been doing it—magically, to wonderful effect—for centuries. It's just a question of walking in someone else's shoes and finding the right voice. It requires you to be sensitive and imaginative—but these are qualities that are essential for all kinds of good writing.

So step one in writing from the opposite gender is to approach the exercise with an open mind. Too many times in our daily lives, we're tempted to lump either men or women into groups. We might say to ourselves, "Men—they're all the same" or "That's such a typical girl thing to do."

Unless you've actually spent time being the other gender, there is a huge gap of experience between the two. Similar divides that have existed in the past, such as racial barriers, are shrinking. More and more people are learning that race is an illusion and has no basis in genetics, for example. The gender gap is something different altogether, because it does have a genetic basis. There's just no denying that men and women are born different, and are certainly treated differently as they grow up. But if we're able to imagine someone from another culture, then we can imagine someone of another gender.

Step two is to always, always, always think of your character as an individual. If you're a man trying to write about women, don't start by thinking, "What are some typical female traits?" and then giving your character those traits. There's no faster way to making a two-dimensional cliché. Instead, think about yourself, and try thinking about gender as a kind of culture. I can say I was raised in a culture of being female, which means certain things about education and the way I've been treated by others. But at the same time, it's not everything about who I am. It's not the be all and end all of me. Remember that for your character: his or her gender is a definite factor in the way he or she thinks and acts. But it's just the tip of the iceberg when it comes to their fears, loves, and desires.

Step three is to observe people around you, and to add that to your own imagination. The good news is that you can very easily learn about the opposite sex by asking questions and by just observing the many people around you. If you have close friends of the opposite sex, go ahead and ask questions about what shaving is like or what they find most attractive about the opposite sex. And keep your eyes open. If you're a woman, observe how men walk, how they move their hands, how they talk, where they're looking. If you're a man, do the same for women. All of these little things, if included subtly in your writing, will help make your character seem genuine, an actual man or woman rather than a cliché. Don't be looking to confirm stereotypes; look with a cool objective eye.

The ultimate goal of having a character of the opposite sex in your story is not to reduce them to that sex, but to humanize them, to make them rise above their gender to become the individuals that they are. Let your character grow and expand beyond the expectations of their gender. Give them thoughts to think that defy stereotypes, or that give new insight into the real experience of being a man or woman.

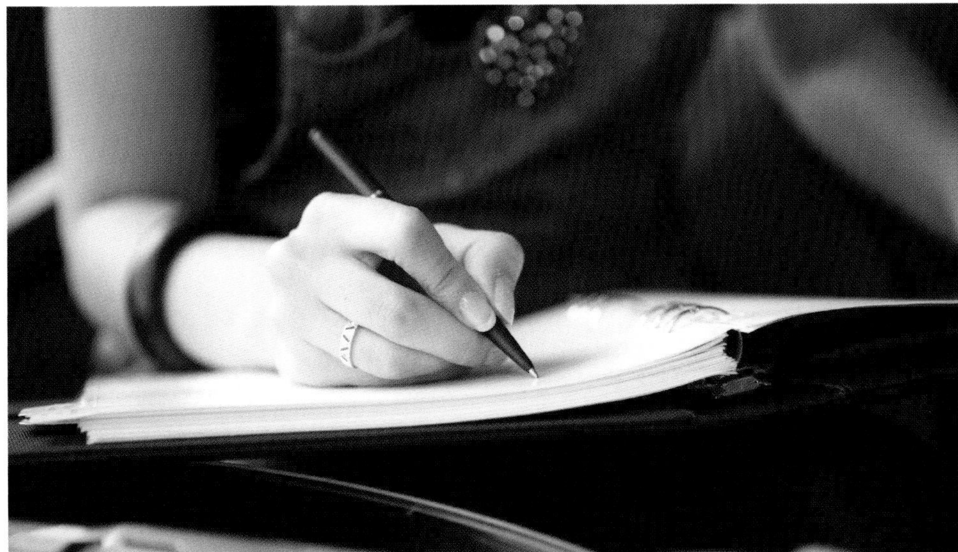

Vocabulary

defy: contradict
gap: divide
insight: inside view
open mind: readiness to accept different ideas
tepid: unenthusiastic

Instant Aging

BY KYLE JAMES

A FIRM IN GERMANY HAS DEVELOPED A SUIT THAT ENABLES THE YOUNG AND FIT TO SEE WHAT IT'S LIKE TO BE OLD AND FRAIL. THOSE TRYING ON THE "AGE EXPLORER" GET A TASTE OF LIFE AT 70.

In the youth-oriented culture of today, there is often a marked lack of sympathy for members of society over 65. As the world continues to be predominantly driven by all things "young," the limitations brought about by old age—arthritis, stiffness, loss of hearing, and a general slowing down—are often met with little understanding, or even outright contempt.

Not so for the guinea pigs who submit themselves for a turn in the Age Explorer, a kind of instant-aging suit developed by the Meyer-Hentschel consulting firm in the German city of Saarbrücken. Ten minutes spent in the Age Explorer is enough to imbue instant sympathy with the elderly in even the most adamant ageist.

"Younger people who try on the suit say, finally, I understand why older people act the way they do," said Hanne Meyer-Hentschel, the suit's creator.

Instant arthritis

The Age Explorer brings about this generational appreciation by propelling its wearers decades into the future by simulating how the body might behave at the age of 70. The suit's red overalls have 13 pounds of weights sewn into them; pads strapped to the elbows and knees stiffen those joints. Walking across a large room wearing the suit becomes a slow, exhausting experience. The thick, red Age Explorer gloves have a Velcro-like substance sewn into them: Putting them on brings about instant arthritis, since any pressure applied to the hand feels like a thousand tiny needles digging into one's flesh.

As if that weren't enough, headphones, similar to the ear protection airport baggage handlers wear, take away a good deal of one's hearing. A welder's mask-like face shield robs the subject of his peripheral vision, its yellow glass leaves the world looking strange and blurred.

"It's all about the physical changes that we're all going to face sooner or later to some degree," said Beate Baltes of Meyer-Hentschel, who babysits those getting their first taste of old age. Not everyone who reaches 70 is going to have arthritis or failing eyesight, but the Age Explorer is meant to simulate a possible future in which things one takes for granted today will not be quite as self-evident.

Not so easy anymore

Simple things like picking up a napkin out of a stack take Age Explorer wearers intense concentration, and about two minutes. Pulling a wallet out of a back

pocket with newly arthritic hands becomes a painful and frustrating experience. Once that's accomplished, despair can be the next emotion to set in when trying to recognize or pick up the different coins there.

After a tedious, tiring walk across a large room, most of the newly aged are ready for a break on a comfortable sofa. But while taking a seat is welcome, the difficulty in getting back up on one's feet again almost makes the sitting not worth the trouble.

"At first it was funny in a way, like you're in some kind of Halloween costume," said Lisa Neundorfer, a marketing researcher who has tried out the suit. "But then you realize how cut off you are from your environment. Suddenly you have a whole new perspective on things."

New understanding for Grandma

The third generation of the suit will take age simulation to the next step. Age Explorer III will be able to mimic certain mental conditions among the elderly, like confusion or interrupted thought processes. Put enough people into the thing, according to one wearer, and it might just spark a renewed hunt for the legendary Fountain of Youth.

Source: *Deutsche Welle*, February 19, 2003

Vocabulary

- **contempt:** disgust
- **guinea pigs:** participants in a research study
- **imbue:** give
- **marked:** notable
- **spark:** inspire to occur
- **takes for granted:** ceases to appreciate due to familiarity
- **tedious:** difficult and boring

READ ON

My Sister's Keeper
by Jodi Picoult

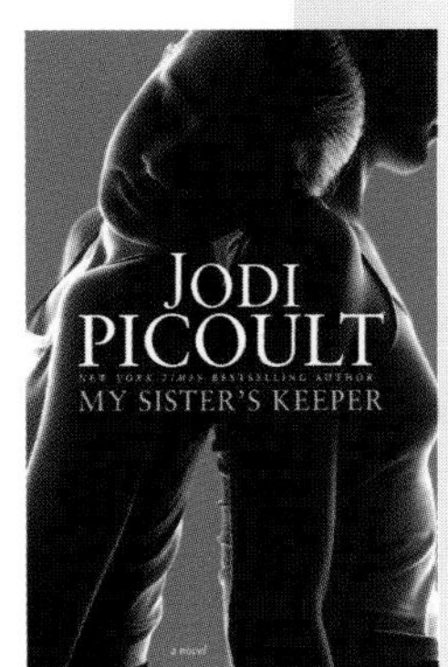

This novel tells the story of Anna, who was genetically engineered to be a perfect blood and bone-marrow match for her older sister, who has a rare form of cancer. When Anna is considered as a kidney donor to save her 16-year-old sister, she hires a lawyer to represent her and allow her to have control over her own body. Written from each of the family members' perspective, this book raises questions about what it means to be part of a family.

Prince Cinders

BY BABETTE COLE

Prince Cinders was not much of a prince. He was small, spotty, scruffy and skinny. He had three big hairy brothers who were always teasing him about his looks. They spent their time going to the Palace Disco with princess girlfriends. They made poor Prince Cinders stay behind and clean up after them. When his work was done, he would sit by the fire and wish he was big and hairy like his brothers.

One Saturday night, when he was washing the socks, a dirty fairy fell down the chimney. "All your wishes shall be granted," cried the fairy. "Ziz Ziz Boom, Tic Tac Ta, this empty can shall be a car. Bif Bang Bong, Bo Bo Bo, to the disco you shall go!"

"That can't be right!" said the fairy.

"Toe of rat and eye of newt, your rags will turn into a suit!" ("Crumbs," thought the fairy, "I didn't mean a SWIM suit!")

"Your greatest wish I'll grant to you. You SHALL be big and hairy too!"

Prince Cinders got big and hairy, all right!

"Rats!" said the fairy. "Wrong again, but I'm sure it all wears off at midnight."

Prince Cinders didn't know he was a big hairy monkey because that's the kind of spell it was. He thought he looked pretty good! So off he went to the disco. The car was too small to drive but he made the best of it.

But when he arrived at the Royal Rave-up, he was too big to fit through the door! He decided to take the bus home. A pretty princess was waiting at the stop.
"When's the next bus?" he grunted.

Luckily, midnight struck and Prince Cinders changed back into himself. The princess thought he had saved her by frightening away the big hairy monkey! "Wait!" she shouted, but Prince Cinders was too shy. He even lost his trousers in the rush!

The princess was none other than the rich and beautiful Princess Lovelypenny. She put out a proclamation to find the owner of the trousers:

"The Princess Lovelypenny decrees that she will marry whoever fits the trousers lost by the prince who saved her from being eaten by the Big Hairy Monkey. Fitting sessions begin today. –P.L."

Every prince for miles around tried to force the trousers on. But they wriggled about and refused to fit any of them! Of course, Prince Cinders' brothers all fought to get into the trousers at once . . .

"Let him try," commanded the princess, pointing at Cinders. "They won't fit that little squirt," sneered his brothers.

. . . But they did! Princess Lovelypenny proposed immediately.

So Prince Cinders married Princess Lovelypenny and lived in luxury, happily ever after ... and Princess Lovelypenny had a word with the fairy about his big hairy brothers, whom she turned into house fairies. And they flitted around the palace doing the housework for ever and ever.

Vocabulary

flitted: moved about rapidly

newt: a small type of salamander

sneered: gave a facial expression of contempt or scorn

squirt: slang, an insult meaning a tiny and weak person

wears off: loses its effect

wriggled: squirmed, twisted

Gender Stereotypes Can Distort Our Memories

Plenty of research has shown that some stereotypes are not only offensive, but they can also have a detrimental effect on people's behaviour.

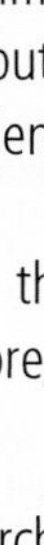

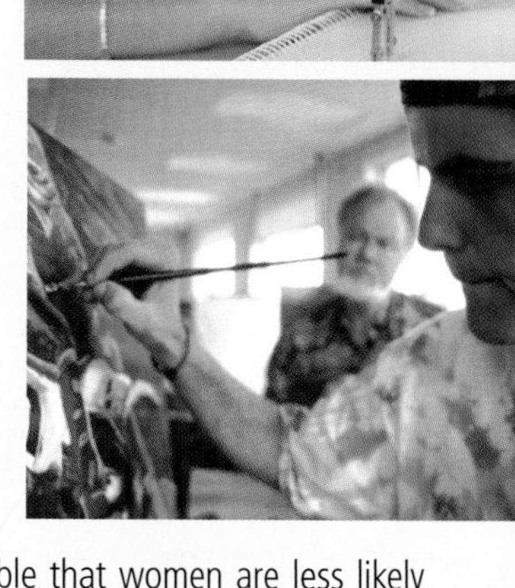

For example, women's math performance suffers after they are reminded of the stereotype that men are better than women at math.

Now, Armand Chatard and his colleagues have taken this line of research a step further by demonstrating that being reminded of gender stereotypes can distort students' memories of their prior exam performance.

An initial study with 73 high-school students (34 boys) showed that those students who more strongly endorsed gender stereotypes in relation to math and the arts subsequently showed a more biased recall of their past exam performance. That is, girls who endorsed the stereotypes underestimated their past math performance, while boys who endorsed the stereotypes tended to underestimate their past arts performance.

A second study with 64 high school students gave some a highly salient reminder of gender stereotypes—that is, they rated their agreement with statements like "Men are gifted in mathematics" and "Women are gifted in the arts," before rating their own abilities. Others were given what was considered a weaker reminder of gender stereotypes—they rated their own performance first, before evaluating men and women in general. Finally, all the students re-called their past exam performance.

Girls given a more salient reminder of gender stereotypes underestimated their actual past math exam performance while boys in this condition overestimated their math performance. No such difference was observed in the weak reminder condition. Regarding the arts, all students overestimated their performance, but among those given a salient reminder of stereotypes, the girls overestimated their arts performance more, and the boys far less.

The researchers said these findings could have real world implications: "It is possible that women are less likely to embrace scientific careers than men because gender stereotypes lead them to underestimate their past achievement."

Source: *British Psychological Society Research Digest*, January 2008

Vocabulary

- **detrimental:** negative, damaging
- **distort:** make false
- **endorsed:** believed in
- **gifted:** having a natural aptitude
- **rated:** evaluated
- **salient:** most important

READ ON

Boy v. Girl?: How Gender Shapes Who We Are, What We Want, and How We Get Along

by George Abrahams, Ph.D., and Sheila Ahlbrand

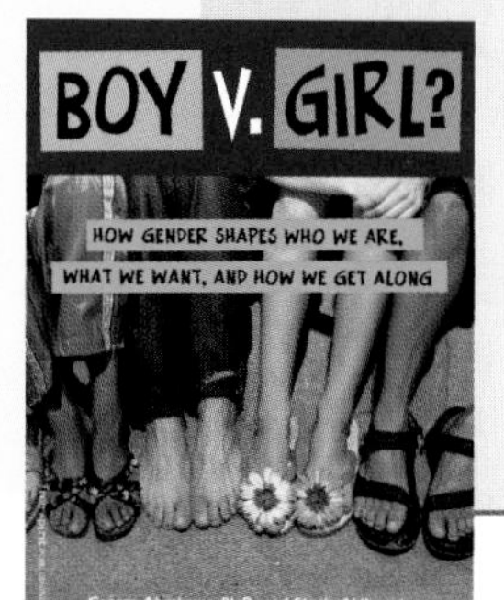

When you think of gender stereotypes, what comes to mind? How do these stereotypes affect your life and your decisions? And what does it mean to be a boy or a girl in today's society? This book encourages you to take a closer look at the barriers each gender's stereotypes create on your journey toward adulthood, and helps you to navigate your own path.

Men and Women: From the Same Planet After All?

The popular media has portrayed men and women as psychologically different as two planets—Mars and Venus. However, these differences are vastly overestimated. According to a review of 46 studies conducted over the last 20 years, the two sexes are, in fact, more similar in personality, communication, cognitive ability and leadership than previously realized.

According to a report in the journal *American Psychologist* (Vol. 60, No. 6), from childhood to adulthood, men and women are more alike than different on most but not all psychological variables. Psychologist Janet S. Hyde, Ph.D., examined psychological differences based on gender in studies that looked at a number of psychological traits and abilities. She compared the data across 20 years' worth of gender studies. Her goal was to determine how much gender influenced an outcome. The traits and variables examined were cognitive abilities; verbal and nonverbal communication; social or psychological traits, like aggression or leadership; psychological well-being, like self-esteem; motor behaviours, like throwing distance; and moral reasoning.

Gender differences accounted for either zero or a very small effect for most of the psychological variables examined, according to Hyde. Only motor behaviours (throwing distance), some aspects of sexuality and heightened physical aggression showed marked gender differences.

Furthermore, gender differences seem to depend on the context they were measured in, said Hyde. In studies where gender norms are removed, researchers demonstrated how important gender roles and social context were in determining a person's actions. In one study where participants were told that they were not identified as male or female, neither sex conformed to a stereotyped image of aggression. They did the opposite to what was expected.

Over-inflated claims of gender difference seen in the mass media affect men and women in work, parenting and relationships, said Hyde. Studies of gender and evaluation of leaders in the workplace show that women who go against the caring, nurturing stereotype may pay for it dearly when being hired or evaluated. This also happens with the portrayals of relationships in the media. Best-selling books and popular magazine articles assert that women and men can't get along because they communicate too differently, said Dr. Hyde. Maybe the problem is that they give up prematurely because they believe they can't change what they mistakenly believe is simply part of being male or female, she added.

Children also suffer the consequences of these exaggerated claims of gender difference. There is a widespread belief that boys are better in math than girls, said Dr Hyde. But according to this meta-analysis, boys and girls perform equally in math until high school, where boys do gain a small advantage. Unfortunately, elementary-aged mathematically-talented girls may be overlooked by parents who have lower expectations for a daughter's success in math versus a son's likelihood to succeed in math. Research has shown that parents' expectations for their children's math success relate strongly to a child's self-confidence and his or her performance.

The misrepresentation of how different the sexes are, which is not supported by the scientific evidence, harms men and women of all ages in many different areas of life, said Dr. Hyde. "The claims can hurt women's opportunities in the workplace, dissuade couples from trying to resolve conflict and communication problems and cause unnecessary obstacles that hurt children's and adolescents' self-esteem."

Source: Adapted from "Men and Women Found More Similar Than Portrayed in Popular Media, According To Research on Gender Differences," APA Online.

Vocabulary

assert: state as fact
gender: sex, as in male or female
harms: hurts
heightened: increased
marked: significant
meta-analysis: study comparing data from a wide range of other studies across a period of time
norms: standards, patterns or types
overlooked: failed to notice
traits: distinguishing features or characteristics
vastly: considerably, greatly

Is This Heaven?

It sure isn't high school. I've been here eight weeks and I've never been happier

by Scott Dobson-Mitchell

Two months ago, on my first official day of university classes, I tried to get ahead of a slower-moving crowd on the way to my physics lecture. When I started to run on the wet grass, there was a brief, frictionless moment when I suddenly realized, "Oh crap, I'm about to fall." And then I tumbled bookbag-first to the ground. I waited for someone to snicker, or say something sarcastic. Instead everyone politely pretended not to notice.

I wasn't in high school anymore. I was in university.

If the same thing had happened just a few months earlier, when I was still in Grade 12, I would have had to change my name, move to Saskatchewan and go into the Geek Protection Program.

Behaviour that was considered uncool in high school—say, speaking in complete sentences—is a good thing in university. All of a sudden, nobody cares all that much about what you're wearing, or if you carry a Ninja Turtle bookbag. (Well, okay, maybe that's just Waterloo.)

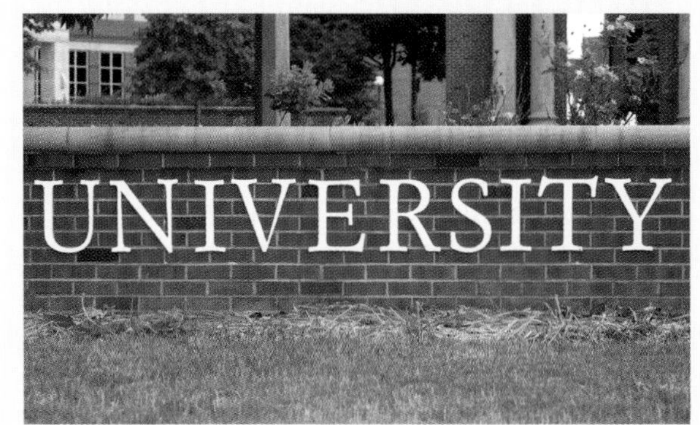

In high school, there are dozens of intricate social rules that you have to stay on top of at all times. But in university? It's common to have hundreds of students in a single class. The place is anonymous, or at least a lot less stifling. No one is paying so much attention to you. The academic pace at university also seems much faster. There haven't been any slow days, at least not yet. When my anthropology professor announced he'd be showing a movie to the class, I assumed I'd have a 50-minute period to relax and brain-coast. But then a documentary about primate social behaviour started up. Unlike high school, it was actually relevant to what we were learning, and not just an excuse to keep a bunch of kids busy while the teacher had an eyes-wide-open snooze.

High school takes as long to complete as an undergraduate degree, but if the pace of my first two months at university is anything to go by, we're going to absorb a lot more material here. In just one biology lecture we reviewed what took more than two months of high-school

classes to cover. I think they should condense all four years into one, and let us escape the clutches of high school sooner. I know, it won't happen. But a guy can dream.

I was surprised when I found out that my first-ever university chemistry lab involved intimidating-sounding chemicals like concentrated hydrochloric acid. At the beginning of the experiment, the lab instructor reminded everyone to mix the nitric acid under the fume hood, since the gas it emits can be toxic. Had this been a high-school chemistry lab, there would have been at least one student mixing nitric acid 10 feet outside of the safety zone. Probably standing right under a ventilation duct, spreading a dense cloud of toxic gases throughout the building. But in the university lab, everyone was so . . . adult. Did the instructor say use the fume hood? Okay, so we'll use the fume hood.

In university, teachers also don't lurk in dark corners, waiting to yell at you about running in the halls, or talking too loudly, or opening your sandwich bag before you reach the legally designated eating area.

When I bumped into someone from my old Grade 12 math class and asked him if he missed high school, he snorted, "Nope. I didn't like school after Grade 8." I knew exactly what he meant. For some of us, high school was all about survival.

I wish I could go back in time and tell my Grade 9 self that there is light at the end of the tunnel. That even if high school seems like it's endless, there really is life beyond it. But it's easy to lose sight of that fact when you're sitting through health class. Oh, and I'd also give myself a warning: Don't try to pass anyone on the first day of class.

Source: *MacLean's*, November 24, 2008

Vocabulary

brain-coast: be lazy
intimidating: frightening and discouraging
intricate: complicated and very detailed
lurk: lie in wait for someone
snooze: nap
stifling: oppressive
uncool: not acceptable to peers

How to Find a Roommate... Safely

You're new to a city, and you can't afford to live alone.

An extremely tight renters' market has forced monthly rents through the roof, so living solo is simply out of the question. But aside from a couple of old college buddies who recently moved to the area (who already have roommates), you haven't yet made friends in your new city. You've got to find a roommate fast if you want to have any chance of scoring an apartment. You'll have to take a deep breath and do what many solo renters do every day: go "potluck." It's a bit frightening, especially for those of us who saw the film "Single White Female" and are still traumatized from the experience.

So how are you supposed to find a roommate? You could always use a roommate service, but even using a professional source is no guarantee that your lifestyles and habits will be compatible. What kinds of sources can you rely upon that won't compromise your personal safety? You've got to start your search early, because it's very rare that you find a roommate immediately. It's going to take time, patience and some careful screening before you find the stranger with whom you'll be sharing living space for the immediate future.

First of all, before you even get started, abandon your illusion of finding the perfect roommate with whom you'll enjoy an instant rapport and certain domestic bliss. Sure, it happens on occasion, but don't weed out potential candidates because you think they'll fall short of that ideal. All you should expect from your roommate is neatness, common courtesy, safe living habits (including the avoidance of drugs, hanging out with and inviting over a dangerous crowd and a willingness to keep the doors locked and the keys to himself/herself) and timely payment of his/her half of the rent. If friendship develops after those ground rules have been established and respected, terrific. If not, you should still consider yourself lucky for finding yourself a good roommate, because that's exactly what you've got.

Let's say you do, in fact, have a friend in the area with whom you could consider living. Should you do it? We've all heard the advice that we should never travel with friends if we want to remain friends. In some cases, that's true for roommates, too. Even if you have separate bedrooms, sharing a common living space (the living room, kitchen and bathroom, in particular) can create a host of problems. You and your friend might be bosom buddies, and while you might swear that you'd remain the best of friends as roommates, avoid it if you can help it. You and your friend could start to view each other in a different light once you're sharing an apartment. New personality characteristics will suddenly come into focus in a much sharper and clearer way. The smaller the living space, the better the chance you'll be at each other's throats before long. In many cases, it's best to reside with someone who knows nothing about your history—an objective audience, so to speak.

This isn't to imply, however, that you should go grab someone off the street and ask him or her to split the rent with you. Instead, start with the local classifieds section. It's a great place to find leads for potential roommates. You'll definitely want to interview candidates; never under any circumstances should you make an offer to someone over the phone, sight unseen. Our telephone personalities can be very different than the ones we project in person. When you do start to interview candidates, have a friend or family member stay with you for two reasons: the first, for your own safety; and second, to offer an additional, objective opinion about your candidates. The sooner you start scanning the classifieds, the better. It's likely that you'll run through many duds before you find yourself a good roommate.

by Courtney Ronan

If you decide to place an ad yourself, set specific hours during which candidates may call. Don't print your name, or if you can help it, your sex, either. This doesn't mean your ad has to be vague, dull and straightforward, though. You can and should make it fun-spirited. Use your creativity and a touch of humour to entertain. You're more likely to receive a positive response from candidates, and a greater number of them.

A potentially safer search technique is to ask all of your friends in the area if they know anyone who's looking for a roommate. If not, or if you know a limited number of people in the area, you could try scanning the bulletin boards of reputable spots like local universities, coffee houses, your church or favourite bookstore. These are all destinations where you stand a better chance of finding someone who's not only goal-oriented and moralistic, but who shares your interests as well.

When showing your place to potential candidates, be sure that you run down the list of required utility expenses, even if the candidates don't ask (and they should). You don't want to offer someone a position as your roommate, then have them leave when they discover just how high their share of the utilities is. Also, if the building in which you live has any particular quirks, eccentric or noisy neighbours, a challenging landlord, a problem with excessive heat in the summertime, be honest and up front about it. You can counter those disclosures with positives about your building and the surrounding neighbourhood.

Your most critical job as a roommate-screener is to listen to your instincts. If the red flags are waving in your brain about any one of your candidates, even if you can't put your finger on the problem, don't make that person an offer. Our instincts often prove to be our most valuable tool. They're there for our survival, so be listening.

It's not easy finding yourself a roommate, especially when time is of the essence. But you can do it safely and responsibly provided you proceed with caution as well as enthusiasm. After all, you've got to sell yourself, too.

Source: *Realty Times*

Vocabulary

afford: have the ability to pay for
disclosures: information a person reveals
dull: boring
quirks: odd, unusual or remarkable features
reside: live with
scoring: getting
screening: checking to see who to eliminate and who to consider
solo: alone
timely: on time
weed out: eliminate

Your Money Is Your Business

Money. Budgets. Savings. Investments. These are all words you may hear tossed around on the news or in your parents' dinner conversations, but where do you fit in when it comes to money? Do you know where your money goes, or how to use it to achieve your goals? Now that you're reaching a point in your life where you will be moving on to bigger and better things, it's time for you to take control of your financial life. Sound complicated? Have no fear—it's as easy as 1-2-3: **Think, Save, Act.**

Think.

You've probably heard the expression: "think first, act later." Achieving good financial health depends on it. What matters most to you? To begin, think about what you want to do with your money. In other words, identify your financial goals. You can then prepare a budget to see whether your goals are realistic, given your income and expenses.

Some goals can be achieved in the short term, like going to the movies or having an evening out with friends. Other goals require a long-term commitment. You have to plan ahead to attain them.

In order to determine your financial goals, you need to:

❖ Identify how much money you need to save and how much time you have to do so.

❖ Make a list of your financial goals, in order of priority.

❖ From time to time, ask yourself if
- your objectives are still realistic;
- changes in your financial situation call for changes to your goals.

It's a fact: writing is remembering. Write down your objectives to motivate yourself!

Once you have set realistic financial goals, and calculated how much you need to save in order to reach them, you're ready to set up a budget and save for your dreams. But before you do that, you have a bit more thinking to do. You need to get a clear picture of what's coming in and what's going out, money-wise.

The big picture, in three easy steps:

❖ List your income, or money coming in, and expenses, or money going out, for each week.

❖ Add them up separately.

❖ Compare the results.

If your income is higher than your expenses, lucky you! You've got money to save. If, however, your expenses are higher than your income but you still want to save money, you have two choices: reduce expenses or commit to trying to raise your income.

Now, it's time to think about how to reach those financial goals. The only way to do that is to save your money!

Save.

Now you're in business! Why not put a bit of money aside? The reward is more freedom and control over your own affairs.

To save money, you first have to set your priorities. You can then prepare a real budget that will help you plan your short- or long-term expenses and set aside some savings. Set up categories of items you spend your money on, and make sure that savings is one of those categories. Then, using your newfound knowledge of your expenses, decide what is reasonable to spend in each of these categories on a weekly basis.

Your budget will let you:

- be autonomous
- have what you want (without always asking your parents for money)
- set clear limits for yourself
- avoid unnecessary expenses
- plan ahead
- understand the value of money

As your financial responsibilities increase, so does the importance of good budgeting. Whether your goals are big or small, it's always a good idea to plan ahead. Learn to reach your personal objectives, and you'll be ready to take on your new responsibilities when the time comes.

Source: L'Autorité des Marchés Financiers

READ ON

What Color Is Your Parachute? For Teens

by Richard Nelson Bolles and Carol Christen with Jean M. Blomquist

Based on Richard Nelson Bolles's *What Color Is Your Parachute?*, the best-selling job-hunting book in the world, this book takes the same self-exploration ideas and teaches them to teens using interactive exercises, worksheets and profiles.

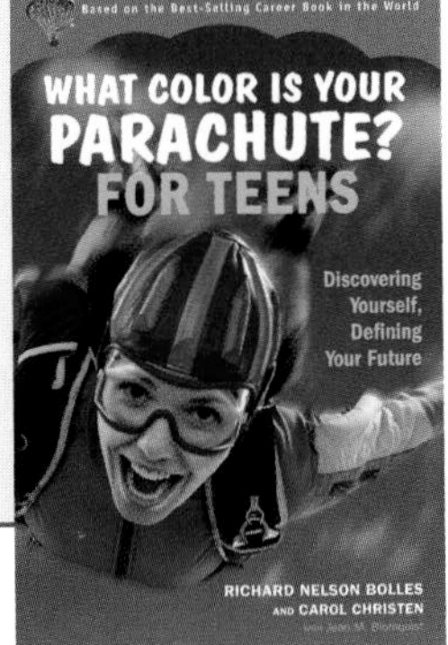

Act.

You have already defined your dreams and determined how much money you could put aside. Now it's time to act! Make your money work for you by investing your savings. It takes money to make money!

No matter what type of account you choose, the important thing is to keep your savings in the account and use the magic of compound interest to make your savings grow.

So, what exactly is compound interest? It sounds complicated, but it couldn't be simpler. To earn compound interest, begin by investing your savings and letting them accumulate interest. Each time the interest on your savings is calculated, it gets added to your savings, or compounded. So over time, you will continue to earn interest not only on your original investment, but also on the interest it has already earned.

For example, if you invest \$1000 in a fund with a 5% annual interest rate, your investment will be worth \$1276.28 in five years!

The sooner and more regularly you start investing money, the more you benefit from the magic of compound interest.

The more informed you are about your own financial situation and the ways you can save for your future, the more knowledgeable you will be of the right moves to make. Ask questions, read about the different savings options, and above all, keep track of where you put your money and how your savings is growing. After all, your money is your business!

Vocabulary

account: agreement with a financial institution to keep money in a safe place

budgets: time-based plans for spending and saving money, organized by categories of spending

commitment: pledge or undertaking

interest: a percentage of the money you save, earned as a reward for keeping your money at a financial institution

savings: money set aside and not spent

Sports Go High Tech

Check out three innovations that could revolutionize sports

Good Pointe

For 350 years, ballerinas have worn the same kind of pointe shoe, which allows them to gracefully pirouette and leap across the stage, all while on tiptoe. Despite pointe shoes' elegant appearance, the slippers' age-old design makes wearing them torture for dancers' feet.

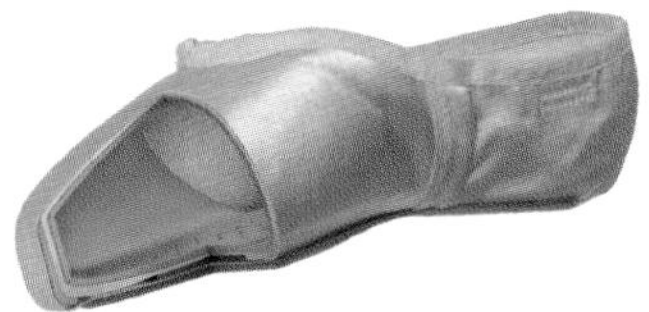

The discomfort comes from the blister-inducing shoes' paper-mâché construction, which uses layers of paper and cloth hardened with paste to form the shoes' unique flat-tipped shape. Thankfully, one ballet shoe manufacturer has updated the design using 21st-century materials—a state-of-the-art foam called D3o.

D3o has already been used to pad snow-boarding beanies, soccer goalie gloves and motorcycle jackets. The polymer does more than just cushion sportswear. When moved slowly, the material remains flexible, but any sudden impact causes its chains of molecules to tangle together. That causes the foam to temporarily stiffen and form a shock-absorbing barrier.

The company's new satin dance shoes look identical to traditional ones, says Richard Palmer, an engineer and inventor of D3o. "The only thing different will be the smile on dancers' faces," he says.

Source: Cody Crane, *Scholastic ScienceWorld*

Better Ball

If you are used to identifying soccer balls by their distinctive black and white geometric pattern, you might do a double take when you see the ball being kicked around by today's pro players. A noted sporting-goods company created the redesigned ball with its swirl and paddle-shaped sections for the 2006 World Cup. Since then, it's become the standard for major championships and leagues.

Why give the classic ball the boot? Older balls consisted of 32 hexagon and pentagon pieces that, when sewn together, formed a sphere. The new balls have just 14 curved pieces that neatly fit together like puzzle pieces. The benefit: Fewer panels make for a much rounder and aerodynamic ball. Since air flows more easily around the ball, it will behave more consistently when kicked. That, according to the inventors, will increase players' accuracy when passing and shooting. Result: Fans will hear "Goooooal," a lot more often during the course of a match.

The streamlined balls are also designed to be waterproof. In rainy conditions, traditional stitched balls soak up water through their seams as players kick them around the field. The waterlogged balls become sluggish and lack spin when kicked, which is a necessary property if you're trying to bend the ball like Beckham. The new ball's panels are fused together with glue and heat so they are watertight. The ball's surface even has a goosebump-like texture that provides a better grip when a player's shoe connects with a wet ball.

Head Gear

Each year, 1.2 million high-school football players hit the gridiron. By the end of the season, about five percent of them will have experienced at least one concussion (mild traumatic brain injury), says Steven Broglio, a professor of kinesiology (study of human movement). He's testing a new high-tech system built into football helmets that could do more to protect players' heads than padding alone.

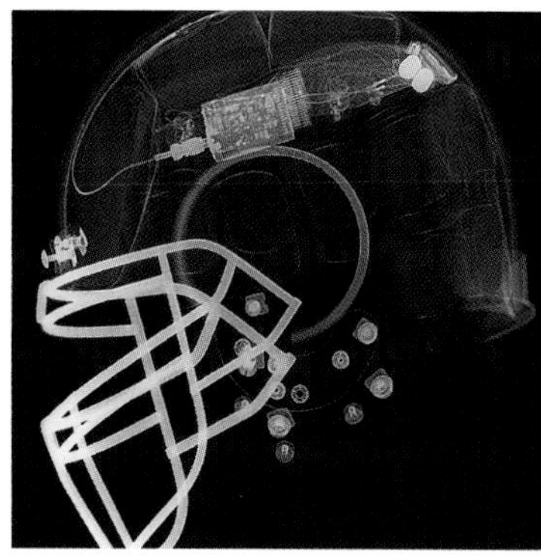

Broglio is working with a local high school football team, one of the first teams to don helmets containing six accelerometers. The sensors are part of the Head Impact Telemetry System (HITS) and measure changes in velocity when a player receives a blow to the head. "HITS can detect where and how hard an impact occurred," says Broglio. An antenna then beams the information to a sideline computer monitored by the team's athletic trainer.

After a hard-hitting tackle, many high-school players try to shake off the telltale signs of concussion, like dizziness or a headache, and get back in the game, says Broglio. Now HITS can alert a coach when a footballer should sit this game out.

Vocabulary

beanies: hats

blister: small liquid-filled bubble on the skin caused by friction

don: put on

goosebumps: little bumps on the skin caused by a reaction to cold or fear

gridiron: football field

soak up: take in

stiffen: become hardened

telltale: certain, typical

waterlogged: full of water

waterproof/watertight: able to keep water out completely

The Science Behind Our Athletes

A lot goes into making an Olympic athlete. Extraordinary skill and determination go a long way in fulfilling gold-medal dreams, but there is more to winning than hard work. Olympic athletes have their own teams of technological experts that help them get to the top of their sport.

For years, NRC has been improving athletic performance behind the scenes in its laboratories and wind tunnels. From bobsledding to speed skating, scientists know that success often depends as much on aerodynamics as on skill. For hockey players, it might be more about their stick than their stick-handling!

Famous faces in NRC's wind tunnels

Researchers at the NRC Institute for Aerospace Research in Ottawa study the effects of wind not only on vehicles and bridges, but also on athletes and their equipment, clothing and positioning. These researchers help athletes use the wind tunnel to check the aerodynamics of their body position, such as how rounded their shoulders are, or if their legs are held tightly together.

In the 1970s and 1980s, Ken Read, Steve Podborski, Rob Boyd and other Canadian downhill skiers—known as the Crazy Canucks for their wild antics on the ski hill—polished up their aerodynamic skills in the NRC wind tunnels. Speed skaters Catriona LeMay Doan and Jeremy Wotherspoon tested the aerodynamic qualities of different suits in the NRC wind tunnel. Catriona later won a gold medal at the Salt Lake City Olympics in 2002.

Most recently, members of Canada's national skeleton team, including gold, silver and bronze medallists, used the wind tunnels to assess the aerodynamics of their sleds, suits and body positioning. In the wind tunnel, the athletes could feel as though they were moving at 125 kilometres an hour and experiment with body position without worrying about falling off their sleds.

Equipment and outfits

It's not only in the wind tunnels that science and technology help Canadian athletes. A lot of innovation goes into the equipment they wear and use while competing.

Before the 1992 Olympics in Albertville, France, a team of scientists at the NRC Integrated Manufacturing Technologies Institute used lasers on bobsled runners to improve their durability and speed. NRC also designed the Olympic torch for the 1988 winter games in Calgary.

A stronger hockey stick

A team of researchers at the NRC Steacie Institute for Molecular Sciences is currently using the cutting-edge science of nanotechnology to make better hockey sticks with carbon nanotubes.

Carbon nanotubes are tiny hollow cylinders made entirely of the element carbon. They get their name from the fact that their diameters are about one nanometre across; one million times smaller than a millimetre. It is almost impossible to imagine things this small. To put it in perspective, if one of these nanotubes were as round as a piece of ordinary dental floss, the person using it would be about 1500 km tall with teeth the size of Mt. Everest!

Despite their size, carbon nanotubes are 100 times stronger than steel and only one sixth of the weight. Adding carbon nanotubes to the composites used in today's hockey sticks can dramatically improve their durability, meaning lighter, tougher and more flexible sticks that won't break at that crucial moment in the game.

Unfortunately, the current market price of nanotubes is more than 20 times that of gold. Only tiny amounts of carbon nanotubes are needed to see significant improvements in sporting good performance, making the benefits outweigh the extra cost. More widespread use of nanotubes in other areas will not come until the cost can be reduced substantially.

That is why NRC scientists are working to develop more cost-effective ways to produce carbon nanotubes and incorporate them into composites. Soon hockey players, golfers, cyclists, tennis players and athletes in other sports will begin to experience the benefits of carbon nanotubes.

Through efforts like these, NRC is helping Canada's athletes become stronger competitors who look, feel and perform better on the international stage.

Source: National Research Council Canada

Vocabulary

antics: absurd or foolish behaviour

dental floss: thin string used to clean between the teeth

skeleton: sport in which participants slide on bobsled tracks lying down, head first

steel: a strong metal alloy made from iron, carbon and other elements

Fairly Safe

What athletes may or may not do ought to be decided on grounds of safety, not fairness.

Another Olympics, another doping debate. And this time it is a fervent one, as recent advances in medical science have had the side-effect of providing athletes with new ways of enhancing performance, and thus of putting an even greater strain on people's ethical sensibilities.

This is especially true of gene therapy. Replacing defective genes holds out great promise for people suffering from diseases such as muscular dystrophy and cancer. But administered to sprightly sportsmen, the treatment may allow them to heave greater weights, swim faster and jump farther. And that would be cheating, wouldn't it?

Two notions are advanced against doping in sport: safety and fairness. The first makes sense, the second less so—particularly when it comes to gene therapy. For instance, some people have innate genetic mutations which give them exactly the same sort of edge. Eero Mantyranta, a Finn, was a double Olympic champion in cross-country skiing. His body has a mutation that causes it to produce far more of a hormone called EPO than a normal person would. This hormone stimulates the production of red blood cells. A synthetic version of it is the (banned) drug of choice for endurance athletes.

Mr. Mantyranta was allowed to compete because his advantage was held to be a "natural" gift. Yet the question of what is natural is no less vexed than that of what is fair. What is natural about electric muscle stimulation? Or nibbling on nutrients that have been cooked up by chemists? Or sprinting in special shoes made of springy carbon fibre? Statistically speaking, today's athletes are unlikely to be any more naturally gifted than their forebears, but records continue to fall. Nature is clearly getting a boost from somewhere.

Given that so much unnatural tampering takes place, the onus is surely on those who want to ban doping (genetic or otherwise) to prove that it is unusually unfair. Some point out, for instance, that it would help big, rich countries that have better access to the technology. But that already happens: Just compare the training facilities available to the minuscule Solomon Islands squad alongside those of mighty Team America. In druggy sports it may narrow the gap. One condition of greater freedom would be to enforce transparency: Athletes should disclose all the pills they take, just as they register the other forms of equipment they use, so that others can catch up.

From this perspective, the sole concern when it comes to enhancing athletic performance should be: Is it safe for the athletes? Safety is easier to measure than fairness: doctors and scientists adjudicate on such matters all the time. If gene doping proves dangerous, it can be banned. But even then, care should be exercised before a judgment is reached.

Many athletes seem perfectly willing to bear the risks of long-term effects on their health as a result of their vocations. Aged Muhammad Ali's trembling hands, for example, are a direct result of a condition tellingly named *dementia pugilistica.* Sport has always been about sacrifice and commitment. People do not admire Mr. Mantyranta because he had the luck of the genetic draw. They admire him for what he achieved with his luck. Why should others be denied the chance to remedy that deficiency?

Source: *The Economist*

Vocabulary

adjudicate: examine, judge
banned: prohibited
boost: lift, assistance
disclose: reveal
doping: taking performance drugs
enhancing: making better
nibbling: chewing
onus: responsibility to act
sprightly: in good physical shape

READ ON

Higher, Further, Faster: Is Technology Improving Sport?

by Stewart Ross

As reports of doping in sports increase, world records are continually broken. Equipment is also getting increasingly sophisticated. Author Stewart Ross, who wrote this book for the Science Museum, London, questions whether sports are becoming more exciting for spectators, or if honest competition has lost its value.

Vegetarians Face an Ethical Dilemma

By Amy Iggulden

Vegetarians who have learned to live without roast beef dinners and bacon sandwiches have been forced to make yet another major sacrifice: chocolate.

It came after the makers of Britain's most popular chocolate bars admitted that they now contain an ingredient derived from a cow's stomach.

The admission by the company who produces these treats presents the country's three million vegetarians with an ethical dilemma over whether to consume more than 20 best-selling products.

This month, the company began using animal rennet to produce the whey needed for its products, rather than a vegetarian alternative. Rennet is extracted from the stomach-lining of slaughtered newborn calves, and is used in traditional cheese production in central Europe. In Britain a microbial alternative made from mould is used.

Liz O'Neill, a spokesperson for The Vegetarian Society, said it was disappointed at the chocolate company's "backward step." "This decision rules out an enormous number of the real favourite chocolate bars, the ones that are very widely available. It is limiting choice." The society's website also urges members to write to the company to complain about the use of animal-derived whey.

Paul Goalby, the corporate affairs manager at the company producing these chocolate confections, told *The Mail on Sunday*: "Since changing the sourcing of our ingredients we are no longer able to ensure our chocolate will be animal rennet-free. So we made the principled decision to admit it was not guaranteed to be vegetarian. If the customer is an extremely strict vegetarian, then we are sorry the products are no longer suitable."

Source: *The Telegraph*, May 14, 2007

Vocabulary

mould: fungus that grows on damp or decaying organic matter

slaughtered: killed

whey: the watery part of milk produced when raw milk goes sour

PROFESSIONAL *wildlife* PHOTOGRAPHERS

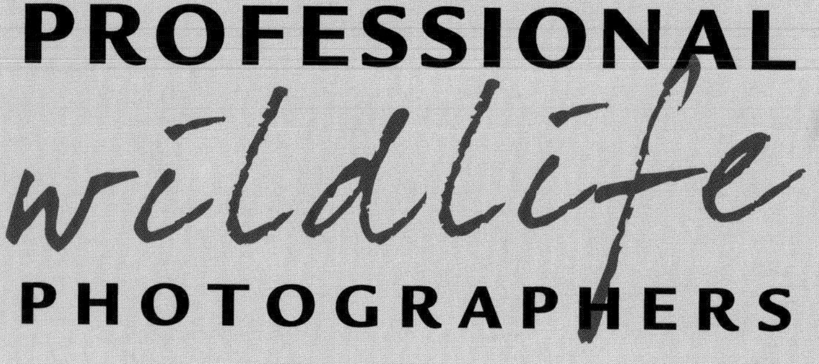

PHOTOGRAPHING WILD ANIMALS VERSUS CAPTIVE ANIMALS

Making a living by photographing wildlife can pose some difficult ethical questions for photographers. There are no specific rules or guidelines to constrain how they conduct themselves when in the field.

Photographing captive animals is one of the trickiest ethical debates facing photographers. There are many opposing opinions about what is considered true wildlife and whether captive animals qualify. If a photographer chooses to photograph a captive animal, there are no hard rules about when or if the conditions under which the image was taken should be revealed.

John E. Marriott, a photographer based in Canmore, Alberta, has spent most of his career capturing photos of Western Canada's wildlife and is an advocate of photographing non-captive wildlife; he has never taken an image for publication of a captive animal.

"I strive to get animals in their natural setting. I never get to choose the lighting or their behaviour. The animal decides if I get to photograph it," he says.

While he holds these values himself, Marriott says that only now, 13 years into his career, can he live off the income generated by his wildlife photography. He says he understands why some professionals photograph captive wildlife since it is much easier than spending days out in the field.

A fairly common practice in the industry, photographing captive wildlife can produce some stunning images of rare and mysterious creatures. While some, such as Marriott, argue these images do not depict real wildlife and can be deceiving, others, like Rebecca Grambo and Robert McCaw, disagree.

Grambo, an award-winning science writer and natural history photographer along with her husband, photographs captive animals which can otherwise be dangerous or elusive. She does this with her safety and that of the animal in mind, and says she is more concerned with the well-being of the creature than making money.

"Our line is always: 'Does this have a negative impact on the animal in some way?'" Grambo says, "We are very careful when it's just us out there. If the animal's behaviour changes, we stop."

Similarly, Robert McCaw, one of Canada's leading wildlife and nature photographers, believes that there is nothing wrong with photographing captive wildlife. Since captive animals are generally used to human interaction, photographing them, says McCaw, means less harm to "real" wildlife, which can be easily startled or frightened by a photographer's presence.

"I see no harm in photographing captive animals. I know how to read the behaviour of animals and whether they're

upset or not," says McCaw. "I think there are a lot of problems when people don't understand the behaviour."

This ethical dilemma does not end at choosing to photograph a captive or wild animal. When a photographer decides to photograph captive wildlife, he or she is then faced with the ethical decision whether or not to reveal the circumstances under which the photo was taken.

Labelling a wildlife image depicting a captive animal can have a stigma attached to it. So, some photographers would argue that it's bad business to divulge the information right away. Other photographers, like Grambo, make it top priority to clearly indicate which images are of captive wildlife.

"There's a real ethical commitment by those of us who really love the outdoors and animals to accurately portray what we're seeing and be very honest about how our pictures are taken," she says.

When a photographer decides to photograph captive wildlife, he or she is then faced with the ethical decision whether or not to reveal the circumstances under which the photo was taken.

BAITING WILDLIFE

Photographers Mike Grandmaison and John E. Marriott spent six days in Churchill, Manitoba, in November 2008, trying to get close-up pictures of the town's famously plentiful polar bears from the safety of a tundra buggy.

Both Marriott and Grandmaison are professionals in the industry, and while they don't focus entirely on wildlife photography, the purpose of this northern excursion was to get some great shots of polar bears. During a free day at the end of their trip, a few tour companies and hotel employees recommended a different kind of photo-op at a sled dog operation outside town.

"The owner feeds polar bears, he says, to get them to not eat his sled dogs, and he charges people to come in and view or photograph the bears," says Marriott, who is based in Canmore, Alberta.

Both photographers felt that this was not an ethical scenario and said no to the opportunity.

Baiting animals to get great shots is a practice that's widespread in the industry, among both professionals and amateurs. While parks and protected areas may have rules about feeding wildlife, it's not an entirely restricted practice in Canada and there are arguments both for and against it.

Grandmaison, a nature photographer based in Winnipeg, has had his work published worldwide and has authored books such as *Georgian Bay*, a photographic exploration of the region. He considers himself a naturalist, stemming from his time spent at Laurentian University studying biology. Grandmaison believes in trying to protect the subject and the environment as much as possible and that baiting could adversely affect animals. "Baiting can certainly be disruptive," he says, "which could lead you to problems since you are changing the behaviour of the animal."

For a photographer to decide whether he or she will coax animals toward their lens with bait, they first must determine what actions

constitute baiting. For some, like Marriot, who avoid the practice, baiting means enticing wildlife with any type of food or water or an illusion of the two. Others tend to think there are more grey areas in the definition of baiting and that photographers must use their discretion based on the situation.

"To me, it is simple: if you attract wildlife with food or water, you are baiting," said photographer Ethan Meleg in an email. "I can't understand how it's different to feed something for the purpose of watching it versus taking a photo."

Ethan Meleg, an established outdoor photographer from Wheatley, Ontario, has had a love for nature and wildlife since he was a child and is currently on a one-and-a-half-year-long photo expedition exploring North and Central America. While Meleg says he doesn't bait often, he does believe it can be an appropriate and useful technique for capturing images in certain situations. However, he also says that the practice requires extensive knowledge and experience to determine which situations are less dangerous – to the animal or the human.

"If you do bait a subject, it is important that you are baiting in a way that mimics or is identical to a natural setting," he said in an email. "A photographer must also be prepared to not bait if it poses a risk to the animal."

Similarly, Grandmaison, while he seldom practises baiting himself, says that some photographers would agree that there could be less adverse effects on certain species if baiting were carried out in an informed and responsible manner. "Sometimes you have to look at the broader situation. It may be different baiting a bear than baiting a chipmunk," he says.

While these photographers might not see eye-to-eye on the many grey areas of baiting in wildlife photography, Marriott, Grandmaison and Meleg all agree that this practice may not be as harmful a technique on certain animals as it is on others.

Grey areas aside, responsibility and knowledge of a species' behaviour are huge factors in determining what the harmful consequences of baiting wildlife are. Some photographers argue that any interference with the animal can have detrimental results, while others, like Meleg, argue that baiting, in the right circumstances and with the proper knowledge, will not cause harm to the animal and may have positive results for both the animal and photographer.

"We are at a time when out society is increasingly losing touch with nature," he said in an email. "The photos or simply the enjoyment that results from responsible feeding of wildlife may help strengthen our connection with the natural world."

Source: Michela Rosano, *Canadian Geographic Photo*

Vocabulary

buggy: vehicle used to navigate through difficult terrain
mimics: imitates
photo-op: slang for opportunity to take a photograph
plentiful: abundant
portray: depict
see eye-to-eye: agree upon
stigma: negative image or idea
stunning: compelling, extremely beautiful
trickiest: most complicated

CIRCUS ANIMALS: Abused and Dangerous

by RaeLeann Smith

Four zebras and three horses recently escaped from the Ringling Bros. and Barnum & Bailey Circus in Colorado and ran loose near a busy interstate highway for 30 minutes. This harrowing incident is just the latest in a long series of escapes and rampages that illustrate the dangers that animals in circuses pose to both themselves and the public. Transporting wild animals from town to town is inherently stressful for these animals, as it requires that they be separated from their families and social groups and intensively confined or chained for extended periods of time. It's no surprise that many animals try to escape.

The modern circus traces its history to the Roman Circus Maximus, an elongated U-shaped arena constructed in a long narrow valley between two of Rome's seven hills. In the arena, both aristocrats and commoners attended chariot races, equestrian events, and, later, wild-animal displays. Although the events staged in the Circus Maximus began as fairly benign popular entertainment, they became increasingly violent spectacles. Little attention was paid to those injured or killed during these events—slaves and animals—because they were "nonpersons" according to Roman law.

The modern circus arose in the early 19th century, beginning with equestrian and acrobatic acts. A circus first claimed to have tamed wild animals in 1820. In 1851 George Bailey added a menagerie, including elephants, to his show. Flying trapeze artists, clowns, and a live orchestra rounded out the fledgling circus. In 1871 a human "freak" show was added.

Although human freak shows have nearly disappeared, animal circuses otherwise continue relatively unchanged. Animals in circuses are still deprived of their basic needs to exercise, roam, socialize, forage, and play. Signs of their mental anguish include a plethora of stereotypical behaviours, such as swaying, pacing, bar-biting, and self-mutilating. Sometimes these animals lash out, injuring and killing trainers, caretakers, and members of the public. They are transported up to 50 weeks a year in stifling, cramped, and dirty trailers and train cars and are forced to perform confusing and physically challenging tricks, such as standing on their heads, riding bicycles, or jumping through rings of fire. In the wild, these animals would be ranging long distances and enjoying rich social lives.

Animal Abuse

The harsh treatment of animals in circuses has spawned protests by humane societies and animal rights groups, which have focused on abusive training and handling practices, the constant confinement endured by the animals, and the dangers that animal circuses pose to the public.

Training methods for animals used in circuses involve varying degrees of punishment and deprivation. Animals perform not because they want to but because they're afraid not to. In the United States, no government agency monitors animal training sessions.

Former Ringling animal crew employees Archele Hundley and Bob Tom contacted PETA [People for the Ethical Treatment of Animals] independently after witnessing what they described as routine animal abuse in the circus, including a 30-minute beating of an elephant in Tulsa, Oklahoma, that left the animal screaming and bleeding profusely from her wounds. Hundley and Tom reported that elephants are chained whenever they are out of public view and are forced to perform while sick or injured. They also reported that horses are grabbed by the throat, stabbed with pitchforks, punched in the face, given painful "lip twists," and whipped. Other Ringling whistleblowers have confirmed these abuses.

PETA obtained undercover video footage of the Carson & Barnes Circus that

shows elephant trainer Tim Frisco beating elephants with a sharp metal training device called a "bullhook" during a training session. The animals cry out in pain. Frisco tells other trainers, "Hurt 'em. Make 'em scream." Frisco also warns other trainers to avoid beating the elephants in public view. Undercover video footage of animal training at various other facilities has revealed the widespread use of abusive techniques, including beating elephants with bullhooks and shocking them with electric prods, striking big cats with whips and sticks and dragging them by heavy chains tied around their necks, smacking and prodding bears with long poles, and kicking chimpanzees and beating them with riding crops.

Animals used in circuses may travel thousands of kilometres a year during extreme weather conditions. They are confined to boxcars and trailers and have no access to basic necessities, such as food, water, and veterinary care. Some elephants spend most of their lives in shackles. One study of travelling circuses reported on an elephant who was forced to spend up to 96 percent of her time in chains. Tigers and lions usually live and travel in cages that are four feet high, seven feet long, and seven feet wide, with two big cats crammed into a single cage. Big cats, bears, and primates are forced to eat, drink, sleep, defecate, and urinate in the same cramped cages.

Constant travel, forced inactivity, and long hours standing on hard surfaces in their own waste lead to serious health problems and early death in captive elephants. At least 25 elephants with Ringling have died since 1992, including four babies. Circuses routinely tear unweaned baby elephants from their mothers to be trained and sent on the road.

Escapes and Attacks

There have been hundreds of incidents involving animal attacks and escapes from animal circuses, often resulting in property damage, injuries, and death for both humans and animals.

Perhaps the most dramatic animal attack involved Tyke, an elephant traveling with Circus International in Honolulu in 1994. In an hour-long episode, Tyke killed her trainer and caused injuries to more than a dozen people. Police fired 87 bullets into Tyke before finally killing her. This was not the first time that Tyke had acted out; she had previously caused $10 000 in damage during a Shriner Circus performance in Altoona, Pa., and attacked a trainer in North Dakota, breaking two of his ribs.

Other attacks by elephants, big cats, primates, and bears are common but haven't received as much media attention because they are rarely videotaped. Many circuses, including Ringling, do not allow video cameras in the arena. In order to avoid publicity, circuses are often quick to settle lawsuits that allege injuries.

Circus Bans

More than a dozen municipalities in the United States have banned performances that feature wild animals. Costa Rica, Sweden, Singapore, Finland, India, and Austria ban or restrict wild animal performances nationwide. Districts in Australia, Argentina, Brazil, Canada, Colombia, and Greece ban some or all animal acts. PETA has been campaigning in the United States for specific bans on the most abusive circus practices, including chaining elephants and using training tools that cause pain and suffering, such as bullhooks and electric prods.

New Trends

Circuses that use animals have been struggling with falling attendance rates and public disillusionment as people learn more about wild animals and their complex physical and emotional needs. Many of the smaller animal circuses have merged or gone out of business. The trend in circus entertainment has been shifting away from the use of animals, as evidenced by the hugely successful Cirque du Soleil. This Montréal-based circus, founded by two street performers in 1984, features only human performers and now has as many as 15 shows running simultaneously around the world. With attendance at animal circuses dwindling, smaller, nonanimal circuses have proliferated, including the New Pickle Circus, the Imperial Circus of China, the Hiccup Circus, and the Flying High Circus.

Source: Encyclopedia Britannica Blog, November 6, 2007

Vocabulary

benign: not harmful
crammed: forced into a small space
dwindling: decreasing
pacing: walking back and forth
plethora: wide range
roam: move about freely
shackles: metal cuffs attached to chains
spawned: given rise to
whistleblowers: people who report abuse from within an organization

READ ON

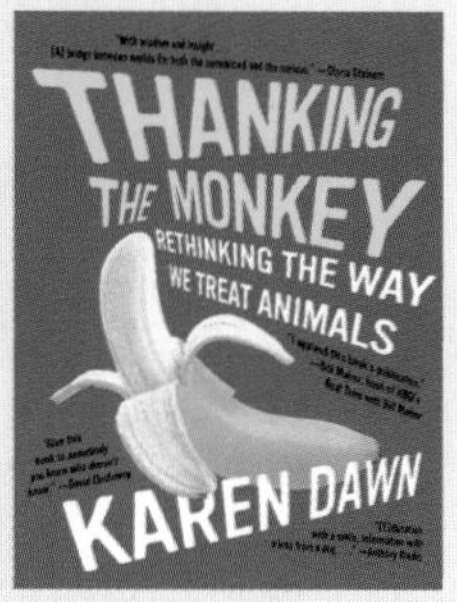

Thanking the Monkey: Rethinking the Way We Treat Animals

by Karen Dawn

Noted animal activist and columnist Karen Dawn takes a lighthearted approach to a very serious subject in this fun and yet thorough book about how humans and animals interact, from having pets to wearing and eating animal products, from animal testing to wildlife studies. Designed for today's generation of socially aware consumers, this book shows how we can do a better job respecting not only the monkey, but the animal kingdom overall.

How to Write Ultimate Protest Songs

You have to use your imagination
To get across the situation
You can simplify or overstate
To make it easier to relate
You can go right over the top
With a list of things you want to stop
Or you can concentrate on just one wrong
And make it easier to sing along

But if you say "I don't like this"
(Or that or the other in a big long list)
Then people write you off as a pessimist
Providing no alternatives
Or if you decide to simplify
And use four-letter words and spit in the sky
Then they'll chant the slogans and won't even try
To understand the reasons why

So perhaps the only way to make clear
The views you'd like everyone to hear
Is by taking a piece of everyday life
And looking at it closer in a different light
Let's take an example—the way we eat
Sat at the table and it's all so neat
Now you can understand that cos that's "how it's done"
And it's probably happened to everyone

Having caught the attention, you now decide
How far to push your thoughts outside
There's loads of angles, like dining out
The hunger of the old man whose cash ran out
The money made by corporations
Selling bombs not food to starving nations
You see there's a worldwide scope of affiliations
Depending how far you wanna stretch imaginations

Insert a little optimism now and then
Before complaining becomes a trend
Repetition defeats the point in the end
It numbs imagination 'til it can't comprehend
So walk the line between humour and gloom
Amongst the debris there's just enough room
To keep your mentality going strong
And create some ultimate protest songs

Source: Citizen Fish, from the album "Free Souls in a Trapped Environment"

Vocabulary

cos: shortened slang for *because*

numbs: takes away pain or feeling

overstate: exaggerate

slogans: memorable words or phrases used for advertising or protests

wanna: slang for *want to*

Music for All Seasons: One Musician's Story

When I was asked if I could sing at a foster care home and a battered women's shelter [for Music for All Seasons, a program providing musical performances for people who are unable to attend concerts], I was happy to be working and I looked forward to spending an afternoon with Dave M., with whom I have worked for 20 years. I accepted the gig and planned my repertoire and outfit. Little did I know when I left my house in the morning that I would return a different person that evening.

The first thing that moved me when I arrived at the foster home was the sign on the front of the building. This sign indicated that it was a safe place to leave a newborn. Tears came to my eyes. Then came the children and young adults who lived there. They were beautiful, clean, innocent beings with longing in their eyes. I know teenagers. These were different. One teenage boy was fixated on the music. He watched as if there were a magic answer contained in each song. And another who looked as if he should be bored with our music—he was mesmerized. And then there were the two beautiful fourteen-year-olds, one with a baby just starting to show. The other had just lost one a few months ago and was almost certain that she was pregnant again. She lost the last one because her boyfriend (now in jail) got mad at her and kicked her until she miscarried. But she has a new boyfriend now and they want this baby. I wanted to hold them both, protect them and teach them that life could be different. I was powerless except to give their teacher my email and ask them to keep in touch. Then we sang a song. They sang backup to my lead vocal. One of them got up and sang the national anthem with talent, strength and potential. She was amazing! I wanted to tell them that there is life outside of this place. They could have a future. All I could do was try to hide my tears.

The battered women's shelter was our next stop. A woman named "Susan" (not her real name) walked in with her three children. I'm not sure that I can be eloquent enough to describe what I felt from this family, but I knew without a doubt that they had just experienced something very big and very ugly. The children stared into space as if they had just seen a huge monster or a ghost. The little girl seemed in another world, and it seemed that she knew something was not right. Susan was shattered. I wanted so badly to sit and talk with her. To ask her what happened. To take her home with me, and give her a safe place. She was devastated. I found my repertoire changing from kids' songs to songs of hope and friendship. Then Susan requested "Bridge Over Troubled Water," which is one of my all-time favourite songs. Unfortunately, I had never performed it. But the very sweet woman in charge went to her computer, printed out the lyrics from a lyric website and Dave and I went for it. I sang it with all my might.

When we were finished with our program, I felt drained and exhilarated at the same time. I wanted to do so much more. I wanted to fix everyone. I wanted to change the world.

As I have said many times since that day, I will give my talents to these people whenever I can. I hope in my lifetime I can do more. If all people could spend one day like this, witnessing the people in these circumstances, the world just might be a better place.

Source: Music for All Seasons

Vocabulary

devastated: completely destroyed emotionally

exhilarated: euphoric

foster care home: place where children whose birth parents are unable to care for them are looked after by parental figures

mesmerized: hypnotized

miscarried: experienced the premature death of a fetus due to medical difficulties

newborn: baby that has just been born

shelter: safe place to stay

Playing for Change: Peace through Music

Mark Johnson: The Music of Inspiration

About 10 years ago in New York City, I was headed to work one morning, and, while in the subway, I witnessed a musical performance by two monks painted white from head to toe. They were wearing brown robes, and one of them was singing in a foreign language while the other man played a nylon guitar. I remember seeing about 200 people—of different cultures, races and genders—stop and listen to the music. Everyone there was so moved by the performance even though I can't imagine many of us knew what they were singing about. It occurred to me that there existed in this moment in time a strong sense of human connection and the ability to overcome our differences as people. I decided right then and there that music is the key to a better world. I also realized it was my calling to go out and find as many of these inspiring human moments as possible. This became the first event that triggered the idea of *Playing for Change: Peace Through Music.*

I remember asking myself a serious question before embarking on the journey of making this film. How can I make a film that inspires everyone on the planet to come together as one? The answer is found in the universal language of music. Throughout the film, we make songs around the world in which musicians from across the globe, who have never before met, unite together to make songs. This act of playing music with people of different cultures, religions, economics and politics is a powerful statement. It further illustrates that we can find

ways of working together and sharing our experiences with one another in a positive way.

Before we were ever different, we were all human beings.

When trying to document music, art and heartfelt dialogue, we found that inspiration and an open mind are essential factors. The driving force for this film is to find a way to inspire the planet to come together as a human race. We wanted to focus on our connections rather than all of our differences. We believe music can break down the walls and barriers between cultures and raise the level of human understanding and connection.

Here are some direct examples of what I am talking about. We travelled to New Orleans shortly after the devastation of Hurricane Katrina. The city felt sad and desolate, yet the music never stopped. The street musicians and music in the clubs kept the city alive and gave it a sense of hope. When we share the struggle of New Orleans with other parts of the world in the context of song, it becomes something that everyone on the planet can understand and be a part of. The same is true in South Africa. When we visited South Africa and witnessed the pain of the aftermath of apartheid, we saw that through music we can raise the issue to a human situation rather than one of race and economics. The South Africans marching down the streets singing in groups of thousands did more to effect positive change than all the guns and weapons ever did. One of the musicians we recorded in South Africa, named Bhekani Memela, offered us this quote, "Because music knows no races, knows no boundaries, it is possible for music to bring peace around the world."

Everywhere on this planet, people play music. Some may play to celebrate life, some may play to stay as far away from the grave as possible. The reasons for playing music may

differ everywhere you go, but the human impact it has on all of our souls is something we share. I believe that when people watch this film, they will feel more connected to the human race and more inspired to help each other. Perhaps nothing can do more do connect a planet so divided by war, economics, religion and race than music! As Bob Marley said,"One great thing about music: When it hits, you feel no pain."

Playing for Change: Peace Through Music is a documentary film which demonstrates that music will change the world and help bring us all peace. The film features more than 100 musicians and includes live performances, from native Indian reservations to South African townships to the Himalayan mountains. Music has always been an integral part of the identity and expression of various cultures on this planet. However, music's greatest power is its ability to transcend cultural boundaries and connect us as a human race.

Jonathan Walls: Figuring Out How to Play for Change

The concept of *Playing for Change* was relayed to me in 1999. I had just finished a directing workshop at the New York Film Academy and was excited to dive into the craft of storytelling on a professional level, but wasn't sure where my path would ignite. I got a call from a childhood friend who was living in Los Angeles at the time and he told me of a documentary idea that his roommate had about street musicians. His roommate was Mark Johnson and his idea was *Playing for Change*. A month later I was living on their couch, trying to find a way to make the film a reality. Now, a decade later, it is not only a reality, but also a way of life. Mark and I have been creative partners on the Playing for Change film series ever since.

Our first film, *Playing for Change: A Cinematic Discovery of Music*, explored the lives, culture and music of American street musicians. In the beginning, my interest in the concept revolved around my fascination with the courage, commitment, freedom and artistic expression street musicians possessed. The lifestyle they lead felt very close to my heart and the way I was intending to live my life as a filmmaker. Spontaneous. Nomadic. Open. True. Free. The essence I felt, at its core, was the understanding to reach a belief in oneself, being exactly who you wanted to be and actively doing what you desire to do, what you desire to express to the world. For the street musicians it was their music, for me it was films.

Since then, the concept has evolved into an exhilarating movement toward peace. *Playing for Change: Peace Through Music* is our second journey, our second film in this everlong vision of connecting the world through music. To whittle down the experiences I had while making these films is an immense task not only because each moment had its story, but also because each moment had its wisdom. Those stories and those wisdoms felt along the way have countless paths of thought that I'm still retracing. To travel the earth and to absorb its spectrum of differences and similarities became frustrating, enlightening and exhilarating all at once. To ponder our path is overwhelming, but when I simplify its core, I realize we are all still humans beings and we are all one. When this understanding sank in, as it did for me while filming, the mysteries of life disappeared. And then I listened to the music.

Sources: *Moving Pictures Magazine; Huffington Post;* Photos by François Vigué, courtesy of the filmmaker

Vocabulary

boundaries: borders
embarking on: beginning
everlong: continuing
heartfelt: sincere
ignite: take off, become active
overcome: move past or surmount
whittle down: reduce to essential details

READ ON

The Cellist of Sarajevo
by Steven Galloway

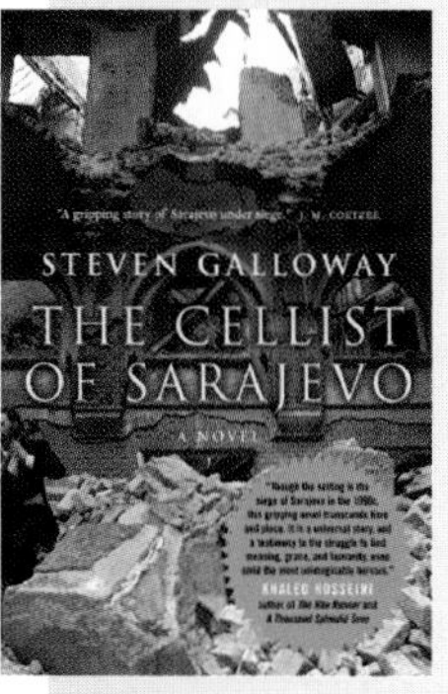

This beautifully written novel tells the story of three people trying to survive in a city torn apart by violence. They are accompanied by a mourning cellist, who vows to honour the dead by playing a piece reconstructed from the fragment of a destroyed musical score, once for each victim. Those who hear his tune cannot help but hold on to the hope that life, and music, will prevail.

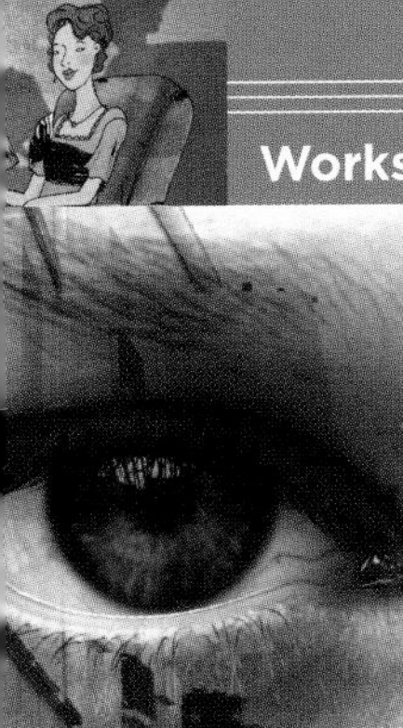

If You Lived Here, You'd Be Home by Now

by Joe Bowers

It was cold. Cold for this time of year anyway. Cold for Louisiana. The wind cut as it blew by. The heat so common to this place, the sticky wet heat and insect buzz that filled most of the year, was gone; cold had come and taken its place. But the sky was still overcast. It usually was. The grey was constant.

The boy was grey, too. He wore an olive green trenchcoat (an army castoff like his boots) over funereal black, greasy hair obscuring his eyes. They must have been grey. He was narrow-shouldered and small, and walked like he was in a trance. I suppose he was. It was trance weather.

He wore headphones. He didn't sing along. He turned left after he crossed the railroad tracks and walked down the road. The ground was covered in leaves, wet and thoroughly dead. They were a hundred shades of light to dark brownish-gold, and might have been almost beautiful on warmer days. As it was, all shades hit the eye together, as a variation of a more familiar colour, an echo of the sky. He walked past Brewbacher's Grill and The Daiquiri Café and into a shop with its shades down.

The writing on the front said: FUST'S COMIC BOOK EMPORIUM: Buy, Sell, and Trade New and Back Issues Sports Trading Cards and More!

The boy went inside and stayed there for quite some time.

When he came out, he had a brown paper bag with him. He sat down in front of the store, pulled a bright coloured magazine from the bag, and began to read. A passerby might have thought the boy was dead. He sat with a blank look on his face, pale and black and green against the vivid paper cover, blasting Action! and Adventure! and sometimes Terror! or Romance! into the atmosphere in lurid red or blue or sharp yellow lettering. He sat still. Very still. Occasionally he would turn a page, with an almost undetectable move of the thumb. He was that way for a long time, breaking his trance every once in a while quickly to exchange the comic in hand for one in the bag. He was never without an open book for long, dropping the used issues on the ground, where they lay swollen with vibrance on the icy concrete.

The daylight was dimmer when he looked up into the real world again and he blinked and shook his head quickly, like one newly awakened, shaking sleep from his mind. He rose slowly, painfully, like an arthritic. He gathered up his books and walked back past the bars, then across the tracks past the Circle K and down the road a ways. He passed a Chinese restaurant, its parking lot filling up for evening business. A group of young people hung around in front of it, getting out of their cars, not much older than he was. They were typical Baton Rouge youth: grinning young men in baseball caps with broad shoulders and cheeks and close-cropped hair. One had his arm around a girl with a painted face and a beautiful scraping false giggle. The boy stopped to watch them in the twilight, hiding himself in the pool of shadow by the side of the building. They shouted good-natured insults at each other in the cold, and went inside. They looked like angels. The boy walked on.

It was almost dark when he got to the hobby shop. It was dark when he came back out of it, carrying a plastic bag with model paints and glue.

Vocabulary

close-cropped: very short

funereal: suggestive of a grave or burial

levee: a barrier that contains the flow of water

life-hum: surrounding sounds blended together

lurid: shining with an unnatural glow

scraping: harsh

squinted: closed the eyes slightly

vibrance: a quality of resonance or strong presence

vivid: bright

He passed the Chinese restaurant again; the evening rush was in full swing. He took his headphones off.

The light was bright and gold through the glass door, and he shaded his face with an arm as he walked by, squinted under it as he passed. God, it looked warm.

It was warm, and busy. Had he walked inside he would have heard the low rumble of a thousand conversations, blending 'til no one word was intelligible. The sounds of people laughing, of small talk and ordering, the sounds of men telling women how beautiful their eyes were, of women telling women how all men were scum, of people complaining about the cold, of people complaining about the food, of people, people, people would all run together into a wonderful life-hum, sweet like night crickets and the rustle of leaves in the wind of summer, sweet like a woman's sigh or the warm beat of her heart. But he passed by the door in the cold and back into the dark, hearing only the wind. There was no sense in warming up if he only had to face the cold again on the way home.

There was no sense in warming up if he only had to face the cold again on the way home.

He put the earphones back on; walked more quickly back past the Circle K and over the railroad tracks, through the leaf-mud on the side of River Road. The levee came into view, separating the dark road from the Mississippi. He hurried past the entrance to a subdivision and past houses and houses, past people eating dinner behind lit windows. He took three turns (a right and two lefts) and then stopped at one of the houses. He didn't go in. He walked around back.

The carport light was on. A bicycle, more rust than dull, chipped red, sat against a moss-covered wall. It hadn't been used since the fall. The moss had frozen to death. He passed through it, stopped when he got to a sliding glass door in the wall. The curtains were down. He opened it and stepped into blackness.

He placed his purchases on the floor beside him, keeping his feet planted firmly in place as if there were things on the ground he would rather not upset. He felt the wall for a switch. Then he spoke.

He cried, "Let There Be Light!

And there was.

And it shone down upon a city and countryside in miniature, a model landscape of houses and green trees spread out on foam grass and dirt over three card tables, a desk and the tops of two dressers. The light was warm and golden, and revealed incredible microscopic detail in brilliant colour, down to a tiny orange Circle K sign in front of the convenience store, down to the painted wavelets of a brilliant blue river, down to a shining red bicycle parked outside a tiny Chinese restaurant. The light shone down from a ceiling painted bright, brilliant blue, the same colour as his eyes.

Source: The EServer Collection: Fiction

The Fisherman *and His Wife*

Once, there was a fisherman who lived with his wife in a miserable little shack near the sea. He went to fish every day, but almost never caught anything. But at last, one day, something tugged at his line. Excited, he hauled it up out of the sea to find a great flounder at the end of the line. The flounder spoke: "Stop, fisherman! Please don't kill me, for I am an enchanted prince! What good will it do for you to kill me, anyway? I won't taste good . . . so put me back in the water and let me swim away!"

"Well," replied the fisherman, "You don't have to go on and on about it. I was ready to put you back the moment you started talking." And so, the fisherman released the flounder back into the shining water, and it sank down to the bottom of the sea, leaving behind a thin trail of blood.

When the fisherman got home, his wife shouted, "What, husband? Have you caught nothing today?"

"No," said the fisherman. "All I caught was a flounder who said he was an enchanted prince, so I let him go."

"Well, what did you wish for, then?" asked his wife.

"What do you mean, what did I wish for?" said the fisherman.

"Oh, husband! He's an enchanted prince, so surely you could have had a wish granted! Do you want to live in a shack like this for the rest of our days? The least you could have done was to wish for a nice cottage! Go back and ask the fish for a pretty cottage. You spared his life—it's the least he can do to repay you!"

The fisherman, feeling quite stupid, reluctantly went back to the sea to find the fish. The sea, oddly, had turned dull and green. The fisherman stood by it and said:

"Flounder, flounder in the sea,
Please, listen to me:
My wife, Ilsebil, wants her own way
No matter what I do or say."

The flounder came swimming to the surface and said, "Well, what do you want?"

"I'm sorry," said the fisherman, "but my wife made me come to call you. She thinks I should have wished for something as I let you go, and she wants a pretty cottage instead of our old shack."

"Go home," said the flounder. "She has her wish."

The fisherman went home and found his wife sitting on a bench outside a lovely little cottage, with a garden full of flowers and vegetables, and a yard with chickens and ducks. Inside, there was a pretty little sitting room, a fine bed in the bedroom, and a kitchen and pantry furnished with everything they could possibly need. His wife said, "There, now, isn't this much better than our old shack?"

The fisherman had to agree, and said, "Yes, and now we can be happy."

His wife replied, "We'll see about that." Then they had a good supper and went to bed.

For a week, everything was fine in their lovely new home. But the fisherman's wife wanted more. "Listen, husband," she insisted, "this cottage is too tiny. The flounder could have given us a bigger house, you know. I want to live in a castle. Go ask him for a big stone castle."

"But wife, what on earth are we going to do in a castle? There is no need for this! Besides, I don't want to make the flounder angry."

"I don't care, I want a castle. If the fish can grant wishes, he can easily grant us this. Now, go back and ask him to give us a castle!"

The fisherman's heart was heavy, but he felt he must do what his wife asked. So he went back to the sea, which had turned a dark violet and grey colour. He stood by the sea and said:

"Flounder, flounder in the sea,
Please, listen to me:
My wife, Ilsebil, wants her own way
No matter what I do or say."

The flounder came swimming to the surface and said, "Now, what do you want?"

"I'm sorry," said the fisherman, half-scared, "but my wife wants a big stone castle."

"Go home," said the flounder. "She is standing at the door of it."

The fisherman went home, thinking he might no longer even have a house, but there was a big stone castle there, and indeed, his wife was standing in the doorway, clothed in a fancy brocade dress. She took him by the hand and showed him the grand hallway, with marble floors everywhere, and rich tapestries hanging in every room. Tables in the dining room were decked out with a feast, and outside the house were stables with carriages and fine horses. There was a beautiful garden outside, and a park full of every kind of animal one could wish to hunt. "Now," said the wife, "Isn't this better?"

"Oh, yes," said the fisherman. "Now we have everything we will ever need."

"We will see about that," said his wife.

And sure enough, the next morning, as his wife looked out their bedroom window at the rolling hills and lovely garden, she said to him, "Husband, why can't we be King over all of this land? I want to be King. Go to the flounder and tell him to make us King! We must be King!"

"But wife, I don't want to be King! I can't ask him that!" said the fisherman.

"You must go. I will be King," insisted his wife.

So the fisherman went, feeling terribly sad the whole way down to the sea, and muttering to himself, "It's just not right." When he reached the sea, it was dark and grey, rough and foul-smelling. He stood there and said:

"Flounder, flounder in the sea,
Please, listen to me:
My wife, Ilsebil, wants her own way
No matter what I do or say."

The flounder said,"Now, what does she want?"

"I'm sorry," said the fisherman, half-scared, "but now she wants to be King."

"Go back," said the flounder. "She is already King."

When the fisherman went back, he was greeted by a sentry, playing trumpets and drums. Velvet hung from the walls, and everything was decorated in marble and gold. His wife was sitting on a bejewelled throne, with a gold crown on her head and a sceptre in her hand. She was surrounded by servants.

Her husband stood before her and said, "I suppose you are King now."

"Yes, I am," she replied uneasily, "but I am bored with it. I can't bear it any longer. I want to be Emperor."

"What?! Isn't it enough for you to be King? I will not ask the flounder for anything more, wife! It isn't right!" cried the fisherman.

"Husband, I will be Emperor, and you will go ask the flounder to make it so."

"But wife, there is only one Emperor in the land! The flounder can't make you Emperor!" whimpered the fisherman.

"Excuse me, but I am King,"shouted the wife," and you are merely a husband. Go tell the flounder to make me Emperor!"

So the husband, feeling weak in the knees and sick to his stomach, went back to the sea. Clouds rushed across the sky, the wind whipped his clothes around him, and in the distance he could hear the distress signals of ships being tossed on the waves. Leaves fell from the trees, and the water foamed and dashed upon the shore. Near the horizon, the clouds were an angry dark red, as in a bad storm. Despairing, the fisherman said:

"Flounder, flounder in the sea,
Please, listen to me:
My wife, Ilsebil, wants her own way
No matter what I do or say."

The flounder said, "What does she want now?"

"I'm sorry," said the fisherman, trembling in his boots, "but she wants to be Emperor."

"Go back," said the flounder."She is Emperor."

When the fisherman returned home, he saw that the palace was surrounded by marble statues, and the doors were guarded by soldiers marching back and forth. Inside, counts, barons and dukes walked about as attendants, and they led him to his wife, who was sitting on a huge throne of pure gold. On her head was a three-crown set, studded with diamonds, and she was surrounded by princes. In one hand, she held a sceptre, and in the other, the golden ball signifying the power of the empire.

Her husband said, "So, wife, are you now Emperor? Is it that much better? Surely you must be content, for there is no higher position you can attain."

"We will see about that," said the wife. And sure enough, when she awoke to see the sun rise, she wanted to make it rise herself. She shook her husband awake and said, "Wake up and go to the flounder. Tell him I must be Lord of the Universe."

"What?" mumbled the fisherman, still half asleep, thinking he must have heard her wrong.

"Husband, if I cannot be Lord of the Universe, and cause the sun and moon to set and rise, I will not be able to stand it. I will never be happy again."

"Wife, control yourself! This is one thing the flounder cannot do! It is not possible!"said the fisherman.

His wife, wild-eyed, flew into a terrible rage, kicking him and screaming. "I won't bear it any longer—go!"

The fisherman pulled on his trousers as fast as he could and ran like a madman out of the room. He rushed to the sea, hardly keeping his balance, as the wind threatened to lift him up and smash him on the rocks. Houses around him quivered, trees swayed, and cliffs began to crumble into the black, boiling sea. The fisherman could barely hear himself shriek:

"Flounder, flounder in the sea,
Please, listen to me:
My wife, Ilsebil, wants her own way
No matter what I do or say."

The flounder said, "What does she want now?"

"I'm sorry," shouted the fisherman over the wild cries of the wind, "but now she wants to be Lord of the Universe."

"Go back," said the flounder. "She is sitting in her old shack, and there she will stay."

And indeed, the fisherman and his wife have been there to this day.

Source: Adapted from The Brothers Grimm

Vocabulary

crumble: fall apart
decked out: covered in a beautiful way
foul-smelling: smelling bad
grant: give
muttering: speaking quietly
pantry: small room to store food and other supplies
shack: small, run-down hut
tugged: pulled

All Summer In a Day

By Ray Bradbury

"Ready?"

"Ready."

"Now?"

"Soon."

"Do the scientists really know? Will it happen today, will it?"

"Look, look; see for yourself!"

The children pressed to each other like so many roses, so many weeds, intermixed, peering out for a look at the hidden sun.

It rained.

It had been raining for seven years; thousands upon thousands of days compounded and filled from one end to the other with rain, with the drum and gush of water, with the sweet crystal fall of showers and the concussion of storms so heavy they were tidal waves come over the islands. A thousand forests had been crushed under the rain and grown up a thousand times to be crushed again. And this was the way life was forever on the planet Venus, and this was the schoolroom of the children of the rocket men and women who had come to a raining world to set up civilization and live out their lives.

"It's stopping, it's stopping!"

"Yes, yes!"

Margot stood apart from them, from these children who could never remember a time when there wasn't rain and rain and rain. They were all nine years old, and if there had been a day, seven years ago, when the sun came out for an hour and showed its face to the stunned world, they could not recall. Sometimes, at night, she heard them stir, in remembrance, and she knew they were dreaming and remembering gold or a yellow crayon or a coin large enough to buy the world with. She knew they thought they remembered a warmness, like a blushing in the face, in the body, in the arms and legs and trembling hands. But then they always awoke to the tatting drum, the endless shaking down of clear bead necklaces upon the roof, the walk, the gardens, the forests, and their dreams were gone.

All day yesterday they had read in class about the sun. About how like a lemon it was, and how hot. And they had written small stories or essays or poems about it:

I think the sun is a flower,
That blooms for just one hour.

That was Margot's poem, read in a quiet voice in the still classroom while the rain was falling outside.

"Aw, you didn't write that!" protested one of the boys.

"I did," said Margot. "I did."

"William!" said the teacher.

But that was yesterday. Now the rain was slackening, and the children were crushed in the great thick windows.

"Where's teacher?"

"She'll be back."

"She'd better hurry, we'll miss it!"

They turned on themselves, like a feverish wheel, all tumbling spokes.

Margot stood alone. She was a very frail girl who looked as if she had been lost in the rain for years and the rain had washed out the blue from her eyes and the red from her mouth and the yellow from her hair. She was an old photograph dusted from an album, whitened away, and if she spoke at all her voice would be a ghost. Now she stood, separate, staring at the rain and the loud wet world beyond the huge glass.

"What're *you* looking at?" said William.

Margot said nothing.

"Speak when you're spoken to." He gave her a shove. But she did not move; rather she let herself be moved only by him and nothing else.

They edged away from her, they would not look at her. She felt them go away. And this was because she would play no games with them in the echoing tunnels of the underground city. If they tagged her and ran, she stood blinking after them and did not follow. When the class sang songs about happiness and life and games her lips barely moved. Only when they sang about the sun and the summer did her lips move as she watched the drenched windows.

And then, of course, the biggest crime of all was that she had come here only five years ago from Earth, and she remembered the sun and the way the sun was and the sky was when she was four in Ohio. And they, they had been on Venus all their lives, and they had been only two years old when last the sun came out and had long since forgotten the color and heat of it and the way it really was. But Margot remembered.

"It's like a penny," she said once, eyes closed.

"No it's not!" the children cried.

"It's like a fire," she said, "in the stove."

"You're lying, you don't remember!" cried the children.

But she remembered and stood quietly apart from all of them and watched the patterning windows. And once, a month ago, she had refused to shower in the school shower rooms, had clutched her hands to her ears and over her head, screaming the water mustn't touch her head. So after that, dimly, dimly, she sensed it, she was different and they knew her difference and kept away.

There was talk that her father and mother were taking her back to Earth next year; it seemed vital to her that they do so, though it would mean the loss of thousands of dollars to her family. And so, the children hated her for all these reasons of big and little consequence. They hated her pale snow face, her waiting silence, her thinness, and her possible future.

"Get away!" The boy gave her another push. "What're you waiting for?"

Then, for the first time, she turned and looked at him. And what she was waiting for was in her eyes.

"Well, don't wait around here!" cried the boy savagely. "You won't see nothing!"

Her lips moved.

"Nothing!" he cried. "It was all a joke, wasn't it?" He turned to the other children. "Nothing's happening today. *Is* it?"

They all blinked at him and then, understanding, laughed and shook their heads. "Nothing, nothing!"

"Oh, but," Margot whispered, her eyes helpless. "But this is the day, the scientists predict, they say, they *know*, the sun. . . ."

"All a joke!" said the boy, and seized her roughly. "Hey, everyone, let's put her in a closet before teacher comes!"

"No," said Margot, falling back.

They surged about her, caught her up and bore her, protesting, and then pleading, and then crying, back into a tunnel, a room, a closet, where they slammed and locked the door. They stood looking at the door and saw it tremble from her beating and throwing herself against it. They heard her muffled cries. Then, smiling, they turned and went out and back down the tunnel, just as the teacher arrived.

"Ready, children?" she glanced at her watch.

"Yes!" said everyone.

"Are we all here?"

"Yes!"

The rain slackened still more.

They crowded to the huge door.

The rain stopped.

It was as if, in the midst of a film, concerning an avalanche, a tornado, a hurricane, a volcanic eruption, something had, first, gone wrong with the sound apparatus, thus muffling and finally cutting off all noise, all of the blasts and repercussions and thunders, and then, second, ripped the film from the projector and inserted in its place a peaceful tropical slide which did not move or tremor. The world ground to a standstill. The silence was so immense and unbelievable that you felt your ears had been stuffed or you had lost your hearing altogether. The children put their hands to their ears. They stood apart. The door slid back and the smell of the silent, waiting world came in to them.

The sun came out.

It was the color of flaming bronze and it was very large. And the sky around it was a blazing blue tile color. And the jungle burned with sunlight as the children, released from their spell, rushed out, yelling, into the springtime.

"Now don't go too far," called the teacher after them. "You've only two hours, you know. You wouldn't want to get caught out!"

But they were running and turning their faces up to the sky and feeling the sun on their cheeks like a warm iron; they were taking off their jackets and letting the sun burn their arms.

"Oh, it's better than the sun lamps, isn't it?"

"Much, much better!"

They stopped running and stood in the great jungle that covered Venus, that grew and never stopped growing, tumultuously, even as you watched it. It was a nest of octopi, clustering up great arms of flesh-like weed, wavering, flowering in this brief spring. It was the color of rubber and ash, this jungle, from the many years without sun. It was the color of stones and white cheeses and ink, and it was the color of the moon.

The children lay out, laughing, on the jungle mattress, and heard it sigh and squeak under them, resilient and alive. They ran among the trees, they slipped and fell, they pushed each other, they played hide-and-seek and tag, but most of all they squinted at the sun until tears ran down their faces, they put their hands up to that yellowness and that amazing blueness and they breathed of the fresh, fresh air and listened and listened to the silence which suspended them in a blessed sea of no sound and no motion. They looked at everything and savored everything. Then, wildly, like animals escaped from their caves, they ran and ran in shouting circles. They ran for an hour and did not stop running.

And then—

In the midst of their running one of the girls wailed.

Everyone stopped.

The girl, standing in the open, held out her hand.

"Oh, look, look," she said, trembling.

They came slowly to look at her opened palm.

In the center of it, cupped and huge, was a single raindrop.

She began to cry, looking at it.

They glanced quietly at the sky.

"Oh. Oh."

A few cold drops fell on their noses and their cheeks and their mouths. The sun faded behind a stir of mist. A wind blew cool around them. They turned

and started to walk back toward the underground house, their hands at their sides, their smiles vanishing away.

A boom of thunder startled them and like leaves before a new hurricane, they tumbled upon each other and ran. Lightning struck ten miles away, five miles away, a mile, a half mile. The sky darkened into midnight in a flash.

They stood in the doorway of the underground for a moment until it was raining hard. Then they closed the door and heard the gigantic sound of the rain falling in tons and avalanches, everywhere and forever.

"Will it be seven more years?"

"Yes. Seven."

Then one of them gave a little cry.

"Margot!"

"What?"

"She's still in the closet where we locked her."

"Margot."

They stood as if someone had driven them, like so many stakes, into the floor. They looked at each other and then looked away. They glanced out at the world that was raining now and raining and raining steadily. They could not meet each other's glances. Their faces were solemn and pale. They looked at their hands and feet, their faces down.

"Margot."

One of the girls said, "Well . . .?"

No one moved.

"Go on," whispered the girl.

They walked slowly down the hall in the sound of cold rain. They turned through the doorway to the room in the sound of the storm and thunder, lightning on their faces, blue and terrible. They walked over to the closest door slowly and stood by it.

Behind the closed door was only silence.

They unlocked the door, even more slowly, and let Margot out.

Source: *A Medicine for Melancholy and Other Stories* by Ray Bradbury

Vocabulary

blessed: holy
blushing: turning red or pink
bore: carried
compounded: added up
cupped: held as if in a cup
dimly: slightly
muffled: softened, less loud
slackening: lessening
squeak: make a high-pitched noise
tatting: tapping

READ ON

To Build a Fire and Other Favorite Stories
by Jack London

Jack London's short stories recount tales of adventure and strength in the face of adversity. These thirteen stories, including the classic "To Build a Fire," represent some of his most gripping work. One of the most widely read fiction writers ever to lay pen to paper, London reveals the essence of the human character: the will to survive.

Shakespeare in Plain English

Sonnet 18 in Shakespeare's Words

Shall I compare thee to a summer's day?
Thou art more lovely and more temperate:
Rough winds do shake the darling buds of May,
And summer's lease hath all too short a date;
Sometime too hot the eye of heaven shines,
And often is his gold complexion dimm'd,
And every fair from fair sometime declines,
By chance or nature's changing course untrimm'd;
But thy eternal summer shall not fade
Nor lose possession of that fair thou ow'st;
Nor shall Death brag thou wand'rest in his shade,
When in eternal lines to time thou grow'st:
So long as men can breathe or eyes can see,
So long lives this, and this gives life to thee.

Sonnet 18 in Plain English

Should I compare you to a summer day? You are lovelier and calmer. Strong winds shake the tender leaf buds of May, and summer is far too short. Sometimes the sun's rays are too hot, and at other times, it is often hidden by clouds. Everything that is beautiful loses its beauty, either by bad luck or simply the change of the seasons, but your beauty is forever and will not fade or lose its strength. Death will never take you, because you are here in my written words, which will last forever. As long as there is someone alive to see and read these lines of poetry, the words will live forever, and therefore, so will you.

Vocabulary

dimm'd: dimmed; made less bright
grow'st: grows
hath: has
ow'st: owes
thee: you
thou: you
untrimm'd: untrimmed; unchanged
wand'rest: wanders

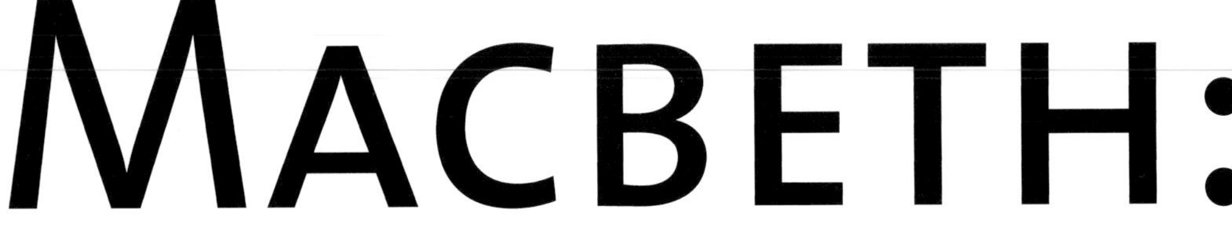

INTRODUCTION

As is frequently pointed out by the critics, *Macbeth* was probably written in haste. No one knows why Shakespeare was in a hurry, unless he was nauseated by all the bloodshed. At any rate, this explains the unusually large number of tragic flaws in the play.

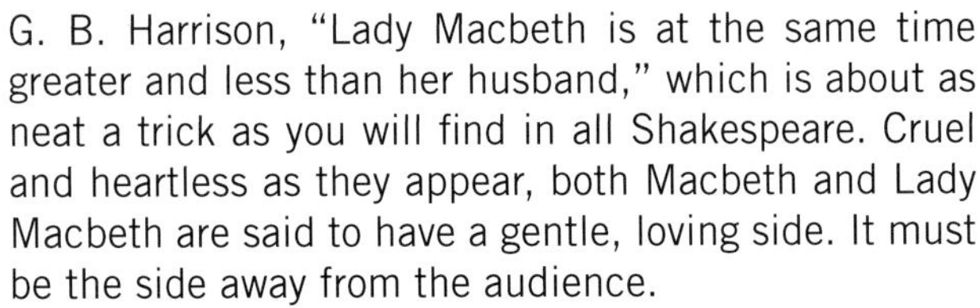

It is the shortest of Shakespeare's major tragedies.* According to one theory, it was long in its original version and subsequently cut. Most of the cutting was doubtless left in the capable hands of Macbeth and the hired murderers, with Lady Macbeth cheering them on.

Shakespeare, who never could think up a plot all by himself, found this one in Holinshed's Chronicles, changing it just enough so that no one would recognize the source.† If, as researchers say, Shakespeare took liberties with Scottish history, most of us who love liberty applaud him for it.

As Kittredge observes, Shakespeare at the beginning of the play "plunges, as usual, *in medias res.*" Whatever this is, he doesn't come up for air until the play is over. Few Elizabethan dramatists had such powers of endurance as Shakespeare, and few modern theatregoers have such powers of endurance as Elizabethans.

The play is full of atmosphere, which helps the characters breathe. Of the characters, the most interesting are Macbeth and Lady Macbeth. The latter is not only her husband's wife but his evil genius.‡ According to G. B. Harrison, "Lady Macbeth is at the same time greater and less than her husband," which is about as neat a trick as you will find in all Shakespeare. Cruel and heartless as they appear, both Macbeth and Lady Macbeth are said to have a gentle, loving side. It must be the side away from the audience.

There are some beautiful passages. One of them is the hallway in Macbeth's castle, where Lady Macbeth loved to fingerpaint on the wall with other people's blood.

* Some don't consider this a flaw.

† He didn't count on the resourcefulness of modern scholars, who have to discover things like this to become associate professors.

‡ All in all, quite a helpmate.

Source: *Twisted Tales from Shakespeare* by Richard Armour

Vocabulary

bloodshed: violence resulting in death

in haste: quickly

passages: 1) lines of text 2) pathways from one room to another

theatregoers: people who go to see plays performed live

READ ON

No Fear Shakespeare Graphic Novels: Romeo and Juliet

by SparkNotes Editors, illustrated by Matt Wiegle

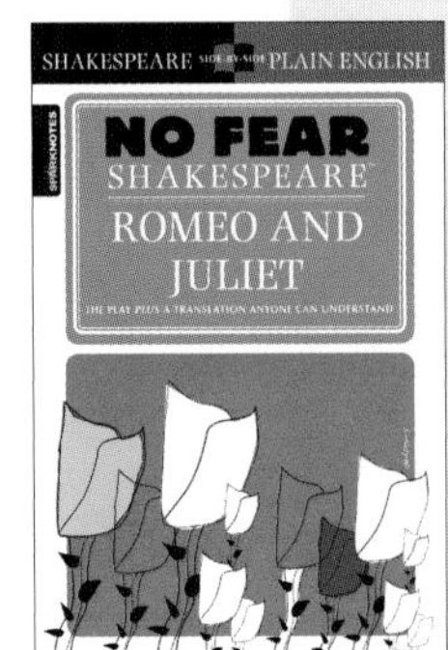

No Fear Shakespeare Graphic Novels is a series based on the *No Fear Shakespeare* series, which translates Shakespeare's plays into modern English. This version of *Romeo and Juliet* brings to life the age-old love story and its tragic events through appealing, yet slightly offbeat illustrations. The book's illustrated cast of characters, its plot summary, and line-by-line translations of the original text, plus graphic representations of each scene, make the story clear and understandable as well as fun to read.

King Lear

(Based on the classic play by William Shakespeare)

When a king puts his daughters' love to the test, his kingdom is torn apart by greed, betrayal and madness

CHARACTERS

Narrator

King Lear: ruler of Britain

Fool: Lear's jester

Goneril: Lear's eldest daughter

Regan: Lear's middle daughter

Cordelia: Lear's youngest and favourite daughter

Kent: nobleman loyal to Lear

Gloucester: Earl loyal to Lear

Edmund: Gloucester's cruel son

Edgar: Gloucester's loyal son

Cornwall: Regan's husband

Albany: Goneril's husband

Duke of Burgundy: Cordelia's suitor

King of France: Cordelia's suitor, and later, husband

Oswald: Goneril's servant

Servant 1: employee of Gloucester

Servant 2: employee of Gloucester

Messenger

Scene 1

Narrator: King Lear calls a meeting with his daughters Goneril, Regan and Cordelia, and his friend, the nobleman Kent. In the room next door, the King of France and the Duke of Burgundy wait to find out which of them gets to marry Cordelia. But first, Lear makes a surprising announcement.

Lear: I have a dark purpose for calling you here. I'm tired of being King, so I am giving up my kingdom to my three daughters.

Narrator: Lear unfolds a map of Britain.

Lear: Who loves me most? She will get the best land.

Goneril: Dad, I love you more than words! More than eyesight!

Lear *(circling part of the map)*: This is yours, Goneril. Regan?

Regan: I love you so much, I can't feel anything else.

Lear *(pointing)*: Very well, this is your kingdom. Now, Cordelia, my youngest and my favourite, what do you have to say?

Cordelia: Nothing, my lord.

Lear: What? Nothing will come of nothing!

Cordelia: You raised me and loved me, so I obey, love, and honour you. No more, no less.

Lear: That's it? Fine! You get nothing, not even a dowry. No one will ever marry you!

Narrator: Cordelia realizes that without a dowry—money that parents give to a daughter's husband—she won't be able to marry.

Kent: Sire, are you crazy? Your behaviour baffles me!

Lear: How dare you question me, Kent! Get out of here!

Narrator: Kent leaves, and the Duke of Burgundy and the King of France enter.

Lear: Burgundy, do you still want a dowry for Cordelia?

Burgundy: Only what you offered.

Lear: Too bad. There is no dowry.

Burgundy: Oh, uh . . .

France: It's very strange that your favourite daughter should fall from favour so suddenly. I didn't know you could be so capricious.

Lear: Better Cordelia was never born than not to have pleased me better.

Burgundy ***(to Cordelia)*****:** I'm sorry that in losing a father you have lost a husband.

Cordelia ***(to Burgundy)*****:** Since you love money more than you love me, I will not be your wife.

France: Cordelia, you are rich though you are poor. Will you marry me and be the Queen of France?

Narrator: Cordelia agrees to marry the King of France. They leave Britain and go to France.

Scene 2

Narrator: Since Lear gave up his throne, he and his knights have been living with Goneril. They spend their days drinking, hunting, and playing—like they're on vacation. Goneril takes her servant Oswald aside.

Goneril: How are we going to get rid of my dad?

Oswald: I don't know.

Goneril: I have an idea! Let's treat him terribly.

Narrator: A while later, Lear and his Fool wait to be served.

Lear: Someone get me something to eat. Where is my daughter Goneril?

Oswald: She doesn't feel well.

Lear: Why don't people do as I say? I asked for a drink an hour ago!

Oswald: Whatever.

Goneril ***(walking in)*****:** Look, Dad. If you want to stay here, get rid of your stupid knights.

Lear: My knights are my kingly privilege.

Goneril: You're not a King anymore.

Lear: Fine, I'll go live with Regan. At least I know she truly loves me.

Fool ***(to Lear)*****:** You've become old before you've become wise.

Narrator: Lear and the Fool go pack their belongings.

Albany: Goneril, my wife, I think you're too hard on your dad.

Goneril: What do you know, husband? I'm Queen of half of Britain now.

Scene 3

Narrator: Lear and his Fool arrive at Regan's castle. They are tired and hungry from their journey.

Lear: Oh Regan, Goneril was so cruel to me!

Regan: I can't imagine my sister behaving badly. You distort the truth.

Fool ***(to Lear)*****:** You've made your daughters your mothers.

Narrator: Lear falls to his knees.

Lear ***(to Regan)*****:** I hate your sister! Please, allow me some food and a place to sleep?

Regan: Good grief!

Lear: (rising): Please, you are so much kinder than Goneril.

Goneril ***(walking in)*****:** What is my sick, old dad saying about me?

Regan: He's whining about how mean you are. ***(to Lear)*** Dad, I sent for Goneril when I heard you were coming. She is here to take you home.

Lear: What about my knights?

Regan: You don't need them.

Lear: Regan, please let me stay!

Regan: No, sorry.

Narrator: Lear stomps off with the fool.

Cornwall: There's a storm coming. Where is he going?

Regan: He's in a high rage!

Goneril: Just let him go.

Regan: No one is allowed to give him shelter tonight. Is that clear?

Narrator: Meanwhile, Gloucester, an Earl who is loyal to Lear, meets with Kent.

Gloucester: I'm worried about our country. Did you know that Cornwall and Albany aren't getting along?

Kent: Cordelia sent me a letter. Now that she is the Queen of France, she has a lot of power. She's coming to Britain with the French Army to make everything right.

Gloucester: What do we do?

Kent: Send your knights to Dover to prepare for her arrival.

Gloucester: Okay. What about Lear? This storm could kill him.

Kent: I'll go find him.

Scene 4

Narrator: Lear and the Fool wander in the storm. They're soaked, hungry, and miserable. Lear seems to be going crazy.

Lear: Foul storm! Is this the best you can do?

Fool: This night will turn us all into fools and madmen.

REGAN, PLEASE LET ME STAY!
NO, SORRY!

Kent ***(walking up)*****:** Who's there?

Lear: A man more sinned against than sinning!

Kent: Come, sire, let's take shelter in this cave.

Lear: Nothing could have brought me to such lowness than my horrid progeny. I'm a discarded father.

Narrator: They huddle together in the cave. Lear looks at the Fool, who shivers violently.

Lear: Fool, are you okay? I may be losing my mind, but I still care about you.

Fool: This night pities neither wise men nor fools.

Narrator: Just then, Gloucester appears.

Gloucester: Sir, I can't obey your daughters' cruel command. Take shelter at my house.

Narrator: Kent and Gloucester take Lear and the Fool to Gloucester's home.

Kent ***(aside to Gloucester)*****:** I think Lear is losing his mind.

Gloucester: Can you blame him? His daughters seek his death. I'm almost nuts myself.

Kent: Maybe some rest will cure him.

Gloucester: I told my son Edmund about our plan to meet Cordelia and the French Army in Dover. Let's send Lear to Dover first thing in the morning. Cordelia will care for him.

Scene 5

Narrator: Armed with the knowledge that his father, Gloucester, is saving Lear and working with the French, Edmund runs to Cornwall, Regan's husband.

Edmund: Did you know that my father, Gloucester, brought Lear to his house last night? He completely ignored Regan's precept!

Cornwall: Oh yeah?

Edmund: Wait, there is more. He plans to help French spies topple the government! Am I a terrible son to betray my own father?

Cornwall: Don't worry. We'll dispose of Gloucester, and I'll be a better father to you than he ever was.

Narrator: Cornwall takes Regan, Goneril and soldiers to Gloucester's house.

Cornwall: We're here for the traitor Gloucester!

Narrator: Soldiers seize Gloucester and tie him to a chair.

Gloucester: What are you talking about?

Regan: We know everything, so don't try to lie. Where is the King?

Gloucester: I sent him to Dover.

Regan: Why?

Gloucester: Because I would not see your cruel hands pluck out his eyes.

Cornwall: After today, you'll never see anything again.

Narrator: Cornwall tears out one of Gloucester's eyes. He is about to tear out the other when a servant stabs him.

Cornwall: How dare you!

Narrator: Cornwall kills the servant, and then plucks out Gloucester's other eye.

Gloucester: I'm blind! Oh, Edmund! Help me, Edmund!

Regan: Edmund hates you. He's the one who told us about your treason.

Cornwall: Help me, Regan. This wound is worse than I thought.

Narrator: Regan tries to help her husband, but he is seriously injured.

Scene 6

Narrator: Edmund talks to Goneril about the coming French invasion. There seems to be something romantic between them.

Goneril: Perhaps you are a better match for me than my coward husband.

Edmund: Perhaps I am, my lady.

Goneril: After this war, I will kill my husband, Albany, so we can be together.

Narrator: Edmund leaves, and Albany enters.

Albany: Goneril, you aren't worth the dust that blows in your face. You and your sister drove your own father nuts!

Messenger ***(running in)*****:** Beg your pardon, Sir, but Cornwall is dead! A servant killed him when he attacked Gloucester! And now Gloucester is blind.

Albany: Poor Gloucester!

Goneril ***(to herself)*****:** Now that my sister is single, she'll want Edmund for herself.

Albany: Why didn't Edmund help his father?

Goneril: You idiot. It was Edmund who betrayed him.

Albany: You're all nuts!

Goneril: If we combine our army with Regan's army, we can beat the French.

Albany: I will dispatch the army at once. To Dover!

Scene 7

Narrator: The blind Gloucester wanders around outside.

Servant 1: Let me bandage your bleeding face.

Gloucester: Leave me alone! Nothing can comfort me.

Servant 2: Sir, you can't see your way. Let us help.

Gloucester: I should have trusted and loved Edgar, not Edmund.

Narrator: Edgar approaches Gloucester. When Edgar sees his blind dad, his heart fills with pity.

Edgar: World, oh what a world!

Narrator: Gloucester doesn't recognize Edgar's voice.

Gloucester: Lead me to the edge of a cliff in Dover, so I may end my life.

Edgar: Give me your arm, I'll take you.

Narrator: They arrive in Dover. Edgar leads Gloucester to a small rock.

Gloucester: When will we get to the top of the cliff?

Edgar: We are there now. Don't you feel how steep the ground is?

Gloucester: Uh, no.

Edgar: How scary to stand so high!

DON'T CRY! I KNOW YOU DON'T LOVE ME. BUT UNLIKE YOUR SISTERS, YOU HAVE A REASON TO HATE ME.
I DON'T HATE YO
I LOVE YOU. ALL
FORGIVEN, FATHE

Edgar ***(to himself)*****:** This is the only way to cure him of his desire to die.

Narrator: Gloucester steps to the edge of the rock.

Gloucester: Goodbye, World!

Narrator: Gloucester jumps, but the rock is only a few feet high. He lands on the ground, unharmed.

Edgar ***(running up)*****:** How are you alive? You fell so far!

Gloucester: Why am I not dead?

Edgar: This is above all strangeness.

Narrator: Just then, Lear wanders by, dressed in wild flowers and babbling to himself.

Gloucester: I know that voice! It's the King! Let me kiss his hand!

Lear: Let me wipe it first. It stinks of mortality.

Gloucester: Lear, it's me, Gloucester!

Lear: You have no eyes, yet you see how this world goes.

Narrator: Just then, Cordelia and some of her soldiers arrive. She takes them all to safety in the French camp, where Edgar reveals his true identity to Gloucester and Lear is put to bed.

Lear *(falling asleep)*: My other daughters flattered me like a dog, but I am as vulnerable to a storm as anyone.

Narrator: When Lear wakes up, Cordelia sits beside his bed.

Cordelia: How do you feel?

Lear: You do me wrong to take me out of the grave.

Cordelia: Do you recognize me?

Lear *(studies her face)*: Cordelia?

Narrator: They embrace. Cordelia cries.

Lear: Don't cry! I know you don't love me. But unlike your sisters, you have a reason to hate me.

Cordelia: I don't hate you. I love you. All is forgiven, Father.

Scene 8

Narrator: Regan and Goneril arrive in Dover with their armies and set up camp. While they prepare for battle, the two sisters flirt with Edmund, who keeps his options open by professing love to Goneril *and* Regan. Later, everyone meets to review the plan of attack.

Albany: I hear that Lear joined the French Army.

Goneril: Does it matter? We must stop the invasion.

Albany: But your sister Cordelia is over there.

Goneril: She's betrayed us.

Albany: I will fight with you, but I don't like this.

Narrator: That night, Edgar sneaks into Albany's tent to reveal a secret.

Edgar: I intercepted a letter from your wife, Goneril. I'm sad to say, she plans to kill you and Regan so she can marry Edmund.

Albany: I will deal with her after the battle.

Edgar: My fight is with my brother, Edmund.

Albany: When the time is right, I'll call you. Be ready.

Scene 9

Narrator: The next day, the battle begins. Unfortunately, Cordelia's army is no match for British forces. She loses, and Edmund takes her and Lear prisoner. Albany takes control of the post-battle situation.

Albany: Where are Lear and Cordelia? We should show them mercy.

Edmund: I sent them away where they will be safe.

Albany: You don't have the rank to make decisions like that!

Regan: Hey, leave him alone. Edmund is going to marry me.

Goneril: What?! Edmund can't marry you!

Regan *(stumbling)*: Oh, I feel sick suddenly. I'm going to rest.

Narrator: Albany takes this as his cue to deal with Edmund's treachery.

Albany: Edgar! The time is now!

Narrator: Edgar steps up to face his brother, Edmund. The two men fight and Edgar wounds Edmund. Goneril runs out crying.

Edgar: I have avenged my father's death.

Albany: Gloucester is dead?

Edgar: When I told him about my plan to fight Edmund, he died of a broken heart.

Messenger *(carrying two bodies)*: Look! Goneril killed herself, but not before she poisoned Regan!

Kent: Where is Lear?

Albany: Edmund, where is Lear?

Edmund *(dying)*: I wish to do some good before I die, so I will tell you the truth. I ordered Lear and Cordelia to be hanged. You need to hurry if you're going to stop it.

Narrator: With that, Edmund dies.

Albany: Run, messenger!

Narrator: The messenger is too late. Lear walks in clutching Cordelia's lifeless body.

Lear: Howl! Howl! Howl! I couldn't save her!

Edgar: What horror is this?

Lear: A plague upon you all!

Kent: Sire, your other daughters are dead, too.

Narrator: Lear falls on Cordelia's body and dies.

Kent: Oh, my heart breaks!

Edgar: He is dead!

Kent: He is finally at peace.

Albany *(to Kent and Edgar)*: Friends of my soul, rule this kingdom with me. Let us heal it together.

Narrator: The men exit slowly in a tragic procession to bury the dead.

Source: Adapted by Kristin Lewis for *Scholastic Scope*, February 2, 2009

Vocabulary

baffles: confuses
clutching: holding
dispatch: send
distort: change
flattered: complimented
progeny: children
treachery: deception

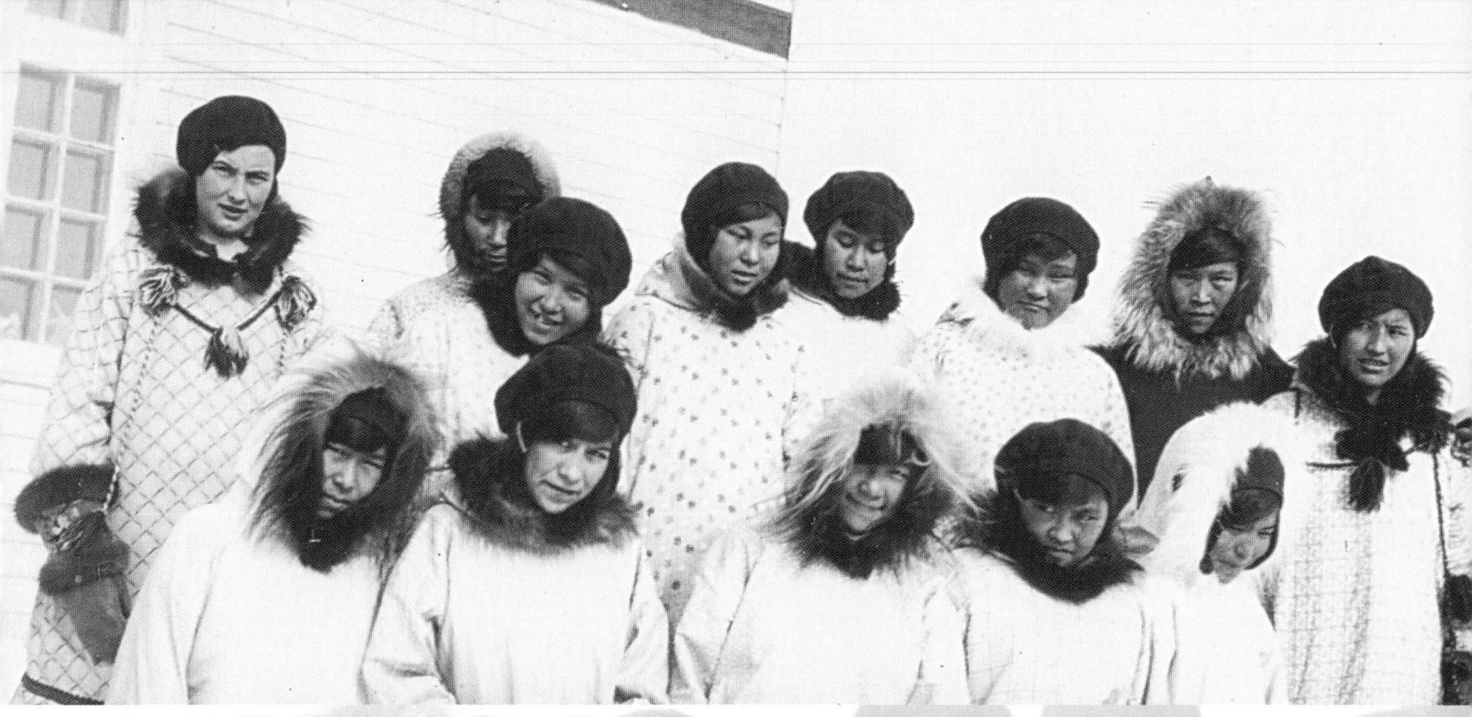

MY LESSON

By Caitlin Therrien

When my younger sister was named, we had planned a potlatch for many weeks. She was very honoured to receive the name which was once my grandmother's. All seemed to be exultant; there was food, gifts, song and dance. I saw smiles on even the oldest of our elders. I didn't believe that anything could go wrong, but as my sister handed the blanket she was wearing to the chief, white man came between them yelling angrily. Apparently, one of the men was of great merit, and he told our chief that it was illegal for us to have such a gathering.

For many years we have had potlatches; it was a way for us to share wealth, to celebrate life, death, marriage and names. Taking away our dances and our traditions was like erasing who we were from the face of the earth. We would not stand for anyone to take away what represented so much to us!

Although the whites had told us to stop, we would sometimes sneak to an area in the bush so we would not be caught, and in that area we would wear our masks, tell our stories and celebrate the way of our people before the white man came.

My mother had once told me that the white man was trying to make us more like them, and I didn't understand why. I didn't understand why they wouldn't let us be when we had not done harm to them. I did not think that it was awful to be different from each other. Now at this age, I know that they were intolerant people, who seemed not to like anything that was different from them.

I remember when I was fourteen, white men told the parents in our community that it would benefit us more if we went to the white man's special

schools. I remember my mother and father both weeping and watching them shrink smaller as we drove further away while my sister and I sat on a trailer with many other children.

At the school, I was given the name Catherine, I was not allowed to speak my own language and I was not allowed to have my own beliefs. I was taught to read, write and pray. If any of us misbehaved, we were beaten; we were not shown love, and we did not show love. To rebel we spoke our language out loud, calling many of the nuns bad names, and some children tried to run away.

During one winter, several children had gotten a fever, and many of the ill children died; my sister was one of them. After my sister died, I was lost; I wished that I could have gone with her but instead I stayed in that purgatory.

When I was finally sent home, I did not know who I was. I did not fit in with white people, nor did I fit in with my own people. My family did not know what to do with me, and I grew into a river of depression, anger and hate. For many years, I drank to try to console myself, but I found that could not help.

I could have continued this way to death. Until my mother, one day, took me to the forest where my sister was named and smudged me. She told me that I needed to find myself, to cleanse myself, and to save myself. I told her that I did not know how to do such things because I didn't know who I was. I told her of how I hated the white man for what they had made me become, which was a monster in my eyes. My mother took my hand and told me the story of our people. She told me not to hate the bottle but to hate the poison in it. She told me I was not lost because if I looked hard enough, I would realize that I was on the path that the creator had chosen for me, and to take each lesson I had endured and to use them to benefit my people. I now know who I am. I know my traditions; I am not ashamed of myself or of my people. I am very old now, and my life has taught me much, so as I give you this story, learn from it. Don't let anyone take away who you are, and if you fall down, or forget, there will always be a reminder to help you pick yourself back up.

I teach you what I have been taught, so you can teach the same to your children. If we continue this, we have truly lost nothing, and we will never be forgotten.

Source: From *Initiations: A Selection of Young Native Writings*, edited by Marilyn Dumont

My mother took my hand and told me the story of our people.

Vocabulary

misbehaved: disobeyed

potlatch: a ceremonial feast

smudged: protected using the smoke from a burning bundle of ceremonial herbs

FROM
FORBIDDEN CITY: A Novel of Modern China

by William Bell

On Friday morning before dawn the phone rang. I heard Lao Xu answer it and start yelling into the receiver. Then he shouted, "Wake up! There is a rumour that Zhao Zi-yang is going to Tian An Men Square to talk to the students!"

We were all up and dressed in moments. "Let's go!" Eddie said.

I grabbed my backpack. No one seemed to notice that I went right along with them. The tall light standards in the square and the lights from the monuments make it easy to see where you're going, although you need extra lights for TV pictures. It took us at least half an hour to push through the throng to the Monument to the People's Heroes, which is where Eddie figured the action would be. Buses were parked in the square now, commandeered by the students for shelter when it rained. It was cold out, and a lot of people had coats on.

Nothing was happening at the moment. Eddie said to Dad, "Let's split up and call on the two-way if we see anything."

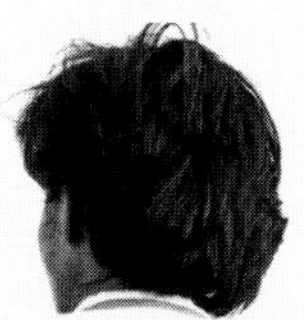

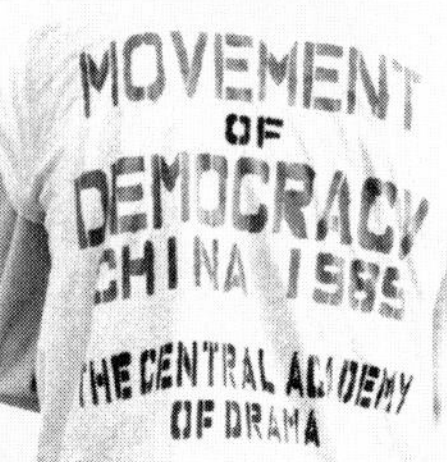

"Okay," answered Dad. "I'll go down towards Qian Men." That's the Front Gate.

"I'll cover the mausoleum," Eddie said. "Lao Xu, let's go."

"Alex, you can come with me," Dad said.

"Why don't I stay here? That way we can cover three areas at once."

"I don't know, Alex. I don't want you to get lost."

What a lame thing to say, I thought. Eddie must have agreed. "Are you kidding, Ted? Your kid knows this city better than most of the residents!"

Dad agreed, reluctantly, and the three of them waded into the crowd. I went up to the base of the monument among a hundred or so students and tried to get a look around. The first tier of the tall building still had a lot of wreaths on it. Nothing unusual seemed to be happening—other than probably half a million people, tents, parked buses, voices yelling over loud-hailers, TV lights sparking up for a few minutes and then fading again.

I fished my camcorder out of my pack. It would be worthwhile to try taping anything that happened. Then I checked my radio to make sure it was on channel one and that it was on receive mode. I put it in my breast pocket.

I stood around for a while, fighting off the chill, before I noticed something going on over at the Great Hall of the People. A blaze of lights had come on,

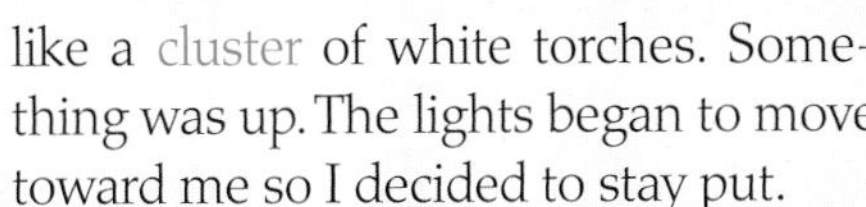

like a cluster of white torches. Something was up. The lights began to move toward me so I decided to stay put.

I took out my radio and keyed it. "Dad, Eddie, this is Alex. Can you see the lights? In the northwest quadrant, moving toward me. Over."

"Alex, Dad here. I can't see them. I'm on the south side of Qian Men. The smell of Kentucky chicken is driving me nuts. Over."

"And I can't see anything," was Eddie's response.

"I'll check it out and let you know. Over and out."

I put the radio in my pocket again. The lights were moving toward me quickly. They were TV lights. Somebody important was coming.

Right near the monument was a bus, and when Zhao Zi-yang got to the bus he stopped. He was at the centre of a tight circle of students wearing the white headbands that said Democracy Now! in Chinese. He reached up and started shaking hands with students in the bus. Amazing. This guy was the second most powerful man in China.

By that time I was making my way toward him. I had to climb down from the monument's base, so I lost sight of Zhao, but the lights were easy to home in on. What wasn't easy was pushing through the crowd. Then I got an idea. I took off my hat and stuffed it in my pocket so my blonde hair would show.

"Press! Press!" I shouted, and held my camcorder up high so it could be seen. "Press! Let me through, please!"

It worked. The crowd of students parted and I got to the bus in time to see that Zhao was talking. He was of medium height, with a high forehead and western style glasses. I put the camcorder to my eye and zoomed in to get a medium close-up of Zhao with students at the bus windows in the background. Even through the viewfinder I could see that he was crying as he spoke to the crowd.

The only thing from his speech that I understood were the words . . . "too late."

I probably don't need to write down how deliriously happy Dad and Eddie were when I hooked my camcorder up to our office TV and showed them the tape. I thought Eddie was going to carry me around the room.

Within an hour Dad had found someone in the hotel who agreed to take the tape to the satellite feed station and Eddie had written a report and faxed it to Toronto.

I was delirious myself. The reporter's bug had really bitten me.

We all wanted to go back to sleep but we couldn't. Too much to do. I skipped school again. Dad went back to the square with Eddie and Lao Xu to try and interview some students about Zhao's visit and ask them what they thought it meant to their movement. I got to clean up the office because Eddie wouldn't let anyone from the hotel in. Pretty demeaning job for someone who got his video report on national TV, if you ask me.

It took me all morning to tidy up the office. It's hard to make an office neat when you know that the people who work in it are used to a mess and that if they ever came back to find an orderly workplace they'd think they were in the wrong office. I also made sure all the battery rechargers were full and charging away.

After lunch Lao Xu came by and started using the phone as he often did. He tried to catch people after the customary afternoon nap, before the lines got too busy again. He was shouting away for an hour or so, saying, "Wei? Wei?" about once a second, then he sat and made some notes.

Eddie and Dad came back later in the afternoon, looking tired. Dad put away his camera in its aluminum case and flopped into one of the armchairs. Eddie said hello and headed for the shower with his pipe still in his mouth.

Just as Eddie padded into the office wearing a towel around his large middle and drying his hair with another towel the phone rang. Lao Xu answered it, yelled for a few seconds, listened some more, and hung up, looking glum.

"There is a rumour that Chairman Zhao Zi-yang has been removed from office," he said quietly. "And my friend says we should turn on the TV."

I pushed the button and the screen came to life. We gathered around.

"That's Li Peng," Lao Xu said. The premier was talking. He looked stern, even angry, but he had a look on his face that seemed to say, "I'm the boss now."

"What's up, Lao Xu?" Dad asked.

Lao Xu kept his eyes on the screen. "Please wait, Ted."

So the three of us stared at Li Peng, dressed in a dark blue Mao suit, collar buttoned up under his chin, chopping the air with his hand, karate-style, as he talked. I could make out a couple of words, like China and student and foreigner. Then it was over.

Dad and Eddie and I turned to Lao Xu. We knew from the look on his face that the news was not good. He spoke in a low voice, as if he couldn't quite believe his own words.

"Premier Li Peng says that Beijing is now under martial law."

"Oh-oh," Dad said.

Eddie let out a low whistle, puffing out his moustache.

Lao Xu continued. "And he has ordered all students and others to clear Tian An Men Square or face the consequences. Their presence is illegal. All demonstrations are illegal. It is also illegal to spread rumours. And," Lao Xu added, looking directly into Eddie's eyes, "foreign correspondents are forbidden to report on anything to do with the students' presence in Tian An Men Square. If they disobey, measures will be taken."

I knew what martial law meant. It meant that all laws were suspended, even the constitution, and the government made policy directly, using the military to carry it out. Martial law meant soldiers on the street corners with guns, searches of persons and houses without any kind of warrant—by soldiers, not police. It meant curfews. And fear mixed with excitement.

Which is what I was starting to feel.

But a couple of things I didn't understand. "What's this stuff about rumours?" I asked Lao Xu.

"It means—"

Eddie cut him off. "Remember what I told you about how the government here controls and manages the news, Alex?" I nodded, a little put out that he was answering for Lao Xu. "Well, the government will now tell more lies to the people than ever and withhold more information than ever. If people start circulating the truth, they are accused of spreading rumours and arrested. It's a way of controlling information."

I looked at Lao Xu. He sat there with a glum look on his face and nodded without saying anything.

"What will happen now?" I asked.

In unison, Eddie and Lao Xu shrugged.

"Lao Xu, can you still work for Dad and Eddie?" I wanted to know. "I mean, won't this make things more difficult for you?"

Lao Xu smiled. "I can continue," he answered, "for the time being, because I have not yet been told anything different by my leader."

I stood at the office window looking at the crowds streaming along Chang An Avenue. Martial law, I thought. That's what Zhao must have meant when he said, "It's too late."

Vocabulary

commandeered: took over
cluster: group
demeaning: lowering one's dignity
glum: depressed
keyed: pressed a button to speak
loud-hailers: loudspeakers
stern: strict in appearance
warrant: document that allows a police officer to arrest a person or search a building

JUST A NUMBER

by Hannah McGechie

Last fall, a coworker and I went to a conference and spoke about a topic we know a lot about—youth culture online. When we had finished our presentation, a man got up to thank us on behalf of the conference organizers. In front of the entire 60-person audience, he told us that he and his colleagues had learned so much from us in the past hour, but that it was safe to say they knew more than us about the "bad guys." And with that, he cast a shadow of doubt over our credibility and reinforced the age division between us and everyone else at the conference. My coworker and I both have degrees in criminology and have worked on the front line with these same "bad guys"; we have spent years in prisons and courtrooms, reading charge sheets and police reports while listening to the stories and experiences of victims and offenders alike. All this was ignored and we were effectively dismissed as too young to be able to understand or even critically think about the complexities of crime.

This wasn't the first (or last) time I have been discriminated against based on my age or how young I appear. I've chaperoned youth events and not been taken seriously because I was mistaken for one of the participants, I've given presentations only to be asked questions about what I intend to do after high school instead of questions about the subject matter, and I can't even begin to count the number of times someone I'm working with has done a double-take when meeting me in person after only communicating via email or telephone. The look I'm given every single time silently asks how I could possibly be old enough to do the work I do and speak with authority about any subject. More often than not, I'm dismissed and my input ignored based not on how I came to have it but because I'm seen as too young to give it.

When I mention my frustration to others, they sympathize but often tell me that when I'm older, I'll appreciate looking younger than I am. The fact is, I'm not offended that I'm frequently mistaken for a 16-year-old even though I'm in my 20s. What offends me is that I'm treated a certain way based on my perceived age, and not based on what I actually say or do. It bothers me equally when individuals who are actually in their teens are dismissed as being too young to have valuable contributions or observations to make.

Ageism—discriminating against someone based on his or her real or perceived age—is not limited to targeting young people but affects older adults as well. It frequently goes unnoticed because it is seen as logical: the idea that experience and wisdom increase with age and then deteriorate after one's 65th birthday is very popular. This is often true, but not always; young people are equally capable of thinking critically and having experiences that give them authority on certain subjects. Unfortunately, this systemic form of ageism is so common that we are not only almost entirely unaware of it, but not questioning it either.

Being the victim of ageism is very frustrating and often damaging. It has not stopped me from doing work I am passionate about or speaking up about subjects I know a lot about, but it has changed my behaviour. By the end of the conference I mentioned, I was worn down and had grown hesitant to ask questions and offer my perspective because I knew

Only one Teenager at a time No hoods or hats,caps or hoodies or no service

I wasn't going to be taken seriously. While other speakers at the conference could wear jeans, I dressed in business clothing the entire time in an attempt to look older. If I have a choice, I prefer to conduct business via email so that whoever I'm communicating with can't see how young I look. Other young people become even more discouraged and stop contributing to discussions and initiatives that they are interested in. It's not a huge surprise to me that the voting turnout rate is lower for young people than for Canadians in general. After living through years of being told to be quiet and listen to the adults who really know what's going on, why would young Canadians be flocking to the polls? We often doubt our abilities to spark change in our communities because we are used to our knowledge and abilities being judged and ignored.

Ageism has resulted in a great deal of disengagement of youth, but several groups are now fighting back. "Apathy is Boring" is an ongoing project that was created in 2004 with the aim of increasing the representation of youth in politics and democracy. The creators saw how their peers were disengaged from the political process and decided to use art, technology and media to get them involved in human rights, social justice and politics. The project has grown and evolved, creating offshoots such as the "Youth Friendly Guide," which provides resources and counsel to those who want to create intergenerational partnerships. Many organizations (such as Ottawa's Youth Services Bureau and the Royal Canadian Mounted Police) have also formed youth advisory committees to ensure that young voices are heard and reflected in policies and projects.

Being subjected to ageism is incredibly discouraging, but we cannot allow it to stop us. We must fight back, get involved and raise our voices even more. We have a lot to offer and from a unique, largely overlooked perspective.

Source: Royal Canadian Mounted Police *deal.org* Webzine, February 2009

USE

Vocabulary

charge sheets: lists of offences that suspects are charged with

flocking: running

mistaken for: confused with

offended: upset

offenders: people who have committed crimes

overlooked: ignored

spark: inspire

voting turnout rate: number of people who cast votes in an election

READ ON

The Boy in the Striped Pajamas
by John Boyne

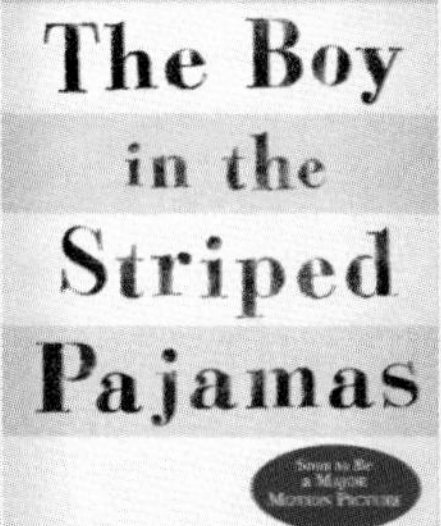

The time is 1942: the place, Berlin, Germany. Young Bruno comes home from school one day to discover that his whole family is moving to Poland. Their new home is next to a huge fence, through which Bruno can see hundreds of people dressed in striped pajamas. Not sure of what his father does for a living, and even more unsure about why all of these people are living behind the fence, Bruno does what any curious nine-year-old would do: He sneaks over to the fence to explore. The friendship that results between Bruno and a boy his age on the other side of the fence has consequences neither of them could have imagined.

Get Comfortable Not Knowing

There once was a village that had among its people a very wise old man. The villagers trusted this man to provide them answers to their questions and concerns.

One day, a farmer from the village went to the wise man and said in a frantic tone, "Wise man, help me. A horrible thing has happened. My ox has died and I have no animal to help me plow my field! Isn't this the worst thing that could have possibly happened?" The wise old man replied, "Maybe so, maybe not." The man hurried back to the village and reported to his neighbours that the wise man had gone mad. Surely this was the worst thing that could have happened. Why couldn't he see this?

The very next day, however, a strong young horse was seen near the man's farm. Because the man had no ox to rely on, he had the idea to catch the horse to replace his ox—and he did. How joyful the farmer was. Plowing the field had never been easier. He went back to the wise man to apologize. "You were right, wise man. Losing my ox wasn't the worst thing that could have happened. It was a blessing in disguise! I never would have captured my new horse had that not happened. You must agree that this is the best thing that could have happened." The wise man replied once again, "Maybe so, maybe not." Not again, thought the farmer. Surely the wise man had gone mad now.

But, once again the farmer did not know what was to happen. A few days later, the farmer's son was riding the horse and was thrown off. He broke his leg and would not be able to help with the crop. Oh no, thought the man. Now we will starve to death. Once again, the farmer went to the wise man. This time he said, "How did you know that capturing my horse was not a good thing? You were right again. My son is injured and won't be able to help with the crop. This time I'm sure that this is the worst thing that could have possibly happened. You must agree this time." But, just as he had done before, the wise man calmly looked at the farmer and in a compassionate tone replied once again, "Maybe so, maybe not." Enraged that the wise man could be so ignorant, the farmer stormed back to the village.

The next day, troops arrived to take every able-bodied man to the war that had just broken out. The farmer's son was the only young man in the village who didn't have to go. He would live, while the others would surely die.

The moral of this story provides a powerful lesson. The truth is, we don't know what's going to happen—we just think we do. Often we make a big deal out of something. We blow up scenarios in our minds about all the terrible things that are going to happen. Most of the time, we are wrong. If we keep our cool and stay open to possibilities, we can be reasonably certain that, eventually, all will be well. Remember: maybe so, maybe not.

Source: *Don't Sweat the Small Stuff—And It's All Small Stuff* by Richard Carlson, Ph.D.

Vocabulary

big deal: something or someone of great importance

blessing: good fortune

blow up: make something more important than it really is

broken out: started

compassionate: showing recognition of stressful circumstances

frantic: desperate

plow: create furrows in the soil for planting crops

The Great Idea

by Ellie Shuo Jin

In the past decade, along with the hottest temperatures came the hottest topic: climate change. It is difficult to deny its ominous presence when the glacial ice caps are slowly slipping into the ocean and forest fires dominate the news channels.

Many studies have been done regarding climate change, and the consensus is that most of the changes are due to human activities, particularly the production of greenhouse gases that contribute to global warming. However, in comparison to the large amount of funds dedicated to the reversal of climate change, the progress has been meagre.

This is largely due to the general misconception that technology will simply resolve all the problems that humans are threatened with. Furthermore, when the available technology fails to rectify the problem, people then take an economic approach and state that not enough funds have been generated to fight global warming. As a result little change has been made in the environment thus far.

This simplistic "techno-economic" approach is insufficient for solving complex environmental problems that are rooted in equally complex social structures. Effective solutions must draw on a broader understanding of social systems and human behaviour. Therefore, more impact can be made on reversing the effects of climate change when the focus is shifted from scientific research to analyzing the links with human social behaviour.

The solution to the issue of global climate change is rooted in understanding human behaviour. The biggest threat to the future of Earth is not global warming, not another SARS outbreak, and definitely not a nuclear war; the biggest concern that humans face is "the selfishness gene." It is this selfishness gene that prevents the people from seeing beyond their generation, trading in their old wagons for new oil-guzzling BMWs. It is also the selfishness gene that stops Canadian politicians from continuing (or in reality, starting) to seriously work on the Kyoto Protocol, because they fear that they will lose votes. It is the selfishness gene that has prevented Earth from changing for the better.

Before any real actions take place, several things regarding the attitude of the general public must change. First, politicians should implement and monitor carbon taxes because once they're in place a clear message is sent out stating that pollution is wrong and conservation helps all. On the same note, the government should reward those who are trying to save the environment by giving them tax breaks; positive reinforcement goes a long way.

Second, more information regarding the necessity of reversing climate change should be transmitted along all the communication networks. People do not know that numerous jobs can be created if everything goes green and that taxes could be lowered due to a decrease in healthcare costs as a direct result of a better environment.

Third, individuals who are already green should apply more pressure on their less green counterparts to encourage them to help with reversing the effects of climate change. This tactic proved to be especially helpful in the anti-smoking movement. When links were established between smoking and many diseases, the smoke-free population began to apply pressure to the smoking population for them to re-evaluate their lifestyle choices and to quit before it was too late. Now smoking is generally something that is frowned upon. This demonstration of social pressure proved to be especially helpful in making drastic changes in the way people lived their lives. Perhaps it is time to do it again.

Scientists say there are only 50 years left before it is too late to reverse the effects of climate change, as the damages caused by human activities are increasing at an exponential rate. However, if people can end their dependency on the highly addictive tobacco, maybe there is still a chance that people will end their dependency on climate-changing products as well.

It is time to stop hoping that technology will save the day and shift the focus to analyzing human behaviour and finding out exactly why the current methods are not effective. Enough money has been spent on scrutinizing the existing data. Humanity should not be examining numbers and figures; they should take a good look at themselves.

Source: *What If Magazine*, Spring 2009

Vocabulary

broader: wider; more inclusive
counterparts: people who are similar
links: connections
meagre: deficient in amount or quality
rooted in: connected in a fundamental way
SARS: Severe Acute Respiratory Syndrome, an illness that attacks the lungs and can be fatal
scrutinizing: looking at carefully; analyzing
selfishness: concern for one's own welfare and disregard for the welfare of others

A FEW RULES FOR PREDICTING THE FUTURE

BY OCTAVIA E. BUTLER

"So do you really believe that in the future we're going to have the kind of trouble you write about in your books?" a student asked me as I was signing books after a talk. The young man was referring to the troubles I'd described in *Parable of the Sower* and *Parable of the Talents*, novels that take place in a near future of increasing drug addiction and illiteracy, marked by the popularity of prisons and the unpopularity of public schools, the vast and growing gap between the rich and everyone else, and the whole nasty family of problems brought on by global warming.

"I didn't make up the problems," I pointed out. "All I did was look around at the problems we're neglecting now and give them about 30 years to grow into full-fledged disasters."

"Okay," the young man challenged. "So what's the answer?"

"There isn't one," I told him.

"No answer? You mean we're just doomed?" He smiled as though he thought this might be a joke.

"No," I said. "I mean there's no single answer that will solve all of our future problems. There's no magic bullet. Instead there are thousands of answers–at least. You can be one of them if you choose to be."

Several days later, by mail, I received a copy of the young man's story in his college newspaper. He mentioned my talk, listed some of my books and the future problems they dealt with. Then he quoted his own question: "What's the answer?" The article ended with the first three words of my reply, wrongly left standing alone: "There isn't one."

It's sadly easy to reverse meaning, in fact, to tell a lie, by offering an accurate but incomplete quote. In this case, it was frustrating because the one thing that I and my main characters never do when contemplating the future is give up hope. In fact, the very act of trying to look ahead to discern possibilities and offer warnings is in itself an act of hope.

LEARN FROM THE PAST

Of course, writing novels about the future doesn't give me any special ability to foretell the future. But it does encourage me to use our past and present behaviours as guides to the kind of world we seem to be creating. The past, for example, is filled with repeating cycles of strength and weakness, wisdom and stupidity, empire and ashes. To study history is to study humanity. And to try to foretell the future without studying history is like trying to learn to read without bothering to learn the alphabet.

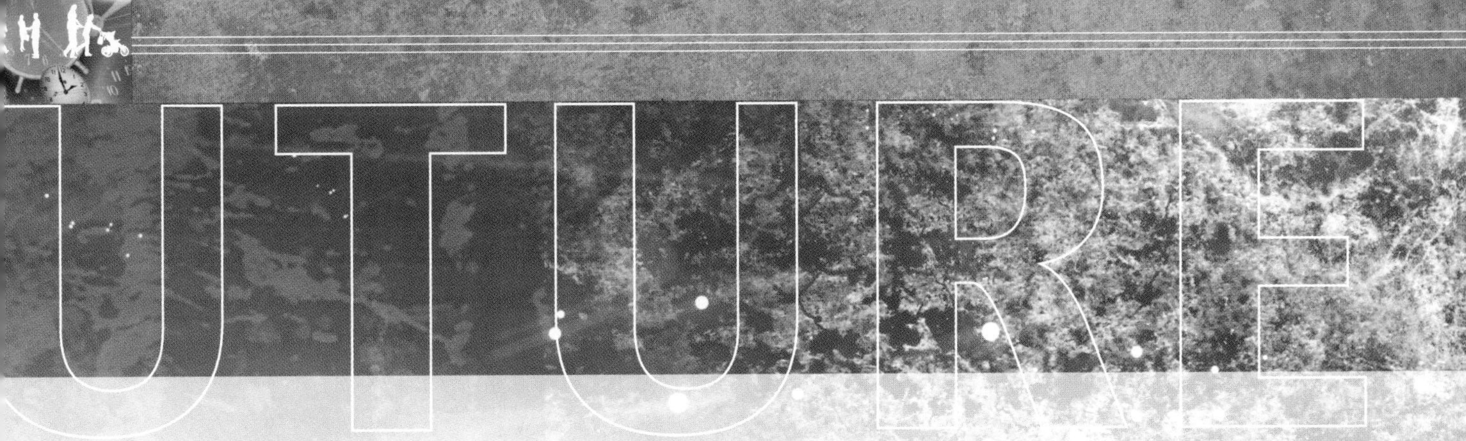

When I was preparing to write *Parable of the Talents*, I needed to think about how a country might slide into fascism-something that America does in *Talents*. So I reread *The Rise and Fall of the Third Reich* and other books on Nazi Germany. I was less interested in the fighting of World War II than in the prewar story of how Germany changed as it suffered social and economic problems, as Hitler and others bludgeoned and seduced, as the Germans responded to the bludgeoning and the seduction and to their own history, and as Hitler used that history to manipulate them. I wanted to understand the lies that people have to tell themselves when they either quietly or joyfully watch their neighbours mined, spirited away, killed. Different versions of this horror have happened again and again in history. They're still happening in places like Rwanda, Bosnia, Kosovo and East Timor, wherever one group of people permits its leaders to convince them that for their own protection, for the safety of their families and the security of their country, they must get their enemies, those alien others who, until now, were their neighbours.

It's easy enough to spot this horror when it happens elsewhere in the world or elsewhere in time. But if we are to spot it here at home, to spot it before it can grow and do its worst, we must pay more attention to history. This came home to me a few years ago, when I lived across the street from a 15-year-old girl whose grandfather asked me to help her with homework. The girl was doing a report on a man who had fled Europe during the 1930s because of some people called-she hesitated and then pronounced a word that was clearly unfamiliar to her-"the Nayzees?" It took me a moment to realize that she meant the Nazis, and that she knew absolutely nothing about them. We forget history at our peril.

RESPECT THE LAW OF CONSEQUENCES

Just recently I complained to my doctor that the medicine he prescribed had a very annoying side effect.

"I can give you something to counteract that," my doctor said.

"A medicine to counteract the effects of another medicine?" I asked.

He nodded. "It will be more comfortable for you."

I began to backpedal. I hate to take medicine. "The problem isn't that bad." I said. "I can deal with it."

"You don't have to worry," my doctor said. "This second medication works and there are no side effects."

That stopped me. It made me absolutely certain that I didn't want the second medicine. I realized that I didn't believe there

were any medications that had no side effects. In fact, I don't believe we can do anything at all without side effects–also known as unintended consequences. Those consequences may be beneficial or harmful. They may be too slight to matter or they may be worth the risk because the potential benefits are great, but the consequences are always there. In *Parable of the Sower*, my character put it this way:

All that you touch/You Change
All that you Change/Changes you
The only lasting truth/Is Change
God/Is Change

BE AWARE OF YOUR PERSPECTIVE

How many combinations of unintended consequences and human reactions to them does it take to detour us into a future that seems to defy any obvious trend? Not many. That's why predicting the future accurately is so difficult. Some of the most mistaken predictions I've seen are of the straight-line variety–that's the kind that ignores the inevitability of unintended consequences, ignores our often less-than-logical reactions to them, and says simply, "In the future, we will have more and more of whatever's holding our attention right now." If we're in a period of prosperity, then in the future, prosperity it will be. If we're in a period of recession, we're doomed to even greater distress. Of course, predicting an impossible state of permanent prosperity may well be an act of fear and superstitious hope rather than an act of unimaginative, straight-line thinking. And predicting doom in difficult times may have more to do with the sorrow and depression of the moment than with any real insight into future possibilities. Superstition, depression and fear play major roles in our efforts at prediction.

It's also true that where we stand determines what we're able to see. Where I stood when I began to pay attention to space travel certainly influenced what I saw. I followed the space race of the late 1950s and the 1960s not because it was a race, but because it was taking us away from Earth, away from home, away to investigate the mysteries of the universe and, I thought, to find new homes for humanity out there. This appealed to me, at least in part, because I was in my teens and beginning to think of leaving my mother's house and investigating the mysteries of my own adulthood.

Apollo 11 reached the moon in July 1969. I had already left home by then, and I believed I was watching humanity leave home. I assumed that we would go on to establish lunar colonies and eventually send people to Mars. We probably will do those things someday, but I never imagined that it would take as long as it has. Moral: Wishful thinking is no more help in predicting the future than fear, superstition or depression.

COUNT ON THE SURPRISES

I was speaking to a group of college students not long ago, and I mentioned the fear we'd once had of nuclear war with the Soviet Union. The kids I was talking to were born around 1980, and one of them spoke up to say that she had never worried about nuclear war. She had never believed that such a thing could possibly happen–she thought the whole idea was nonsense.

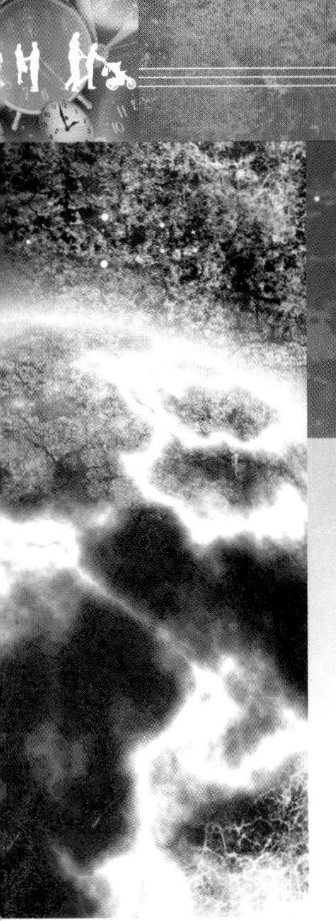

She could not imagine that during the Cold War days of the sixties, seventies and eighties, no one would have dared to predict a peaceful resolution in the nineties. I remembered air-raid drills when I was in elementary school, how we knelt, heads down against corridor walls with our bare hands supposedly protecting our bare necks, hoping that if nuclear war ever happened, Los Angeles would be spared. But the threat of nuclear war is gone, at least for the present, because to our surprise our main rival, the Soviet Union, dissolved itself. No matter how hard we try to foresee the future, there are always these surprises. The only safe prediction is that there always will be.

So why try to predict the future at all if it's so difficult, so nearly impossible? Because making predictions is one way to give warning when we see ourselves drifting in dangerous directions. Because prediction is a useful way of pointing out safer, wiser courses. Because, most of all, our tomorrow is the child of our today. Through thought and deed, we exert a great deal of influence over this child, even though we can't control it absolutely. Best to think about it, though. Best to try to shape it into something good. Best to do that for any child.

Source: *Essence*, May 2000

Vocabulary

air-raid drills: emergency practice procedures to prepare people for bombing attacks
backpedal: modify one's opinion
bludgeoned: beaten with a blunt instrument
counteract: oppose by doing the contrary
doomed: destined to meet a tragic end
drifting: moving slowly
foretell: predict
illiteracy: inability to read
magic bullet: instant solution to a problem
mined: made to collapse
quoted: cited

READ ON

Parable of the Sower

by Octavia E. Butler

In this story of a future gone wrong, Lauren Olamina, a 15-year-old Black girl, dreams of a better world. Los Angeles, her city, has become overrun by homeless scavengers and violent addicts who, frustrated by the lack of jobs and water, set fires everywhere they go. Lauren, who suffers from "hyperempathy," a genetic condition that makes her feel the pain of others, flees north with a group of refugees. She is determined to create a safe haven and, one day, allow humans to escape to the stars. This sensitive, graceful portrayal of the struggle to keep hope alive shows what humanity can do in the face of failure.

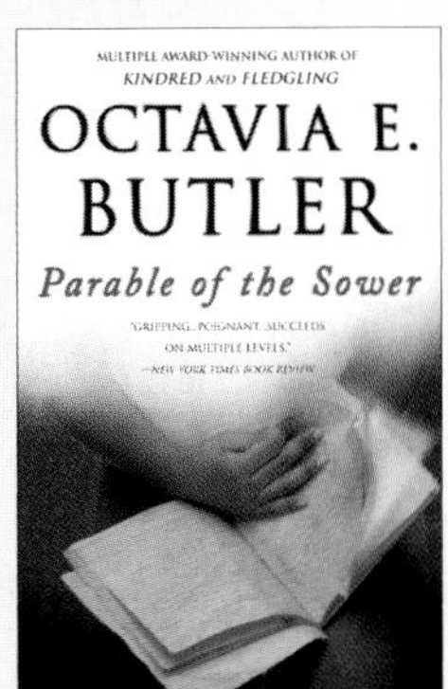

ANNABEL LEE

It was many and many a year ago,
In a kingdom by the sea,
That a maiden there lived whom you may know
By the name of Annabel Lee;
And this maiden she lived with no other thought
Than to love and be loved by me.

I was a child and *she* was a child,
In this kingdom by the sea:
But we loved with a love that was more than love—
I and my Annabel Lee;
With a love that the winged seraphs of heaven
Coveted her and me.

And this was the reason that, long ago,
In this kingdom by the sea,
A wind blew out of a cloud, chilling
My beautiful Annabel Lee;
So that her highborn kinsmen came
And bore her away from me,
To shut her up in a sepulchre
In this kingdom by the sea.

The angels, not half so happy in heaven,
Went envying her and me—
Yes!—that was the reason (as all men know,
In this kingdom by the sea)
That the wind came out of the cloud by night,
Chilling and killing my Annabel Lee.

But our love it was stronger by far than the love
Of those who were older than we—
Of many far wiser than we—
And neither the angels in heaven above,
Nor the demons down under the sea,
Can ever dissever my soul from the soul
Of the beautiful Annabel Lee:

For the moon never beams, without bringing me dreams
Of the beautiful Annabel Lee;
And the stars never rise, but I feel the bright eyes
Of the beautiful Annabel Lee;
And so, all the night-tide, I lie down by the side
Of my darling—my darling—my life and my bride,
In her sepulchre there by the sea,
In her tomb by the sounding sea.

—EDGAR ALLAN POE

ABOUT THE AUTHOR

Edgar Allan Poe

Edgar Allan Poe (1809–1849) was a poet, short-story writer, editor and literary critic who is best known today for his gothic-style tales of horror. His most famous stories include "The Black Cat," "The Tell-Tale Heart" and "The Cask of Amontillado." He is also famous for poems such as "The Bells" and "The Raven." Born in Boston, Massachusetts, his parents died when he was young, and he was raised by foster parents. He was one of the first well-known American writers to have attempted to live on the earnings of his writing alone. This led him to move frequently for jobs and caused him to have financial difficulties. In 1835, he married his 13-year-old cousin, Virginia Clemm. She died of tuberculosis in 1847, and Poe's subsequent writings appear to have been influenced by the illness and loss of his wife, most clearly in the poem "Annabel Lee." The cause of the author's own illness and death in 1849 remains a mystery.

Vocabulary

coveted: wanted
dissever: separate
sepulchre: tomb
seraphs: angels

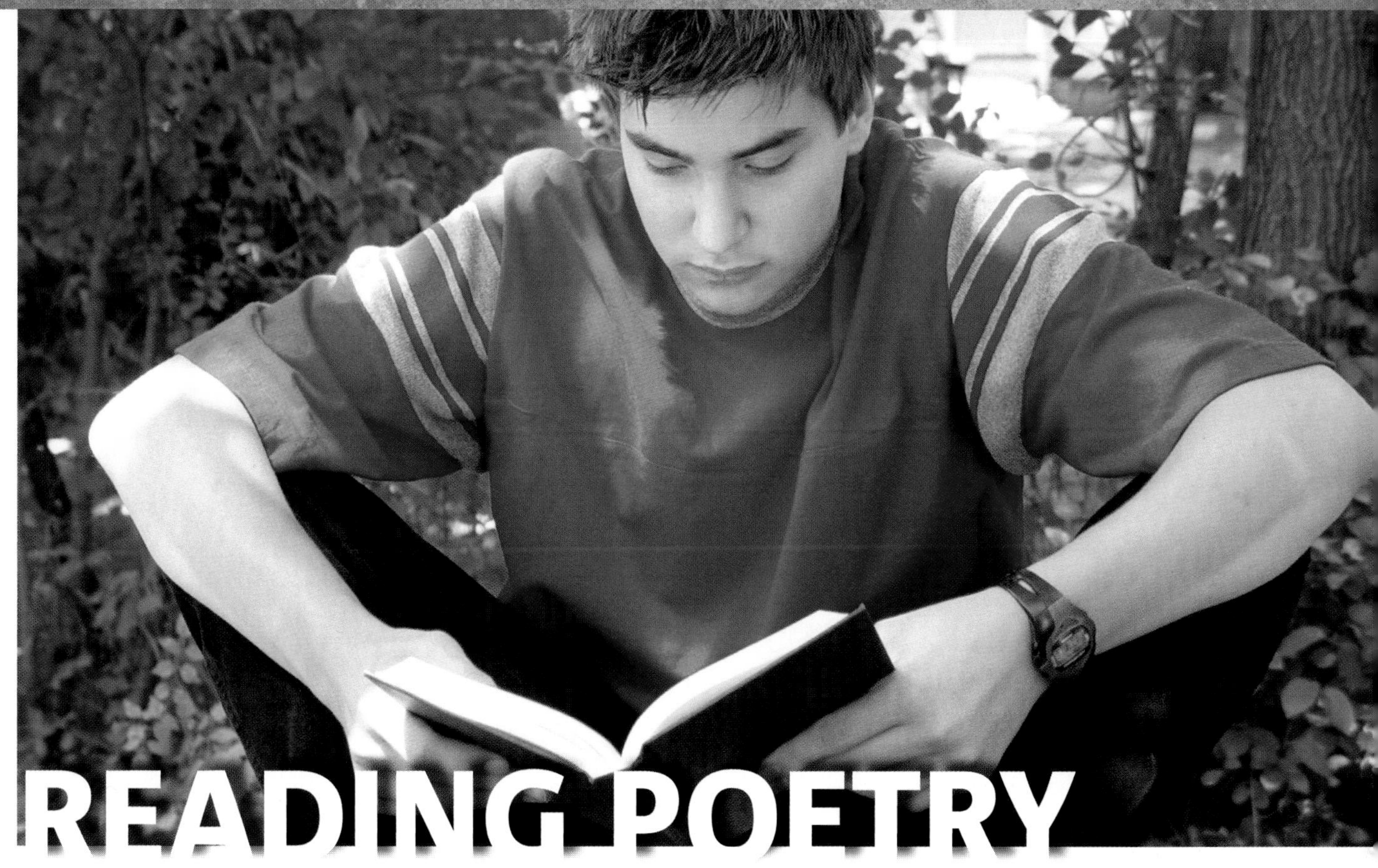

READING POETRY

The experience you get from reading poetry is not exactly like any other. Sometimes poetry gives the impression of saying more than words can say. This mysterious-seeming effect is caused by the fact that in poetry, words are used in a way that is different from the way words are usually used. Poetry is art, and so has a different purpose from that of the regular way of talking and writing, and has a different effect.

by Kenneth Koch and Kate Farrell

Most of the difficulties that people have in reading poetry come from their not understanding this. It is easier to understand using a rock to make sculpture, or sound to make music, than it is to understand using words to make poetry. Words already have meanings and ways of being put together to get something across. So, when you read words, it is natural to expect the ordinary kind of intellectual sense that you are used to—a kind of sense you don't expect, for instance, when you listen to music. Once you understand what poetry is and how it is different from other writing, it won't seem to you so confusing and difficult.

Usually when you talk or write, you start with an idea, then try to express it in words and in a style that will make it clear to the people you are talking or writing to. Sometimes that's easy. You say, "I would like a glass of water." Sometimes it's hard. Talking about strong or complicated feelings—about being in love, for instance, or feeling sad—you may end up with a feeling that you haven't really said what you meant, that there isn't any way to put what you feel into words. The more personal the thing that you want to say, and the more particular it is to your own way of thinking and feeling and seeing things, the less likely it is that you can express it with the ordinary way of talking.

Suppose you decide to find a way of talking in which you can express perfectly your own sense of things, your thoughts or way of seeing, or your own particular experience. And that it becomes more important to you to get those things right than to make sure somebody else understands them. Suppose you want to get an experience into words so that it is permanently there, as it would be in a painting—so that every time you read what you wrote, you re-experienced it. Suppose you want to say something so that it is right and beautiful—even though you may not understand exactly why. Or suppose words excite you—the way stone excites a sculptor—and inspire you to use them in a new way. And that for these or other reasons you like writing because of the way it makes you think or because of what it helps you to understand. These are some of the reasons poets write poetry.

It doesn't make sense to read poetry the way you read a newspaper article. It is good, in general, to read a poem with the kind of freedom, openness and sensitive attentiveness to your own thoughts and feelings that you have when you write a poem yourself or when you listen to a friend talking, or when you hear music. You understand the meaning of the words in the poem with your intellect, but you also respond to the poem with a part of your intelligence that includes your feelings and imagination and experience.

You can like a poem before you understand it, and be moved by it, and in fact, that is a sign that you're starting to understand it, that you're reading the poem in a good way. Being moved by a poem—laughing or feeling sad or full of longing—or being excited by it, or feeling (maybe you don't know why) the "rightness" of the poem is a serious part of reading and liking poetry. You may find what you read to be beautiful, or be reminded of places and times, or find in it another way to look at things. All this can help you to understand the poem because it brings it closer to you, makes it a part of your experience. And the better you understand a good poem, the more you'll like it.

The best way to begin is by reading the poem several times to get used to the style. After you get a sense of the whole poem, there are some things you can do to help yourself understand anything that's unclear—if anything still is unclear, which often it won't be. There may be a word or two you don't understand, or a reference to a person or a place that you're not familiar with. These you can look up in a dictionary or encyclopedia or ask someone about. There may be a sentence that's so long it's hard to follow, or a sentence that's left incomplete; words may be in an unusual order, or a sentence may be hard to see because it's divided into different lines. For these problems, just go through the poem slowly, seeing where the different sentences begin and end. If you understand part of a poem and not another part, try to use what you do understand to help you see what the rest means.

If the poem still seems hard to you, it may be because you're looking for something that isn't there. You may think that the poem makes a point, that it comes to some conclusion about life in general, when the point may only be to get into that poem the look of a locust tree in the early spring. Or you may be looking for a hidden meaning that isn't there. The suggestiveness of poetry often makes people think there is one specific hidden meaning. There isn't one. A good poem means just what it says, and it suggests what it suggests. The search for deep meanings behind what is said is usually painful and unrewarding. Poems don't usually have hidden meanings. One main trouble with "finding" such meanings when they're not really there is that they end up hiding what really is there. One of Wallace Stevens's poems begins:

The houses are haunted
By white nightgowns.

He means, in fact, as you realize after you read the poem a few times and get to know it, that people are wearing conservative white night clothes which make them look like ghosts. It's a witty way of making fun of them for being so conservative and dull. If you start off looking for hidden meanings, however, you may never know this. You may start thinking of a supernatural phenomenon, of real ghosts, maybe even of Lazarus and his rising from the grave, and you'll lose the poem completely. It's like looking for the real meaning behind a sailboat race on the bay. You'd probably miss the beauty and excitement of the boats, the water, the sky, the day. Remember (writing poems of your own will help you to know it) that poets are not big, dark, heavy personages dwelling in clouds of mystery, but people like yourself who are doing what they like to do and do well. Writing poetry isn't any more mysterious than what a dancer or a singer or a painter does. If a poet writes well, what he says is to be found in the words that are actually there, almost always in the commonest meanings.

Sometimes, too, people make the mistake of analyzing the poem word by word before they've got an idea of what the whole poem is like. This seems scholarly and scientific but is as misleading as analyzing each of a person's words in a conversation before you know who he is and what he is talking about. Better than starting right in to analyze according to some already existing idea is to think of how the poem is affecting you—think of your own responses to it. Also, when first reading a poem, you don't have to be concerned with its technique, with how it is made—that is to say, its rhyme, its meter, its imagery, and so on. That can be interesting to talk or write about later, but when you're first reading a poem you don't need to do it.

Even when they don't know much about poetry, people sometimes have strong ideas about what poetry ought to be like. This can keep them from enjoying all the different ways poetry can be. If you read poetry expecting it to be always the same, you will be confused. It is an art, like music or painting with all kinds of possible variations.

Everything you like about a poem will be enhanced, and what you understand of it will be increased, by reading other poems by the same poet. As you get used to a poet's style and so on, you can hear everything in his poems more clearly. If you don't feel intimidated, understanding or figuring things out can be enjoyable in itself. Think of the rather pleasant process of figuring out a part of town you've never been in or a person you've just met.

Reading poetry is not a completely passive pleasure, as is sitting in the sun or watching television. It is more like the pleasure you get from playing tennis or listening to music. There is a difference between what you feel the first time you play tennis and the fiftieth time. Or between the first time you go to a concert and later on, when you know more about the music and are used to concerts. Poetry is like that. The more you know about it and the more you read it, the more at ease you'll feel with it, the better you'll get at reading it, and the more you'll like it. When you read a poem, the poet's experience becomes, in a way, your own, so you see things and think things you wouldn't see and think otherwise. It's something like travelling—seeing new places, hearing things talked about in new ways, getting ideas of other possibilities. It can change you a little and add to what you know and are.

Source: From *Sleeping on the Wing: An Anthology of Modern Poetry with Essays on Reading and Writing* by Kenneth Koch and Kate Farrell

Vocabulary

enhanced: increased or intensified in value or beauty

meter: the pattern of stressed syllables in lines of poetry

misleading: taking the reader in the wrong direction

From *The Grapes*

BY JOHN STEINBECK

The concrete highway was edged with a mat of tangled, broken, dry grass, and the grass heads were heavy with oat beards to catch on a dog's coat, and foxtails to tangle in a horse's fetlocks, and clover burrs to fasten in sheep's wool; sleeping life waiting to be spread and dispersed, every seed armed with an appliance of dispersal, twisting darts and parachutes for the wind, little spears and balls of tiny thorns, and all waiting for animals and for the wind, for a man's trouser cuff or the hem of a woman's skirt, all passive but armed with appliances of activity, still, but each possessed of the anlage of movement.

The sun lay on the grass and warmed it, and in the shade under the grass the insects moved, ants and ant lions to set traps for them, grasshoppers to jump into the air and flick their yellow wings for a second, sow bugs like little armadillos, plodding restlessly on many tender feet. And over the grass at the roadside a land turtle crawled, turning aside for nothing, dragging his high-domed shell over the grass. His hard legs and yellow-nailed feet threshed slowly through the grass, not really walking, but boosting and dragging his shell along. The barley beards slid off his shell, and the clover burrs fell on him and rolled to the ground. His horny beak was partly open, and his fierce, humorous eyes, under brows like fingernails, stared straight ahead. He came over the grass leaving a beaten trail behind him, and the hill, which was the highway embankment, reared up ahead of him. For a moment he stopped, his head held high. He blinked and looked up and down. At last he started to climb the embankment. Front clawed feet reached forward but did not touch. The hind feet kicked his shell along, and it scraped on the grass, and on the gravel. As the embankment grew steeper and steeper, the more frantic were the efforts of the land turtle. Pushing hind legs strained and slipped, boosting the shell along, and the horny head protruded as far as the neck could stretch. Little by little the shell slid up the embankment until at last a parapet cut straight across its line of march, the shoulder of the road, a concrete wall four inches high. As though they worked independently, the hind legs pushed the shell against the wall. The head upraised and peered over the wall to the broad smooth plain of cement. Now the hands, braced on top of the wall, strained and lifted, and the shell came slowly up and rested its front end on the wall. For a moment the turtle rested. A red ant ran into the shell, into the soft skin inside the shell, and suddenly head and legs snapped in, and the armoured tail clamped in sideways. The red ant was crushed between body and legs. And one head of wild oats was clamped into the shell by a front leg. For a long moment the turtle lay still, and then the neck crept out and the old humorous

# of Wrath

frowning eyes looked about and the legs and tail came out. The back legs went to work, straining like elephant legs, and the shell tipped to an angle so that the front legs could not reach the level cement plain. But higher and higher the hind legs boosted it, until at last the center of balance was reached, the front tipped down, the front legs scratched at the pavement, and it was up. But the head of wild oats was held by its stem around the front legs.

Now the going was easy, and all the legs worked, and the shell boosted along, waggling from side to side. A sedan driven by a forty-year-old woman approached. She saw the turtle and swung to the right, off the highway, the wheels screamed and a cloud of dust boiled up. Two wheels lifted for a moment and settled. The car skidded back onto the road, and went on, but more slowly. The turtle had jerked into its shell, but now it hurried on, for the highway was burning hot.

And now a light truck approached, and as it came near, the driver saw the turtle and swerved to hit it. His front wheel struck the edge of the shell, flipped the turtle like a tiddly-wink, spun it like a coin, and rolled it off the highway. The truck went back to its course along the right side. Lying on its back, the turtle was tight in its shell for a long time. But at last its legs waved in the air, reaching for something to pull it over. Its front foot caught a piece of quartz and little by little the shell pulled over and flopped upright. The wild oat head fell out and three of the spearhead seeds stuck in the ground. And as the turtle crawled on down the embankment, its shell dragged dirt over the seeds. The turtle entered a dust road and jerked itself along, drawing a wavy shallow trench in the dust with its shell. The old humorous eyes looked ahead, and the horny beak opened a little. His yellow toe nails slipped a fraction in the dust.

Source: Chapter Three of *The Grapes of Wrath* by John Steinbeck

ABOUT THE AUTHOR

John Steinbeck

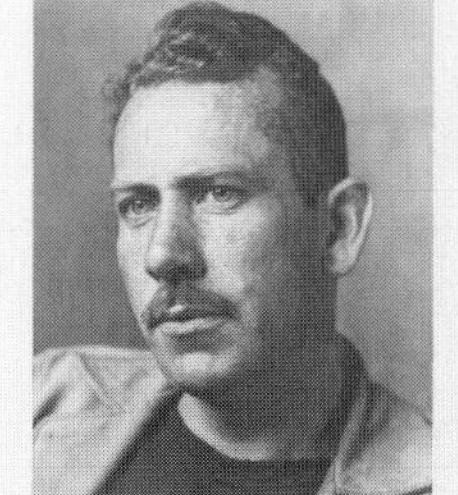

John Steinbeck (1902–1968) was an American writer who won the Pulitzer prize for his novel *The Grapes of Wrath* and is also known for his novel *Of Mice and Men*, among other works. Having grown up in California surrounded by farms where migrant workers lived and toiled, his writing has a distinctly rural flavour. Steinbeck worked on a ranch as a young man, and became familiar with the struggles of the working class and the prejudices they experienced at the hands of the rich. Steinbeck also served as a war correspondent during World War II. His later novels, including *East of Eden* and *The Winter of Our Discontent*, combined a desire to share the heritage of his country with the notion that this very same country was in a state of moral decline. Steinbeck won the Nobel Prize for Literature in 1962. He died in New York City in 1968.

Vocabulary

anlage: part of a plant that starts its development
burrs: thorny parts of a plant
embankment: long mound of earth next to a road that supports it and holds back water
fetlocks: projection behind and above a horse's hoof
foxtails: plants with tall stems and fuzzy tops that resemble a fox's tail
hind: rear
jerked: moved quickly
oat beards: the part of the oat plant that contains the seed
plodding: moving slowly
sedan: type of closed car
skidded: slid
swerved: turned aside suddenly
tiddly-wink: a small round plastic counter flipped on its edge into a cup
waggling: swaying

From *Stardust* by Neil Gaiman

The wind blew from Faerie and the East, and Tristran Thorn suddenly found inside himself a certain amount of courage he had not suspected that he had possessed. "You know, Miss Forester, I get off in a few minutes," he said. "Perhaps I could walk you a little way home. It's not much out of my way." And he waited, his heart in his mouth, while Victoria Forester's grey eyes stared at him, amused. After what seemed like a hundred years she said, "Certainly."

Tristran hurried into the parlor and informed Mr. Brown that he would be off now. And Mr. Brown grunted in a not entirely ill-natured way and told Tristran that when he was younger he'd not only had to stay late each night and shut up the shop, but that he had also had to sleep on the floor beneath the counter with only his coat for a pillow.

Tristran agreed that he was indeed a lucky young man, and he wished Mr. Brown a good night, then he took his coat from the coat-stand and his new bowler hat from the hat-stand, and stepped out onto the cobblestones, where Victoria Forester waited for him.

The autumn twilight turned into deep and early night as they walked. Tristran could smell the distant winter on the air—a mixture of night mist and crisp darkness and the tang of fallen leaves.

They took a winding lane up toward the Forester farm, and the crescent moon hung white in the sky and the stars burned in the darkness above them.

"Victoria," said Tristran, after a while.

"Yes, Tristran," said Victoria, who had been preoccupied for much of the walk.

"Would you think it forward of me to kiss you?" asked Tristran.

"Yes," said Victoria bluntly and coldly. "Very forward."

"Ah," said Tristran.

They walked up Dyties Hill, not speaking; at the top of the hill they turned and saw beneath them the village of Wall, all gleaming candles and lamps glimmering through windows, warm yellow lights that beckoned and invited; and above them the lights of the myriad stars, which glittered and twinkled and blazed, chilly and distant and more numerous than the mind could encompass.

Tristran reached down his hand and took Victoria's small hand in his. She did not pull away.

"Did you see that?" asked Victoria, who was gazing out over the landscape.

"You are the most lovely woman in all the world," said Tristran, from the bottom of his heart.

"Get along with you," said Victoria, but she said it gently.

"What did you see?" asked Tristran.

"A falling star," said Victoria. "I believe they are not at all uncommon at this time of year."

"Vicky," said Tristran. "Will you kiss me?"

"No," she said.

"You kissed me when we were younger. You kissed me beneath the pledge-Oak, on your fifteenth birthday. And you kissed me last May Day, behind your father's cow-shed."

"I was another person then," she said. "And I shall not kiss you, Tristran Thorn."

"If you will not kiss me," asked Tristran, "will you marry me?"

There was silence on the hill. Only the rustle of the October wind. Then a tinkling sound: it was the sound of the most beautiful girl in the whole of the British Isles laughing with delight and amusement.

"Marry you?" she repeated, incredulously. "And why ever should I marry you, Tristran Thorn? What could you give me?"

"Give you?" he said. "I would go to India for you, Victoria Forester, and bring you the tusks of elephants, and pearls as big as your thumb, and rubies the size of wren's eggs.

"I would go to Africa, and bring you diamonds the size of cricket balls. I would find the source of the Nile and name it after you.

"I would go to America—all the way to San Francisco, to the gold-fields, and I would not come back until I had your weight in gold. Then I would carry it back here, and lay it at your feet.

"I would travel to the distant northlands did you but say the word, and slay the mighty polar bears, and bring you back their hides."

"I think you were doing quite well," said Victoria Forester, "until you got to the bit about slaying polar bears. Be that as it may, little shop-boy and farm-boy, I shall not kiss you; neither shall I marry you."

Tristran's eyes blazed in the moonlight. "I would travel to far Cathay for you and bring you a huge junk I would capture from the king of the pirates, laden with jade and silk and opium.

"I would go to Australia, at the bottom of the world," said Tristran, "and bring you. Um." He ransacked the penny dreadfuls in his head, trying to remember if any of their heroes had visited Australia. "A kangaroo," he said. "And opals," he added. He was fairly sure about the opals.

Victoria Forester squeezed his hand. "And whatever would I do with a kangaroo?" she asked. "Now, we should be getting along, or my father and mother will be wondering what has kept me, and they will leap to some entirely unjustified conclusions. For I have not kissed you, Tristran Thorn."

"Kiss me," he pleaded. "There is nothing I would not do for your kiss, no mountain I would not scale, no river I would not ford, no desert I would not cross."

He gestured widely, indicating the village of Wall below them, the night sky above them. In the constellation of Orion, low on the Eastern horizon, a star flashed and glittered and fell.

"For a kiss, and the pledge of your hand," said Tristran, grandiloquently, "I would bring you that fallen star."

He shivered. His coat was thin, and it was obvious he would not get his kiss, which he found puzzling. The manly heroes of the penny dreadfuls and shilling novels never had these problems getting kissed.

"Go on, then," said Victoria. "And if you do, I will."

"What?" said Tristran.

And Victoria laughed at him, then, and took back her hand, and began to walk down the hill toward her father's farm.

Tristran ran to catch her up. "Do you mean it?" he asked her.

"I mean it as much as you mean all your fancy words of rubies and gold and opium," she replied. "What is an opium?"

"Something in cough mixture," said Tristran. "Like eucalyptus."

"It does not sound particularly romantic," said Victoria Forester. "Anyway, should you not be running off to retrieve my fallen star? It fell to the East, over there." And she laughed again. "Silly shop boy. It is all you can do to ensure that we have the ingredients for rice pudding."

"And if I brought you the fallen star?" asked Tristran lightly. "What would you give me? A kiss? Your hand in marriage?"

"Anything you desire," said Victoria, amused.

"You swear it?" asked Tristran.

They were walking the last hundred yards now, up to the Foresters' farmhouse. The windows burned with lamplight, yellow and orange.

"Of course," said Victoria, smiling.

The track to the Foresters' farm was bare mud, trodden into mire by the feet of horses and cows and sheep and dogs. Tristran Thorn went down on his knees in the mud, heedless of his coat or his woollen trousers. "Very well," he said.

The wind blew from the east, then.

"I shall leave you here, my lady," said Tristran Thorn. "For I have urgent business, to the East." He stood up, unmindful of the mud and mire clinging to his knees and coat, and he bowed to her, and then he doffed his bowler hat.

Victoria Forester laughed at the skinny shop-boy, laughed long and loud and delightfully, and her tinkling laughter followed him back down the hill, and away.

ABOUT THE AUTHOR

Neil Gaiman

When Neil Gaiman was a young boy, he was told by the adults around him to stop inventing things that weren't there. Luckily for readers worldwide, he didn't listen, and continues to invent tales of ghosts who raise children, parallel universes, and falling stars that look remarkably like human beings. Born and raised in England, he grew up reading science fiction and fantasy novels by authors like J.R.R. Tolkien, Ursula K. Le Guin, Harlan Ellison and Samuel R. Delany. He was also an avid reader of comic books. These literary influences first brought him to journalism, where he reviewed fantasy books, and then to writing his own comic book series, the most well-known of which is *The Sandman*. Gaiman is also the author of the award-winning novels *Coraline* and *The Graveyard Book*. He now lives in Minneapolis, Minnesota, with his wife and three children.

Vocabulary

bluntly: plainly

cobblestones: round stones used to pave a road

cricket: an English game played with a bat and a ball

ford: cross

grandiloquently: in a grandiose manner

grunted: said in a low, hoarse voice

mire: mud and trampled grass mixed together

parlor: front room

penny dreadfuls: stories sold for a penny that told tales of heroes

pledge-Oak: tree under which promises were made

ransacked: searched frantically

scale: climb

shilling novels: inexpensive adventure novels

tinkling: making the sound of a tiny bell

A Haunted House

Whatever hour you woke there was a door shutting. From room to room they went, hand in hand, lifting here, opening there, making sure–a ghostly couple.

by Virginia Woolf

"Here we left it," she said. And he added,"Oh, but here too!" "It's upstairs," she murmured."And in the garden," he whispered "Quietly," they said, "or we shall wake them."

But it wasn't that you woke us. Oh, no."They're looking for it; they're drawing the curtain," one might say, and so read on a page or two. "Now they've found it," one would be certain, stopping the pencil on the margin. And then, tired of reading, one might rise and see for oneself, the house all empty, the doors standing open, only the wood pigeons bubbling with content and the hum of the threshing machine sounding from the farm. "What did I come in here for? What did I want to find?" My hands were empty. "Perhaps it's upstairs then?" The apples were in the loft. And so down again, the garden still as ever, only the book had slipped into the grass.

But they had found it in the drawing room. Not that one could ever see them. The window panes reflected apples, reflected roses; all the leaves were green in the glass. If they moved in the drawing room, the apple only turned its yellow side. Yet, the moment after, if the door was opened, spread about the floor, hung upon the walls, pendant from the ceiling—what? My hands were empty. The shadow of a thrush crossed the carpet; from the deepest wells of silence the wood pigeon drew its bubble of sound. "Safe, safe, safe," the pulse of the house beat softly. "The treasure buried; the room . . ." the pulse stopped short. Oh, was that the buried treasure?

A Haunted House

A moment later the light had faded. Out in the garden then? But the trees spun darkness for a wandering beam of sun. So fine, so rare, coolly sunk beneath the surface the beam I sought always burnt behind the glass. Death was the glass; death was between us; coming to the woman first, hundreds of years ago, leaving the house, sealing all the windows; the rooms were darkened. He left it, left her, went North, went East, saw the stars turned in the Southern sky; sought the house, found it dropped beneath the Downs. "Safe, safe, safe," the pulse of the house beat gladly. "The treasure yours."

The wind roars up the avenue. Trees stoop and bend this way and that. Moonbeams splash and spill wildly in the rain. But the beam of the lamp falls straight from the window. The candle burns stiff and still. Wandering through the house, opening the windows, whispering not to wake us, the ghostly couple seek their joy.

"Here we slept," she says. And he adds, "Kisses without number." "Waking in the morning—" "Silver between the trees—" "Upstairs—" "In the garden—" "When summer came—" "In winter snowtime—" The doors go shutting far in the distance, gently knocking like the pulse of a heart.

Nearer they come; cease at the doorway. The wind falls, the rain slides silver down the glass.

Our eyes darken; we hear no steps beside us; we see no lady spread her ghostly cloak. His hands shield the lantern. "Look, " he breathes." Sound asleep. Love upon their lips."

Stooping, holding their silver lamp above us, long they look and deeply. Long they pause. The wind drives straightly; the flame stoops slightly. Wild beams of moonlight cross both floor and wall, and, meeting, stain the faces bent; the faces pondering; the faces that search the sleepers and seek their hidden joy.

"Safe, safe, safe," the heart of the house beats proudly. "Long years—" he sighs." Again you found me." "Here," she murmurs, "sleeping; in the garden reading; laughing, rolling apples in the loft. Here we left our treasure—" Stooping, their light lifts the lids upon my eyes. "Safe! safe! safe!" the pulse of the house beats wildly. Waking, I cry "Oh, is this your buried treasure? The light in the heart."

Vocabulary

cloak: coat
murmured: said in a quiet voice
pendant: light hanging from the ceiling
shield: cover
stooping: leaning over
threshing machine: grain separator
thrush: a type of small bird

ABOUT THE AUTHOR

Virgina Woolf

Virginia Woolf (1882–1941) was an English writer who was a member of the influential Bloomsbury group in London, a group of writers who shared similar ideas about writing and life. She is most famous for her novels *Mrs. Dalloway*, *To the Lighthouse*, and *Orlando*, as well as her long essay, "A Room of One's Own." The quote, "a woman must have money and a room of her own if she is to write fiction," comes from this essay. Woolf's husband, Leonard, was very supportive of her writing, and also tried to help her through her many depressive episodes, which made it difficult for her to socialize. Her writing abilities remained intact throughout her bouts of illness, but in 1941, she finally succumbed to what is now thought to have been bipolar disorder, committing suicide. Woolf's work is known today for its lyrical language and descriptive qualities, as well as its narrative experimentation, and it has been translated into over 50 languages.

From

"Lies My Father Told Me"

by Ted Allan

If it rained on Sunday my mother wouldn't let me go out, so every Saturday evening I prayed for the sun to shine on Sunday. Once I almost lost faith in God and in the power of prayer but Grandpa fixed it. For three Sundays in succession it rained. In my desperation, I took it out on God. What was the use of praying to Him if He didn't listen to you? I complained to Grandpa.

"Perhaps you don't pray right," he suggested.

"But I do. I say, Our God in Heaven, hallowed be Thy name, Thy will on earth as it is in heaven. Please don't let it rain tomorrow."

"Ah! In English you pray?" my grandfather exclaimed triumphantly.

"Yes," I answered.

"But God only answers prayers in Hebrew. I will teach you how to say that prayer in Hebrew. And, if God doesn't answer, it's your own fault. He's angry because you didn't use the holy language. " But God wasn't angry because next Sunday the sun shone its brightest and the three of us went for our Sunday ride.

On weekdays, Grandpa and I rose early, a little after daybreak, and said our morning prayers. I would mimic his sing-song lamentations, sounding as if my heart were breaking and wondering why we both had to sound so sad. I must have put everything I had into it because Grandpa assured me that one day I would become a great cantor and a leader of the Hebrews. "You will sing so that the ocean will open up a path before you and you will lead our people to a new paradise."

I was six then and he was the only man I ever understood even when I didn't understand his words. I learned a lot from him. If he didn't learn a lot from me, he made me feel he did.

I remember once saying, "You know, sometimes I think I'm the son of God. Is it possible?"

"It is possible," he answered, "but don't rely on it. Many of us are sons of God. The important thing is not to rely too much upon it. The harder we work, the harder we study, the more we accomplish, the surer we are that we are sons of God."

At the synagogue on Saturday his old, white-bearded friends would surround me and ask me questions. Grandpa would stand by and burst with pride. I strutted like a peacock.

"Who is David?" the old men would ask me.

"He's the man with the beard, the man with the bearded words." And they laughed.

"And who is God?" they would ask me.

"King and Creator of the Universe, the All-Powerful One, the Almighty One, more powerful even than Grandpa." They laughed again and I thought I was pretty smart. So did Grandpa. So did my grandmother and my mother.

So did everyone, except my father. I didn't like my father. He said things to me like, "For God's sake, you're smart, but not as smart as you think. Nobody is that smart." He was jealous of me and he told me lies. He told me lies about Ferdeleh.

"Ferdeleh is one part horse, one part camel, and one part chicken," he told me. Grandpa told me that was a lie, Ferdeleh was all horse. "If he is part anything, he is part human," said Grandpa. I agreed with him. Ferdeleh understood everything we said to him. No matter what part of the city he was in, he could find his way home, even in the dark.

"Ferdeleh is going to collapse one day in one heap," my father said. "Ferdeleh is carrying twins." "Ferdeleh is going to keel over one day and die." "He should be shot now or he'll collapse under you one of these days," my father would say. Neither I nor Grandpa had much use for the opinions of my father.

On top of everything, my father had no beard, didn't pray, didn't go to the synagogue on the Sabbath, read English books and never read the prayer books, played piano on the Sabbath and sometimes would draw my mother into his villainies by making her sing while he played. On the Sabbath this was an abomination to both Grandpa and me.

One day I told my father, "Papa, you have forsaken your forefathers." He burst out laughing and kissed me and then my mother kissed me, which infuriated me all the more.

I could forgive my father these indignities, his not treating me as an equal, but I couldn't forgive his telling lies about Ferdeleh. Once he said that Ferdeleh "smelled up" the whole house, and demanded that Grandpa move the stable. It was true that the kitchen, being next to the stable which was in the back shed, did sometimes smell of hay and manure but, as Grandpa said, "What is wrong with such a smell? It is a good healthy smell."

It was a house divided, with my grandmother, mother and father on one side, and Grandpa, Ferdeleh and me on the other. One day a man came to the house and said he was from the Board of Health and that the neighbours had complained about the stable. Grandpa and I knew we were both beaten then. You could get around the Board of Health, Grandpa informed me, if you could grease the palms of the officials. I suggested the obvious but Grandpa explained that this type of "grease" was made of gold. The stable would have to be moved. But where?

As it turned out, Grandpa didn't have to worry about it. The whole matter was taken out of his hands a few weeks later.

Next Sunday the sun shone brightly and I ran to the kitchen to say my prayers with Grandpa. But Grandpa wasn't there. I found my grandmother there instead—weeping. Grandpa was in his room ill. He had a sickness they call diabetes and at that time the only thing you could do about diabetes was weep. I fed Ferdeleh and soothed him because I knew how disappointed he was.

That week I was taken to an aunt of mine. There was no explanation given. My parents thought I was too young to need any explanations. On Saturday next I was brought home, too late to see Grandpa that evening, but I felt good knowing that I would spend the next day with him and Ferdeleh again.

When I came to the kitchen Sunday morning Grandpa was not there. Ferdeleh was not in the stable. I thought they were playing a joke on me so I rushed to the front of the house expecting to see Grandpa sitting atop the wagon waiting for me.

But there wasn't any wagon. My father came up behind me and put his hand on my head. I looked up questioningly and he said, "Grandpa and Ferdeleh have gone to heaven. . . ."

When he told me they were never coming back, I moved away from him and went to my room. I lay down on my bed and cried, not for Grandpa and Ferdeleh, because I knew they would never do such a thing to me, but about my father, because he had told me such a horrible lie.

ABOUT THE AUTHOR

Ted Allan

Ted Allan (born Alan Herman, 1916–1995) was a Canadian playwright, actor, screenwriter, novelist, and biographer who grew up in Montréal. When asked to write a story quickly for the Canadian Jewish Congress Bulletin in 1949, Allan initially refused: The editor wanted the story that evening! Allan eventually relented, creating a story in just a few hours. The story, "Lies My Father Told Me," was based on his relationship with his grandfather, a religious Jew, and Allan later rewrote it as a screenplay for the Academy-award-winning film of the same name. His son, Norman Allan, rewrote the story with him as a novella.

Stress: WHAT IT IS AND HOW TO MANAGE IT

Feeling like there are too many pressures and demands on you? Losing sleep worrying about tests and schoolwork? Eating on the run because your schedule is just too busy? You're not alone. Everyone experiences stress at times—adults, teens, and even kids. But there are things you can do to minimize stress and manage the stress that's unavoidable.

WHAT IS STRESS?

Stress is a feeling that's created when we react to particular events. It's the body's way of rising to a challenge and preparing to meet a tough situation with focus, strength, stamina, and heightened alertness.

The events that provoke stress are called stressors, and they cover a whole range of situations—everything from outright physical danger to making a class presentation or taking a semester's worth of your toughest subject.

The human body responds to stressors by activating the nervous system and specific hormones. This natural reaction is known as the stress response. Working properly, the body's stress response enhances a person's ability to perform well under pressure. But the stress response can also cause problems when it overreacts or fails to turn off and reset itself properly.

GOOD STRESS AND BAD STRESS

The stress response (also called the fight or flight response) is critical during emergency situations, such as when a driver has to slam on the brakes to avoid an accident. It can also be activated in a milder form at a time when the pressure's on but there's no actual danger, like sitting down for a final exam. A little of this stress can help keep you on your toes, ready to rise to a challenge. And the nervous system quickly returns to its normal state, standing by to respond again when needed.

But stress doesn't always happen in response to things that are immediate or that are over quickly. Ongoing or long-term events, like coping with a divorce or moving to a new neighbourhood or school, can cause stress, too. Long-term stressful situations can produce a lasting, low-level stress that's hard on people. This can wear out the body's reserves, leave a person feeling depleted or overwhelmed, weaken the body's immune system, and cause other problems.

WHAT CAUSES STRESS OVERLOAD?

Although just enough stress can be a good thing, stress overload is a different story—too much stress isn't good for anyone. For example, feeling a little stress about a test that's coming up can motivate you to study hard. But stressing out too much over the test can make it hard to concentrate on the material you need to learn.

Pressures that are too intense or last too long, or troubles that are shouldered alone, can cause people to feel stress overload. Here are some of the things that can overwhelm the body's ability to cope if they continue for a long time:

- being bullied or exposed to violence or injury
- relationship stress, family conflicts, or the heavy emotions that can accompany a broken heart or the death of a loved one
- ongoing problems with schoolwork related to a learning disability or other problems, such as attention deficit disorders (usually once the problem is recognized and the person is given the right learning support, the stress disappears)
- crammed schedules, not having enough time to rest and relax, and always being on the go

SIGNS OF STRESS OVERLOAD

People who are experiencing stress overload may notice some of the following signs:

- **anxiety or panic attacks**
- **a feeling of being constantly pressured, hassled, and hurried**
- **irritability and moodiness**
- **physical symptoms, such as stomach problems, headaches, or even chest pain**
- **allergic reactions, such as eczema or asthma**
- **problems sleeping**
- **drinking too much, smoking, overeating, or doing drugs**
- **sadness or depression**

Everyone experiences stress a little differently. Some people become angry and act out their stress or take it out on others. Some people internalize it and develop eating disorders or substance abuse problems. And some people who have a chronic illness may find that the symptoms of their illness flare up under an overload of stress.

KEEP STRESS UNDER CONTROL

What can you do to deal with stress overload or, better yet, to avoid it in the first place? Stress-management skills work best when they're used regularly, not just when the pressure's on. Here are some things that can help you keep stress under control.

- **Take a stand against overscheduling.** If you're feeling stretched, consider cutting out an activity or two, opting for just the ones that are most important to you.
- **Be realistic.** Don't try to be perfect—no one is. And expecting others to be perfect can add to your stress level, too (not to mention put a lot of pressure on them!). If you need help on something, like schoolwork, ask for it.
- **Get a good night's sleep.** Getting enough sleep helps keep your body and mind in top shape, making you better equipped to deal with any negative stressors. Your biological "sleep clock" may cause you to prefer staying up a little later at night, but if you still need to get up early for school, you may not get all the hours of sleep you need.
- **Learn to relax.** The body's natural antidote to stress is called the relaxation response. It's your body's opposite of stress, and it creates a sense of well-being and calm. You can help trigger the relaxation response by learning simple breathing exercises to use in stressful situations. And ensure you stay relaxed by building time into your schedule for activities that are calming and pleasurable.

- **Treat your body well.** Experts agree that getting regular exercise helps people manage stress. (Excessive or compulsive exercise can contribute to stress, though, so as in all things, use moderation.) And eat well to help your body get the right fuel to function at its best. Under stressful conditions, the body needs its vitamins and minerals more than ever. In addition, alcohol or drugs may seem to lift stress temporarily, but they actually promote more stress because they wear down the body's ability to bounce back.
- **Watch what you're thinking.** Your outlook, attitude, and thoughts influence the way you see things. Is your cup half full or half empty? A healthy dose of optimism can help you make the best of stressful circumstances. Even if you're out of practice, or tend to be a bit of a pessimist, everyone can learn to think more optimistically and reap the benefits.
- **Solve the little problems.** Learning to solve everyday problems can give you a sense of control. But avoiding them can leave you feeling like you have little control and that just adds to stress. Develop skills to calmly look at a problem, figure out options, and take some action toward a solution.

BUILD YOUR RESILIENCE

Ever notice that certain people seem to adapt quickly to stressful circumstances and take things in stride? If you want to build your resilience, work on developing these attitudes and behaviours:

- Think of change as a challenging and normal part of life.
- See setbacks and problems as temporary and solvable.
- Believe that you will succeed if you keep working toward your goals.
- Take action to solve problems that crop up.
- Build strong relationships and keep commitments to family and friends.
- Have a support system and ask for help.
- Participate regularly in activities for relaxation and fun.

Learn to think of challenges as opportunities and stressors as temporary problems, not disasters. Practise solving problems and asking others for help and guidance rather than complaining and letting stress build. Make goals and keep track of your progress. Make time for relaxation. Be optimistic. Believe in yourself. Be sure to breathe. And let a little stress motivate you into positive action to reach your goals.

Source: Adapted from "Stress," TeensHealth, Nemours Foundation.

Before You Sign *Any* Contract:

10 Things You Need to Know

You've decided to get that cellphone, credit card, or gym membership. Do you know exactly what you are getting into? Before you sign any contract on the dotted line, here are the 10 things you need to know:

1 Shop around!

Understand exactly what each company is offering. The more you know, the more you can negotiate. Compare price, guarantee/warranty, duration of contract, and any terms or conditions that are important to you.

2 Know who you're dealing with.

Reputation is important, so ask friends or family for references. If you are not sure about a company's reputation, check with the Better Business Bureau or investigate a company online.

3 Negotiate!

Most contracts can be negotiated. Use the information you gathered while shopping around to get the best service and price. If the company or individual wants your business, they will listen to your arguments. Don't feel pressured—it is your decision to make!

4 Pay attention to details before signing a written contract.

Don't rely on verbal promises; make sure any agreements or claims made by the salesperson are written into the contract. Strike out elements you do not want to sign for and have them initialled by you and the salesperson before you sign. Fill all blank spaces so that details cannot be added later by the salesperson.

5 Understand everything in the contract before agreeing to it.

Ask more questions or ask someone knowledgeable for advice if there are elements you don't understand. And don't forget the fine print; it is part of the contract too! If you feel you need to, have a lawyer review the contract.

6 Find out whom to call for help or to lodge a complaint.

Ask the salesperson for a customer service phone number and the steps to take if you need to make a complaint.

7 A contract means you are responsible.

It is a legal document, so you will have to live with what you agreed to. Generally, a contract cannot be changed or broken unless you and the other party both agree (see next tip).

8 Know how to get out of it.

Usually, a short period of time is allowed to end a contract without penalty; it's called the "cooling off period" and it should be described in the contract. If not, it doesn't mean you don't have access to it, so check with the Consumer Protection Act of your province. Otherwise, to end a contract before it is over, both parties have to agree and most of the time, it will cost you!

9 Sleep on it!

Is this what you really need and want? It's okay to change your mind before signing or agreeing to a contract.

10 Once you've agreed to a contract, make sure you get a copy – and keep it!

You may need it later on for reference, or to launch a complaint if you have a problem.

Source: Financial Consumer Agency of Canada

The Truth about "Rehab" and Drug Addiction

THE REALITY IS FAR FROM GLAMOROUS

Popular culture is filled with stories about the glitzy lives of celebrities, from the designer clothes they wear to their latest romances. It's easy to assume that everything they do is glamorous—including going to "rehab."

"Rehab" is a commonly used term that can refer to a range of drug treatment options. While some of the centres you see in the news might seem like five-star resorts, there is a big difference: These centres are designed to treat drug and alcohol addiction, which is anything but glamorous. The reality is that it's a serious disease that affects the brain and body. Addiction can destroy what people love most—their personal relationships, their careers, and, for some, their lives.

The good news is that, with treatment, people suffering from drug and alcohol addiction can recover and live long, healthy lives.

WHAT IS DRUG ADDICTION?

People who are addicted to drugs have a compulsive and sometimes uncontrollable craving for them. Using drugs changes the brain. Once addicted, a person wants to use drugs even when he or she faces extremely negative consequences.

That was the case with Edward, 31, who is recovering from drug addiction. Looking back at his teen years, he remembers that his drug addiction led him to miss school, receive bad grades, and get into trouble at home and with the law. He recalls dismissing all of the bad things that happened because of his drug use. "Once I was addicted, nothing could stop me from taking drugs. I saw the negative consequences I faced from taking drugs as obstacles to my [drug] use and lifestyle rather than as a wake-up call," Edward says.

TREATING A CHRONIC DISEASE

Even after successfully completing a drug treatment program, people who are addicted to drugs may relapse. This is because drug addiction is a chronic disease, like asthma or diabetes—it requires long-term treatment to help people get to a point where they can manage their recovery and regain their lives. Also, as with other chronic diseases, patients can relapse. Relapse does not mean that treatment failed—rather it's a signal that treatment should be started again or modified to make it more effective. The chronic nature of addiction means that people may need treatment or support throughout their lives, and patients often need treatment multiple times to manage the disease.

ISSUES WITH GETTING HELP

Many people who need treatment for drug or alcohol abuse do not receive it. In 2007, 23.2 million people age 12 or older needed treatment, but only 2.4 million individuals—about 10.3 percent of people in need—actually received treatment for their addiction problems.

Why are some teens and adults not getting the help they need? Some people won't admit they have a problem. Sometimes people don't know how to get help. Others know they have a problem and how to get help but don't seek treatment for a range of different reasons.

It is important to get help as soon as there is a problem. As Dr. Nora D. Volkow, Director of the National Institute on Drug Abuse (NIDA), points out, "You don't have to wait until you've hit rock bottom to get help. The earlier you get help, the sooner you can begin to recover."

WHERE TREATMENT OCCURS

Residential treatment centres—places where people live and receive intensive treatment and supervision for varying amounts of time—are just one place to get help. People may also receive treatment in hospitals and outpatient clinics. Treatment centres may offer multiple types of treatment, including one-on-one behavioural therapy, group therapy and, when available and appropriate, the use of medications.

Once someone decides to get help, it may take time to determine the best treatment program. There is no quick fix for drug addiction. As with other chronic diseases, it often requires long-term, continuous treatment.

TREATMENT

Whether at a residential treatment centre or an outpatient program, behavioural therapy can play a major role in helping a person manage his or her drug addiction. In one type of behavioural therapy, known as Cognitive Behavioural Therapy, patients come to terms with the harmful consequences of their addiction to drugs. They also learn coping skills for avoiding "triggers" and remaining drug-free.

Avoiding triggers means staying away from things that might cause, or trigger, a person to begin abusing drugs again. As with asthma patients, who avoid dust or smoke to prevent an asthma attack, a person recovering from drug addiction needs to avoid hanging out with friends who abuse drugs and, when possible, avoid extreme stress, which can also trigger a relapse.

Cognitive Behavioural Therapy can also help individuals deal with depression and other mood or anxiety disorders that sometimes go hand in hand with a drug addiction.

For support, people often turn to others in recovery in group therapy settings. People recovering from drug addiction share their experiences and struggles with others facing the same issues.

It was this type of therapy that finally worked for Edward. He received treatment at all types of facilities, including outpatient programs, 28-day and 60–90 day residential drug treatment centres, and a halfway house, before he figured out what worked best.

ROAD TO RECOVERY

Even when a variety of treatments are available, relapses may be part of a person's path to recovery from drug addiction. "I was in and out for several years," says Edward. But treatment for drug addiction does work. The most successful treatment addresses each patient's individual drug-abuse patterns and drug-related medical, psychiatric and social problems. For Edward, becoming willing to accept help from others was the key to long-term recovery. As he explains, "Once I was ready to accept help from other people, I didn't have a relapse. I've been in recovery for seven years now."

Source: Scholastic *Choices*, April 1, 2009

BY JULIA MCKINNELL

Finally, a Food Bank for Vegetarians

Vegetarian Jessica Smith faced a dilemma in June 2006. She and her vegetarian husband were forced to go to a food bank in Toronto. "And of course the inevitable came up: the tuna fish," says Smith, who doesn't eat fish or meat. "My husband is a boxer. He needs to eat. So do I. I have hypoglycemia. It was do or die." The 32-year-old said the couple ate the fish in small bites and swallowed quickly in order not to choke. "We looked at it this way. It was an emergency. It was either we eat it or we're going to get sick."

When Smith heard that a vegetarian food bank was opening in Scarborough, Ontario, she telephoned the food bank's unlikely founder, Malan Joseph, a Catholic real estate agent who eats meat. "It completely blew my mind," says Smith. "I asked if there were other vegetarian food banks. He said no, 'we'll be the only one in Canada.'" (Marzena Gersho, director of national partnerships and programs at the Canadian Association of Food Banks in Toronto, confirms there are no other vegetarian food banks in the country.)

Joseph credits his Hindu vegetarian wife for drawing his attention to the plight of low-income vegetarians. "If you eat meat, you can eat vegetarian and non-vegetarian. But if you are vegetarian, you only have one choice. I've had a dream for 10 years to open up a food bank for vegetarians only," he says. "For many, many low-income vegetarians, it is emotionally disturbing if they go to a regular food bank and are given meat or sausages." The vegetarian food bank is non-profit and receives no government funding. Joseph pays out of his own pocket to rent the warehouse space, a two-level unit in a strip mall.

Smith, who after talking to Joseph signed on as the new food bank's volunteer coordinator, believes she was born with a natural aversion to meat. Growing up in Sarnia, Ontario, she remembers, "I'd eat my broccoli and spinach and all the foods that usually little kids hate. My mother used to have to hide meat in my spinach to get me to eat it."

Among the Ontario Vegetarian Food Bank's potential clients are those who have never eaten meat and would not—even if abstaining from it jeopardized their health. "Anecdotally," says Smith, "we know about people who will not touch meat or fish even if it means they get sick." The food bank's Hindu clients, for instance, believe in the consequences of karma and are unable to inflict injury on any type of creature.

"I don't want to put down a standard food bank. These people do good work," says Smith. "But you won't see any fresh produce there. You get things like peanut butter, canned beans and canned soup." Unfortunately, a lot of canned goods contain chicken and beef broth, says David Alexander, director of operations for the Ontario Vegetarian Association.

Joseph canvasses grocery stores to donate fresh fruit and vegetables. "I've got green vegetables, too many to name. Potatoes, onions, soups, tofu. I've asked for cooking oil but so far no one has donated that because it's a little bit expensive. We've got spices in little packets."

"We're looking at tofu, tempeh, lentils, chickpeas, cottage cheese. Food that has lots of protein," says Smith, adding, "There's this concept that vegetarian food is cheap and that even a low-income person can afford it. Actually, fruits and vegetables can be expensive, and will increase as transportation and oil prices go up."

In April of 2008, a food bank in Golden, B.C., began a pilot project, stocking clients' food hampers with fresh fruits and vegetables, thanks to the generosity of a 90-year-old woman, Ruth Wixon, who bequeathed her house and garden to the city. Food bank volunteers tend to the garden twice a week; clients pick up food hampers on Wednesdays and are overjoyed to find the fresh produce, says Sister Jelaine Christensen, a food bank volunteer. It used to be some clients would look through their hamper, saying, "I can't eat that. I can't eat that." Now, she says, "people are excited!"

The food bank also receives donations from local residents who are participating in the nationwide Plant a Row Grow a Row program. "People are planting vegetables in their gardens and planting a row for the food bank," explains Sister Christensen. "We just had someone call this morning. They had peas they wanted to bring over."

Source: *MacLean's*, August 18, 2008

Another World of Farming

For many Québec family farms, hosting a visitor from another culture is a fascinating trip.

BY **ANDREW MCCLELLAND**

FOR Julie Miller, a sheep producer from Ulverton, life is full of learning opportunities and new experiences. But having a grain producer from Mali visiting and observing her farm for two full weeks was perhaps one of the most rewarding exchanges of a lifetime.

Miller and her family participated in UPA (*L'Union des producteurs agricoles*) International Development's "*Viens marcher ma terre*" ("Come walk our land") program, which pairs agricultural producers from developing countries with family farms who act as hosts to farmers from around the world. The program allows a meeting of minds and perspectives between such diverse nations as Senegal, El Salvador and Guinea with rural communities in Québec such as Saint-Isidore D'Auckland, Compton and Saint-Blaise.

That's how Miller, along with her husband Andrew Smith and their family, got to meet and share production techniques with Amadou Oumar Maïga, a grain producer from Mali, a former French colony in northwestern Africa.

"It was interesting to learn the real similarities between farming in Mali and farming here in Canada," says Miller. "I realized that many farmers don't have a huge cost of production there; in Mali they let their sheep or goats roam in the forest. Amadou was shocked to learn how much debt farmers can incur here."

UPA DI paired Maïga with Miller's Bergerie Hexagone farm to let the Malian grain producer get a feel for Québec agriculture as the conclusion to his month-long stay in late September of 2005. Maïga was not alone in his trip from Africa to

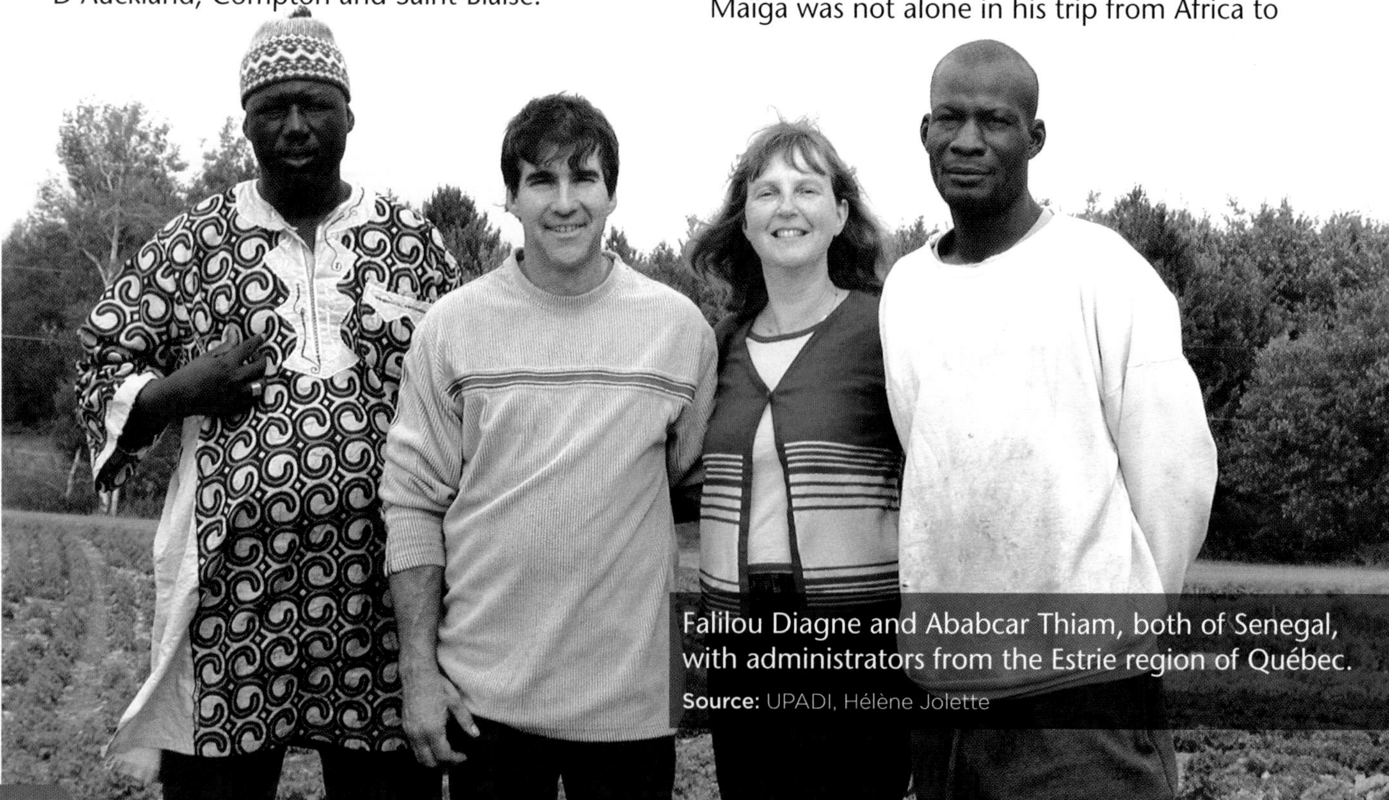

Falilou Diagne and Ababcar Thiam, both of Senegal, with administrators from the Estrie region of Québec.
Source: UPADI, Hélène Jolette

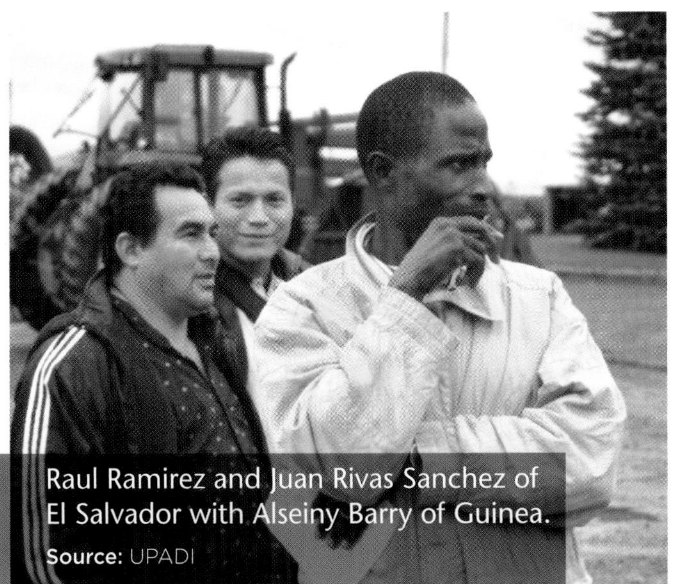
Raul Ramirez and Juan Rivas Sanchez of El Salvador with Alseiny Barry of Guinea.
Source: UPADI

the province. A handful of agricultural producers from developing nations came and stayed with selected host families as part of the *"Viens marcher ma terre"* program, which last year focused on the Estrie region. Visiting farmers spend the first weeks of their trip learning about the UPA, Québec's agricultural and political system, and the advantages of trade unions and collective marketing systems.

Acting as the head of marketing for the Baabahuu Jici cooperative in Mali, the importance and struggle for union organization was one that Maïga knew well.

"I asked him once: 'What are the challenges in setting up your marketing system?'" recounts Miller. "He answered: 'Pride.' He said that in Mali they don't value the farmer. I think that the farming life is so difficult there that if anyone manages to formally educate their children, they go off to the city and don't want to know anything about farming."

Host families in the exchange program are also offered a training session of their own. Before meeting their visiting producer, Québec farmers learn about their exchangee's profile and are offered a brief introduction to their social and cultural background. As any participant in the *"Viens marcher ma terre"* program will attest to, having a visitor from another continent can be a great eye-opener.

"Amadou walked into our house in his robes and turban and told us right away that he was Muslim and that he prayed five times a day, which he did every day he was here," says Miller. "We talked about Islam and Christianity, and I asked about customs and the way of life in Mali. We even listened to a CD of Malian music that I already had and we compared what we liked and what we didn't like on it!"

"Viens marcher ma terre" is put on every year by UPA DI. Support from the union's regional syndicates and specialized federations has been enormous, with financial contributions coming from many of them. With help from the Québec Farmer's Association, UPA DI also hopes to organize exchanges between Québec anglophones and farmers living in former British colonies in Africa—where English is more predominant.

"It was a great experience," says Miller. "I won't pretend that it wasn't difficult, because there was a certain degree of culture shock. Culture shock for Amadou—but also for me. I was experiencing culture shock in my own house. Without a doubt, it introduced me to another world."

Source: *Québec Farmers' Advocate*, April 2006

Vocabulary

culture shock: a very different experience than one is used to in one's own environment

exchangee: person who visits from another country as part of an exchange program

eye-opener: an experience that raises awareness of an issue

hosts: people who have guests from another country stay with them

predominant: most widely used

roam: wander

Emily Carr:

A Biographical Sketch

Emily Carr's life story has all the qualities of an excellent biography — tragedy, inspiration, triumph, resolve, eccentricity — yet the details of her life have been clouded by her own autobiographical sketches and journals. Carr's writings describe events as she herself liked to remember them. Since the publication of Maria Tippett's *Emily Carr: A Biography* in 1979, numerous scholars, biographers, novelists and playwrights have attempted to make sense of her recollections and capture her life in print. As a result, the image of Carr the artist, with her magical forests and magnificent totems; Carr the author, with her stories of nineteenth-century Victoria and her beloved pets; and Carr the eccentric, animal-loving recluse play an important part in the Canadian imagination. The celebrity status she enjoys today would come as a great shock to Carr, who for most of her life felt like an outcast, known more for her eccentricities than her artistic achievements.

Emily Carr at age 21, 1893.
Source: British Columbia Archives

Emily Carr was born on December 13, 1871, in Victoria, British Columbia, to Richard and Emily Saunders Carr. She was the fifth child in a family of five girls. A brother, Dick, was born in 1875. Her father was a British immigrant who, after years of aimless travel, had found success in Alviso, California, selling supplies to miners during the Gold Rush. He met Emily Saunders, married her in England and in 1863 moved his young family to Victoria, where he established a wholesale grocery and liquor store. Emily Carr was a rambunctious child who enjoyed running through the fields and playing with the animals on her family's land. In her early life she did not spend much time with her mother, who had tuberculosis and was frequently bedridden. Carr was extremely close to her father before an incident in her adolescence — which remains unclear but which Carr later referred to as the "brutal telling" — forever destroyed their relationship. Her sensitivity and her devotion to art isolated her from her sisters, who did not understand either her work or her desire to keep doing it in spite of the fact that she earned very little money. Throughout her life, Carr continued to devote herself to art despite her family's lack of support.

Although she produced most of her art during the years she spent in British Columbia, Carr did not go to art school there. In her late teens, after the death of both parents, rather than be subjected to the demands of her overbearing sister Edith, Carr approached her legal guardian for money to attend the California School of Design. She spent more than three years in San Francisco, where she received a traditional education, creating still-life drawings and portraying landscapes. After returning to Victoria for a brief time, Carr travelled to England and studied at the Westminster School of Art and in the private studios of a number of British watercolourists. Here, too, she studied in the nineteenth-century British watercolour tradition. Her year of study in France between 1910 and 1911 proved to be more inspiring: Carr learned from a number of instructors how to paint in a Post-Impressionist style.

She returned to Vancouver in 1911, committed to documenting the First Nations cultures of British Columbia, an exercise that she started in 1907. During an ambitious six-week sketching trip in the summer of 1912, she produced a great number of watercolours and corresponding studio canvases in her new French style. These works met a mixed reception and had limited sales, so Carr returned to Victoria to build and manage an apartment house with her share of the family estate. She was consigned to a life of domestic drudgery for nearly fifteen years until 1927, when her work was included in a National Gallery of Canada exhibition and she first met the Group of Seven. She found the work of Lawren Harris to be particularly inspiring, as were his words of encouragement and his pronouncement that she was "one of them." She returned from this eastern trip to begin the most productive period of her career. At this time, she created the inspired, powerful canvases for which she is best known. She also began a lifelong friendship and correspondence with Harris, who acted as her mentor and spiritual guide, especially in the few years after their first meeting.

Emily Carr, *Tree Trunk*, c. 1931

Carr's health began to deteriorate in 1937, when she suffered the first of many heart attacks. As her sketching trips and studio painting became physically harder, she started to focus on writing. Ira Dilworth, teacher and CBC executive, became her confidant and literary advisor, replacing Harris as the most important male figure in her life. Dilworth's support of her autobiographical sketches gave her both the confidence and the means to try publishing her work. Her writing, initially broadcast on CBC Radio, garnered popular appeal, and the audience that for years had been hostile to her art began to love her work. Emily Carr died in Victoria on May 2, 1945, after checking herself into St. Mary's Priory to rest, with no idea that she would ultimately become a Canadian icon.

Carr experimented with many styles throughout her long career, following the trends in development of modernism in the first half of the twentieth century. Despite changes in her style, approach and intent, she continued to use two principal and often overlapping themes in her work: the "disappearing" First Nations cultures and the western landscape. She is perhaps best known for the work she produced in the last decade of her life — dark and rhythmic forests, vast spiritual skies and monumental totemic structures — when she developed a style that was entirely her own.

Carr slowly began to achieve commercial and critical success in the final years of her career. However, the fame she enjoyed then barely compares to the esteem in which she is held so widely today. Her life is irrevocably connected with the Canadian West, the place where she was born and where she chose to spend her life, with only a few brief interruptions. Her independence as a woman when domesticity was expected, her resolve to travel frequently and unaccompanied to isolated First Nations villages, and her devotion to art despite the obstacles, distractions and criticism, remain inspirational.

Source: Adapted from Vancouver Art Gallery, Emily Carr Exhibit

Vocabulary

aimless: without direction
bedridden: confined to bed by illness
clouded: made inaccurate
drudgery: unpleasant manual work
hostile: showing strong dislike
overbearing: bossy
overlapping: having some similar qualities
portraying: making an image of
rambunctious: active
recollections: memories
sketches: short texts
watercolourists: painters who use watercolour paints

The Day is

by Henry Wadsworth Longfellow

The day is done, and the darkness
Falls from the wings of Night,
As a feather is wafted downward
From an eagle in his flight.

I see the lights of the village
Gleam through the rain and the mist,
And a feeling of sadness comes o'er me
That my soul cannot resist:

A feeling of sadness and longing,
That is not akin to pain,
And resembles sorrow only
As the mist resembles the rain.

Come, read to me some poem,
Some simple and heartfelt lay,
That shall soothe this restless feeling,
And banish the thoughts of day.

Not from the grand old masters,
Not from the bards sublime,
Whose distant footsteps echo
Through the corridors of Time.

For, like strains of martial music,
Their mighty thoughts suggest
Life's endless toil and endeavor;
And to-night I long for rest.

Done

Read from some humbler poet,
Whose songs gushed from his heart,
As showers from the clouds of summer,
Or tears from the eyelids start;

Who, through long days of labor,
And nights devoid of ease,
Still heard in his soul the music
Of wonderful melodies.

Such songs have power to quiet
The restless pulse of care,
And come like the benediction
That follows after prayer.

Then read from the treasured volume
The poem of thy choice,
And lend to the rhyme of the poet
The beauty of thy voice.

And the night shall be filled with music,
And the cares, that infest the day,
Shall fold their tents, like the Arabs,
And as silently steal away.

Vocabulary

- **akin:** to like
- **banish:** be rid of
- **bards:** storytellers
- **corridors:** hallways
- **devoid:** empty
- **endeavour:** effort
- **gleam:** shine
- **gushed:** came out rapidly
- **humbler:** less popular
- **infest:** take over
- **lay:** short lyric or narrative poem meant to be sung
- **martial:** military
- **o'er:** over
- **soothe:** ease
- **steal:** sneak
- **toil:** difficult work
- **wafted:** drifted

ABOUT THE AUTHOR

Henry Wadsworth Longfellow

Henry Wadsworth Longfellow (1807–1882) was an American educator and poet. He is most known for his works "Paul Revere's Ride," *The Song of Hiawatha*, and "Evangeline." He was one of the five members of a group of poets known as the Fireside Poets. He was born in Portland, Maine, and throughout his childhood there, knew that he wanted to write poetry. He became a literature professor at Harvard College, but retired from teaching to focus on his writing. Longfellow's lyric poems, which are known for their musicality, are often based on legends and myths. He was the most popular poet of his day, and his works continue to be read worldwide.

REFERENCE SECTION

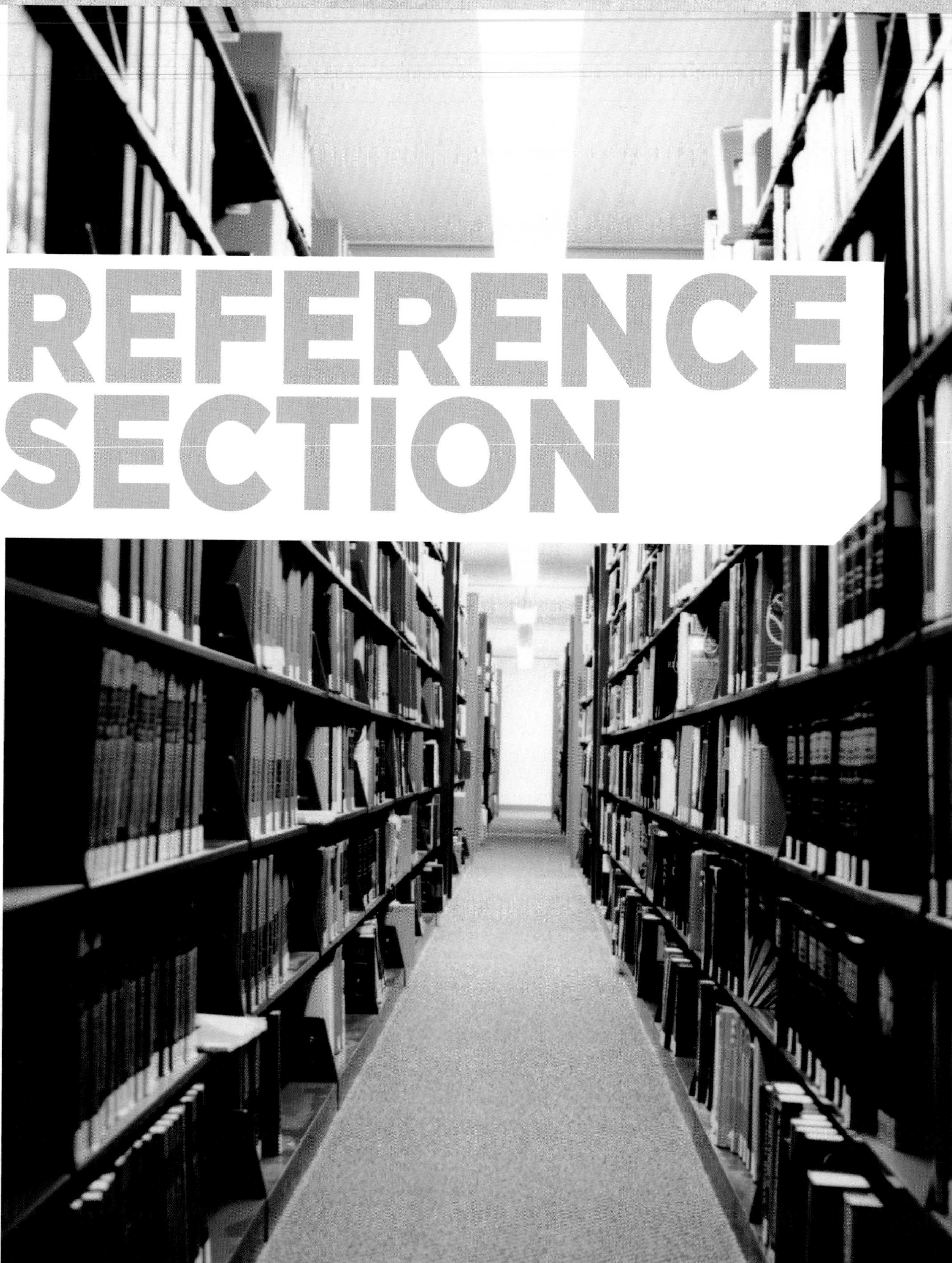

Table of Contents

Grammar

The Simple Tenses

You use the simple tenses to describe facts or events in the past, present or future.

Past	*We **went** to the movies last night.*	*Megan **was** late for practice yesterday.*
Present	*We often **go** to the movies.*	*Megan **is** always late.*
Future	*We **will** probably **go** next weekend.*	*She **will be** late tomorrow.*

The Simple Present

You can use the simple present to describe

• a recurring action, habit or routine	*She **takes** the bus to school.*
• a fact	*The Earth **orbits** around the Sun.*
• a present state or an opinion	*Marc **is** late. I **think** he **is** lost.*

Formation

Affirmative	Negative*	Interrogative
I/You/We/They understand	*I/You/We/They **do not** understand*	***Do** I/you/we/they understand?*
He/She/It understands	*He/She/It **does not** understand*	***Does** he/she/it understand?*

* In everyday English and for most texts, use the contractions *don't* and *doesn't*. Otherwise, the sentence is considered formal.

Affirmative: Use the base form of the verb in all cases. For the third person singular, add an *s* to the base form.

Negative: To make a negative statement, use *do not* (the simple present of the auxiliary verb *to do*) with the base form of the main verb. Use *does not* for the third person singular.

Interrogative: To ask a question, start with the auxiliary *do* or *does*, followed by the subject and the base form of the main verb. For information questions, see page 328.

Time markers: adverbs of time and frequency, such as *all the time, always, at night, every day, frequently, generally, in the morning, never, normally, often, rarely*

Reminder: The verb *to be* does not follow the same rules. Because it is used as an auxiliary verb in many tenses, it is also important to know the contracted form.

Affirmative*		Negative*		Interrogative
I am	*I'm*	*I am not*	*I'm not*	*Am I?*
You are	*You're*	*You are not*	*You're not*	*Are you?*
He/She/It is	*He/She/It's*	*He/She/It is not*	*He/She/It's not*	*Is he/she/it?*
We are	*We're*	*We are not*	*We're not*	*Are we?*
You are	*You're*	*You are not*	*You're not*	*Are you?*
They are	*They're*	*They are not*	*They're not*	*Are they?*

* In everyday English, use the contracted form of the verb *to be*. The following negative contractions are also used: *You/We/They aren't, He/She/It isn't.*

GRAMMAR

The Simple Past

You can use the simple past to describe

• an action or event completed in the past	*Last year, she **worked** as a manager in a clothing store.*
• a past state or opinion	*I **thought** that dogs **were** dangerous but I **was** wrong.*

Formation

Affirmative	Negative*	Interrogative
*I/You/He/She/It/We/They watch**ed***	*I/You/He/It/She/We/They **did not** watch*	***Did** I/you/he/she/it/we/they watch?*
*I/You/He/She/It/We/They **sang***	*I/You/He/She/It/We/They **did not** sing*	***Did** I/you/he/she/it/we/they sing?*

* In everyday English, use the contraction *didn't*.

Affirmative: For regular verbs, the simple past is formed by adding *ed* to the base form of the verb. Irregular verbs in the simple past vary and must be learned. See Common Irregular Verbs on page 317.

Negative: To make a negative statement, use *did not* (the simple past of the auxiliary verb *to do)* with the base form of the main verb.

Interrogative: To ask a question, start with the auxiliary *did*, followed by the subject and the base form of the main verb. For information questions, see page 328.

Time markers: *a year/week/month ago, last summer/Monday/week/month/year, then, yesterday,* etc.

Reminders: To form the affirmative of verbs ending in *e*, add *d* (*to place* = *placed*). For verbs ending in *y*, change the *y* to *ied* (*to try* = *tried*). Some one-syllable verbs that end in a consonant double the consonant before adding *ed* (*stop* = *stopped*).

The verb *to be* does not follow the same rules. Because it is used as an auxiliary verb in many tenses, it is also important to know the contracted form.

Affirmative	Negative*		Interrogative
*I **was***	*I **was not***	*I **wasn't***	***Was** I?*
*You **were***	*You **were not***	*You **weren't***	***Were** you?*
*He/She/It **was***	*He/She/It **was not***	*He/She/It **wasn't***	***Was** he/she/it?*
*We **were***	*We **were not***	*We **weren't***	***Were** we?*
*You **were***	*You **were not***	*You **weren't***	***Were** you?*
*They **were***	*They **were not***	*They **weren't***	***Were** they?*

* In everyday English, use the contracted form of the verb *to be* for negative statements.

The Future

You can use the future to describe

• an intended action	*We **will visit** my grandmother this summer.*
• a future state	*She **will be** very happy.*
• predictable future events	*Winter **will come** soon. People **will eat** too much during the holidays.*
• probable future results	*If we read often, our spelling and writing **will improve**.*

Formation

Affirmative*	Negative*	Interrogative
*I/You/He/She/It/We/They **will** watch*	*I/You/He/She/It/We/They **will not** watch*	***Will** I/you/he/she/it/we/they watch?*

* In everyday English, use the contracted form of *will* (*'ll*) and *will not* (*won't*).

Affirmative: Use the auxiliary *will* with the base form of the main verb in all cases.

Negative: Add *not* after the auxiliary to make a negative statement.

Interrogative: To ask a question, start with the auxiliary *will*, followed by the subject and the base form of the main verb. For information questions, see page 328.

Time markers: *in a week/month, next Monday/week/month/year, soon, this summer/winter, tomorrow,* etc.

Reminder: The verb *to be* follows the same rules as other verbs for the future.

*I **will be** at the meeting. **Will** you **be** there? Jason **won't be**.*

LEARN MORE

The auxiliary verb *shall* is sometimes used instead of *will* in formal English, especially in the interrogative.

*Where **shall** we **meet** after class?*

Another way of expressing or asking about future intentions is to use the simple present of the auxiliary verb *to be* + *going to* and the base form of the main verb.

*We **are going to study** very hard to ace that test.*

***I'm not going to waste** any more time.*

***Are** you **going to help** me with the project?*

You can use the present continuous to talk about definite plans in the near future. See The Present Continuous on page 305.

*We **are meeting** friends at the arena after school.*

***Is** Sheryl **coming** to the concert this weekend?*

You can use the simple future tense to express opinions, assumptions or guesses about the future.

Use verbs like *to believe, to think, to suppose, to doubt, to expect, to hope* and *to know* in the present tense to introduce your idea. Use the simple future for your prediction.

*I believe we all **will pass** the exam.*

*I doubt that I **will get** an A.*

The Continuous Tenses

You use the continuous tenses to describe ongoing actions in the past, present or future.

Past	*I **was reading** when you called.*	*It **was snowing** when I woke up.*
Present	*I **am reading** a great book.*	*It **is snowing** again.*
Future	*I **will be reading** it until you arrive.*	*It **will be snowing** all day.*

GRAMMAR

The Present Continuous

You can use the present continuous to describe

• an action that is happening right now	*It **is** still **raining**.*
• an ongoing action	*We **are writing** a play for English class.*
• definite plans in the near future	*Jen **is tutoring** Max this afternoon.*

Formation

Affirmative*	Negative*	Interrogative
*I **am** think**ing***	*I **am not** think**ing***	***Am** I think**ing**?*
*You **are** think**ing***	*You **are not** think**ing***	***Are** you think**ing**?*
*He/She/It **is** think**ing***	*He/She/It **is not** think**ing***	***Is** he/she/it think**ing**?*
*We **are** think**ing***	*We **are not** think**ing***	***Are** we think**ing**?*
*You **are** think**ing***	*You **are not** think**ing***	***Are** you think**ing**?*
*They **are** think**ing***	*They **are not** think**ing***	***Are** they think**ing**?*

* In everyday English, use the contracted form of the auxiliary verb *to be: I'm, you're, he's, she's, it's, we're, they're; I'm not, he/she/it isn't, you/we/they aren't.*

Affirmative: Use the simple present of the auxiliary verb *to be* and the present participle of the main verb. See Present Participles on page 314.

Negative: Add *not* after the auxiliary verb to make a negative statement.

Interrogative: To ask a question, start with the auxiliary verb, followed by the subject and the present participle of the main verb. For information questions, see page 328.

Time markers: *again, always, at the moment, later, now, right now, still, this morning/afternoon/evening, today, tonight,* etc.

Reminder: Some verbs, such as *to agree, to believe, to remember, to understand, to desire, to like, to mind, to fear,* are generally not used in the continuous tenses.

LEARN MORE

You can use the present continuous **in the negative** to indicate that an action that is not occurring perhaps should be. For example, *We are not trying* could indicate that we should be trying harder.

You can use the present continuous **in the interrogative** to ask a question about an action that is occurring but perhaps should not be. The question *Are you leaving?* could imply that you should not be leaving.

The Past Continuous

You can use the past continuous to describe

• an action that was happening at a specific point in the past	*The plane **was landing**.*
• an ongoing action in the past	*Simon **was travelling** around Europe.*

Formation

Affirmative	Negative*	Interrogative
*I/He/She/It **was thinking***	*I/He/She/It **was not thinking***	***Was** I/he/she/it **thinking**?*
*You/We/They **were thinking***	*You/We/They **were not thinking***	***Were** you/we/they **thinking**?*

* In everyday English, use the contracted form *(wasn't, weren't) for negative statements.*

Affirmative: Use the simple past tense of the auxiliary verb *to be* and the present participle of the main verb. See Present Participles on page 314.

Negative: Add *not* after the auxiliary verb to make a negative statement,

Interrogative: To ask a question, start with the auxiliary verb, followed by the subject and the present participle of the main verb. For information questions, see page 328.

Time markers: *that morning/afternoon/evening, then, when, while,* etc.

Reminder: Some verbs, such as *to agree, to believe, to remember, to understand, to desire, to like, to mind, to fear,* are generally not used in the continuous tenses.

The Future Continuous

You can use the future continuous to describe

• an action that will be happening at a specific point in the future	*Ben **will be meeting** Noah tomorrow.*
• an ongoing action in the future	*They **will be performing** all week.*

Formation

Affirmative*	Negative*	Interrogative
*I/You/He/She/It/We/They **will be thinking***	*I/You/He/She/It/We/They **will not be thinking***	***Will** I/you/he/she/it/we/they **be thinking**?*

* In everyday English, use the contracted form of *will ('ll)* and *will not (won't).*

Affirmative: Use *will be* (the future tense of the auxiliary verb *to be*) and the present participle of the main verb. See Present Participles on page 314.

Negative: Use *will not be* with the present participle of the main verb to make a negative statement.

Interrogative: To ask a question, start with the auxiliary *will*, followed by the subject, *be*, and the present participle of the main verb. For information questions, see page 328.

Time markers: *in (three) days/weeks/months, soon, by then/tomorrow/Monday, later, all afternoon/day/month,* etc.

The Perfect Tenses

You use the perfect tenses to describe past actions in relation to the past, present or future.

Past	*We **had seen** this movie before but we still enjoyed it.*
Present	*Pascale **has gone** to Paris many times.*
Future	*The train **will** probably **have left** when we get there.*

The Present Perfect

You can use the present perfect to describe

• a recently completed action	*I **have done** all my homework.*
• an action completed at an unspecified time in the past	*She **has** already **read** this book.* *We **have seen** this movie many times.*

Formation

Affirmative*	Negative*	Interrogative
*I/You/We/They **have played***	*I/You/We/They **have not played***	***Have** I/you/we/they **played**?*
*He/She/It **has played***	*He/She/It **has not played***	***Has** he/she/it **played**?*

* In everyday English, you can use the contracted form of *have* (*'ve*) and *has* (*'s*).
For example: *I**'ve not** played hockey since I was nine years old. She**'s** played for years.*

Affirmative: Use *have/has* (the simple present of the auxiliary verb *to have*) and the past participle of the main verb. See Past Participles on page 314.

Negative: Add *not* after the auxiliary verb to make a negative statement.

Interrogative: To ask a question, start with the auxiliary verb, followed by the subject and the past participle of the main verb. For information questions, see page 328.

Time markers: *already, always, before, for, lately, never, recently since, yet,* etc.

Reminder: The past participle of regular verbs ends in *ed* (*worked, moved*). For irregular verbs, the past participles vary and must be learned. See Common Irregular Verbs on page 317.

LEARN MORE

You can also use the present perfect to describe an unfinished action that began in the past and will probably continue.

*This library **has served** the community for 30 years.*

*Martine **has** always **lived** in Sherbrooke.*

GRAMMAR

GRAMMAR

The Past Perfect

You can use the past perfect to describe an action that happened in the past before some other past event.

*Malika **had sent** me an email before she called.*

*This **had happened** many times before.*

Formation

Affirmative*	Negative*	Interrogative
*I/You/He/She/It/We/They **had played***	*I/You/He/She/It/We/They **had not played***	***Had** I/you/he/she/it/we/they **played**?*

* In everyday English, you can use the contracted form of *had* (*'d*).
For example: ***I'd** never played hockey before, but she**'d** played the game before.*

Affirmative: Use *had* (the simple past of the auxiliary verb *to have*) and the past participle of the main verb. See Past Participles on page 314.

Negative: Add *not* after the auxiliary verb to make a negative statement.

Interrogative: To ask a question, start with the auxiliary verb, followed by the subject and the past participle of the main verb. For information questions, see page 328.

Time markers: *already, always, as soon as, before, for, never, the moment, until, when,* etc.

Reminder: The past participle of regular verbs ends in *ed* (*worked, moved*). For irregular verbs, the past participles vary and must be learned. See Common Irregular Verbs on page 317.

The Future Perfect

You can use the present perfect to describe an action that will occur in the future before some other future event.

*We **will have finished** our presentation when the bell rings.*

*By June, you **will have mastered** the perfect tenses.*

Formation

Affirmative*	Negative*	Interrogative
*I/You/He/She/It/We/They **will have played***	*I/You/He/She/It/We/They **will not have played***	***Will** I/you/he/she/it/we/they **have played**?*

* In everyday English, use the contracted form of *will* (*'ll*) and *will not* (*won't*).
For example: *By the end of June, they**'ll** have finished high school.*

Affirmative: Use *will have* (the future of the auxiliary verb *to have*) and the past participle of the main verb. See Past Participles on page 314.

Negative: Use *will not have* with the past participle of the main verb to make a negative statement.

Interrogative: To ask a question, start with the auxiliary *will*, followed by the subject, *have*, and the past participle of the main verb. For information questions, see page 328.

Time markers: *by a certain date (e.g. by Friday, by next year, by the end of January), by that time, by then, when,* etc.

The Conditional Tenses

You use the conditional tenses to describe probable, possible or unreal actions or situations.

Present	*Myriam* ***would study*** *more if she had time.* *The stores* ***should*** *still* ***be*** *open.* *If I* ***could afford*** *a car, I* ***would get*** *my driver's permit.*
Perfect	*I* ***would have told*** *you if I had known.* *You* ***would have liked*** *that movie.* *They* ***could have waited*** *for us.*

The Present Conditional

You can use the present conditional to describe

• an unreal event	*If I had more money, I* ***would travel*** *this summer.*
• a probable event	*The plane* ***should land*** *at 10:15 a.m.*
• a possible event	*It* ***could be*** *a bit late.*
• a request or advice	*You* ***should get*** *a tutor if you are having problems with math.*

Formation

Affirmative	Negative*	Interrogative
I/You/He/She/It/We/They ***would*** *walk*	*I/You/He/She/It/We/They* ***would not*** *walk*	***Would*** *I/you/he/she/it/we/they walk?*
I/You/He/She/It/We/They ***should*** *walk*	*I/You/He/She/It/We/They* ***should not*** *walk*	***Should*** *I/you/he/she/it/we/they walk?*
I/You/He/She/It/We/They ***could*** *walk*	*I/You/He/She/It/We/They* ***could not*** *walk*	***Could*** *I/you/he/she/it/we/they walk?*

* In everyday English, you can use the contracted form of *would not* (*wouldn't*), *should not* (*shouldn't*) or *could not* (*couldn't*). For example: *You* ***shouldn't*** *jump to conclusions.*

Affirmative: Use the modal auxiliary *would/should/could* and the base form of the main verb. See Modal Auxiliaries on page 312.

Negative: Add *not* after the modal auxiliary to make a negative statement.

Interrogative: To ask a question, start with the modal auxiliary, followed by the subject and the base form of the main verb. For information questions, see page 328.

Time markers: *if, probably, perhaps, then,* etc.

LEARN MORE

You use the present conditional in indirect speech to report statements made about the future. For example, to report that a friend said, "I will come by to see you tomorrow":

She said that she ***would come*** *by to see us tomorrow.*

To report that a friend said, "I can probably come by tomorrow":

She said that she ***could*** *probably* ***come*** *by tomorrow.*

You can use the present conditional to report past thoughts about the future.

Peter hoped that he ***would*** *eventually* ***study*** *law.*

The Perfect Conditional

You can use the perfect conditional to describe

• an unreal past event	*If he had received your email, he **would have responded**.*
• a probable past event	*The plane **should have landed** at 10:15 a.m.*
• a possible past event	*She **could have missed** the bus.*
• advice about a past event	*You **should have told** me about this earlier.*

Formation

Affirmative	Negative*	Interrogative
*I/You/He/She/It/We/They **would have** walked*	*I/You/He/She/It/We/They **would not have** walked*	***Would** I/you/he/she/it/we/they **have** walked?*
*I/You/He/She/It/We/They **should have** walked*	*I/You/He/She/It/We/They **should not have** walked*	***Should** I/you/he/she/it/we/they **have** walked?*
*I/You/He/She/It/We/They **could have** walked*	*I/You/He/She/It/We/They **could not have** walked*	***Could** I/you/he/she/it/we/they **have** walked?*

* In everyday English, you can use the contracted form of *would not* (*wouldn't*), *should not* (*shouldn't*) or *could not* (*couldn't*).

Affirmative: Use *would/should/could have* and the past participle of the main verb. See Past Participles on page 314.

Negative: Use *would/should/could not have* and the past participle of the main verb to make a negative statement.

Interrogative: To ask a question, start with the modal auxiliary *would/should/could,* followed by the subject, *have,* and the past participle of the main verb. For information questions, see page 328.

Conditional Sentences

Conditional sentences have two parts: the if-clause, which describes the condition, and the main clause, which describes the potential result.

You can use conditional sentences to describe

• a probable event	*If she hurries* (condition), *she will catch the bus.*
• a possible event	*He could pass the final exam if he studies harder* (condition).
• an unreal event	*We would eliminate poverty if we could* (condition).

For Probable or Possible Events

- **If-clause:** Use the simple present.
- **Main clause:** Use the future to indicate an intention or a probable result.

  *If my passport is ready, I **will leave** the country.*

  *Your English **will improve** a lot if you practise.*
- You can indicate that events in the main clause are more or less probable by using the modal auxiliaries *may*, can or *should* with the base form of the verb.

  *If my passport is ready, I **may leave** the country.* (possibility)

  *Your English **should improve** a lot if you practise.* (strong probability).

For Unreal Events

To refer to present or future conditions that could still be fulfilled but are improbable:

- **If-clause:** Use the simple past.
- **Main clause:** Use the present conditional.

*If we had a pool, I **would go** swimming every day.*

*Your English **would improve** a lot if you practised.*

To refer to past conditions that were not fulfilled:

- **If-clause:** Use the past perfect.
- **Main clause:** Use the perfect conditional.

*If we had had a pool, I **would have gone** swimming every day.*

*Your English **would have improved** a lot if you had practised.*

Modal and Auxiliary Verbs

Modals are part of a group of words called auxiliary verbs. Auxiliary verbs combine with ordinary verbs to form tenses or expressions.

Basic Auxiliaries

The basic auxiliaries (*to be, to have, to do*) combine with the present participle, past participle or base form of verbs to form progressive tenses (*She **is** sleeping*), perfect tenses (*They **had** tried*) and simple tenses (*I **do not** understand*).

Formation

	Present*	Past*
to be	*I **am** sleeping* *He/She/It **is** sleeping* *You/We/They **are** sleeping*	*I/He/She/It **was** sleeping* *You/We/They **were** sleeping*
to have	*I/You/We/They **have** tried* *He/She/It **has** tried*	*I/You/He/She/It/We/They **had** tried*
to do	*I/You/We/They **do** not understand* *He/She/It **does not** understand*	*I/You/He/She/It/We/They **did not** understand*

* In everyday English, you can use the contracted form of these auxiliary verbs: *am ('m), is ('s) are ('re), is not (isn't), are not (aren't); was not (wasn't), were not (weren't); have ('ve), has ('s), had ('d); do not (don't) does not (doesn't), did not (didn't)*. For example: *We'**ve** told everyone that we **aren't** going on the ski trip.*

Negative: Add *not* after the auxiliary verb to make a negative statement.

*We **didn't** work last Friday. They **had not** asked us to.*

Interrogative: To ask a question, start with the auxiliary, followed by the subject and the base form or participle of the main verb. Question words go at the beginning of the sentence. See Information Questions on page 328.

***Has** he called yet? When **did** you send that letter?*

Modal Auxiliaries

You can use modal auxiliaries (*can, could, may, might, must, will, would, shall, should*) to express an ability, intention, obligation, advice, a possibility, permission or request.

Modal	To Express	Example
can	ability	***Can*** *you speak Spanish?*
could	possibility advice past ability request	*She's late. She* ***could*** *have missed the bus.* *You* ***could*** *do additional research on the topic.* *When I was six, I* ***could*** *spend hours playing.* ***Could*** *you send me Simon's address?*
may	permission possibility	*You* ***may*** *use your dictionaries for this task.* *It* ***may*** *snow later today.*
might	lesser possibility	*They* ***might*** *drop by tomorrow.*
must	obligation advice	*We* ***must*** *hand in our essays tomorrow.* *You really* ***must*** *see that movie: it's great!*
will	definite intention	*I* ***will*** *travel a lot when I am older.*
would	desire request	*They* ***would*** *travel more if they could.* ***Would*** *you hold the door, please?*
shall	request for advice or agreement	***Shall*** *we meet in the study hall?* *Let's meet at eight,* ***shall*** *we?*
should	advice strong possibility	*We* ***should*** *look it up in the reference section.* *If we practise our presentation, it* ***should*** *go well.*

Formation

Affirmative: Use the modal auxiliary with the base form of the verb.

Negative: Add *not* after the modal auxiliary to make a negative statement. In everyday English, you can use the contracted form of *will not (won't), would not (wouldn't), should not (shouldn't), cannot (can't)* and *could not (couldn't)*.

Paul ***couldn't*** *remember her address. He* ***might not*** *arrive on time.*

Interrogative: To ask a question, start with the modal auxiliary, followed by the subject and the base form of the main verb. Question words go at the beginning of the sentence. See Information Questions on page 328.

May *I leave now? When* ***should*** *I come back?*

LEARN MORE

Some short phrases are used like modals with the base form of verbs to express capability (*be able to*), intention (*be going to*), permission (*be allowed to*) or necessity (*have to*). Unlike modals, they must be conjugated.

We ***will be able to*** *help you after school.*
Was *Ravi* ***able to*** *help you?*
He ***was allowed to*** *keep his cellphone.*
You ***are not allowed to*** *keep your textbook.*

I ***am going to*** *work harder this term.*
They ***were going to*** *work late.*
She ***has to*** *hand in her essay by Friday*
When ***will*** *we* ***have to*** *hand in our project?*

The Active and Passive Voices

The Active Voice

You use the **active voice** when the subject is agent or doer of the action.

*Jean **wrote** a letter.*

Jean (the subject, or doer of the action) *wrote* (the action) *a letter.*

The Passive Voice

You use the **passive voice** when the subject is not the agent or doer of the action **or** when the agent is not identified.

*The letter **was written** by Jean.* (The subject is not the agent.)

The letter was written. (The agent is not identified.)

You can use the passive voice for reports, such as science reports, in which the agent is less important than the facts or analysis. The passive voice is also useful for instructions and rules.

*Your application must **be received** by Monday.*

Formation

- The passive voice uses the auxiliary verb *to be* with the past participle of the main verb. See Past Participles on page 314. The following chart lists the active and passive forms of the verb *to give* in the third person singular.

Verb Form	Active Voice	Passive Voice
Simple present	*gives*	*is given*
Present continuous	*is giving*	*is being given*
Simple past	*gave*	*was given*
Past continuous	*was giving*	*was being given*
Present perfect	*has given*	*has been given*
Past perfect	*had given*	*had been given*
Future	*will give*	*will be given*
Present conditional	*would give*	*would be given*
Perfect conditional	*would have given*	*would have been given*
Present infinitive	*to give*	*to be given*
Perfect infinitive	*to have given*	*to have been given*
Present participle/gerund	*giving*	*being given*
Perfect participle	*having given*	*having been given*

- To change a sentence from active to passive, you have two options:

1. Move the agent to the end of the sentence and introduce it with the preposition *by*.

   *The janitor **cleans** the pool every week.* → *The pool **is cleaned** by the janitor every week.*

2. Eliminate the agent and describe only the action.

   *The pool **is cleaned** every week.*

Participles

You use participles to form the continuous and perfect tenses, the passive voice, or as adjectives.

Present Participles

You use present participles with the auxiliary verb *to be* to form the continuous tenses.

*They are **skiing**. I had been **studying**. We will be **working**.*

You can use present participles as adjectives to modify a noun.

*We watched a very **boring** documentary about the impact of **dripping** taps.*

You can also use present participles after verbs of sensation, such as *to feel, to see, to hear, to listen, to smell, to watch,* to modify the object of the verb.

*I could smell the bacon **sizzling** and the coffee **brewing** in the kitchen.*

You can use present participles to replace a main clause.

She looked up and saw a large crow land on a branch. → ***Looking** up, she saw a large crow land on a branch.*

Formation

- Add *ing* to the base form of the verb: *work**ing**, play**ing**, hear**ing**, cry**ing***, etc.
- If a verb ends in *e*, the *e* is dropped: *to slide = slid**ing**, to prepare = prepar**ing**.*
- If a verb ends in a consonant preceded by a single vowel, the consonant is usually doubled before adding *ing*: *to bet = bett**ing**, to forget = forgett**ing**.*

Past Participles

You use past participles with the auxiliary verb *to have* to form the perfect tenses.

*We have **negotiated**. They had **refused**. We will have **tried**.*

You also use past participles to form the passive voice.

*Summer jobs are **posted** on the site. They will be **updated** every week.*

You can use some past participles as adjectives to modify a noun.

*The **broken** windows and **torn** curtains made the house look **abandoned**.*

You can use past participles to replace a passive main clause.

George was frightened by the sudden crash. He ran away. → ***Frightened** by the sudden crash, George ran away.*

Formation

- Add *ed* to the base form of regular verbs: *look**ed**, work**ed**, play**ed**, talk**ed***, etc. If a verb ends in *e*, simply add *d*: *to change = change**d**, to prepare = prepare**d**.*
- Past participles of irregular verbs vary and must be learned: *been, chosen, heard, lost, taught*, etc. See Common Irregular Verbs on page 317.

Gerunds and Full Infinitives

Gerunds and full infinitives are verb forms that you use like nouns.

Gerunds

You can use a gerund as the subject of a sentence.

__Hunting__ is an outdoor sport.

You can use a gerund as the object of a verb or after a preposition.

I enjoy __walking__ in the rain but I am tired of __slipping__ on ice.

Gerunds are also used in compound words to indicate purpose: ***running** shoes, **diving** board, **walking** stick, **swimming** pool*, etc.

Formation

- Add *ing* to the base form of the verb: *sing**ing**, walk**ing**, try**ing***, etc.
- If a verb ends in *e*, the *e* is dropped: *to make = mak**ing**, to declare = declar**ing***.
- If a verb ends in a consonant preceded by a single vowel, the consonant is usually doubled before adding *ing: to let = let**ting**, to swim = swim**ming***.

Full Infinitives

You can use a full infinitive as the subject of a sentence:

__To write__ in English may be difficult at first.

You can use a full infinitive as the object of a verb.

I wanted __to call__ you but I forgot __to bring__ your phone number.

You can also use a full infinitive after certain adjectives, such as *happy, lucky, sad, sorry,* and after certain nouns, such as *ability, decision, plan* and *refusal.*

I was so happy __to hear__ about your new job.

Her plan __to go__ to music school fell through.

Reminder: Do not mix gerunds and infinitives in the same sentence.

*She enjoyed **dancing** and **singing**.* (**not** *She enjoyed dancing and to sing.*)

She liked ***to dance*** and ***to sing***. (**not** *She liked to dance and singing.*)

LEARN MORE

Gerunds are often used on signs to indicate that an action is not permitted.

No __smoking__ *No __fishing__ allowed* *No __loitering__*

Some verbs can be followed by an infinitive or a gerund: *to allow, to begin, to continue, to forget, to hate, to like, to love, to mean, to need, to prefer, to regret, to remember, to start, to try.*

Some verbs can only be followed by a gerund: *to admit, to avoid, to consider, to defend, to deny, to enjoy, to finish, to imagine, to mind, to practise, to risk, to suggest.*

Some verbs can only be followed by a full infinitive: *to agree, to ask, to choose, to decide, to expect, to hope, to learn, to plan, to promise, to seem, to want, to wish.*

GRAMMAR

Phrasal Verbs

Phrasal verbs are expressions that combine verbs and prepositions or adverbs. Phrasal verbs often combine a verb and a direction, such as *after, against, around, away, back, down, for, in, off, on, out, over, up*. They have a different meaning from the original verb. For example, the verb *to break* can mean different things depending on the word that follows it.

break away: separate from

break down: divide into parts or lose control emotionally

break in: enter, sometimes forcibly

break off: separate from or end a connection or relationship

break out: burst or escape

break up: end a relationship or take apart

Phrasal verbs can be either transitive (followed by an object) or intransitive (not followed by an object). Depending on their use, some can be both.

Transitive	Intransitive
Look out *for me at the concert.*	***Look out!*** *The ice is cracking.*
I'm going to ***give up*** *eating candy.*	*Don't* ***give up****. You can pass the exam if you try.*
Take off *your hat in class.*	*The plane will* ***take off*** *at 4:05.*

Common Phrasal Verbs

Phrasal Verb	Meaning	Example
be against	be opposed to	*Most people* ***are against*** *the use of sweatshops.*
be over	finish	*The presentation* ***will be over*** *in ten minutes.*
call off	cancel	*They* ***should call off*** *the elections.*
cut off	discontinue	*My Internet connection* ***was*** *suddenly* ***cut off****.*
die out	become extinct	*Many bird species* ***are dying out****.*
fill in	complete	*Please* ***fill in*** *the Venn diagram.*
go over	examine, study	*Let's* ***go over*** *the instructions together.*
leave out	omit	*Marc* ***left out*** *his address on the form.*
look up	search for	*I* ***am going to look up*** *that word in the dictionary.*
make up	invent	***Did*** *she* ***make up*** *an excuse for being late?*
put off	postpone	*The exam* ***has been put off*** *until next Friday.*
stand for	represent	*The symbol C1* ***stands for*** *ESL Competency 1.*
take off	remove	*You* ***can take off*** *your coat.*
take up	start doing	*I* ***should take up*** *a sport.*
try out	test	***Try out*** *your plan before you propose it.*
turn down	refuse, reject	*She* ***turned down*** *a job as a camp counsellor.*
wipe out	destroy	*A hurricane* ***can wipe out*** *whole communities.*
work out	calculate	*We need* ***to work out*** *the cost of our ski trip.*

Common Irregular Verbs

Base Form	Simple Past	Past Participle	Base Form	Simple Past	Past Participle
be	was, were	been	lie	lay	lain
beat	beat	beaten	light	lit	lit
become	became	become	lose	lost	lost
begin	began	begun	make	made	made
bend	bent	bent	mean	meant	meant
bite	bit	bitten	meet	met	met
bleed	bled	bled	pay	paid	paid
blow	blew	blown	put	put	put
break	broke	broken	read	read	read
bring	brought	brought	ride	rode	ridden
build	built	built	ring	rang	rung
buy	bought	bought	rise	rose	risen
catch	caught	caught	run	ran	run
choose	chose	chosen	say	said	said
come	came	come	see	saw	seen
cost	cost	cost	seek	sought	sought
cut	cut	cut	sell	sold	sold
deal	dealt	dealt	send	sent	sent
dig	dug	dug	set	set	set
do	did	done	shake	shook	shaken
draw	drew	drawn	shine	shone	shone
drive	drove	driven	shoot	shot	shot
drink	drank	drunk	show	showed	shown
eat	ate	eaten	shut	shut	shut
fall	fell	fallen	sing	sang	sung
feel	felt	felt	sink	sank	sunk
fight	fought	fought	sit	sat	sat
find	found	found	sleep	slept	slept
fly	flew	flown	slide	slid	slid
forbid	forbade	forbidden	speak	spoke	spoken
forget	forgot	forgotten	spend	spent	spent
forgive	forgave	forgiven	spin	spun	spun
freeze	froze	frozen	stand	stood	stood
get	got	gotten	steal	stole	stolen
give	gave	given	stick	stuck	stuck
go	went	gone	stink	stank	stunk
grow	grew	grown	swear	swore	sworn
hang	hung	hung	swim	swam	swum
have	had	had	take	took	taken
hear	heard	heard	teach	taught	taught
hide	hid	hidden	tear	tore	torn
hit	hit	hit	tell	told	told
hold	held	held	think	thought	thought
hurt	hurt	hurt	throw	threw	thrown
keep	kept	kept	understand	understood	understood
know	knew	known	wake	woke	woken
lay	laid	laid	wear	wore	worn
leave	left	left	win	won	won
let	let	let	write	wrote	written

Adverbs

Types of Adverbs

You use adverbs to add meaning by describing, intensifying or clarifying what you say or write. Adverbs can modify a verb, an adjective, another adverb or a whole sentence.

Type of Adverb	Used to Express	Examples
Manner	**how something** happens or is done	*badly, carefully, fast, neatly, quickly, quietly, seriously, slowly, well*
Degree	**how much** something happens or is done	*almost, completely, enough, extremely, just, rather, really, so, too, very*
Time	**when** something happens	*before, immediately, now, recently, since, soon, still, then, today, yet*
Frequency	**how often** something happens	*always, frequently, never, occasionally, often, once, seldom, sometimes*
Place	**where** something happens	*away, down, everywhere, far, here, near, north, somewhere, there, up*
Sentence	**how** the speaker feels about something	*certainly, definitely, luckily, naturally, sadly, surely, (un)fortunately*

Formation

- Some adverbs have the same form as adjectives: *fast, fine, well, hard, early, late, much, enough*, etc.
- Many adverbs are formed by adding *ly* to an adjective: *smartly, quickly, loudly, really, independently, extremely*, etc.

Position

- An adverb that modifies a verb can follow or precede it, depending on the type of adverb and the emphasis desired.
  *They worked **late** on Thursday and **completely** forgot to call.*
- An adverb that modifies an adjective or another adverb usually precedes it.
  *I was **very** happy that you had done **so** well.*

The Comparative and Superlative of Adverbs

You can use the comparative and superlative forms of adverbs to express degree.

Formation	Comparative	Superlative
Adverbs of one syllable: *fast, near*	Add ***er***: *fast**er**, near**er***	*Add **est**:* *fast**est**, near**est***
Adverbs of two or more syllables: *often, directly*	Add ***more/less***: ***more/less*** often, ***more/less*** directly	*Add **most/least**:* ***most/least*** often, ***most/least*** directly
Irregular adverbs: *badly, far, little, much, well*	Their form varies: *worse, further, less, more, better*	Their form varies: *worst, furthest, least, most, best*

Nouns

Types of Nouns

There are four types of nouns in English:

- **Common nouns**, which identify physical things: *boy, elephant, book, car, water*
- **Proper nouns**, which identify specific people, institutions, places, etc., and always start with a capital: *Anne-Marie, Chicoutimi, Africa, Museum of Fine Arts*
- **Abstract nouns**, which identify feelings, qualities and concepts: *anger, pride, hope, faith, belief, result*
- **Collective nouns**, which are singular words that represent more than one person, creature or thing: *group, pair, trio, herd, team*

Singular, Plural

To change a singular noun to the plural form, follow these rules.

Formation	Examples
For most nouns, you usually add ***s***. This includes nouns that end in a ***vowel*** + ***y***.	*artist**s**, house**s**, manager**s**, prop**s**, street**s**, boy**s**, monkey**s**, tray**s***
For nouns ending in a ***consonant*** + ***y***, drop the ***y*** and add ***ies***.	*cherry = cherr**ies**, city = cit**ies**, country = countr**ies**, fly = fl**ies***
For most nouns ending in ***f*** or ***fe***, drop the ***f*** or ***fe*** and add ***ves***.	*half = hal**ves**, thief = thie**ves**, knife = kni**ves**, life = li**ves**, wife = wi**ves***
Nouns that end in ***ff*** and some nouns that end in ***f*** or ***fe*** are exceptions. You simply add ***s***.	*cliff**s**, staff**s**, chief**s**, handkerchief**s**, proof**s**, safe**s***
For nouns ending in ***o***, ***ch***, ***sh***, ***ss*** or ***x***, add ***es***.	*potato**es**, watch**es**, wish**es**, dress**es**, box**es***
Some words of foreign origin ending in ***o*** are exceptions. You simply add ***s.***	*kilo**s**, kimono**s**, photo**s**, piano**s***
A few common nouns form the plural by changing their form.	*child = child**ren**, man = m**en**, woman = wom**en**, foot = f**ee**t, tooth = t**ee**th, mouse = m**ic**e*
The names of a few creatures do not change in the plural.	*deer, moose, sheep*
Some words are always plural.	*clothes, glasses, pants, scissors*

LEARN MORE

Compound nouns are made up of two nouns or a gerund and a noun. You use hyphens for compound nouns that otherwise would be unclear: *call waiting, city-state, diving board, kitchen table, mother-in-law.*

The plural of most compound nouns is formed by putting the last word in the plural: *city-state**s**, diving board**s**, kitchen table**s***, but *mother**s**-in-law.*

Compound nouns ending in a gerund (*call waiting, weight training*) cannot be made plural. See Countable, Uncountable on page 320.

Countable, Uncountable

A **countable noun** is a noun that **can** be preceded by a number like *one, two, three,* or an indefinite article (*a/an*): *girl, car, flower, week, cloud, layer, part,* etc.
A countable noun can be made plural.

An **uncountable noun** is a noun that **cannot** be preceded by a number like *one, two, three,* or an indefinite article (*a/an*): *snow, ice, advice, help, furniture, weather, shopping,* etc.
Uncountable nouns cannot be made plural.

Examples of Uncountable Nouns	
Substances	*dust, milk, paper, sand, water, wood*
Abstract nouns	*courage, information, knowledge, pity*
Gerunds	*camping, fishing, swimming, surfing*
Other examples	*baggage, garbage, luggage, weather*

Reminder: Some words can fall into both categories. The meaning of the word in a sentence determines if it is countable or uncountable.

*She ate toast with **jam**.* (In this sentence, ***jam*** is an uncountable substance.)

*They sell a wide variety of **jams**.* (In this sentence, ***jam*** refers to varieties of jams and is countable.)

Possessive Form

You use the possessive form of nouns to show ownership. Instead of *the arm of the person,* write or say *the person's arm.*

Formation	Examples
For all nouns that do not end in ***s***, add an **apostrophe** + ***s***	*Marie**'s** boat, the children**'s** toys, today**'s** lesson*
If a plural noun ends in ***s***, add an **apostrophe** only.	*the students**'** essays, the visitors**'** dressing room, the workers**'** representative*
For singular nouns ending in ***s***, add an **apostrophe** + ***s*** if it is natural to pronounce an extra ***s***.	*Thomas**'s** car, the boss**'s** memo, the headmistress**'s** speech, the actress**'s** lines*
If not, add an **apostrophe** only.	*Brussels' parks, Ulysses' travels*

Reminder: The possessive form (***'s***) is mainly used for people, animals, regions and nations: *a conductor**'s** hat, the horse**'s** tail, Charlevoix**'s** attractions, Montréal**'s** architecture, Canada**'s** role.*

It can also be used in time expressions: *a month**'s** vacation, tomorrow**'s** schedule, today**'s** weather, a summer**'s** day, fifteen minutes' break.*

For inanimate objects, use ***of*** to indicate possession: *the walls **of** my house, the front wheels **of** the car.*

Articles

You use **indefinite articles** (*a, an*) with singular countable nouns to refer to unspecified people or things. There is no plural form of the indefinite article. It is simply omitted.

*Anne bought **a** new coat. She loves sales.*

You use the **definite article** (*the*) with singular or plural nouns to refer to specific people or things.

*Anne bought **the** green coat she had seen last Friday.*

- Use ***a*** before a word that starts with a consonant sound: ***a*** *car,* ***a*** *hotel,* ***a*** *union.*
- Use ***an*** before a word that starts with a vowel sound: ***an*** *activity,* ***an*** *error,* ***an*** *hour.*
- Use ***the*** before both singular or plural nouns: ***the*** *group,* ***the*** *procedure,* ***the*** *dishes.*

Exceptions: Do not use an article before the following nouns.

Sports	*She watches **hockey** and **curling** every weekend.*
Places	*We have never been to **Spain** or **Portugal**. We have seen **Paris**.*
Nationalities and languages	***South Americans** and **Spaniards** speak a very different form of **Spanish**.*
Meals	*Let's meet for **lunch**. I didn't have time to have **breakfast**.*

Reminder: Do not use ***a/an*** with uncountable nouns. See Countable, Uncountable on page 320.

Pronouns

You use pronouns to replace nouns in a sentence. They can help you avoid repetition. Use pronouns only when necessary. A sentence can become confusing and meaningless if too many pronouns are used.

Personal Pronouns

You can use personal pronouns as subject pronouns and object pronouns.

Subject Pronouns	*I*	*you*	*he/she/it*	*we*	*you*	*they*
Object Pronouns	*me*	*you*	*him/her/it*	*us*	*you*	*them*

- **Subject pronouns** replace subject nouns.

  *Tom works every day after school. = **He** works every day after school.*

  *Martine and I went to the movies last night. = **We** went to the movies last night.*
- An **object pronoun** replaces a noun that is the direct or indirect object of a verb or the object of a preposition.

  *The teacher asked Leo and Patricia for help. The teacher asked **them** for help.*

  *I received an email from Marc. = I received an email from **him**.*

GRAMMAR

Reflexive Pronouns

You use reflexive pronouns as the direct or indirect object of a verb when the subject and object are the same.

Subject Pronouns	*I*	*you*	*he/she/it*	*we*	*you*	*they*
Reflexive Pronouns	*myself*	*yourself*	*himself/ herself/ itself*	*ourselves*	*yourselves*	*themselves*

Singular reflexive pronouns refer back to a singular subject.

*The computer protects **itself** from viruses.*

*Jenny, please entertain **yourself** while I finish this work.*

Plural reflexive pronouns refer to a plural subject.

*Marc and Lucie, please entertain **yourselves** while I finish this work.*

Reflexive pronouns also follow prepositions.

*Frederic promised to take care of **himself** while on holiday.*

Reminder: You can use reflexive pronouns to give extra emphasis by placing them directly after a noun or pronoun.

*The pop star **himself** made an appearance to accept the award.*

Relative Pronouns

You use relative pronouns to replace a noun or pronoun as the subject or object of a relative clause.

*The person **who** sat next to me kept talking all the time.*

*The game **that** we saw last week was more exciting.*

*A girl, **whose** name I forget, came by with your book.*

Use	Subject Pronoun	Object Pronoun*	Possessive Case
For people	*who*	*whom/who*	*whose*
For things	*that/which*	*which*	*whose/of which*

* In everyday English, the object pronoun is often omitted: *The counsellor (who) I met was very helpful. He was amused by the plan (that) I proposed.* In formal English, we often change ***who*** to ***whom*** for direct objects or objects of prepositions. *The person to whom I spoke gave me this information.*

Reminder: Relative pronouns are often confused with interrogative pronouns *(who, whom, whose, what, which).* The difference is that relative pronouns introduce relative clauses, while interrogative pronouns introduce information questions. See Relative Clauses on page 327.

Possessive Pronouns

You use possessive pronouns to replace a noun and a possessive adjective. It draws attention to the possessor and will help you avoid repeating the noun.

Your shoes are dark green; ***mine*** *(my shoes) are black.*

François forgot his textbook, so Jane lent him ***hers*** *(her textbook).*

You can use possessive pronouns as the subject or object of a verb. Their form remains the same in both cases.

Subject pronouns	*I*	*you*	*he/she/it*	*we*	*you*	*they*
Possessive pronouns	*mine*	*yours*	*his/hers*	*ours*	*yours*	*theirs*
Possessive adjectives	*my*	*your*	*his/her/its*	*our*	*your*	*their*

Reminder: Possessive pronouns in English vary according to their possessor, not according to the noun they modify.

It's Leanna's watch. = It's ***hers****.* but *It's David's watch. = It's* ***his****.*

I got my grades. = I got ***mine****.* but *They got their grades. = They got* ***theirs****.*

Demonstrative Pronouns

You use demonstrative pronouns to replace a noun and a demonstrative adjective. It draws attention to the noun without repeating it.

Who is that teacher? ***That*** *is Mrs. Ling, the gym teacher.*

You can also use demonstrative pronouns to replace a phrase or sentence.

They are cleaning up the park. They do ***this*** *every spring.*

Use ***this*** and ***that*** for singular nouns, and ***these*** and ***those*** for plural nouns.

Reminder: When followed by a noun, *this, that, these* and *those* are demonstrative adjectives. See Demonstrative Adjectives on page 324.

This test is easy. Those shoes are great.

When used alone, they are demonstrative pronouns.

This *is easy.* ***Those*** *are great shoes.*

Interrogative Pronouns

You use interrogative pronouns (*who, whom, whose, what, which*) at the beginning of a sentence to ask for information about people, events or things.

Who *did this?* ***What*** *happened?* ***Which*** *do you want?*

You can use interrogative pronouns to replace a noun and an interrogative adjective to avoid repeating the noun.

Whose cellphone is this? And ***whose*** *is this one?*

Reminder: Interrogative adverbs (*how, when, where, why*) and interrogative adjectives (*what, which, whose*) are also used to ask for information. See Information Questions on page 328.

Adjectives

You use adjectives mainly to modify nouns and pronouns.

Qualitative Adjectives

Qualitative adjectives (*slim, blue, damp, light, round*) provide information about the size, age, shape, colour, origin, material or purpose of a person, creature or thing.

*Martine lives in a **red brick** house by the river.*

You can also use qualitative adjectives after verbs like *to be, to seem, to become* or *to get*.

*When Leo was **young**, the village seemed very **big** to him.*

Qualitative adjectives always remain the same. They do not change to indicate number (singular or plural) or gender (feminine or masculine): *a **tall** girl, a **tall** boy, **tall** trees.*

You can use several adjectives to modify a noun but it is generally best to use no more than three adjectives with a noun. Qualitative adjectives usually follow this order.

Order of Adjectives*	Examples			
1. attitude/emotion	*interesting*	*funny*	*fine*	*sad*
2. size/weight	*small*	*large*	*light*	*heavy*
3. age	*old*	*young*	*new*	*recent*
4. shape	*round*	*square*	*long*	*short*
5. colour	*red*	*green*	*dark*	*pale*
6. origin	*English*	*Roman*	*Ontarian*	*Italian*
7. material	*leather*	*nylon*	*wooden*	*plastic*
8. purpose	*electronic*	*swimming*	*portable*	*technological*

* Adjectives of quantity, demonstrative adjectives and possessive adjectives precede qualitative adjectives: *I bought **these three** great striped T-shirts at the mall.*

Other Types of Adjectives

- **Quantitative adjectives** (*much, many, few, some, any, no,* and most numbers) indicate the number or amount of a noun.

  *This country has **many** natural resources.*

  *They could arrive at **any** time.*

  ***No** dogs are allowed in this area.*

  *I counted **twenty** large black birds in that tree.*

- **Distributive adjectives** (*each, every, either, neither, both, all*) specify inclusions and exclusions.

  *I liked **both** movies a lot; the film critic liked **neither** movie.*

  ***Every** student will receive an information booklet.*

- **Demonstrative adjectives** (*this, that, these, those*) are used with a noun to draw attention to or identify a person, creature or thing.

  *I am not afraid of **that** man.*

  *Look at **these** examples.*

- **Possessive adjectives** (*my, your, his, her, its, our, their*) are used with a noun to indicate a relationship (*my dad, her friend*) or possession (*their car, his theory*).

  *This is **our** apartment. **My** sister and I share a room.*

  *Every day has **its** challenges.*

Reminder: Possessive adjectives in English vary according to their possessor, not according to the noun they modify.

*Mary's mother = **her** mother*	*but*	*Mike's mother = **his** mother*
*Joshua's book = **his** book*	*but*	*Marc and Lorna's book = **their** book*

Remember that the possessive adjective *its* does not take an apostrophe. Do not confuse it with the contracted form of the verb *to be* (*it's*).

- **Interrogative adjectives** (*what, which, whose*) are used with a noun to ask for information about specific people or things. See Information Questions on page 328.

  ***Which** topic did you choose?*

  ***What** college do you plan to attend?*

  ***Whose** dog is that?*

The Comparative and Superlative of Adjectives

You can use the comparative and superlative forms of adjectives to indicate superiority.

Formation	Comparative	Superlative
Adjectives of one syllable: *warm, light*	Add ***er***: *warmer, lighter*	Add ***est***: *warmest, lightest*
Adjectives of two syllables ending in *y*: *happy, hungry*	Change ***y*** to ***ier***: *happier, hungrier*	Change ***y*** to ***iest***: *happiest, hungriest*
Adjectives of two or more syllables: *wonderful, interesting*	Add ***more/less***: ***more** wonderful, **less** interesting*	Add ***most/least***: ***most** wonderful, **least** interesting*
Irregular adjectives: *bad, good, little, many*	Their form varies: *worse, better, less, more*	Their form varies: *worst, best, least, most*

For comparisons of superiority, use the comparative with ***than***.

*The month of July is **warmer than** August.*

For comparisons of inferiority, use ***less*** or ***less . . . than*** with the basic form of the adjective.

*The month of June was **less warm**, but it was **less rainy than** July.*

For comparisons of equality, use the basic form of the adjective with ***as . . . as***:

*We are **as hungry as** you are.*

GRAMMAR

Prepositions

You use prepositions before nouns, pronouns or gerunds to indicate time or place.

- **Prepositions of time** can indicate time, date, duration or elapsed time: *after, at, before, during, for, in, on, since, until.*

  *The test will be **on** Friday, **at** 2:30 p.m.* (date, time)

  *Sara has been attending university **since** September.* (elapsed time)

  *We will wait for you **until** evening.* (duration)

- **Prepositions of place** can indicate place, position, destination, means or movement: *above, across, against, along, behind, below, beside, between, beyond, by, from, in, in front of, near, next to, on, over, through, to, under, with.*

  *They met her **at** the market.* (place)

  *Sit **next to** me.* (position)

  *We will travel **from** New York **to** Washington **by** bus.* (movement, destination, means)

Reminder: You can combine prepositions with verbs to form verbal phrases that modify the original meaning of the verbs. See Phrasal Verbs on page 316.

*Sheila **took off** her glasses.* *Steve **took up** golf.*

Conjunctions and Other Transition Words

You use conjunctions and other transition words to connect two sentences, phrases or words. They have different uses.

Use	Examples of Transition Words
To add another idea	*and, also, besides, furthermore, in addition, moreover*
To compare two different ideas	*but, however, instead, on the other hand, nevertheless, yet*
To contrast ideas	*although, despite the fact that, even if, even though*
To indicate a reason	*as, because, for, since*
To state a consequence	*as a result, because of this, consequently, for this reason, therefore*
To advance a narrative	*after, after that, as soon as, at first, before, during, finally, for a while, immediately, in the late afternoon, later, later on, meanwhile, next,. quickly, suddenly, then, when, while*

- **Coordinating conjunctions** connect two words, phrases or clauses. The main coordinating conjunctions are *and, but, or, nor*. The following phrases are also coordinating conjunctions: *both . . . and, either . . . or, neither . . . nor, not only . . . but also.*

  *We will visit Spain **and either** Italy **or** France.*

  ***Both** Steve **and** Carole are excellent swimmers, **but** they don't compete.*

- **Subordinating conjunctions** introduce subordinate clauses. The most common subordinating conjunctions are *if, that, although, unless, when, for, because, when, while, as.* See Other Subordinate Clauses on page 328.

  *I told her **that** I would arrive on Monday.* *You were out **when** he called.*

- Other transition words, such as some adverbs (*however, so, therefore*) and prepositions (*besides*) can act as conjunctions.

  ***Besides** being an athlete, she is an A student, **so** she deserves a scholarship.*

Sentence Structure

Types of sentences

A sentence may contain one or more clauses. Sentences can be divided into three basic structures: simple, compound and complex.

- **Simple** sentences contain one main clause.

  He (subject) *went* (verb) *to the party*.

- **Compound** sentences contain two or more main clauses, usually connected by a conjunction (*and, but, or, nor,* etc.).

  He (subject) *went* (verb) *to the party* ***and*** *danced* (verb) *all night.*

- **Complex** sentences contain at least one main clause and one subordinate or relative clause, usually connected by a subordinating conjunction or relative pronoun. See Subordinating Conjunctions on page 326, and Relative Pronouns on page 322.

  I think (main clause) ***that*** *I will stay at home tonight* (subordinate clause).

  At the party, he met the woman (main clause) ***who*** *later became his wife* (relative clause).

Reminder: A subordinate clause must include a subject and verb. Subordinate clauses also include relative clauses and if-clauses. See Conditional Sentences on pages 310–311.

Relative Clauses

Relative clauses are introduced by relative pronouns (*who, whom, whose, that, which, of which*). You use them to provide information about people, things or events.

- **Defining** clauses complete a sentence by giving essential information that identifies a person or thing in the main clause.

  I returned the book ***that*** *Bertrand had lent me*. (The relative clause identifies which book.)

  The musician ***who*** *wrote that song isn't well known.* (The relative clause identifies which musician.)

- **Non-defining** clauses add non-essential information to a sentence and are separated from the main clause by commas. They do not change the meaning of the main clause.

  The party, ***which*** *was attended by many students,* (non-essential information) *was held on April 14.*

  My mother, ***who*** *is an optimist*, (non-essential information) *thinks the economy will improve soon.*

- **Connective** clauses continue the story but do not add information that identifies the person, event or thing in the main clause. They are separated by a comma.

  At the party I spoke to Marie, ***who*** *said she was tired of school.*

GRAMMAR

Other Subordinate Clauses

Types of Clauses	Examples
Clauses of reason and result (introduced with *as, because, since, that, so*) explain why something happened or the result.	*You arrived late* ***because*** *you overslept.* ***Since*** *you didn't arrive, I started without you.* *I worked so hard* ***that*** *I got an A.*
Clauses of time (introduced with *after, as soon as, before, once, since, until, when, whenever, while*) explain when something happened.	*She will return* ***as soon as*** *she can.* *We can't start* ***until*** *the rain stops.* *I'll choose the images* ***when*** *you finish writing the text.*
Clauses of comparison (formed with a comparative and *than*, or with *as . . . as*) explain the basis of comparison.	*The conference was more interesting* ***than*** *I had thought.* *They have* ***as*** *much homework* ***as*** *we do.*
Clauses of concession (introduced with *although, though, however, even though/if*) explain why an event was unlikely.	*We went skiing* ***even though*** *it was raining.* ***Although*** *she tried to like rap music, she never did enjoy it.*
Noun clauses (introduced with *that*) are used as the subject or object of the verb in the main clause.	*It's a good thing* ***that*** *I checked the time.* *They hope* ***that*** *you will call them soon.* *She said* ***that*** *he was not there.*

Information Questions

You use **question words** and the **interrogative form** of verbs to ask for information.

To ask an information question, start with the question word, followed by the auxiliary, subject, main verb and the rest of the sentence. The auxiliary and the form of the main verb will depend on the tense. See pages 302–311.

Question words include interrogative pronouns (*who, whom, what, which, whose*), adjectives (*what, which, whose*) and adverbs (*where, when, why, how*). See Interrogative Pronouns on page 323.

To Ask About	Question Word	Example
Identity of persons, things or events	*Who** *What** *Which*	***Who*** *did you see at the party?* ***What*** *will Joanne do next?* ***Which*** *story do you prefer?*
Possession	*Whose*	***Whose*** *essay is the teacher reading?*
Place	*Where*	***Where*** *have you put my MP3 player?*
Time	*When*	***When*** *is the next practice?*
Reason	*Why*	***Why*** *do you like surfing?*
Means, manner, degree	*How*	***How*** *can I use this software to plan my project?* ***How*** *well did they do at the auditions?*

* When *who* or *what* is the subject, use the affirmative form of the verb instead of the interrogative: *Who* ***wrote*** *this short story? What* ***happens*** *next?*

Direct and Indirect Speech

Direct Speech

You use **direct speech** to repeat the speaker's exact words. Use quotation marks to identify the words said and capitalize the first word that the speaker says.

Direct speech is introduced or followed by a verb explaining how the words are spoken, such as *to say, to complain, to object, to mutter, to reply, to shout*.

Indirect Speech

You use **indirect speech** to report what someone says or writes without using the exact words. To do this, you must make certain changes.

Formation

- Remove the quotation marks and the comma.
- Change the tense of the speaker's original words (verb, time markers) if necessary.
- Change pronouns and possessives as needed.
- if there is no introductory verb, add an appropriate verb to introduce the reported speech (*to say, to reply, to declare*, etc.). Add the word *that* after the introductory verb.

Direct Speech	Indirect Speech
Simple present →	**Simple past**
The young man proudly said, "I ***write*** *stories for a magazine."*	*The young man proudly said that he* ***wrote*** *stories for a magazine.*
Simple past →	**Past perfect**
The young man proudly said, "I ***wrote*** *stories for a magazine."*	*The young man proudly said that he* ***had written*** *stories for a magazine.*
Future →	**Present conditional**
The young man proudly said, "I ***will write*** *stories for a magazine."*	*The young man proudly said that he* ***would write*** *stories for a magazine.*
Present continuous →	**Past continuous**
The young man proudly said, "I ***am writing*** *stories for a magazine."*	*The young man proudly said that he* ***was writing*** *stories for a magazine.*

LEARN MORE

To use indirect speech to report an information question, you will also need to

- change the verb *said* to *asked* or to another verb of inquiry (*inquired, wondered*)
- change the interrogative form of the verb to the affirmative form
- replace the question mark with a period

To report a yes/no question, add the word *if* or *whether*.

Direct Speech	Indirect Speech
Interrogative →	**Affirmative**
Anne-Marie ***said****, "When do you find time to write?"*	*Anne-Marie* ***asked*** *when he found time to write.*
She ***said****, "Do you also write novels?"*	*She* ***asked whether*** *he also wrote novels.*

GRAMMAR

Punctuation and Capitalization

Punctuation

Punctuation marks have different uses in written texts.

Punctuation Mark	Uses	Example
Period (.)	• To end a sentence • Abbreviations • Initials	*The rest is history.* *U.S.A.* *H.G. Wells*
Exclamation mark (!)	• To show surprise or emotion • To warn	*That's great!* *Look out!*
Question mark (?)	• To ask a question	*When is he leaving?*
Comma (,)	• To separate items in a list • Before or within a quotation • To separate clauses • To separate introductory elements • To separate parts of a date	*lettuce, tomatoes, cucumbers* *"Let's go," said Max.* *If he phones, tell him I'll call later.* *Tell me, do you like jazz?* *Monday, November 8, 2010*
Apostrophe (')	• To show possession • To indicate a missing letter or letters in a contraction	*Marianne's presentation* *It's true that we've had our share of good luck, isn't it?*
Parentheses (( ))	• To add information or examples	*The simple tenses (present, past and future) are easy to learn.*
Colon (:)	• To introduce a list • To introduce an explanation or summary of information • To introduce a long quotation	*There are three main sections: texts, grammar and exercises.* *The formula is simple: work hard and you will succeed.* *In his address to the nation, President Obama stated:*
Semi-colon (;)	• To link closely related sentences (main clauses)	*Martin didn't know what to do; he couldn't move.*
Quotation marks (" ")	• To indicate direct speech	*"When is the next train leaving for Toronto?" Terry asked.*

Capitalization

Capitalize the first word of every sentence.	*Remember to hand in your assignment.*
Capitalize most words in titles and subtitles of works.	*War and Peace* *Canadian Oxford Dictionary*
Capitalize proper nouns (persons, organizations, geographical names, days of the week, months, holidays).	*The House of Commons will be in session in Ottawa starting on the first Monday in October and until the Christmas holidays.*
Capitalize proper names, races, nationalities and languages.	*Kyoko is Japanese, but she speaks excellent English and French.*
Capitalize adjectives and common nouns used as essential parts of proper nouns.	*The National Gallery* *The First World War*
Capitalize trade names.	*Blackberry, Apple, Koolaid*

Some Spelling Rules

GRAMMAR

Distinguishing between *ie* and *ei*

Some words, like *receive, achieve* and *thief,* have syllables that sound the same but are spelled differently.

The basic rule: Put ***i*** before ***e***, except after ***c***, or when the syllable is pronounced "*ay*" like in *vein* and *eight.*

- ***i* before *e*:** *believe, hygiene, grief, thief, friend, chief*
- ***ei* after *c*:** *ceiling, conceive, perceive, receive, deceive, receipt*
- ***ei* pronounced like "*ay*":** *neighbour, freight, sleigh, eight, weight, vein*

Doubling consonants

Double the consonant of

- words of one syllable ending in a single consonant

  stop, stopping *bat, batted* *big, bigger, biggest*
- most words of two or three syllables ending in a single stressed consonant

  begin, beginning *emit, emitting* *refer, referred*
- words ending in ***l*** preceded by a single vowel or two distinct vowels

  travel, travelling *cruel, cruelly* *signal, signalled*

Do not double the final consonant when there are two vowels or a vowel and another consonant before the final consonant.

drift, drifting *retreat, retreated* *result, resulting*

Changing *y* to *i*

Change ***y*** to ***i***

- to form the comparative or superlative of adjectives ending in ***y*** before adding ***er***, ***est***

  happy, happier, happiest *shiny, shinier, shiniest* *scary, scarier, scariest*
- to form the simple past and past participle of most verbs ending in ***y*** preceded by a consonant

  hurry, hurried *carry, carried* *satisfy, satisfied*

  say, said *pay, paid* *try, tried*

Exceptions: *obey, obeyed; play, played*

Do not change the ***y*** to ***i*** to form the present participle of verbs ending in ***y***.

hurry, hurrying *carry, carrying* *say, saying*

Changing *y* to *ies*

Change ***y*** to ***ies*** to form the plural of nouns and the simple present (third person singular) of verbs ending in ***y*** preceded by a consonant.

party, parties *fly, flies* *hurry, hurries*

Dropping the *e*

Drop the ***e*** to form the gerund or present participle of verbs ending in ***e*** before adding ***ing***.

amaze, amazing *surprise, surprising* *supervise, supervising*

Vocabulary

Word Quest Vocabulary

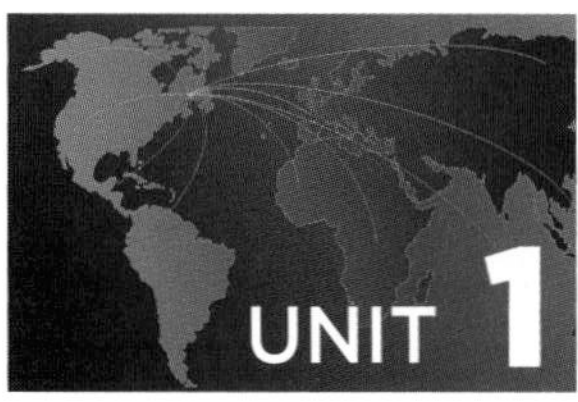

UNIT 1 Ticket to the World Word Quest

accommodation: place to stay

airline: company that transports people by plane

backpacking: travelling with your possessions in a backpack

ballooning: travelling by hot-air balloon

currency: money

exchange: swap

fare: price paid to travel

handbook: instruction manual

hitchhike: to get free rides in strangers' cars

journey: trip, voyage

landmark: something that helps you recognize where you are

off the beaten track: away from towns

road trip: journey by car

sightseeing: visiting interesting places

suitcase: case for carrying clothes

tour guide: person paid to accompany tourists

traveller: someone on a journey

trend: fashion

wilderness: undeveloped area of land

UNIT 2 Bounce Back Word Quest

addiction: dependence

conquer: defeat

cope: deal with something difficult

disease: illness

faith: belief

friendship: relationship between friends

hardship: problems or difficulties

help line: telephone service providing information or advice

obstacle: barrier preventing you from going somewhere or doing something

ordeal: painful or difficult experience

overcome: conquer

peer pressure: influence from a group

psychologist: professional who studies how the mind works

resort to: do something out of desperation

self-esteem: pride in oneself

skill: talent

social worker: professional who helps people with problems

substance abuse: consumption of illegal drugs or too much alcohol

support network: group of people who help a person

Word Quest Vocabulary

Gender Stereotypes Word Quest

communication: sending and receiving messages

compassion: sympathy

consideration: reflection

femininity: femaleness

ignorant: not knowing

interaction: working together or communicating with each other

machismo: great pride in being male

masculinity: maleness

oblivious: not aware

perceptive: observant

Moving On Word Quest

advice: opinion about what someone should do

career: long-term occupation or profession

conscientious: dependable, thorough

dependability: reliability

dilemma: difficult choice

endeavour: try to do something

exploit: make use of

guidance: advice

independence: freedom from someone else's control

occupation: job

predicament: complicated or difficult situation

quest: search

trade: skilled manual work

volunteering: doing something without pay

Humans, Animals and Ethics Word Quest

accountable: having to explain your actions

animal kingdom: the world of animals

attachment: connection

bond: friendly relationship

contact: touch, get in touch

cruel: hurtful, causing pain

essential: indispensable

harvest: collect, gather

inevitable: unavoidable

issue: subject

link: something connecting different things

required: wanted

Word Quest Vocabulary

UNIT 6 Songs of Change Word Quest

agreement: accord

camaraderie: friendship

commitment: promise to do something

complaint: objection

compromise: negotiation

concede: give up

concern: anxiety

conciliation: agreement

crisis: catastrophe

disagreement: difference of opinion

discord: disagreement

dispute: argument

dissent: opposition, disagreement

find the middle ground: compromise

protest: demonstration

spirit: general feeling

surrender: admit defeat

topic: theme

understanding: knowledge

unity: agreement, solidarity

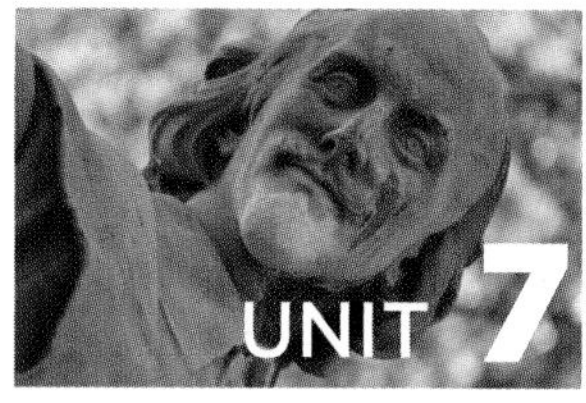

UNIT 7 Shakespeare Lives On Word Quest

characterization: creation of a fictional person by a writer

comic relief: humour coming after tension

houselights: lights in the area where the audience sits

lead role: protagonist

musical: theatrical show or film with music and singing

part: role

performance: the act of playing a role

play: theatrical show

playbill: poster advertising a play

playwright: writer of plays

plot: series of events in a story

script: written form of a play

setting: place or time where the events in a play happen

Shakespearean: in the style of William Shakespeare

star: actor who plays the protagonist

storyline: plot, sequence of events

supporting actor: actor who plays a secondary character

theatregoers: audience

tragedy: serious play with a sad ending

usher: person who shows people to their seats

Word Quest Vocabulary

UNIT 8 When Human Rights Go Wrong Word Quest

acquittal: decision that someone is not guilty

conviction: decision that someone is guilty

duty: obligation

just: fair

pardon: absolution

quandary: difficult situation in which it is hard to decide what to do

reprieve: official order stopping a punishment

resolution: conclusion

responsibility: duty

suffer: feel pain

way out: means of escape

warranted: deserved

UNIT 9 Fast Forward 20 Word Quest

achievement award: prize given for accomplishment(s)

birth: beginning

breakthrough: advance beyond previous limits

childhood: period of life when you are a child

corporate world: business world

entrepreneurial: enterprising

fame: celebrity

fulfillment: contentment

happiness: joy

high school sweetheart: boyfriend or girlfriend in secondary school

housing development: buildings where people live

income: revenue

investments: things you buy and hope will become more valuable

leisure: relaxation, pleasure

parenthood: the state of having children

relationships: connections

relocate: move to another place

scholarship: bursary

single: alone

suburbs: residential areas near a city

training: practical education

VOCABULARY

Common Idioms

VOCABULARY

1. **at first sight:** immediately
When we went to the animal shelter, we knew at first sight that Charlie was the dog we wanted to adopt.
2. **change one's mind:** to change a decision
Amanda changed her mind and decided that she would come to the movies with us after all.
3. **cough up:** to have to pay for
Cassie had to cough up the money he owed for the broken window.
4. **don't count your chickens before they're hatched:** don't make plans based on uncertain events
When I said that I wanted to go to medical school, my teacher told me not to count my chickens before they were hatched.
5. **feel blue:** to be sad
Fred feels blue whenever he thinks of the Expos baseball team leaving Montréal.
6. **fishy:** suspicious
I thought his story smelled a little fishy and sure enough it wasn't true.
7. **give someone a hand:** to be helpful
Could you give me a hand with the groceries? They're very heavy.
8. **have a lot of nerve:** to be bold or impudent
Jennifer has a lot of nerve to call me after she was so unkind.
9. **black and white:** clear
The rules are black and white: you have to attend every practice.
10. **in no time:** quickly
Rebecca did her homework in no time because she wanted to go out.
11. **kill two birds with one stone:** to achieve two things with a single action
I killed two birds with one stone: I went to Toronto on a school trip and visited my cousin who lives there.
12. **knock on wood:** said to keep bad things from happening
George's hockey team should win the tournament. Knock on wood!
13. **let sleeping dogs lie:** to leave things as they are to avoid conflict
My mother suspected that I was angry with my brother but she decided to let sleeping dogs lie.
14. **nosy:** inquisitive
My sister is so nosy. She always tries to read my emails over my shoulder.
15. **piece of cake:** very easy
You'll probably find the exam a piece of cake because you worked so hard.
16. **put/lay one's cards on the table:** to be truthful
I finally decided to put my cards on the table and tell my parents that I wanted to leave school.
17. **save face:** to avoid humiliation
Sarah tried to save face by apologizing to her teacher after everyone else had left.
18. **smart aleck:** person who shows irritating cleverness
Cathy's such a smart aleck. She always corrects the teacher.
19. **sixth sense:** intuition
Harry's sixth sense told him that someone was watching him.
20. **take a stand:** to take a position
We took a stand against vending machines in the cafeteria and circulated a petition to have them removed.
21. **three strikes and you're out:** to have three chances to do something
Remember: Three strikes and you're out. So if you get a third detention, you'll be suspended.
22. **through the grapevine:** from rumours
We heard through the grapevine that the gym teacher was leaving.
23. **tip of the iceberg:** a small visible portion of something large
I took hundreds of photos on the school trip. These are just the tip of the iceberg.
24. **turn over a new leaf:** to move on
We decided to turn over a new leaf and work harder this term.
25. **twenty-four/seven (24/7):** all of the time
My best friend will no longer be around twenty-four/seven (24/7). He's moving to another city.
26. **under the weather:** sick
Brandon is staying in bed today because he's under the weather.

Cognates: True and False

True Cognates

True cognates are words that are spelled the same or similarly in two or more languages and have the same meaning. Below are some true cognates in English and French.

abandon	direction	horrible	opinion	silence
absent	discussion	identification	option	slogan
accident	distance	ignorant	oral	solution
action	durable	illustration	original	sophisticated
animal	effort	imagination	ozone	species
attention	encouragement	immediate	pardon	support
bizarre	excellent	immense	parent	surprise
brave	expert	impatient	participant	technique
catastrophe	exploration	important	pollution	unique
cause	fatal	independence	principal	urgent
central	festival	information	privilege	vacant
certain	final	job	problem	ventilation
conservation	format	logo	public	verbal
correction	fruit	modern	question	violent
cousin	frustration	motivation	recyclable	vision
crime	gadget	muscle	respect	vote
date	garage	musical	responsibility	yoga
defence	guide	narration	routine	zoo
develop	gym	national	sandwich	zoom
dialogue	hockey	objection	science	

False Cognates

False cognates are words that are spelled the same or similarly in two or more languages but have different meanings. Below are some false cognates in English and French.

Word	Definition
actually	in fact
advertisement	publicity
assist	help
attend	take part in
blessed	having a special ability
chance	opportunity
college	place that provides higher learning, similar to a university
crayon	stick of coloured wax
deranged	in an unhealthy mental state
envy	want something that someone else has

Word	Definition
eventually	at a later time
formidable	posing a challenge
gentle	kind, tender
library	place where you can borrow books or work quietly
notes	information copied or written to use for studying or as a reminder
rest	take a break
rate	evaluate or classify
sensible	practical, responsible

Common Prefixes, Suffixes, and Compound Words

VOCABULARY

Prefixes

A prefix comes before a word. It adds something to the meaning.

Prefix	Meaning	Examples
ab-	far from, against	***ab****normal*, ***ab****surdity*
ad-	to, headed for	***ad****vancement*, ***ad****vantage*
anti-	against	***anti-****nuclear*
bi-	two	***bi****cycle*, ***bi****lingual*
co-	together	***co****operate*, ***co-****driver*
de-	away, down	***de****value*, ***de****rail*
dis-	separate from, out	***dis****gusted*, ***dis****play*
ex-	out	***ex-****wife*, ***ex****terior*
homo-	similar, like	***homo****nyms*, ***homo****genous*
in-, im-	not	***in****valid*, ***im****mortal*
inter-	between	***inter****national*, ***inter****provincial*
mal-	bad, evil	***mal****evolent*, ***mal****practice*
mis-	badly, wrongly	***mis****behave*, ***mis****understand*
mono-	one	***mono****lingual*, ***mono****tone*
non-	not	***non****smoker*, ***non****stop*
over-	too much	***over****crowded*, ***over****weight*
per-	all the way through	***per****sistence*, ***per****mission*
post-	after	***post-****game*, ***post****dated*
pre-	before	***pre****historic*, ***pre****war*
pro-	in favour of	***pro-****government*, ***pro-****environment*
re-	again	***re****do*, ***re****write*
semi-	half	***semi-****conscious*, ***semi-****skilled*
sub-	below	***sub****marine*, ***sub****way*
super-	big, more	***super****market*, ***super****sonic*
trans-	across	***trans****atlantic*, ***trans****plant*
un-	not	***un****fair*, ***un****happy*
under-	too little	***under****cooked*, ***under****paid*

Suffixes

A suffix comes at the end of a word. It changes the function of the word.

Noun Suffix	Meaning	Examples
-ence, -ance, -ency	condition of	*urg****ency***, *experi****ence***
-er	person who performs action	*teach****er***, *writ****er***
-dom	position or condition of	*free****dom***, *king****dom***
-ism	belief, act	*Buddh****ism***, *patriot****ism***
-ist	one who supports a belief or performs an act	*human****ist***, *art****ist***
-ity	status of	*de****ity***, *dign****ity***
-hood	situation of	*child****hood***, *neighbour****hood***
-ment	abstraction of	*pay****ment***
-ness	circumstances of	*loneli****ness***, *complete****ness***
-tion	presentation of an act or activity	*participa****tion***, *elec****tion***

Common Prefixes, Suffixes, and Compound Words

Adjective/Adverb Suffix	Meaning	Examples
-able, -ible	capable of	*lov**able**, respons**ible***
-al	of, relating to	*industri**al**, nation**al***
-ful	filled with, full of	*meaning**ful**, doubt**ful***
-ic, -ac	like, related to	*idiot**ic**, mani**ac***
-ish	like, connected to, coming from	*snobb**ish**, Ir**ish***
-ive	having the power of	*vindict**ive**, collect**ive***
-less	without	*clue**less**, tooth**less***
-ly	like	*neat**ly**, quick**ly***
-ory, -ary	linked to, like	*arm**ory**, contr**ary***
-ous, -ose	full of, similar	*melodi**ous**, overd**ose***
-ward	in the direction of	*up**ward**, down**ward***
-y	having	*speed**y**, sleep**y***

Verb Suffix	Meaning	Examples
-ate	act, behave in a certain way	*confisc**ate**, deleg**ate***
-en	make happen	*weak**en**, awak**en***
-ify, -efy	transform into, shape	*beaut**ify**, stup**efy***
-ize	perform an action	*apolog**ize**, modern**ize***

Compound Words

A compound word is a word made up of two different words that, together, form a new word. The meaning of this new word is constructed from the meaning of the original words.

Below are the most common words used in compound words:

Word	Compound Word Examples	Meaning
ache	*ear**ache***	your ears hurt
	*stomach**ache***	your stomach hurts
	*head**ache***	your head hurts
back	*paper**back***	a book with a soft cover
	***back**room*	a room at the back of a store
	***back**yard*	the yard behind a house
board	*score**board***	a board where you keep the score of a game
	*bill**board***	a large board on which you advertise
	***board**walk*	a raised path made of wood
day	***day**light*	the light of day
	*birth**day***	the day of your birth
hair	***hair**do*	a style for hair
	***hair**piece*	an artificial piece of hair
	***hair**brush*	a brush for hair
head	***head**master/**head**mistress*	the person in charge of a school
	***head**band*	a band used for holding hair back on your head
night	***night**time*	time of the day when it is dark
	***night**light*	a small light put in a child's room
place	*birth**place***	place of birth
	*fire**place***	a place where you make a fire
room	***room**mate*	someone you share a room with
	*bed**room***	a room where you sleep
	*board**room***	a room where the board of directors can meet
storm	*snow**storm***	a storm with snow
	*thunder**storm***	a storm accompanied by thunder
tea	***tea**pot*	a container for making and serving tea
	***tea**spoon*	a small spoon originally used for tea

VOCABULARY

Strategies

Strategy Definitions

Strategy	Definition	Page
Communication Strategies		
Gesture	Use actions to help convey your message.	341
Recast	Check that you understand by repeating the information.	341
Rephrase	Use other words to convey the same message.	341
Stall for time	Take time to think of your response.	341
Substitute	Use different words and expressions.	341
Learning Strategies		
Activate prior knowledge	Use what you already know about the topic.	343
Ask for help, repetition, clarification, confirmation	Ask for assistance and/or more details.	347
Ask questions	Request more information.	347
Compare	Focus on similarities and differences.	346
Cooperate	Work with others to accomplish a common goal.	346
Delay speaking	Take time to answer.	344
Develop cultural understanding	Communicate with English speakers to learn more about their culture.	347
Direct attention	Decide to pay attention to what you have to do and avoid distractions.	343
Encourage yourself and others	Be positive. Focus on success.	342
Infer	Make deductions from context clues.	343
Lower anxiety	Relax and be positive. Focus on your progress.	342
Pay selective attention	Decide in advance to focus on specific details.	345
Plan	Think about the steps needed to do the task.	346
Practise	Reuse language in authentic situations.	346
Predict	Make intelligent guesses based on what you know.	346
Recombine	Put language or ideas together in a new way.	347
Reward yourself	Congratulate yourself when you succeed.	342
Scan	Look for specific details.	346
Seek or create practice opportunities	Use more English (outside the classroom).	344
Self-evaluate	Reflect on what you have learned.	344
Self-monitor	Check and correct your own work.	344
Set goals and objectives	Set short-term and long-term goals to improve your English.	342
Skim	Get a general idea.	343
Take notes	Write down important information.	345
Take risks	Don't be afraid to make a mistake.	342
Transfer	Use language and/or information in a new context.	344
Use semantic mapping	Organize your ideas.	345

STRATEGIES

Communication Strategies

How do we find the adventure travel options on this website?

Just go to the right-hand sidebar, scroll down and click on Adventure Opportunities.

Recast

Check that you understand by repeating the information.

I'm sorry, you went a little fast. Where is it again? In the right-hand sidebar?

Rephrase

Use other words to convey the same message.

Gesture

Use actions to help convey your message.

Yes, move your cursor all the way down to the bottom of the sidebar. There it is, right at the bottom of the Travel Categories list: Adventure Opportunities.

If you were to take a long journey, would you sail or would you do a bike…um…wait a second, what's it called again? You know, a journey by bicycle.

Stall for time

Take time to think of your response.

Do you mean a tour?

Yes, that's it.

Substitute

Use different words and expressions.

STRATEGIES

Learning Strategies

Encourage yourself and others

Be positive. Focus on success.

That was brave of you to talk about how your parents' divorce affected you.

Lower anxiety

Relax and be positive. Focus on your progress.

Reward yourself

Congratulate yourself when you succeed.

It's not easy to discuss it, but the more I talk about it, the easier it gets. I'm proud that I can express myself in English, even if the subject is a tough one.

Take risks

Don't be afraid to make a mistake.

Usually, I try not to make mistakes when I write, but we're not supposed to think about that when we do a quick write. Just get the ideas on the page.

Set goals and objectives

Set short-term and long-term goals to improve your English.

It's totally different from the way we usually think about writing, isn't it? But it makes me want to write more. I plan on writing another story in English when I'm done with this one.

My uncle went to Namibia. He says it's very hot and dry.

Yes, I saw a documentary once and it's mostly desert there.

Activate prior knowledge

Use what you already know about the topic.

Okay. We need to find out about the people who live there, so let's focus on that.

Direct attention

Decide to pay attention to what you have to do and avoid distractions.

Skim

Get a general idea.

This section's about the inhabitants.

Infer

Make deductions from context clues.

Some of the people are called Hereros. This place is called Hereroland. I guess they must live there.

STRATEGIES

Transfer

Use language and/or information in a new context.

This ad reinforces the idea that girls don't need to think about anything but their looks.

Delay speaking

Take time to answer.

Self-evaluate

Reflect on what you have learned.

That stereotype really makes me angry, but I need to think about what I want to say before I say it. If I take a moment to collect my thoughts, I do a much better job expressing myself.

This cover letter emphasizes my strengths and my work experience.

Self-monitor

Check and correct your own work.

I could use it as the starting point for a script for making phone calls when I start my summer job search. If I make the calls in English, that will show that I'm proficient in two languages, and it will be good practice.

Seek or create practice opportunities

Use more English (outside the classroom).

Pay selective attention

Decide in advance to focus on specific details.

Use semantic mapping

Organize your ideas.

I think we should construct our responses to our opponents, using a bulleted list. We can give a response to each point they make in their argument. What do you think?

Let's start by focusing on our opponents' idea that people who use high-tech prosthetics have an unfair advantage in sports.

Take notes

Write down important information.

Well, I always start by asking who, what, when, where, why and how. Then I write down the answers to those questions. That gives me the information I need to remember, and I can go back to my notes if I forget something.

We need to write down the important details about how animals are being treated in the circus. Where should we start?

Cooperate

Work with others to accomplish a common goal.

Plan

Think about the steps needed to do the task.

Compare

Focus on similarities and differences.

Practise

Reuse language in authentic situations.

Let's decide how we're going to divide up the task.

First we should read the two songs and then we should note the differences and similarities.

Both of these songs are about love.

But this one's a folk song and this one's a rap.

Let's sing them. It's a good way to practise our English.

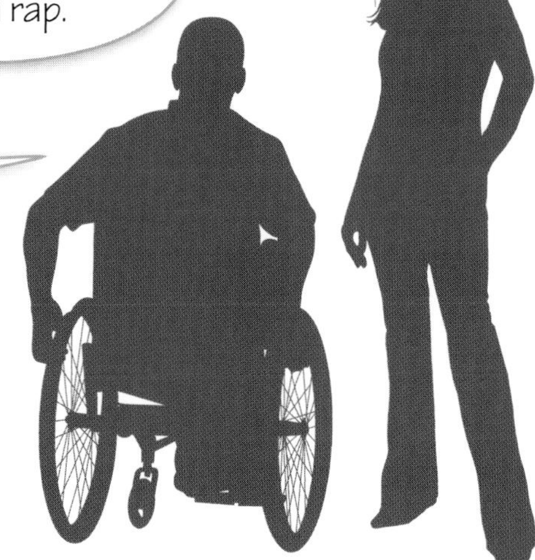

STRATEGIES

Scan

Look for specific details.

Predict

Make intelligent guesses based on what you know.

If we scan through the first page of this story, we can find a lot of words that describe the main character. "Stubborn" is one of them.

I'll bet the main character is going to get herself in trouble, then, by the end of this story!

Maybe not ... sometimes being stubborn can be a good thing, like when you have to really push yourself to do well at something you find difficult.

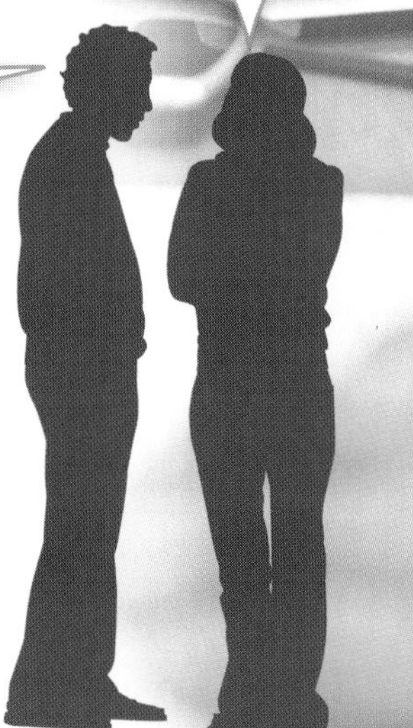

Develop cultural understanding

Communicate with English speakers to learn more about their culture.

Recombine

Put language or ideas together in a new way.

Ask questions

Request more information.

I want to write an email to that rap singer who rewrote some of Shakespeare's plays into rap songs. His version of Romeo and Juliet is amazing!

Yeah, I've never heard Romeo and Juliet explained like that before. I wonder how he knew what to write?

Well, I'm going to ask him how he did it in my email. Maybe he can give me some tips for writing my own Shakespeare rap!

Ask for help, repetition, clarification, confirmation

Ask for assistance and/or more details.

Do you understand everything in this Human Rights Declaration? I don't get this first part.

Can you explain this first section to me?

I understand most of it, but there are a few words at the end that I'm not sure of. I'm going to ask the teacher about those words.

Sure! I understand all of the words in that part.

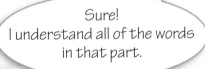

Processes

The Response Process

There are three different types of texts:

- Literary texts, such as biographies, novels, short stories, plays, poetry and journals
- Information-based texts, such as advertisements, atlases, dictionaries, thesauruses, instructions, magazine and newspaper articles, surveys and news broadcasts
- Popular texts, such as cartoons, emails, letters, posters, songs, and articles about culture and everyday life

1. Explore the text.

First explore the text on your own, creating your own understanding. Then share your ideas and responses with others to broaden your understanding of the text.

Before

Before you listen to, read or view the text, do the following:

- **Look at the title and illustrations:** Direct your attention to these components and write down your observations.
- **Determine the topic:** Predict and infer what the text is about, using your observations.
- **Think of what you already know:** Activate your prior knowledge about similar texts.
- **Determine the general message:** Skim and scan the text to get a general idea of what the message is. Be sure to note keywords you already know.
- **Establish your learning goal:** Set a goal for reading, whether it be for information or for pleasure.
- **Create your reading plan:** Select strategies that will help you explore the text.
- **Choose your resources:** Select resources to use while exploring the text, such as guiding questions, dictionaries and the Internet.

During

As you listen to, read or view the text, do the following:

- **Make predictions and inferences:** Check to see if the text confirms your ideas.
- **Note details related to the guiding questions:** Pay selective attention to details that will help you answer the questions.
- **Pay attention to important text elements:** Direct your attention to important details that support the main idea of the text.
- **Use semantic mapping:** Organize your ideas, using tools such as note charts, T-charts, and mind maps.
- **Define keywords:** Use the resources you selected to make sure you understand the text.

The Response Process

After

After you listen to, read or view the text, do the following:

- **Read the guiding questions:** Write down your answers.
- **Explain your reactions:** Write down your ideas, reactions, questions and other important information.
- **Assess your understanding:** Write down the ideas that you found difficult to understand.
- **Read it again:** Reread any parts of the text that you found difficult to understand.
- **Note your discoveries:** Write down new ideas from the text.
- **Make a list of your questions:** Write down your questions and share them with your classmates.
- **Seek another perspective:** Share your ideas and reactions with your classmates, and listen to their impressions of the text. Discuss ideas from the text that you find interesting or important.

2. Connect with the text.

First establish a personal connection with the text by relating it to your own or someone else's experience. Then tell others about your connection. Use the following ideas to explain your response and discuss your connection with your classmates:

- **Explore the element of surprise:** Discuss anything you found unusual or surprising.
- **Elaborate on your interests:** Discuss the points you found interesting, and explain your ideas to your classmates.
- **Establish your personal connection:** Relate the text to your experience or someone else's experience and share this connection with your classmates.
- **Give your opinion:** Relate the text to your opinions and share them with your classmates.

3. Generalize beyond the text.

Relate what you have learned to your community and to life in general. Share your viewpoint about the following ideas with others:

- **Connect with your community:** Discuss how this topic can be related to your own life and your community.
- **Look at the big picture:** Discuss the bigger issues this topic raises related to your own community or your role in society as a whole. Explore similar issues in history or in literature. Share your ideas with your classmates.
- **Analyze actions:** Relate the text to the way people around you act, and think about how you would act in the same situation. Share your ideas with your classmates.
- **Inspire awareness:** With your classmates, discuss ideas for sharing this topic and increasing awareness within your school or your community.

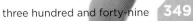

PROCESSES

The Writing Process

The writing process has five phases: prepare to write, write a draft, revise, edit and publish. During the writing process, you may need to go back and forth between the phases as you develop your text.

1. Prepare to write.

Before you start to write your text, do the following:

- **Choose your topic:** Decide what you want to write about.
- **Reflect on your purpose:** Think about why you are writing your text. Possible reasons include one or more of the following: to express ideas, to give information, to direct, to teach, to persuade, to entertain, to narrate, to describe.
- **Identify your audience:** Think about who will read your text. Possible readers include: your teacher, your classmates, your family and friends, groups of people that are particularly interested in your topic, the general public.
- **Select the appropriate text type:** Decide which text type will best convey your message. Possible text types include: a letter, a poem, a story, a play, a persuasive essay, a comic strip or a news article.
- **Set the tone for your language:** Your message should determine whether your language should be simple or complex, formal or informal.
- **Plan your text:** Make an outline or use a graphic organizer to arrange your ideas in the correct order and place information where you need it.
- **Investigate possible resources:** Think about what you will use to research your topic. You may need to consult your tracking sheet, use a dictionary or the Internet, visit the library, check your ideas with your classmates or ask your teacher for guidance.

2. Write a draft.

As you start to write, focus on your message. Use the following steps to create your draft.

Write:

- Include your ideas, opinions, thoughts and feelings.
- Leave space to make adjustments and add new ideas.
- Support your ideas with facts, examples and arguments.

Compare:

- Check your outline or graphic organizer to make sure your draft follows the same structure.
- Check your instructions to make sure you are following them properly.
- Check the model text, if one has been provided.
- Add new ideas to your draft.

Cooperate:

- Discuss your ideas with your classmates.
- Modify your draft with new ideas or changes that result from your discussion.

The Writing Process

3. Revise your text.

Read your text and make sure that your message is clear. Hint: Reading the text aloud will help you identify errors more quickly. Use the list below to help you revise your text.

Check:		Be sure:
Clarity	✓	The message and your ideas are clear.
Organization	✓	Your text is well organized.
Language	✓	Your choice of words is appropriate.
Purpose	✓	Your text achieves your intended purpose.
Audience	✓	Your text reaches your target audience.
Feedback	✓	You considered feedback from your classmates or your teacher.
Rewriting	✓	You added, substituted, removed and rearranged ideas and words when you reworked your draft.

4. Edit your text.

Focus on the formulation of the text. As you edit, do the following:

- **Use resources:** Possible resources to use while editing include model texts, dictionaries, a thesaurus, grammar references, your classmates and your teacher.
- **Get feedback:** Have your classmates and teacher look at your text and make comments and suggestions.
- **Use an editing checklist:** This step ensures that you look for errors in spelling, capitalization, punctuation, grammar and sentence structure. Check each item off your list as you do it.
- **Create your final copy:** Correct your errors and write your final copy.

5. Publish your text (optional).

If you decide to publish your text, use the following publication techniques:

- **Presentation format:** Consider possible formats for presenting your text before choosing the best one for your audience.
- **Resources and strategies:** Remember to use resources and strategies to create your final copy and present your text.
- **How to reach your target audience:** When you present your text, remember who your target audience is. Think about how you will best reach them.
- **Self-evaluation:** Reflect on the writing process and your final product. This will help you to see how you can improve for the next time.

The Production Process

In the production process, you will create a media text. Some examples of media texts are posters, videos, computer presentations, Web pages and books.

The production process has three phases: pre-production, production and post-production. Depending on the type of text, you may not need to include all three phases.

1. Pre-production: Plan your media text.

Before you start to produce a media text, do the following:

- **Choose your topic:** Decide what you want to talk about. Think about what you already know about the topic.
- **Reflect on your purpose:** Think about why you are producing your media text. Possible reasons include one or more of the following: to express ideas, to give information, to direct, to teach, to persuade, to entertain, to narrate, to describe.
- **Identify your audience:** Think about who will read, watch or listen to your media text. Possible viewers include: your teacher, your classmates or the general public.
- **Select the appropriate text type:** Decide which text type will best convey your message. Possible text types include: a poster, a brochure, a video, a radio program, a podcast or a web page.
- **Set the tone for your language:** Your message should determine whether your language should be simple or complex, formal or informal.
- **Plan your visuals and techniques:** Think about what types of images and media techniques will best convey your message.
- **Decide which strategies you will use:** Think about the strategies that will best help you produce your media text, such as taking notes, using semantic mapping or inferring.
- **Research possible production resources:** Think about the kinds of production resources you will need. Use an example of your text type to help you decide what you need for production. Check your ideas with your classmates or ask your teacher for guidance. Look at the writing process to see which steps you will need to include.
- **Investigate possible research resources:** Think about what you will use to research your topic. You may need to consult your tracking sheet, use a dictionary or the Internet, visit the library, check your ideas with your classmates or ask your teacher for guidance.
- **Think about how to cooperate with your team:** Discuss your ideas with your classmates.
- **Establish the roles and responsibilities of each team member:** Decide what each team member will do to help create your media text.
- **Write a focus sentence for your text:** For example: *Our group is going to create a commercial to convince student groups to talk about human rights in our school.*
- **Decide whether to create a script or a storyboard for your text:** Create a visual plan of the production that includes elements such as the action shown through a series of frames or a dialogue between two characters.

The Production Process

2. Production: Produce your media text.

As you produce your text, do the following:

- **Decide how to create the text:** Be sure to follow the decisions that you made in the pre-production phase.
- **Choose the media conventions and techniques you will use:** Think about the elements and techniques you need to use, such as logos, images, symbols and narration. Check your ideas with your classmates or ask your teacher for guidance.
- **Check your resources:** Make sure your resources are appropriate for the kind of text you are producing. Consider feedback from your classmates or ask your teacher for guidance.
- **Identify the editing techniques you will use for your text:** Check the Peer Editing Guide on page 355 and consider what final touches you can add to your text.

3. Post-production: Present and reflect on your media text.

Present your media text to your target audience. Then reflect on your media text, using the following ideas to guide your reflection:

- **Audience feedback and reactions to your text:** Your audience's feedback helps you decide if your text was effective or needs work.
- **Teamwork:** Think about how everyone performed their assigned roles in the team.
- **How to improve your text:** Based on the feedback you receive, discuss what you could do to improve your media text.
- **Your goals for future media texts:** Reflect on the production process and your final product. This will help you to see how you can improve for the next time.

PROCESSES

Editing Tools

Code	Description	Example
1. SV	Subject-verb agreement	Ari ride his bike every day. (SV)
2. SP	Spelling mistake	Alison is my favourite cusin. (SP)
3. CAP	Capitalize	I'll see you on saturday night. (CAP)
4. NO CAP	Do not capitalize	Do you like folk Music? NO CAP
5. WW	Wrong word	Safiya slipped and blessed her ankle. (WW)
6. ¶	New paragraph	When she finished writing her story, she was exhausted from working so hard on the ending. It was very late, so she went to bed. ¶ Tali's stepfather woke up early the next morning. He decided to surprise her with breakfast.
7. ⋏	Insert one or more words	My grandfather lives on ⋏(the) southern coast of France.
8.	Delete	In five days, I will get my ~~my~~ driver's license.
9. #	Add a space	Did you enjoy the benefit#concert?
10. ∼	Change order	Scott goes to the School International.
11. T	Wrong verb tense	Last year my family go to Morocco. (T)
12. rep	Avoid repetition	Then we went to the reading. Then we met the author. Then we asked her for her autograph. (rep)
13. P	Punctuation	What is the answer to question 2. P
14. ?	Not clear	Denis is confused why his program not working next year. ?

Peer Editing Guide

When you edit a classmate's paper, it is important to remember that you are there to help. Constructive criticism is the key to a successful editing experience.

Before you edit, however, you need to read and hear the text. The easiest way to catch errors in the text and make sure that the writer has expressed his or her thoughts well is to use the following double-reading process:

- First, the editor reads the text aloud to the writer.
- Then the writer reads the text aloud to the editor.

The first reading allows both the editor and the writer to hear the text as it is actually written. It is easier to catch errors when you hear a text read aloud. This first reading also avoids a common problem: writers often read their texts the way they should have written them rather than the way they are actually written.

The second reading allows the editor to hear how the writer really wants the text to sound. The writer uses tone of voice to highlight details that are important in the text. This second reading helps the editor to give suggestions to the writer for making the text a complete success.

Here are some general rules to help both the editor and the writer to get the most out of the editing process.

Writer

1. Have the editor read the text aloud to you. Listen carefully and do not interrupt the reading.
2. If you notice errors in the text as the editor reads, write them down so that you will remember them.
3. When the editor has finished reading, it's your turn. Read the text aloud to the editor.
4. If you notice errors in the text as you read, correct them on the text immediately. Then continue reading aloud.
5. After the two readings, listen carefully to the editor's response to the text. Take notes while the editor responds. Do not interrupt the editor.
6. When the editor has finished responding, ask any questions you may have. Ask for any further suggestions for improvement. Write down the editor's answers.
7. Remember: Try to be open to changes and suggestions. The goal of the editing process is to make your text do what you want it to do!

Editor

1. Read the text aloud to the writer.
2. If you notice errors in the text as you read, correct them on the text immediately. Then continue reading aloud.
3. When you have finished reading, have the writer read the text aloud to you. Listen carefully and do not interrupt the reading.
4. During the reading, if you notice that the writer is highlighting certain ideas in the text, note down your observations. These are the ideas that the writer feels are important.
5. After the two readings, respond to the writer's text using the following steps:
   - Respond to the text as a whole.
   - List the text's strong points.
   - List the text's weak points.
   - Point out errors in sentence structure, word choice, descriptions, or general organization.
   - Suggest areas for improvement.
   - Suggest ways the writer can better express the most important ideas in the text. (Remember, you wrote these down during the second reading.)
6. When you have finished responding, listen carefully to the writer's reactions to your response. Answer any questions the writer may have. Give further suggestions for improvement.
7. Remember: Always suggest a way to solve the problem or improve the text. Always give examples of what you think works well in the text. Be sure to listen to the writer's concerns. The goal of the editing process is to help the writer succeed!

Text Types

There are three text types.

1. **Literary texts** include poems, novels, biographies, legends, mysteries and plays.
2. **Information-based texts** are non-fiction texts such as newspapers, advertisements, application forms, dictionaries, documentaries, textbooks, radio and TV broadcasts, and surveys.
3. **Popular texts** are part of popular culture and everyday life. They include emails, comic strips, movies and magazines.

Texts follow certain patterns and have the same features.

Internal features	External features
• **Topic:** the subject of the text • **Language:** the kind of words and language used • **Components:** the elements that organize the text	• **Purpose:** why the text was created • **Audience:** who the text was created for • **Culture:** the background and interests of the intended audience

Features of a Literary Text

1. A short story

The **topic** is a ghost-couple looking through their old house to find a treasure.

The **language** is simple, familiar and descriptive.

A Haunted House 1

by Virginia Woolf 2

Whatever hour you woke there was a door shutting. From room to room they went, hand in hand, lifting here, opening there, making sure—a ghostly couple. 3

"Here we left it," she said. And he added, "Oh, but here too!" "It's upstairs," she murmured. "And in the garden," he whispered. "Quietly," they said, "or we shall wake them." 4

But it wasn't that you woke us. Oh, no. "They're looking for it; they're drawing the curtain," one might say, and so read on a page or two. "Now they've found it," one would be certain, stopping the pencil on the margin. And then, tired of reading, one might rise and see for oneself, the house all empty, the doors standing open, only the wood pigeons bubbling with content and the hum of the threshing machine sounding from the farm. "What did I come in here for? What did I want to find?" My hands were empty. "Perhaps it's upstairs then?" The apples were in the loft. And so down again, the garden still as ever, only the book had slipped into the grass.

But they had found it in the drawing room. Not that one could ever see them. The window panes reflected apples, reflected roses; all the leaves were green in the glass. If they moved in the drawing room, the apple only turned its yellow side. Yet, the moment after, if the door was opened, spread about the floor, hung upon the walls, pendant from the ceiling—what? My hands were empty. The shadow of a thrush crossed the carpet; from the deepest wells of silence the wood pigeon drew its bubble of sound. "Safe, safe, safe," the pulse of the house beat softly. "The treasure buried; the room. . ." the pulse stopped short. Oh, was that the buried treasure?

A moment later the light had faded. Out in the garden then? But the trees spun darkness for a wandering beam of sun. So fine, so rare, coolly sunk beneath the surface the beam I sought always burnt behind the glass. Death was the glass; death was between us; coming to the woman first, hundreds of years ago, leaving the house, sealing all the windows; the rooms were darkened. He left it, left her, went North, went East, saw the stars turned in the Southern sky; sought the house, found it dropped beneath the Downs. "Safe, safe, safe," the pulse of the house beat gladly. "The treasure yours."

The wind roars up the avenue. Trees stoop and bend this way and that. Moonbeams splash and spill wildly in the rain. But the beam of the lamp falls straight from the window. The candle burns stiff and still. Wandering through the house, opening the windows, whispering not to wake us, the ghostly couple seek their joy. **5**

"Here we slept," she says. And he adds, "Kisses without number." "Waking in the morning—" "Silver between the trees—" "Upstairs—" "In the garden—" "When summer came—" "In winter snowtime—" The doors go shutting far in the distance, gently knocking like the pulse of a heart.

Nearer they come; cease at the doorway. The wind falls, the rain slides silver down the glass. Our eyes darken; we hear no steps beside us; we see no lady spread her ghostly cloak. His hands shield the lantern. "Look," he breathes. "Sound asleep. Love upon their lips."

Stooping, holding their silver lamp above us, long they look and deeply. Long they pause. The wind drives straightly; the flame stoops slightly. Wild beams of moonlight cross both floor and wall, and, meeting, stain the faces bent; the faces pondering; the faces that search the sleepers and seek their hidden joy. **6**

"Safe, safe, safe," the heart of the house beats proudly. "Long years—" he sighs. "Again you found me." "Here," she murmurs, "sleeping; in the garden reading; laughing, rolling apples in the loft. Here we left our treasure—" Stooping, their light lifts the lids upon my eyes. "Safe! safe! safe!" the pulse of the house beats wildly. Waking, I cry, "Oh, is this your buried treasure? The light in the heart." **7**

The **components** are
1 a **title**,
2 the **author's name**,
3 an **introduction**,
4 a **triggering action**,
5 **rising action**,
6 **falling action** and
7 the **resolution**.

The **purpose** of this text is to entertain.

The intended **audience** is readers of short fiction, and literature students.

The text refers to the **culture** of home and what it means to people.

Blue = internal features
Green = external features

TEXT TYPES

2. A sonnet

The **topic** is the poet's feelings of love for his lady.

The **components** are
1 a **title**,
2 the **author's name**,
3 **four lines** of poetry following an **ABAB rhyme scheme**,
4 **four lines** of poetry following a **CDCD rhyme scheme**,
5 **four lines** of poetry following an **EFEF rhyme scheme**,
6 and a **concluding couplet**, or two lines of poetry, following a **GG rhyme scheme** and giving a **changed perspective** on the poem's theme.

The **language** is lyrical and descriptive.

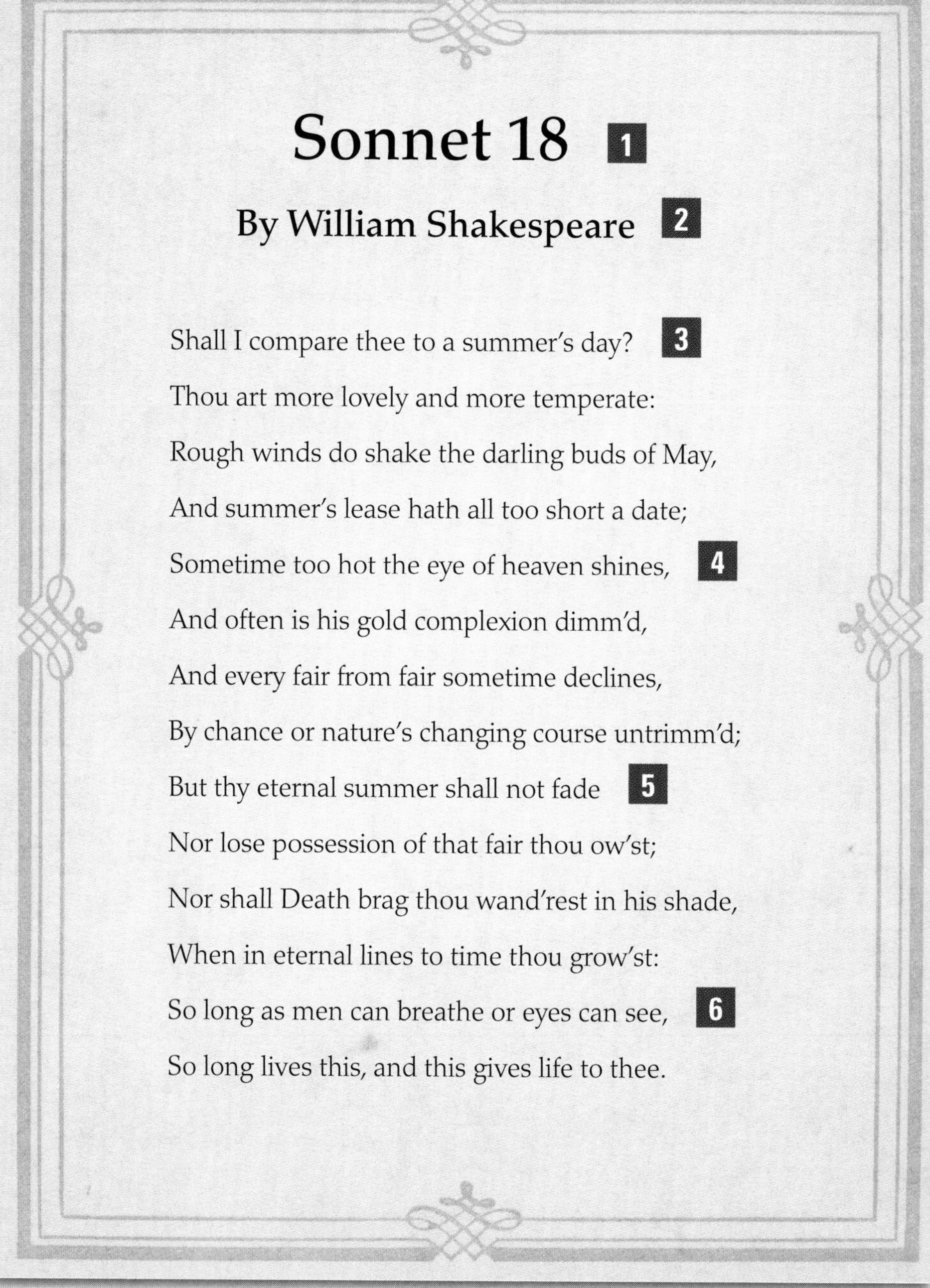

Sonnet 18 1

By William Shakespeare 2

Shall I compare thee to a summer's day? 3
Thou art more lovely and more temperate:
Rough winds do shake the darling buds of May,
And summer's lease hath all too short a date;
Sometime too hot the eye of heaven shines, 4
And often is his gold complexion dimm'd,
And every fair from fair sometime declines,
By chance or nature's changing course untrimm'd;
But thy eternal summer shall not fade 5
Nor lose possession of that fair thou ow'st;
Nor shall Death brag thou wand'rest in his shade,
When in eternal lines to time thou grow'st:
So long as men can breathe or eyes can see, 6
So long lives this, and this gives life to thee.

The **purpose** of this text is to express emotions.

The intended **audience** is readers of poetry.

The text refers to the **culture** of love and relationships in Shakespeare's time.

3. A travel journal entry

August 24, 2009 **1**

Nice, France **2**

After doing all of the things that tourists usually do in Nice, like lie on the beach, eat socca, hang around the marketplace and buy souvenirs, we decided to **3** do something completely different today. My dad knows an astrophysicist from his days at university, and she offered to take us on a tour of **4** the Côte d'Azur Observatory, at the summit of Mont Gros in Nice. I've never been inside an observatory before, and Dr. Regimbau was the perfect person to tell us all about it. She studies pulsars, a kind of star, and says that they can give us information about how the universe was formed. **5**

Dr. Regimbau showed us the telescope and explained that, when it was finished in 1888, it was the biggest refractor telescope in the world—76 centimetres. She also told us that Gustave Eiffel, the same guy who designed the famous Eiffel tower in Paris, designed the dome of the observatory. It's the largest dome in Europe! **6**

Unfortunately, we didn't get to look through the telescope...after all, it was in the middle of the day, and we wouldn't have seen anything unless it was dark outside. But it made me want to learn more about the stars Dr. Regimbau observes, and how they can tell us more about the universe. I even asked my dad if he'd buy me a telescope for my birthday next year. Too bad it won't be as big as the one in Nice! **7**

Tomorrow, it's back to the usual tourist attractions in the south of France...we're going to see if we can spot stars of a different kind in Cannes. Time to get out my sunglasses and make sure the camera batteries are charged! **8**

The **topic** is the attractions that the writer has visited in a particular place.

The **components** are

1 the **date**,

2 the **place** where the journal entry is being written,

3 **details about area tourist attractions**,

4 the **name of the attraction** visited that day,

5 details about **the tour guide**,

6 details about the **visit**,

7 the writer's **reactions and thoughts** and

8 details about the **next attraction to visit**.

The **language** is informal and informative.

The **purpose** of this text is to inform the reader about a particular attraction in Nice: the Côte d'Azur Observatory.

The intended **audience** is the writer herself, her family and friends, and anyone interested in reading travel accounts.

The text refers to the **culture** of tourist attractions, astronomy and the role of the observatory.

Features of an Information-Based Text

1. A resumé

The **topic** is a job candidate's contact information, educational background and qualifications.

The **language** is concise, professional and direct.

The **components** are
1 the candidate's **contact information**,
2 the candidate's **objective**,
3 the candidate's **education history**,
4 the candidate's **extra-curricular activities**,
5 the candidate's **volunteer work and employment history**, and
6 the candidate's **skills and languages**.

The intended **audience** is the person in charge of hiring interns or part-time employees at a legal library.

The text refers to the **culture** of the job search process.

Denise Pelletier 
879 Sherman Street
Montréal, QC H3W 7Y8
(555) 555-1111

Objective: 2
To increase knowledge of cataloguing work and contribute to the day-to-day efficiency of a legal library through a part-time job or internship experience

Education: 3
Santa Maria High School, Montréal, Québec
Selected Courses:
Communication Skills (2009-2010) – Secondary Cycle Two, Year 1
Multimedia Journalism (2010-2011) – Secondary Cycle Two, Year 2
Media Technology (2011-2012) – Secondary Cycle Two, Year 3
Dance and Art Electives

Activities: 4
- Debate Club (2009-2012), Captain (2012), Santa Maria
- Library Committee (2008-2012), Santa Maria
- Literary Magazine (2007-2012), Santa Maria
- Social Action Committee (2007-2012), Santa Maria
- Historical Documents Committee (2010-2012), Santa Maria Community Centre

Volunteer Work and Job History: 
Santa Maria Community Centre, Cataloguer (part time, 2010-2012)
Montréal, Québec
Santa Maria High School Library, Volunteer (2010-2012)
Montréal, Québec

Community Library Association, Volunteer (2009-2012)
Montréal, Québec

Skills and Languages: 
- French – First language
- English – Intermediate level
- Communication skills
- Experience in care of historical documents
- Cataloguing skills
- Researching and resource skills
- Computing and media technology skills

The **purpose** of this text is to show the job candidate's objective for the job search, state educational background and work history, list relevant qualifications for the position, and detail language proficiencies and skills.

2. A thesaurus entry

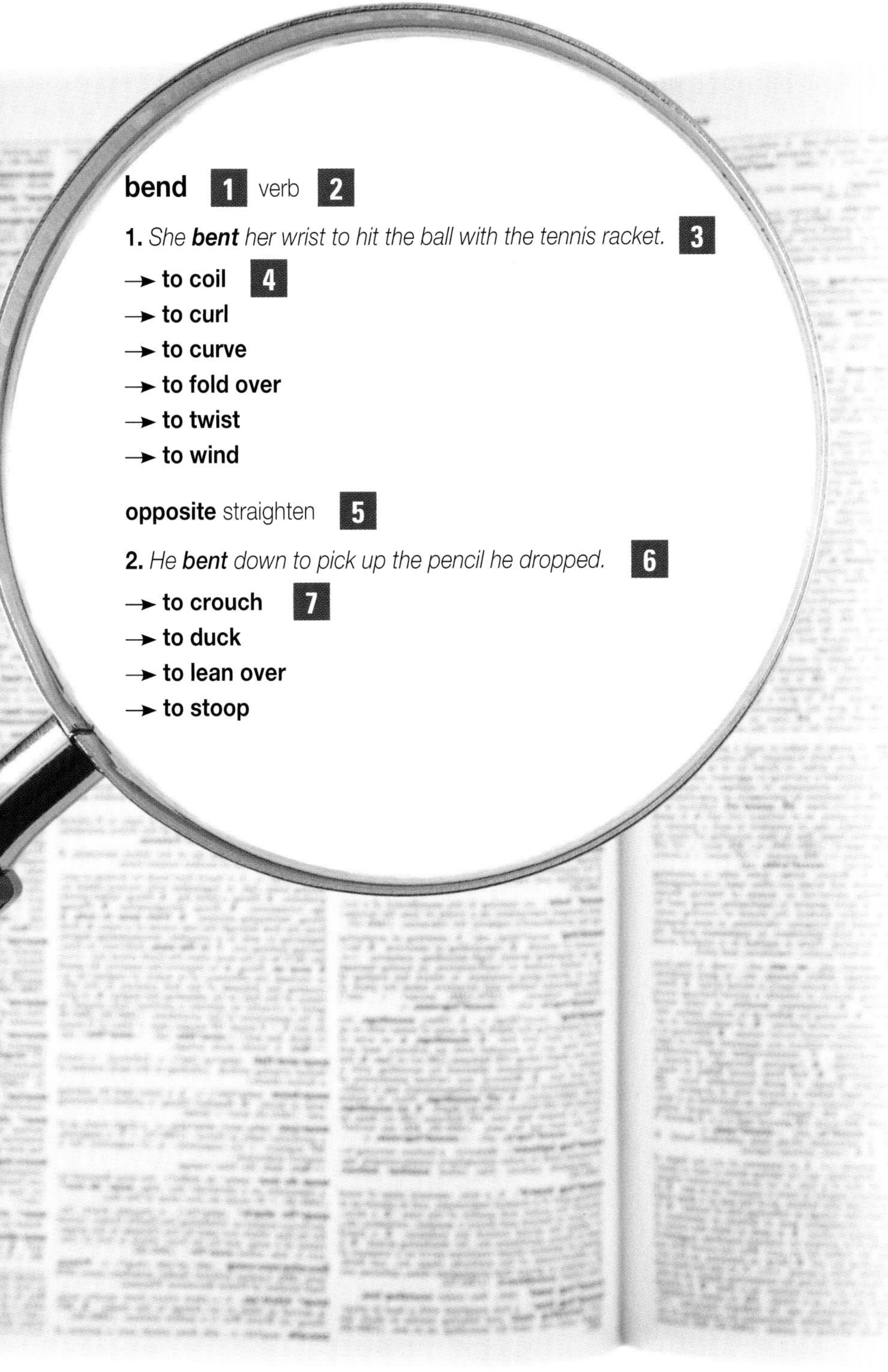

bend 1 verb 2
1. She bent her wrist to hit the ball with the tennis racket. 3
→ to coil 4
→ to curl
→ to curve
→ to fold over
→ to twist
→ to wind
opposite straighten 5
2. He bent down to pick up the pencil he dropped. 6
→ to crouch 7
→ to duck
→ to lean over
→ to stoop

The **topic** is the word you look up and alternative words that mean the same thing.

The **language** is concise and informative.

The **components** are

1 the **word**,

2 the word's **part of speech**,

3 an example of the word's **first meaning**,

4 **alternate words** for the first meaning,

5 the **opposite** of the word,

6 an example of the word's **second meaning** and

7 **alternate words** for the second meaning.

The intended **audience** is anyone who wants to find an alternative word to use in place of a commonly used word, or wants to find the exact word that fits within a particular context.

The text refers to the **culture** of writing in English.

The **purpose** is to inform.

TEXT TYPES

Features of a Popular Text

1. A cover letter

The **topic** is a job candidate's interest in an internship position at a local company.

The **language** is polite, professional and direct.

The **components** are

1 the **date**,
2 the **recipient's name and address**,
3 the **greeting**,
4 the **introduction**,
5 the **body**,
6 the **closing**,
7 the **signature**,
8 the **sender's name and contact information** and
9 an **enclosure mention**.

The text refers to the **culture** of the job search process.

October 25, 2012 **1**

Ms. Tania Lozeau
Personnel Officer
Human Resources Department
Tarryn, Tarryn & Shaw Legal Services
2451 W. Sherbrooke Street
Montréal, QC H7T 9Z2 **2**

Dear Ms. Lozeau: **3**

An article in the Montréal Gazette recently reported that Tarryn, Tarryn & Shaw Legal Services is opening a new law library in the near future. I am very interested in internship opportunities which may become available as a result of this new addition to your company. **4**

My work experience includes several volunteer positions in the field of library science, as well as a part-time paid position at my community centre, cataloguing historical documents for their library. I provide efficient and accurate cataloguing services, and I can work independently as well as with a team of volunteers. When my neighbourhood library had to close due to water damage, I worked very hard to make sure that the books were quickly reshelved at their new location in the correct order. Both the team leader of this community project and my current supervisor have told me that I have excellent data entry skills and take instruction well. I also pay close attention to details and have a positive attitude. In addition, as you can see by my resumé, I have a strong interest in the legal field, and am a top competitor in my school's debate team. **5**

Enclosed is a copy of my resumé and my school transcripts. I look forward to the possibility of contributing to your new cataloguing team, and will call you early next week to discuss possible openings. Thank you for your consideration. **6**

Sincerely,

[signature] **7**

Denise Pelletier **8**

Denise Pelletier
879 Sherman Street
Montréal, QC H3W 7Y8
(555) 555-1111

Encl. Resumé and transcripts **9**

TEXT TYPES

The intended **audience** is the person in charge of hiring interns at the company.

The **purpose** of this text is to introduce the job candidate's interest in a particular position, state her relevant qualifications for the position and express intent to follow up on her request for an interview.

2. A television show script

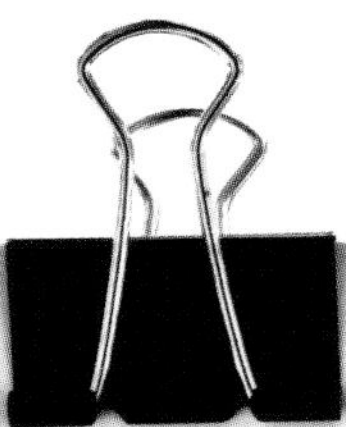

1 **Just Write! Tonight Show Script,** Week 5

[**2** Introduction, 2 minutes 30 seconds, **3** camera on both show hosts]

4 **Jeannie Marston:** **5** Hello, fellow readers and writers, and welcome to Just Write! Tonight, the show where we tell you how your favourite writers got where they are today, and what you can learn from their successes. I'm Jeannie Marston, your cohost. If you want to write, you'll want to tune in to Just Write! Tonight!

4 **Roch Lemay:** **5** And I'm Roch Lemay, getting ready to host yet another exciting show full of interviews, tips, and live readings that will get you writing! We'll be your guides to who's hot and who's not in the world of teen fiction.

Jeannie Marston: That's right, Roch, and tonight's line-up is no exception! We'll be talking to Stephenie Meyer, the author of the super-hot *Twilight* series, about how vampire stories seem to have shot to the top of every teen's reading list.

Roch Lemay: And we'll give you tips on how to think up events that serve as the perfect turning point for your own stories. You'll learn how to keep your readers guessing how the story ends: what details to give away, and where to put them in your story for the maximum effect.

Jeannie Marston: Finally, our guest in the studio for tonight's live reading is Neil Gaiman, reading an excerpt from his newest award-winning novel, *The Graveyard Book*. It's all suspense, all the time on Just Write! Tonight, so stay tuned...you won't want to miss one single minute. We'll be right back!

6 **[Camera pans away from hosts to Just Write! Tonight studio background, cut to advertisement]**

The **topic** is a description of what will happen on a weekly television show about writing fiction, featuring the techniques that successful authors use to create stories.

The **language** is informal, informative and direct.

The **components** are

1 the **show title and week number**,

2 the **show segment title and duration**,

3 **camera instructions for the segment's start**,

4 the **names of the show hosts**,

5 the **lines spoken by each host** and

6 **camera instructions for the end of the segment**.

The intended **audience** is television viewers interested in writing and teen fiction.

The **purpose** of this text is to introduce the schedule of guests and features for the show.

The text refers to the **culture** of reading and writing fiction in English.

TEXT TYPES

Sources

Photos

Key: top = t; bottom = b; centre = c; left = l; right = r

Cover

(tl): Robert Kohlhuber/Istockphoto; (tc): Win Initiative/Getty Images; (tr): Mel Curtis/Getty Images; (bl): Private Collection/Ken Welsh/The Bridgeman Art Library; (bc): Courtesy NRC; (br): diego cervo/Istockphoto

Preliminary Pages

p. iii (tr): Image Source/Getty Images; (cr): Andresr/Shutterstock; (cc): Matt Gray/Getty Images; (bc): Win Initiative/Getty Images; (b): Ableimages/David Harrigan/Getty Images • p. iv: (tl): Courtesy NRC; (cl): ADREES LATIF/Reuters/Corbis; (cc): Kena Betancur/Corbis; (bl): Stockbyte Getty Images; (b): Jupiter Images • p. v (tr): STOCK4B-RF/Getty Images; (cr): Craig van der Lende/Getty Images; (br): Jose Luis Pelaez Inc/Getty Images; (b): Digital Vision

Unit 1

p. 2-3: Image Source/Getty Images • p. 3 (tl): Jennifer Trenchard/Istockphoto; (tr): Andy Hwang/Istockphoto; (tc): Armin Rose/Istockphoto; (b): Christopher Halloran/Shutterstock • p. 4 (l): Ashok Rodrigues/Istockphoto; (r): Y. Marcoux/Publiphoto • p. 7: © 2008 Lisa Gizara • p. 8: Chase Jarvis/Firstlight • p. 9 (l): Dave & Les Jacobs/Getty Images; (c): Heath Korvola/Getty Images; (r): Johner Royalty-Free/Getty Images • p. 10: Andrew Holbrooke/Corbis • p. 11 (t): Al Harvey/The Slide Farm; (c): Courtesy Projects Abroad North America; (b): Courtesy Projects Abroad courtesy Hands Up Holidays • p. 12 (tl): Eddi Boehnke/zefa/Corbis; (cl): Peter Banks/Istockphoto; (tr): Simon Greenwood/Lonely Planet Images; (cr): Sandeep Subba/Istockphoto: (br): Masterfile; (bl): Jacob Wackerhausen/Istockphoto; (r): Daniel Brunner/Istockphoto • p. 13 (t): Eddi Boehnke/zefa/Corbis; (b): Sandeep Subba/Istockphoto • p. 14 (t): Peter Banks/Istockphoto; (bl): Masterfile; (br): Simon Greenwood/Lonely Planet Images • p. 15 (l): Gelpi/Shutterstock: (r): Micha Fleuren/Shutterstock • p. 16 (t): Istockphoto; (cl): Prikhodko/Istockphoto; (cr): Diego Cervo/Istockphoto; (b): Igor Balasanov/Istockphoto

Unit 2

p. 18-19: Andresr/Shutterstock • p. 19 (tl): © 2009 Masterfile Corporation; (tr): Kristy-Anne Glubish/Design Pics/Corbis; (cl): Quavondo Nguyen/Istockphoto; (b): John Lund/Tiffany Schoepp/Blend Images/Corbis • p. 20: CP PHOTO/Ryan Remiorz • p. 22: Igor Balasanov/Istockphoto • p. 24 (bl): Jack Hollingsworth/Corbis; (bc): Birgid Allig/zefa/Corbis; (br): Goodshoot/Corbis • p. 25: Brand X/Corbis • p. 27: Pali Rao/Istockphoto • p. 28: Galina Barskaya/Shutterstock • p. 29: WireImage/Getty Images • p. 32 (t): Istockphoto; (b): Jacob Wackerhausen /Istockphoto

Workshop 1

p. 34: Photos.com • p. 35 (tl): Banana Stock/SuperStock; (tc): Matt Gray/Getty Images; (tr): Nancy Louie/Istockphoto; (b): Altrendo images/Getty Images • p. 36: Jose Luis Pelaez/Getty Images • p. 37: Young Hian Lim/Istockphoto • p. 38: PhotosIndia Collection/maXx images • p. 41: Yuri Arcurs/Shutterstock • p. 45 (bl): Manfred Rutz/Getty Images; (bc): Langdu/Shutterstock; (br): Tetra Images/maXx images

Unit 3

p. 46-47 (t): Win Initiative/Getty Images • p. 46 (b): Vyacheslav Osokin/Shutterstock • p. 47 (tl): Courtesy Dr Gerianne Alexander; (tc): Donn Thompson/Getty Images; (tr): Erik Dreyer/Getty Images; (bl): Ronen/Shutterstock • p. 49 (t): Siri Stafford/Getty Images; (b): Andrew K Davey/Getty Images • p. 50 (l): Petro Feketa/Shutterstock; (r): Lise Gagne/Istockphoto • p. 51: MARVEL/SONY PICTURES/THE KOBAL COLLECTION • p. 52: Victoria & Albert Museum, London, UK/The Bridgeman Art Library • p. 53 (cc): Diego Cervo/Istockphoto; (cr): Rebecca Abell/Shutterstock; (bl): Vadim Ponomarenko/Shutterstock; (br): Randy Faris/Corbis • p. 54: Artsiom Kireyau/Shutterstock • p. 57: Olivier Douliery/ABACAUSA.COM/CP PHOTO • p. 58: Galina Barskaya/Istockphoto • p. 60 (t): Lawrence Manning/CORBIS; (cl): Zholobov Vadim/Shutterstock; (cr): Fred Goldstein/Shutterstock; (b): Istockphoto

Unit 4

p. 62: Ableimages/David Harrigan/Getty Images • p. 63 (tc): Odilon Dimier/Getty Images; (cc): PhotoAlto/Alix Minde/Getty Images; (tr): PhotoDisc/Getty Images; (b): PhotoDisc/Getty Images • p. 64: Jacob Wackerhausen/Istockphoto • p. 65: Nicholas Monu/Istockphoto • p. 66 (t): Asia Images Group/Getty Images; (b): Lisa Kyle Young/Istockphoto • p. 67 (t): Alex Brosa/Istockphoto; (b): Tavrov Konstantin/Istockphoto • p. 68: Istockphoto • p. 71: Istockphoto • p. 72: George Peters/Istockphoto • p. 73: Silvia Bukovac/Istockphoto • p. 74: Louis Michaud/Shutterstock • p. 75: ImageShop/Corbis • p. 76 (t): Tyler Stalman/Istockphoto; (b): Erwin Ps/Istockphoto • p. 77: © Claire Maria Ford • p. 78 (t): Tom Young/Istockphoto; (b): Mark Bowden/Istockphoto

Workshop 2

p. 80 (tr & br): AFP/Getty Images • p. 81 (tl): Getty Images; (tc): Courtesy NRC; (tr): Courtesy NRC; (b): AFP/Getty Images • p. 82 (l): CP PHOTO/Paul Chiasson; (r): AP Photo/Lennox McLendon • p. 86: AP Photo/Mark J. Terrill • p. 87: Courtesy of Speedo ® a division of the Warnaco Swiwmear Group • p. 88: AP Photo/Eugene Hoshiko • p. 89: AP Photo/Andrew Medichini • p. 91 (cl): AP Photo/CP/Aaron Harris; (cr): Nice One Productions/Corbis • p. 93: Chris Schmidt/Istockphoto • p. 95 (bl): Getty Images; (bc): Courtesy Adidas; (br): Getty Images

Unit 5

p. 96-97: ADREES LATIF/Reuters/Corbis • p. 97 (tl): Randy Wells/CORBIS; (cl): Dean Conger/CORBIS; (tr): Altrendo images/Getty Images; (bl): Elliot Westacott/Shutterstock • p. 98: Ian Shaw/Getty Images • p. 99: Susan Roy • p. 100: Emmanuelle Bonzami/Istockphoto • p. 101: MICHAEL CLAYTON-JONES • p. 102: (l): Brian Leatart/Jupiter Images; (r): Rachel Weill/Jupiter Images • p. 106: Photos courtesy of www.purr-n-fur.org.uk • p. 107: Waltraud Grubitzsch/epa/Corbis • p. 108: Christopher Futcher/Shutterstock • p. 109: DLILLC/Corbis • p. 110 (tl): PATRICE LATRON/Corbis; (tr): Hanna Monika/Istockphoto; (c): Julius/CORBIS/Jupiter images; (b): Richard Hamilton Smith/CORBIS

Unit 6

p. 112: Kena Betancur/Corbis • p. 113 (tl): © Scott McDermott/Corbis; (c): CP PHOTO; (tr): JP Laffont/Corbis; (b): Xsandra/Shutterstock • p. 115 (cl): Gai Terrell/Redferns; (clc): MIKE PRIOR/Redferns; (crc): WireImage/Getty Images; (cr): Neal Preston/CORBIS; (b): Lise Gagné/Istockphoto • p. 116: Gai Terrell/Redferns • p. 117: MIKE PRIOR/Redferns • p. 118: WireImage/Getty Images • p. 119: Neal Preston/CORBIS • p. 120: Mario Tama/Getty Images • p. 121: Getty Images • p. 122: Steven Clevenger/Corbis • p. 123: Time & Life Pictures/Getty Images • p. 124: Andrew Winning/Reuters • p. 127: Jaimie Duplass/Shutterstock • p. 128 (t): Stephen Hird/Reuters/Corbis; (cl): CP PHOTO; (cr): Jon Hrusa/epa/Corbis; (b): CP PHOTO

Workshop 3

p. 131 (tc): Bettmann/CORBIS; (tr): ASTRAL FILMS/GROUP 1/THE KOBAL COLLECTION; (b): CP PHOTO/Zach Zito/Everett Collection • p. 132 (bl): The Granger Collection, New York; (bc): CinemaPhoto/Corbis; (br): Ullstein Bild/The Granger Collection, New York • p. 133 (bl): The Granger Collection, New York; (br): CP PHOTO/Sony Pictures/courtesy Everett Collection • p. 136: Chris Schmidt/Istockphoto • p. 148 & 149: Photos.com • p. 151 (bl): CP PHOTO/Everett collection; (bc): Photos.com; (br): CINEMAGINAIRE INC./THE KOBAL COLLECTION/THIJS, JAN

Unit 7

p. 152: Jupiter Images • p. 153 (tc): Wire Image/Getty Images; (tr): Zuma Press.com/Keystone Press; (cc): Zuma Press.com/Keystone Press; (b): English Photographer/Getty Images • p. 154: akg-images • p. 156 (c): Stapleton Collection/Corbis; (b): Zuma Press.com/Keystone Press • p. 158 (tc): Hulton Archive/Getty Images; (tr): Paramount/The Kobal Collection; (bl): UNITED ARTISTS/THE KOBAL COLLECTION/RAHMN, K.O.; (bc): MIRISCH-7 ARTS/UNITED ARTISTS/THE KOBAL COLLECTION; (br): Everett/CP Photo • p. 159 (tl): SAM GOLDWYN/RENAISSANCE FILMS/BBC/THE KOBAL COLLECTION; (tc): MIRAMAX FILMS/UNIVERSAL PICTURES/THE KOBAL COLLECTION; (tr): Courtesy of Jaret Entertainment/Keystone Press; (b): Chuck Savage/CORBIS • p. 160 (t): Paramount/The Kobal Collection; (b): 20TH CENTURY FOX/THE KOBAL COLLECTION/TURSI, MARIO • p. 161 (t): Getty Images; (b): Express UK/Zuma/Keystone Press • p. 162 (t): CP Photo; (b): Everett/CP Photo • p. 165: Peter Viisimaa/Istockphoto • p. 166: Wes Thompson/Corbis • p. 168: Bettmann/CORBIS

Unit 8

p. 170: STOCK4B-RF/Getty Images • p. 171 (tc): Per-Anders Pettersson/Getty Images; (tr): A.G.E. Foto Stock/Firstlight; (cc): Courtesy CMHR; (b): AP Photo/Martin Cleaver • p. 172: Andresr/Shutterstock • p. 173: Blend Images/Masterfile • p. 176 (l): AP Photo/CAF pap; (r): Bettmann/CORBIS • p. 177: ATHAR HUSSAIN/Reuters/Corbis • p. 178: Tony Comiti/Sygma/Corbis • p. 179: Stefan Rousseau/Pool/Reuters/Corbis • p. 180: AP Photo/Themba Hadebe • p. 181 (l): Pharand/Megapress; (r): P. Sheandell/maxx images • p. 182: Stockbyte/Getty Images • p. 183: Istockphoto • p. 184 (t): AP Photo/NTB; (cl): Phillipe Lissac/Godong/Corbis; (cr): OLEG POPOV/Reuters/Corbis; (b): BananaStock/SuperStock

Unit 9

p. 186 & 187: Craig van der Lende/Getty Images • p. 187 (tl): Jean Luc Morales/Getty Images; (tr): Asia Images Group/Getty images; (cc): Dmitriy Shironosov/Istockphoto; (b): Nikolay Titov/Shutterstock • p. 188: Istockphoto • p. 189 (l): Car Culture/Corbis; (r): Colin Anderson/Getty Images • p. 190: CURAphotography/Shutterstock • p. 191 (bl): Istockphoto; (ct): Aldo Murillo/Istockphoto; (cc & cb): Istockphoto • p. 192: Eric Gevaert/Istockphoto • p. 196: CP PHOTO/Sherbrook La Tribune/Files • p. 197 (bl): Carol Kohen/Getty Images • p. 198 (ct): Justin Horrocks/Istockphoto; (cl): Massimo Listri/CORBIS; (cr): A. Chederros/Getty Images; (bl): Colin Anderson/Getty Images

Reading Folio

Opening Page

p. 200 (tl): Nadezda Firsova/Istockphoto; (tr): mtr/Shutterstock; (trc): Spectrum Photofile; (cl): Timothy W. Stone/Shutterstock; (clc): lucwa/Shutterstock; (cr): U.P.images_photo/Shutterstock; (bl & bc): Louisanne/Shutterstock; (br): Rue des Archives/RDA

Unit 1

p. 202: Courtesy Worldwide Quest • p. 203 (t): Spectrum Photofile; (b): Dr. Morley Read/Shutterstock • p. 204 (tl & tcl): Kris Dreessen; (ccl): Amazon-Images/Alamy; (bl): Kris Dreessen; (br): Istockphoto • p. 205: Rue des Archives/RDA • p. 206: Courtesy Penguin Group UK

Unit 2

p. 207: Hannamariah/Shutterstock • p. 208: Lance Sullivan/The Province • p. 209: altrendo images/Getty Images • p. 210 (t): Kevin Russ/Istockphoto; (b): Courtesy Free Spirit Publishing

Workshop 1

p. 211: Dena Steiner/iStockphoto • p. 212 & 213: webphotographeer/iStockphoto • p. 214 (t): Claudia Kunin/Getty Images; (r): Courtesy Meyer-Hentschel Institute, www.ageexplorer.com • p. 215 (l): Courtesy Meyer-Hentschel Institute, www.ageexplorer.com; (r): Courtesy Simon and Schuster

Unit 3

p. 216: Jose Marines/Shutterstock • p. 217: Istockphoto • p. 218 (tr): Klaus Mellenthin/Getty Images; (cr): Dream Pictures/Getty Images; (b): courtesy Free Spirit Publishing • p. 219: mtr/Shutterstock

Unit 4

p. 220 (t): PhotoAlto/Sigrid Olsson/Getty Images; (b): AN NGUYEN/Shutterstock • p. 221: Joy Brown/Shutterstock • p. 223: Stephen Rudolph/Shutterstock • p. 224: Supri Suharjoto/Shutterstock • p. 225: Reprinted with permission from What Color Is Your Parachute? 2009 by Richard Nelson Bolles. Copyright © 2009 by Richard Nelson Bolles, Ten Speed Press, Berkeley, CA. www.tenspeed.com

Workshop 2

p. 226 (t): Courtesy Capulet World; (r): Courtesy Simbex Company; (b): Courtesy Adidas • p. 227 & 228: Courtesy NRC • p. 229 & 230: Jeremy Chevalier/Eastwing • p. 230 (b): Courtesy sciencemuseum.org.uk

Unit 5

p. 231: Lasse Kristensen/Shutterstock • p. 232: Four Oaks/Shutterstock • p. 233: Steve Mann/iStockphoto • p. 234: Eric Naud/iStockphoto • p. 235 & 237: Courtesy PETA • p. 238 (t): Stephane Cardinale/People Avenue/Corbis; (b): Courtesy Harper Collins Canada

Unit 6

p. 239: U.P.images_photo/Shutterstock • p. 240 (t): Istockphoto; (c): Photodisc/Getty Images • p. 241 (t): Musician is Sur Sudha from Kathmandu, Nepal/photo by William Aura; (b): Musician is Phakama Africa from Umlazi, South Africa/photo by François Vigué • p. 242 (t): Musician is Roger Ridley from Nevada, USA/photo by Tahitia Hicks; (b): The Cellist of Sarajevo by Steven Galloway. Copyright © 2008 Steven Galloway. Jacket Photography: Mikail Evstafiev. Reprinted by permission of Knopf Canada

Workshop 3

p. 243 & 244: Louisanne/Shutterstock • p. 245, 246, 247 & 248: The Fisherman and His Wife © 2007 The Reader's Digest Association • p. 249 & 250: Sebastian Kaulitzki/Shutterstock • p 251: lucwa/Shutterstock • p 252 (t): Lane V. Erickson/Shutterstock; (b): Dover Publications

Unit 7

p. 253: Aleksandar Velasevic/Istockphoto • p 254 (t): Illustration by Campbell Grant Twisted Tales of Shakespeare by Richard Armour, p. 44; (b): No Fear Shakespeare Courtesy Barnes & Nobel • p 256, 257 & 258: From SCHOLASTIC SCOPE, February 2. 2009 issue. Copyright © 2009 by Scholastic Inc Reprinted by permission of Scholastic Inc

Unit 8

p. 260 & 261: The General Synod Archives, Anglican Church of Canada • p 261 (cr): Sigrid Olsson/ZenShui/Corbis • p 262 (t): Jacques Langevin/CORBIS SYGMA; (b): Dario Mitidieri/Getty Images • p 264 (t): Bettmann/CORBIS; (b): Dario Mitidieri/Getty Images • p 265: Courtesy Hannah McGechie/RCMP • p 266 (tl): Courtesy Ben Pascoe; (b): The Boy in the Striped Pajamas © Random House Inc.

Unit 9

p. 267: Renars Jurkovskis/Shutterstock • p. 268: Juan Manuel Ordóñez/Shutterstock • p 269: CAN BALCIOGLU/Shutterstock • p 270: Chicago Tribune/MCT/Landov • p 271: Geoffrey Holman/Istockphoto • p. 272 & 273: Qiwen/Shutterstock • p. 273 (b): Parable of the Sower by Octavia Butler Courtesy Hachette Book Group

Texts of General Interest

p. 274 (t): Courtesy Poe Museum; (b): akg-images • p. 275: Istockphoto • p. 276: Brooke Fasani/Getty Images • p. 278 & 279: A.G.E. Foto Stock/Firstlight Bryan Reinhart/Masterfile (b): Bettmann/CORBIS • p. 280: Bryan Reinhart/Masterfile • p. 281: Bill Frymire/Masterfile • p. 282: © Sophia Quach • p. 283 (t): Sasha Martynchuk/Istockphoto; (b): Istockphoto • p. 284: Bettmann/CORBIS • p. 285 & 286: Timothy W. Stone/Shutterstock • p. 286 (b): © Lois Siegel • p. 287: koch valérie/Istockphoto • p. 289: Birgitte Magnus/Istockphoto • p. 290: Dejan Nikolic/Istockphoto • p. 291: Konstantin Sutyagin/Shutterstock • p. 293: Dominic Nahr/Oeil Public • p. 294: Hélène Jolette/UPA DI • p. 295: UPA DI • p. 296: Image B-01601 Coutesy of Royal BC Museum, BC Archives • p. 297: Emily Carr, Tree Trunk, 1931, oil on canvas, 129.1 x 56.3 cm, Collection of the Vancouver Art Gallery, Emily Carr Trust, VAG 42.3.2 Photo: Trevor Mills, Vancouver Art Gallery

Reference Section

p. 300: Digital Vision • p. 341 (t): Ben Blankenburg/Istockphoto; (b): Istockphoto • p. 342 (t): René Mansi/Istockphoto; (b): Jacob Wackerhausen/Istockphoto • p. 343 (t): Andrea Prandini/Istockphoto; (b): © Anthony Bannister/Gallo/AfriPics.com. All Rights reserved • p. 344 (t): © Anthony Bannister/Gallo/AfriPics.com. All Rights reserved • p. 344 (t): Michael Martin/zefa/Corbis; (b): Vince Hobbs/Corbis • p. 345 (t): Celin Serbo/Aurora Photos/Corbis; (b): Alyn Stafford/Istockphoto • p. 346 (t): Jörgen Isaksson/Istockphoto; (b): Istockphoto • p. 347 (t): Oleg Prikhodko/Istockphoto; (b): Chris Schmidt/Istockphoto • p. 349: Catherine Servel/Getty Images • p. 353: Lise Gagne/Istockphoto • p. 354: Susan Trigg/Istockphoto • p. 361: Anton Prado PHOTO/Shutterstock

Texts

Unit 2

pp. 22 & 23: Fondation de l'Hôpital de Montréal pour enfants - Danielle Gabrielle Roy: droy@fhme.com

p. 28: "Inspirations" by Tom Krause from *Chicken Soup for the Teenage Soul III*, Jack Canfield, Mark Victor Hansen, Kimberly Kirberger, 2000, USA

Workshop 1

pp. 39 & 40: Copyright 1969 by Paul Zindel. Used by permission of HarperCollins Publishers.

Unit 4

pp. 74 & 75: Reprinted with permission of Vanier College (The Learning Centre) 2009.

Unit 5

p. 99: ctv.ca Staff

p. 100: Stefan Lovgren/National Geographic Image Collection

p. 101: CityNews.ca Staff

p. 106: Cat Aids Crew of the HMS Amethyst by Simone, Montréal, Québec. Veterans Affairs Canada

Unit 6

p. 116: "Where Have All the Flowers Gone?" by Pete Seeger. © 1961 (Renewed) Fall River Music Inc. All Rights Reserved

p. 117: "Guiltiness" by Bob Marley. Courtesy of Blue Mountain Music Publishing

p. 118: "World On Fire". Performed by Sarah McLachlan. Courtesy of Nettwerk Productions

p. 119: "Last To Die" by Bruce Springsteen. Copyright © 2007 Bruce Springsteen (ASCAP). Reprinted by permission. International copyright secured. All rights reserved.

p. 123: Madeline Hendrickson, Chino Valley, Arizona

Workshop 3

pp. 137–145: Play adapted from "A Wicked Woman" by Jack London, originally published in 1906.

Unit 7

p. 167: All Things Considered, November 20, 2006. Copyright © NPR

Unit 8

p. 177: Universal Declaration of Human Rights. Public domain

Unit 9

p. 190: Courtesy AARP

pp. 192 & 193: Mike Michalowicz, Author of The Toilet Paper Entrepreneur.com and CEO of Obsidian Launch

p. 196: Canwest News Service

p. 197: Peanuts: © United Feature Syndicate, Inc.; PEARLS BEFORE SWINE © Stephan Pastis/Dist. by United Feature Syndicate, Inc.

Reading Folio

Unit 1

p. 202: © The Canadian Press

pp. 203 & 204: © Kris Dreessen, Earthwatch Institute Volunteer

pp. 205–206: From *Around The World in Eighty Days*, Jules Verne, first published in 1872

Unit 2

p. 207: From *Don't Sweat The Small Stuff For Teens* by Richard Carlson, Ph.D. Copyright © 2000 Richard Carlson, Ph.D. Reprinted by permission of Hyperion. All rights reserved.

p. 208: Lora Grindlay, *The Province*, Monday, April 25, 2005. A division of Canwest Publishing.

pp. 209 & 210: Adapted from *The Struggle to be Strong* by Al Desseta, M.A., and Sybil Wolin, Ph.D., ©2000. Used with permission of Free Spirit Publishing Inc., Minneapolis, MN. All rights reserved.

Workshop 1

p. 211: From *Don't Sweat The Small Stuff For Teens* by Richard Carlson, Ph.D. Copyright © 2000 Richard Carlson, Ph.D. Reprinted by permission of Hyperion. All rights reserved.

pp. 212 & 213: Blair Hurley, Creative Writing Corner (www.blairhurley.com)

pp. 214 & 215: Kyle James, *Deutsche Welle*'s website, 2003

Unit 3

pp. 216–217: *Prince Cinders* by Babette Cole (1987). Used by permission of Puffin Books, a division of Penguin Group (USA) Inc.

p. 218: The British Psychological Society's Research Digest (www.researchdigest.org.uk/blog), written by Dr Christian Jarrett.

p. 219: Copyright © 2005 by the American Psychological Association. Adapted with permission. APA Online, September 18, 2005. http://www.apa.org/releases/gendersim0905.html.

Unit 4

pp. 220 & 221: "Is This Heaven?" by Scott Dobson-Mitchell, in *MacLean's*, November 24, 2008. © Scott Dobson-Mitchell

pp. 222 & 223: *Realty Times*, How to Find a Roommate . . . Safely. Courtney Ronan. Publ. Nov. 2000.

pp. 224 & 225: Autorité des marchés financiers

Workshop 2

p. 226: "Sports Go High Tech" by Cody Crane, Scholastic *ScienceWorld*, November 10/24, 2008. Copyright by Scholastic Inc. Reprinted by permission of Scholastic Inc.

pp. 227 & 228: National Research Council Canada

pp. 229 & 230: *The Economist,* July 31, 2008 print edition.

Unit 5

p. 231: "Vegetarians face an ethical dilemma" by Amy Iggulden. The Telegraph, 14 May 2007. © Telegraph Media Group Limited 2007

pp. 232–234: "Professional Wildlife Photographers Face Ethical Dilemmas" by Michela Rosano. Canadian Geographic.

pp. 235–237: © RaeLeann Smith, Britannica, 2006

Unit 6

p. 239: "How To Write Ultimate Protest Songs" by Citizen Fish, from the album "Free Souls in a Trapped Environment". Bluurg Records.

p. 240: Music For All Seasons: One Musician's Story, from http://www.musicforallseasons.org/through_eyes.html

pp. 241 & 242: Mark Johnson: The Music of Inspiration. Moving Pictures Magazine. © The Huffington Post

Workshop 3

pp. 243 & 244: © Joe Bower – eserver

pp. 249–252: Reprinted by permission of Don Congdon Associates, Inc. Copyright 1954, renewed 1982 by Ray Bradbury.

Unit 7

p. 254: Introduction to Macbeth, from *Twisted Tales from Shakespeare* by Richard Armour (McGraw-Hill Book Company, 1957)

pp. 255–259: From Scholastic Scope, February 2, 2009 issue. Copyright 2009 by Scholastic Inc. Reprinted by permission of Scholastic Inc.

Unit 8

pp. 260 & 261: © Marilyn Dumont

pp. 262–264: Extracted from *Forbidden City* by William Bell. Copyright © 1990 by William Bell. Reprinted by permission of Doubleday Canada.

p. 265: © (2009) HER MAJESTY THE QUEEN IN RIGHT OF CANADA as represented by the Royal Canadian Mounted Police (RCMP). Reproduced with the permission of the RCMP.

Unit 9

pp. 268 & 269: "The Great Idea!". Written by Ellie Shuo Jin, North York, ON. Originally published in *What If?* Canada's Creative Magazine for Teens

pp. 270–273: "A Few Rules for Predicting the Future" by Octavia E. Butler. Original essay appeared in May 2000 issue of *Essence Magazine.*

Texts of General Interest

pp. 275–277: From SLEEPING ON THE WING: AN ANTHOLOGY by Kenneth Koch and Kate Farrell, copyright © 1981 by Kenneth Koch and Kate Farrell. Used by permission of Random House, Inc.

pp. 278 & 279: from THE GRAPES OF WRATH by John Steinbeck, copyright 1939, renewed © 1967 by John Steinbeck. Used by permission of Viking Penguin, a division of Penguin Group (USA) Inc.

pp. 280–283: From Stardust, by Neil Gaiman. Copyright © 1998 by Neil Gaiman. By permission of HarperCollins Publishers.

pp. 285 & 286: Reproduced with the permission of Norman Allan.

pp. 287–289: © 2007-2009 The Nemours Foundation. All rights reserved.

p. 290: "Before You Sign Any Contract: 10 Things You Need to Know," Financial Consumer Agency of Canada, 2008. Reproduced with permission of the Minister of Public Works and Government Services, 2009.

pp. 291 & 292: From Scholastic *Scope*, March 23, 2009 issue. Copyright 2009 by Scholastic Inc. Reprinted by permission of Scholastic Inc.

p. 293: © Julia McKinnell

pp. 294 & 295: Reprinted from the *Quebec Farmers' Advocate.*

pp. 296 & 297: © Vancouver Art Gallery, all rights reserved. http://www.virtualmuseum.ca/Exhibitions/EmilyCarr/en/about/index.php

pp. 298 & 299: "The Day is Done" by Henry Wadsworth Longfellow (1807-1882)